The Place Where We

Reading and Writing about New York City

Second Edition

Juanita But

Mark Noonan

New York City College of Technology

City University of New York

Foreword by Brian Keener

KENDALL/HUNT PUBLISHING COMPANY
4050 Westmark Drive   Dubuque, Iowa 52002

CONTENTS

Section II: Literary New York

Alternate Thematic Sequences

The American Dream
Anzia Yezierska, America and I
Junot Diaz, New York: Science Fiction
Edwidge Danticat, New York Was Our
City on the Hill
Alfred Lubrano, Bricklayer's Boy
June Jordan, For My American Family
"Shadows Lines"
Eric Liu, A Chinaman's Chance: Reflections on
the American Dream
Colin Powell, My American Journey

Family
Junot Diaz, New York: Science Fiction
Edwidge Danticat, New York Was Our
City on the Hill
Alfred Lubrano, Bricklayer's Boy
June Jordan, For My American Family
Colin Powell, My American Journey

Community
Ian Frazier, Take the F
June Jordan, For My American Family
Mark Naison, From Doo Wop to Hip Hop:
The Bittersweet Odyssey of African-Americans
in the South Bronx
Angie Cruz, My First address

Work
John Steinbeck, The Making of a New Yorker
Anzia Yezierska, America and I
Edwidge Danticat, New York Day Woman
Alfred Lubrano, Bricklayer's Boy
Colin Powell, My American Journey
Herman Melville, Bartleby, the Scrivener:
A Story of Wall Street

Cultural Identity
Suki Kim, Facing Poverty with a
Rich Girl's Habits
Mohammed Naseehu Ali, My Name
Is Not Cool Anymore
Ralph Ellison, Prologue to the Invisible Man
Michael T. Kaufman, Of My Friend Hector and
My Achilles' Heel
Monique Ferrell, Tu Sabes? A Story in Three Parts
Langston Hughes, Theme for English B
Frances Chung, Yo Vivo En El Barrio Chino

Language
Anzia Yezierska, America and I
Suki Kim, Facing Poverty with a Rich Girl's
Habits
Esmeralda Santiago, When I Was Puerto Rican
Frances Chung, Riding the Subway Is an
Adventure

Ethics
Emma Lazarus, The New Colossus
Jacob Riis, How the Other Half Lives
Peter Marin, Helping and Hating the Homeless
Jonathan Kozol, Savage Inequalities
Herman Melville, Bartleby, the Scrivener:
A Story of Wall Street

Subway
Ralph Ellison, New York, 1936
Anna Quindlen, Pregnant in New York
Ian Frazier, Take the F
Ezra Pound, In the Station of a Metro
Langston Hughes, Subway Rush Hour
Frances Chung, Riding the Subway Is an
Adventure
Victor Hernandez Cruz, Going Uptown to
Visit Miriam

F O R E W O R D

O. Henry once observed that New York City will be great—once it is completed! In truth, however, an essential part of this city's greatness is precisely that it is continually evolving, changing, and growing. I believe that this reader, *The Place Where We Dwell,* conveys this quality of New York City as well as a number of others including its energy, diversity, beauty, promise, and culture. At the same time, in order to portray our city fully—potholes and all—we must also admit its poverty, inequality, harshness, despair, and, inescapably, in the light of recent events, vulnerability.

You have noticed that I have used the pronoun "our" in referring to New York City because this foremost is a reader by, for, and about New Yorkers. Accordingly, this reader was created with students like those at our school, the New York City College of Technology, located in downtown Brooklyn just a walk across the bridge from Manhattan, in mind: students who have arrived at our college from near and far and who, for the time being at least, identify themselves as New Yorkers. The selections here are primarily about New York City and even if they are not specifically so, they could be. At the same time, this anthology is not for New Yorkers alone. The selections here should have wide appeal not only because so many Americans nowadays live in cities, but because what happens in New York seems sooner or later to affect almost everyone.

A useful composition text engages its readers, inspiring them to read insightfully, think critically, and write effectively. *The Place Where We Dwell* does so by providing a range of selections organized around various features of New York City. The first chapter, "New Yorkers," presents New York City head on: its relentless flux in Colson Whitehead's "The Colossus of New York"; its contradictoriness in Ralph Ellison's "New York, 1936"; and its sounds, subway, and architecture in E. B. White's 1949 panoramic "Here is New York." The second, "Crossings," provides a number of variations on the immigrant experience, both hopeful and sobering, beginning with Emma Lazarus' ringing sonnet "The New Colossus" and concluding with illuminating essays by Suki Kim and Mohammed Naseehu Ali. The third chapter, "Class Matters," contrasts the New York City of the "haves" and "have nots," from Andrew Carnegie's paean to great fortunes ("Wealth") to Jacob Riis' scathing exposé of tenement misery, "How the Other Half Lives." It then analyzes modern urban myths about class and the homeless in essays by Janny Scott, David Leonhardt, and Peter Marin.

Chapter Four, "Urban Education," examines the school system from DeWitt Clinton's noble concept, "Free Schools," to the current reality of Jonathan Kozol's "Savage Inequalities." It also includes essays on the specific problems of the school system as well as plans to improve it. Chapter Five, "Violence and Resistance," explores tensions that persist in New York City: the issue of race in Langston Hughes' apocalyptic poem "Harlem" and Ellison's *Prologue to the Invisible Man;* the conditions that foster juvenile delinquency in Nicky Cruz's searing "Into the Pit" and Mark Berkey-Gerard's "Youth Gangs"; and the deterioration of a one-time model housing development in Mark Naison's "From Doo Wop to Hip Hop." Chapter Six, "Current Issues," contains Mayor Bloomberg's recent "state of the city" address as well as essays on gentrification, immigration, and technology. Finally, the reader concludes with samples of memorable New York City literature including poems by Langston Hughes and Herman Melville's haunting depiction of an urban dead soul, "Bartleby, the Scrivener."

In summary, I believe that this compact reader contains a range of provocative and timely pieces that will lead to lively classroom discussions and, more importantly, serve as models for student writing. Most of the reading selections are essays since they are what students learn to write in composition courses; nevertheless, it includes other genres—short stories, poems, news articles—so that students may get a wider sense of the possibilities of written language. It provides divergent points of view on the issues in order to encourage students to keep an open mind and to respect diversity. Since most of the students using this book share the urban experience, they will be able to form learning communities exploring common ground from individual points of view. As for the teacher, he or she may approach these selections thematically in the way they are arranged or, choosing to look at them through the prism of rhetorical modes, may find plentiful examples of narration, analysis, comparison/contrast, and argumentation. In any case, there is a great deal here that speaks directly to both student and teacher. And if this reader should stand the test of time, the editors will have no difficulty finding updated material for subsequent editions. Our restless New York City will see to that.

Brian Keener
Chair, English Department
New York City College of Technology
City University of New York

PREFACE

Do we need another composition anthology? This seems to be a legitimate question to ask when composition textbooks are in proliferation. But as we search seriously, having in mind the unique intellectual needs of our students in an intensely urban environment, we realize that we have not yet found that one textbook with which we need not look any further. And it turns out that the end of our fruitless search has also become the birth of *The Place Where We Dwell: Reading and Writing about New York City*. This homegrown anthology brings together materials about issues that have always concerned New Yorkers; it is a collection that aims to engage our diverse urban student body in a community of active reading, writing, and thinking critically about their immediate surroundings. After several semesters of careful selection of and classroom experiment with the readings and assignments in this book, we are fully convinced that this edition will not be just another reader that our students have to work through, but something that they can connect to and be able to enjoy.

The Place Where We Dwell collects a variety of voices that speaks to every New Yorker and addresses every aspect of life in New York City. It intends to open animated discussion and sustain dynamic conversation through different topics and selections across genres. In Section One, the thematic organization of each chapter allows students to make connections among reading selections and examine specific topics such as city life, immigration, the class divide, urban violence, education, and current issues from multiple perspectives. The first chapter, "New Yorkers," consists mainly of narrative and descriptive works. Aside from being rich and engaging reading, the modeling of these rhetorical patterns is designed to call attention to the use of details and critical reflection of the kind students should incorporate into their own writing. The varied, eloquent, and occasionally elaborate sentences, careful language use, and richly developed paragraphs of writers such as Colson Whitehead, Ian Frazier, and E. B. White make this chapter an ideal place to begin improving college reading and writing skills. Chapter Two, "Crossings," is a chapter that can be effectively used to work on the rhetorical strategy of comparison and contrast. For example, writers such as Edwidge Danticat and Anzia Yezierska critically reflect on the transformations that occur upon leaving their native land and adopting New York as their new home. The writing assignments at the end of the chapter allow students to compare and contrast two or more instances of crossings in connection to their own transformations living in the city. Chapters Three through Five—"Class Matters, Urban Education, Violence and Resistance"—allow students to work with argumentative essays on controversial issues. Written from multiple perspectives, these works simultaneously serve as exemplary models of exposition, analysis, and argumentation and offer a large context for student response. Chapter Six, "Current Issues," allows students to develop their critical thinking and writing skills by entering into recent debates on urban issues and examining them further through research.

Even as we insist that students be involved in understanding and critically inquiring into topics concerning their home city, we also recognize that they need to be introduced to the treasures of New York's literary world. Accordingly, Section Two, entitled "Literary New York," offers a sampling of imaginative writing that both expands upon many of the themes found throughout the reader and offers readers new visions of the urban experience.

Editorial Apparatus

- A range of *interesting topics and texts* about New York City for students to choose from to develop and apply their critical reading, writing, and thinking skills.

- Every chapter begins with an *introduction* that provides a larger context for each reading selection to help students understand, enjoy, and connect the selections.

- Author's *biography* precedes each selection.

- *Pre-reading* questions prepare students to read and think critically about the topic presented in the selection that follows.

- *Discussion questions* are designed to promote thinking about the meaning and implications of the text and to ask students to relate some aspects of the text to a value, practice, or belief in their personal experience or other readings.

- *Writing tasks* are related to the topic of the reading selection. These assignments encourage students to continue to articulate and develop their own perspectives on the topic by using the text to situate their discussion.

- *Connecting ideas* questions at the end of each chapter ask students to compare the texts they are reading either with other texts included in the chapter or with the students' own experiences.

- A *Researching New York* section provides additional resources such as Web sites, books, articles, and films for students' research assignments.

- *Alternate thematic sequences* offer more options and greater flexibility for lesson plans.

The Place Where We Dwell: Reading and Writing about New York City is designed for use in a first-year course in composition, particularly one that emphasizes the urban experience. From our experience of using New York City as a subject in our writing classes, we have found that our classroom readings not only inspire and generate thoughtful student work but serve to cultivate a growing community of writers writing about New York City.

Juanita But
Mark Noonan
English Department
New York City College of Technology
City University of New York

ACKNOWLEDGEMENTS

We would like to thank the following friends and colleagues whose comments, advice, and support helped us make this a better and more useful anthology. From the CityTech English Department, we especially want to thank: Berit Anderson, Albert Angeloro, Paul Broer, Elizabeth Gold, George Guida, Richard Hanley, Gina Liebowitz, Jane Mushabac, Mary O'Riordan, and Nancy Thompson. Special thanks also to Allen Durgin and Jack Shuler, from the CUNY Graduate Center. Our editors at Kendall/Hunt, Carrie Maro, Sue Ellen Saad and Colleen Zelinsky were also very helpful. Lastly, we would like to thank Estella Rojas, Director of the Learning Community, without whose support this project would not have come to fruition.

Section I:

Here Is New York

"Woolworth Building in the Clouds"/CORBIS

"Giovanni Verazzano Discovers the Bay" (1524)

After proceeding one hundred leagues, we found a very pleasant situation among some steep hills, through which a very large river, deep at its mouth, forced its way to the sea; from the sea to the estuary of the river, any ship heavily laden might pass, with the help of the tide, which rises eight feet. But as we were riding at anchor in a good berth, we would not venture up in our vessel, without a knowledge of the mouth; therefore we took the boat, and entering the river, we found the country on its banks well peopled, the inhabitants not differing much from the others, being dressed out with the feathers of birds of various colours. They came towards us with evident delight, raising loud shouts of admiration, and showing us where we could most securely land with our boat. We passed up this river, about half a league, when we found it formed a most beautiful lake three leagues in circuit, upon which they were rowing thirty or more of their small boats, from one shore to the other, filled with multitudes who came to see us. All of a sudden, as is wont to happen to navigators, a violent contrary wind blew in from the sea, and forced us to return to our ship, greatly regretting to leave this region which seemed so commodious and delightful, and which we supposed must also contain great riches, as the hills showed many indications of minerals.

CHAPTER 1

New Yorkers

I'm crazy about this City.

Daylight slants like a razor cutting the buildings in half. In the top half I see looking faces and it's not easy to tell which are people, which the work of stonemasons. Below is shadow where any blasé thing takes place: clarinets and lovemaking, fists and the voices of sorrowful women. A city like this one makes me dream tall and feel in on things. Hep. It's the bright steel rocking above the shade below that does it. When I look over strips of green grass lining the river, at church steeples and into the cream-and-copper halls of apartment buildings, I'm strong. Alone, yes, but top-notch and indestructible—like the City in 1926 when all the wars are over and there will never be another one. The people down there in the shadow are happy about that. At last, at last, everything's ahead. The smart ones say so and people listening to them and reading what they write down agree: Here comes the new. Look out. There goes the sad stuff. The bad stuff. The things-nobody-could-help stuff. The way everybody was then and there. Forget that. History is over, you all, and everything's ahead at last.

Toni Morrison
From *Jazz* (1992)

I'd rather be a lampost in New York than the Mayor of Chicago.

Mayor James J. Walker

New Yorkers

This chapter sees New York City as much the capital of the world and the ultimate metropolis as the home where we live, and move, and have our being. The voices collected here are from the eternally loyal, those who can honestly say, as Toni Morrison's narrator in *Jazz* puts it, "I'm crazy about this City." The readings remind us of the fact that New York is more than just a place that inspires awe, imagination, or even envy. Admit it or not, we do take this city personally.

In "The Colossus of New York," Colson Whitehead suggests that the moment we personalize our memories of New York, we have already become a New Yorker. For him, it is the individual reality and history of the city we carry that makes New York what it is. On the contrary, John Steinbeck's "The Making of a New Yorker" describes a process in which the city shapes a person into one of its own. Embracing the city's "every vice and blemish and beauty," Steinbeck, a converted New Yorker, wonders, "What more could you ask?" Brimming with the pride of a New Yorker is Edward Field's poem "New York." It articulates the solidarity as well as aloofness of individuals living in the city.

In New York, a subway ride is more than just a subway ride. Visiting from Alabama, Ralph Ellison considers his first subway experience in "New York, 1936" as both daunting and liberating. He realizes that in New York's crowded subway cars racial segregation is neither an imperative nor an option. For both Anna Quindlen and Ian Frazier, the subway is a place of happenings, where one observes or partakes in unanticipated encounters and mini-spectacles. From an insider's perspective, Quindlen's "Pregnant in New York" explores the character of the city in terms of gender difference and etiquette. With a good sense of humor, she illustrates what it means to be "disabled" in New York. Ian Frazier's "Take the F" is an essay filled with meticulous details. Frazier guides our eyes to the normally invisible and presents a set of dynamic and diverse images of our neighbors in New York.

E. B. White's "Here is New York" is a monumental piece that breathes the spirit of the city. This essay is at the same time an inward expression, an outward description, as well as a thorough assessment of New York. White's essay checks the pulses of the city and offers an insightful prognosis of urban life.

The Colossus of New York

Colson Whitehead

Colson Whitehead (b.1969) was born and raised in New York City. He is the author of *The Intuitionist* and *John Henry Days* and is a recipient of a Whiting Award and a MacArthur Fellowship. He lives in Brooklyn.

Pre-reading

What was your first memory of New York City?

I'm here because I was born here and thus ruined for anywhere else, but I don't know about you. Maybe you're from here, too, and sooner or later it will come out that we used to live a block away from each other and didn't even know it. Or maybe you moved here a couple years ago for a job. Maybe you came here for school. Maybe you saw the brochure. The city has spent a considerable amount of time and money putting the brochure together, what with all the movies, TV shows and songs—the whole If You Can Make It There business. The city also puts a lot of effort into making your hometown look really drab and tiny, just in case you were wondering why it's such a drag to go back sometimes.

No matter how long you have been here, you are a New Yorker the first time you say, That used to be Munsey's, or That used to be the Tic Toc Lounge. That before the internet café plugged itself in, you got your shoes resoled in the mom-and-pop operation that used to be there. You are a New Yorker when what was there before is more real and solid than what is here now.

You start building your private New York the first time you lay eyes on it. Maybe you were in a cab leaving the airport when the skyline first roused itself into view. All your worldly possessions were in the trunk, and in your hand you held an address on a piece of paper. Look: there's the Empire State Building, over there are the Twin Towers. Somewhere in that fantastic, glorious mess was the address on the piece of paper, your first home here. Maybe your parents dragged you here for a vacation when you were a kid and towed you up and down the gigantic avenues to shop for Christmas gifts. The only skyscrapers visible from your stroller were the

1

legs of adults, but you got to know the ground pretty well and started to wonder why some sidewalks sparkle at certain angles, and others don't. Maybe you came to visit your old buddy, the one who moved here last summer, and there was some mix-up as to where you were supposed to meet. You stepped out of Penn Station into the dizzying hustle of Eighth Avenue and fainted. Freeze it there: that instant is the first brick in your city.

I started building my New York on the uptown No. 1 train. My first city memory is of looking out a subway window as the train erupted from the tunnel on the way to 125th Street and palsied up onto the elevated tracks. It's the early seventies, so everything is filthy. Which means everything is still filthy, because that is my city and I'm sticking to it. I still call it the Pan Am Building, not out of affectation, but because that's what it is. For that new transplant from Des Moines, who is starting her first week of work at a Park Avenue South insurance firm, that titan squatting over Grand Central is the Met Life Building, and for her it always will be. She is wrong, of course—when I look up there, I clearly see the gigantic letters spelling out Pan Am, don't I? And of course I am wrong, in the eyes of the old-timers who maintain the myth that there was a time before Pan Am.

History books and public television documentaries are always trying   5
to tell you all sorts of "facts" about New York. That Canal Street used to be a canal. That Bryant Park used to be a reservoir. It's all hokum. I've been to Canal Street, and the only time I ever saw a river flow through it was during the last water-main explosion. Never listen to what people tell you about old New York, because if you didn't witness it, it is not a part of your New York and might as well be Jersey. Except for that bit about the Dutch buying Manhattan for twenty-four bucks—there are and always will be braggarts who "got in at the right time."

There are eight million naked cities in this naked city—they dispute and disagree. The New York City you live in is not my New York City; how could it be? This place multiplies when you're not looking. We move over here, we move over there. Over a lifetime, that adds up to a lot of neighborhoods, the motley construction material of your jerry-built metropolis. Your favorite newsstands, restaurants, movie theaters, subway stations and barbershops are replaced by your next neighborhood's favorites. It gets to be quite a sum. Before you know it, you have your own personal skyline.

Go back to your old haunts in your old neighborhoods and what do you find: they remain and have disappeared. The greasy spoon, the deli, the dry cleaner you scouted out when you first arrived and tried to make those new streets yours: they are gone. But look past the windows of the travel agency that replaced your pizza parlor. Beyond the desks and computers and promo posters for tropical adventures, you can still see Neapolitan slices cooling, the pizza cutter lying next to half a pie, the map of Sicily on the wall. It is all still there, I assure you. The man who just paid for a trip to Jamaica sees none of that, sees his romantic getaway, his family vacation, what this little shop on this little street has granted him. The disappeared pizza parlor is still here because you are here, and when the beauty parlor replaces the travel agency, the gentleman will still have his vacation. And that lady will have her manicure.

You swallow hard when you discover that the old coffee shop is now a chain pharmacy, that the place where you first kissed So-and-so is now a discount electronics retailer, that where you bought this very jacket is now rubble behind a blue plywood fence and a future office building. Damage has been done to your city. You say, It happened overnight. But of course it didn't. Your pizza parlor, his shoeshine stand, her hat store: when they were here, we neglected them. For all you know, the place closed down moments after the last time you walked out the door. (Ten months ago? Six years? Fifteen? You can't remember, can you?) And there have been five stores in that spot before the travel agency. Five different neighborhoods coming and going between then and now, other people's other cities. Or fifteen, twenty-five, a hundred neighborhoods. Thousands of people pass that storefront every day, each one haunting the streets of his or her own New York, not one of them seeing the same thing.

We can never make proper good-byes. It was your last ride in a Checker cab and you had no warning. It was the last time you were going to have Lake Tung Ting shrimp in that kinda shady Chinese restaurant and you had no idea. If you had known, perhaps you would have stepped behind the counter and shaken everyone's hand, pulled out the camera and issued posing instructions. But you had no idea. There are unheralded tipping points, a certain number of times that we will unlock the front door of an apartment. At some point you were closer to the last time than you were to the first time, and you didn't even know it. You didn't know that each time you passed the threshold you were saying good-bye.

I never got a chance to say good-bye to some of my old buildings.   10
Some I lived in, others were part of a skyline I thought would always be there. And they never got a chance to say good-bye to me. I think they would have liked to—I refuse to believe in their indifference. You say you know these streets pretty well? The city knows you better than any living person because it has seen you when you are alone. It saw you steeling yourself for the job interview, slowly walking home after the late date, tripping over nonexistent impediments on the sidewalk. It saw you wince when the single frigid drop fell from the air conditioner twelve stories up and zapped you. It saw the bewilderment on your face as you stepped out of the stolen matinee, incredulous that there was still daylight after such a long movie. It saw you half-running up the street

after you got the keys to your first apartment. The city saw all that. Remembers, too.

Consider what all your old apartments would say if they got together to swap stories. They could piece together the starts and finishes of your relationships, complain about your wardrobe and musical tastes, gossip about who you are after midnight. 7J says, So that's what happened to Lucy—I knew it would never work out. You picked up yoga, you put down yoga, you tried various cures. You tried on selves and got rid of them, and this makes your old rooms wistful: why must things change? 3R goes, Saxophone, you say—I knew him when he played guitar. Cherish your old apartments and pause for a moment when you pass them. Pay tribute, for they are the caretakers of your reinventions.

Our streets are calendars containing who we were and who we will be next. We see ourselves in this city every day when we walk down the sidewalk and catch our reflections in store windows, seek ourselves in this city each time we reminisce about what was there fifteen, ten, forty years ago, because all our old places are proof that we were here. One day the city we built will be gone, and when it goes, we go. When the buildings fall, we topple, too.

Maybe we become New Yorkers the day we realize that New York will go on without us. To put off the inevitable, we try to fix the city in place, remember it as it was, doing to the city what we would never allow to be done to ourselves. The kid on the uptown No. 1 train, the new arrival stepping out of Grand Central, the jerk at the intersection who doesn't know east from west: those people don't exist anymore, ceased to be a couple of apartments ago, and we wouldn't have it any other way. New York City does not hold our former selves against us. Perhaps we can extend the same courtesy.

Our old buildings still stand because we saw them, moved in and out of their long shadows, were lucky enough to know them for a time. They are a part of the city we carry around. It is hard to imagine that something will take their place, but at this very moment the people with the right credentials are considering how to fill the craters. The cement trucks will roll up and spin their bellies, the jackhammers will rattle, and after a while the postcards of the new skyline will be available for purchase. Naturally we will cast a wary eye toward those new kids on the block, but let's be patient and not judge too quickly. We were new here, too, once.

What follows is my city. Making this a guidebook, with handy color-coded maps and minuscule fine print you should read very closely so you won't be surprised. It contains your neighborhoods. Or doesn't. We overlap. Or don't. Maybe you've walked these avenues, maybe it's all Jersey to you. I'm not sure what to say. Except that probably we're neighbors. That we walk past each other every day, and never knew it until now.

15

Discussion Questions

1. Colson Whitehead writes that everyone's New York is different. What is his "private" New York like? What was the "first brick" in his city?

2. According to Whitehead, when does someone become a New Yorker?

3. What is the significance of the title?

4. According to the author, why are there no "proper good-byes" in New York?

5. How does the author establish the tone of the essay?

6. In paragraph 3 what are skyscrapers compared to? Can you find any other metaphors in the essay?

7. Whitehead uses many expressive verbs such as "roused" (para. 3), "erupted," and "palsied" (para. 4). What are the effects of these words?

8. In paragraph 10 the author writes, "The city knows you better than any living person because it has seen you when you are alone." Find other examples of personification in the essay and comment on them.

Writing Tasks

1. Recount your first memory of being in New York. Focus on a particular image, sensation, event, or encounter.

2. What changes have you noticed in your neighborhood? How do you feel about them?

3. In New York, many neighborhoods have been undergoing economic development in which run-down buildings and vacant lots have been turned into upscale residential areas and chain stores (such as Starbucks Coffee). What do you feel are the advantages and disadvantages of this change known as gentrification?

New York

Edward Field

Edward Field was born on June 7, 1924, in Brooklyn, New York. His books of poetry include *Magic Words: Poems* (Harcourt, 1997); *Counting Myself Lucky: Selected Poems 1963–1992* (1992); *New and Selected Poems from the Book of My Life* (1987); *A Full Heart* (1977), nominated for the Lenore Marshall Prize; and *Stand Up, Friend, with Me* (1963), which was the 1962 Lamont Poetry Selection of The Academy of American Poets.

Pre-reading

Can you think of any misconceptions people have about New York?

NEW YORK

I live in a beautiful place, a city	1
people claim to be astonished	
when you say you live there.	
They talk of junkies, muggings, dirt, and noise,	
missing the point completely.	5
I tell them where they live it is hell,	
a land of frozen people.	
They never think of people.	
Home, I am astonished by this environment	
that is also a form of nature	10
like those paradises of trees and grass	
but this is a people paradise	
where we are the creatures mostly	
though thank God for dogs, cats, sparrows, and roaches.	
This vertical place is no more an accident	15
than the Himalayas are.	
The city needs all those tall buildings	
to contain the tremendous energy here.	
The landscape is in a state of balance.	
We do God's will whether we know it or not:	20
Where I live the streets end in a river of sunlight.	
Nowhere else in the country do people	
show just what they feel—	
we don't put on any act.	

Look at the way New Yorkers   25
walk down the street. It says,
I don't care. What nerve,
to dare to live their dreams, or nightmares,
and no one bothers to look.
True, you have to be an expert to live here.   30
Part of the trick is not to go anywhere, lounge about,
go slowly in the midst of the rush for novelty.
Anyway, beside the eats the big event here
is the streets which are full of love—
we hug and kiss a lot. You can't say that   35
for anywhere else around. For some
it is the sex part they care about and get—
there's all the opportunity in the world if you want it.
For me it is different:
Out walking, my soul seeks its food.   40
It knows what it wants.
Instantly it recognizes its mate, our eyes meet,
and our beings exchange a vital energy,
the universe goes on Charge
and we pass by without holding.   45

Reprinted by permission of the author.

Discussion Questions

1. From the poem, what aspects of New York fascinate the poet? Do you share the same opinion?

2. Do you agree with Field that people in New York are different from elsewhere in the country? From your experience, do you think that his claims are valid?

3. In line 30, Field suggests that to live in New York, "you have to be an expert." What exactly does he mean?

4. In line 40, the poet writes that "my soul seeks its food." What is it in New York that specially nourishes his soul? To what extent do you identify with his experience?

Writing Task

1. Write an essay in which you show the uniqueness of New York as compared to other cities in the nation.

2. Compare this poem to Walt Whitman's "Mannahatta" written in the 19th century. How are they similar? How do they differ?

Roaches

Edward Field

Pre-reading

Can you recall an encounter you have had with either rats or roaches in this city?

Roaches

An old decrepit city like London
doesn't have any.
They ought to love it there
in those smelly, elegant buildings.
Surely I myself have smuggled some in my luggage
but they obviously don't like the English—
for that alone I should love them.
They are among the brightest
and most attractive of small creatures
though you have to be prepared
for the look of horror
on the faces of out-of-town guests
when a large roach walks across the floor
as you are sipping drinks.
You reach out and swat,
and keeping the conversation going
pick up the corpse and drop it into an ashtray
feeling very New Yorky doing it.
After all, you've got to be tough to live here—
the visitor didn't make it.

Roaches also thrive on it here:
They set up lively communes
in open boxes of rice, spaghetti, and matzohs.
You come in to make coffee in the morning
and find a dead one floating in the kettle
and dots or roach shit on the dishes,
hinting at roachy revels the night before.

If you let them alone
they stop running at the sight of you
and whisker about
taking a certain interest in whatever you are doing,
and the little ones, expecting like all babies to be adored,
frolic innocently in the sink,
even in daytime when grownup roaches rest
after a night of swarming around the garbage bag.
The trouble with this approach is
they outbreed you and take over,
even moving sociably right into your bed.
Which brings up the question, Do they bite?
Some say yes, and if yes,
do they carry oriental diseases?
Even though you have tried to accept them
there comes a point when you find your eyes
studying labels of roach killers on supermarket shelves,
decide to try a minimal approach, buy one,
but when you attack with spray can aimed
they quickly learn to flee.
The fastest of course live to multiply
so they get cleverer all the time
with kamikaze leaping into space,
or zigzagging away,
race into far corners of the apartment
where they drop egg-sacks in their last throes
and start ineradicable new colonies.

When you light the oven
they come out and dance on the hot stove top
clinging with the tips of their toes,
surviving by quick footwork until you swat them.
Or if you spray it first
you have the smell of roaches roasting slowly.

And when you wash them down the drain
without their being certifiably dead
do they crawl up when the coast is clear?
Some even survive the deadliest poisons devised by man
and you have weird, white mutations running about.
Dying, they climb the walls, or up your legs, in agony,
making you feel like a dirty rat,
until they fall upside down with frail legs
waving in the air.
No more half-measures—
it's them or us you finally realize
and decide on nothing less than total fumigation:

The man comes while you are out
and you return to a silent apartment, blissfully roach-free.
You vacuum up the scattered bodies of the unlucky,
pushing down guilty feelings, lonely feelings,
and congratulate yourself.
    You booby,
they have only moved over to the neighbor's
and she too is forced to fumigate,
and just when you are on the princess phone crowing to
    your friends,
back they come, the whole tribe of them,
many gone now
due to their trivial life-span and chemical adversaries
but more numerous than ever with the new born
and all the relatives from next door and the neighborhood
    with them,
you standing there outraged, but secretly relieved
as they swarm into the kitchen from every crevice,
glad to be home, the eternal innocents,
greeting you joyfully.

Discussion Questions

1. Discuss the passages or lines you find particularly entertaining.

2. In what ways are cockroaches like any other New Yorker?

Writing Tasks

1. Write about how Field pays careful attention to language, form, and imagery in his two poems.

2. Write your own New York poem.

The Making of a New Yorker

John Steinbeck

John Steinbeck was born in Salinas, California in 1902 and many of his novels, including *The Grapes of Wrath* and *Of Mice and Men,* are set there. Nonetheless, he retained a lifelong interest in New York City. Following his graduation from Stanford University in 1925, he lived in the Fort Greene section of Brooklyn, working first as a construction worker and later as a reporter. He returned to New York in 1941 after winning the Pulitzer Prize and lived on the Upper East Side and Upper West Side until his death in 1968.

Pre-reading

Have you ever lived (or traveled) anywhere else before?
What was the first thing that struck you as different?

N ew York is the only city I have ever lived in. I have lived in the country, in the small town, and in New York. It is true I have had apartments in San Francisco, Mexico City, Los Angeles, Paris, and sometimes stayed for months, but that is a very different thing. This is a matter of feeling.   1

The transition from small town to New York is a slow and rough process. I am writing it not because I think my experience was unique; quite the contrary. I suspect that millions of New Yorkers who were not born here have had much the same experience—at least parallel experiences. . . .

When I came the first time to New York in 1925, I had never been to a city in my life. I arrived on a boat, as a tourist, with only one hundred dollars. It was November. . . .

From a porthole, then, I saw the city, and it horrified me. There was something monstrous about it—the tall buildings looming to the sky and the lights shining through the falling snow. I crept ashore—frightened and cold and with a touch of panic in my stomach. . . .

I wasn't really bad off. I had a sister in New York and she had a good   5
job. She had a husband and he had a good job. My brother-in-law got me

a job as a laborer and I found a room three flights up in Fort Greene Place in Brooklyn. This is about as alone as you can get. The job was on Madison Square Garden which was being finished in a hurry. There was time and a half and there was double time. I was big and strong. My job was wheeling cement—one of a long line—one barrow behind another, hour after hour. I wasn't that big and strong. It nearly killed me and it probably saved my life. I was too tired to see what went on around me. . . .

My knowledge of the city was blurred—aching, lights and the roar of the subway, climbing three flights to a room with dirty green walls, falling into bed half-washed, beef stew, coffee and sinkers in a coffeepot, a sidewalk that pitched a little as I walked, then the line of wheelbarrows again. It's all mixed up like a fever dream.

I don't even remember how long the job went on. It seems interminable and was maybe a month or six weeks. Anyway, the Garden got finished for the six-day bicycle races and Tex Rikard congratulated us all, without respect to race or color. I still get a shiver from the place sometimes.

About that time, my rich and successful uncle came to town from Chicago. He was an advertising man with connections everywhere. He was fabulous. He stayed in a suite at the Commodore, ordered drinks or coffee and sandwiches sent up any time he wanted, sent telegrams even if they weren't important. My uncle got me a job on a newspaper—The New York *American* down on William Street. I didn't know the first thing about being a reporter. I think now that the twenty-five dollars a week that they paid me was a total loss. They gave me stories to cover in Queens and Brooklyn and I would get lost and spend hours trying to find my way back. I couldn't learn to steal a picture from a desk when a family refused to be photographed and I invariably got emotionally involved and tried to kill the whole story to save the subject.

But for my uncle, I think they would have fired me the first week. Instead, they gave me Federal courts in the old Park Row Post Office. Why, I will never know. It was a specialist's job. Some of the men there had been on that beat for many years and I knew nothing about courts and didn't learn easily. I wonder if I could ever be as kind to a young punk as those men in the reporters' room at the Park Row Post Office were to me. They pretended that I knew what I was doing, and they did their best to teach me in a roundabout way. I learned to play bridge and where to look for suits and scandals. They informed me which judges were pushovers for publicity and several times they covered for me when I didn't show up. You can't repay that kind of thing. I never got to know them. Didn't know where they lived, what they did, or how they lived when they left the room. . . .

I had a reason for that, a girl. I had known her slightly in California and she was most beautiful. I don't think this was only my memory. For she

10

got a job in the Greenwich Village Follies just walking around—and she got it with no trouble whatever. . . .

Now New York changed for me. My girl lived on Gramercy Park and naturally I moved there. The old Parkwood Hotel had some tiny rooms—six walk-up flights above the street—for seven dollars a week. I had nothing to do with New York. It was a stage set in which this golden romance was taking place. The girl was very kind. Since she made four times as much money as I did, she paid for many little dinners. Every night I waited for her outside the stage door.

We would sit in Italian restaurants—she paid—and drink red wine. I wanted to write fiction-novels. She approved of that in theory, but said I should go into advertising—first, that is. I refused. I was being the poor artist, shielding his integrity.

During all this time, I never once knew or saw one New Yorker as a person. They were all minor characters in this intense personal drama. Then everything happened at once. The girl had more sense than I thought. She married a banker from the Middle West and moved there. And she didn't argue. She simply left a note, and two days later I was fired from *The American*.

And now at last the city moved in on me and scared me to death. I looked for jobs—but good jobs, pleasant jobs. I didn't get them. I wrote short stories and tried to sell them. I applied for work on other papers, which was ridiculous on the face of it. And the city crept in—cold and heartless, I thought. I began to fall behind in my room rent. I always had that one ace in the hole. I could go back to laboring. I had a friend who occasionally loaned me a little money. And finally, I was shocked enough to go for a job as a laborer. But by that time short feeding had taken hold. I could hardly lift a pick. I had trouble climbing the six flights back to my room. My friend loaned me a dollar and I bought two loaves of rye bread and a bag of dried herrings and never left my room for a week. I was afraid to go out on the street—actually afraid of traffic—the noise. Afraid of the landlord and afraid of people. Afraid even of acquaintances.

Then a man who had been in college with me got me a job as a work-away on a ship to San Francisco. And he didn't have to urge me, either. The city had beat the pants off me. Whatever it required to get ahead, I didn't have. I didn't leave the city in disgust—I left it with the respect plain unadulterated fear gives.

My second assault on New York was different but just as ridiculous as the first. I had had a kind of success with a novel after many tries. Three of my preceding novels did not make their advance and the advance was four hundred dollars. The largest amount I ever got for a short story was ninety dollars, for "The Red Pony." When royalties for "Tortilla Flat" went over a thousand dollars, and when Paramount bought the book for $3,000–$2,700 net, I should have been filled with joy but instead I was frightened. During the preceding years I had learned to live comfortably, and contentedly, on an absolute minimum of money—thirty-five to fifty dollars a month. When gigantic sums like $2,700 came over the horizon I was afraid I could not go back to the old simplicity.

Whereas on my first try New York was a dark, hulking frustration, the second time it became the Temptation and I a whistle-stop St. Anthony.* As with most St. Anthonys, if I had not been drawn toward luxury and sin, and to me they were the same thing, there would have been no temptation. I reacted without originality: today I see people coming to success doing the same things I did, so I guess I didn't invent it. I pretended and believed my pretense, that I hated the city and all its miles and traps. I longed for the quiet and contemplation of the West Coast. I preferred twenty-nine-cent wine and red beans. And again I didn't even see New York. It had scared me again but this time in another way. So I shut my eyes and drew virtue over my head. I insulted everyone who tried to be kind to me and I fled the Whore of Babylon with relief and virtuous satisfaction, for I had convinced myself that the city was a great snare set in the path of my artistic simplicity and integrity.

Back to the West I plunged, built a new house, bought a Chevrolet and imperceptibly moved from twenty-nine-cent wine to fifty-nine-cent wine. Now I made a number of business trips to New York and I was so completely in my role of country boy that I didn't look at it because I must have been enjoying my triumph over the snares and pitfalls. I had a successful play but never saw it. I believed I wasn't interested but it is probable that I was afraid to see it. I even built up a pleasant fiction that I hated the theatre. And the various trips to New York were very like the visits of the Salvation Army to a brothel—necessary and fascinating but distasteful.

The very first time I came to the city and settled was engineered by a girl. Looking back from the cool position of middle age, I can see that most of my heroic decisions somehow stemmed from a girl. I got an apartment on East 51st Street between First and Second Avenues, but even then I kept contact with my prejudices. My new home consisted of the first and second floors of a three-story house and the living room looked out on a small soot field called a garden. Two triumphant Brooklyn trees called ailanthus not only survived but thumbed their noses at the soft coal dust and nitric acid which passed for air in New York.

---

*The 13th-century Patron Saint Anthony is known for preaching against the vices of luxury and greed.

I was going to live in New York but I was going to avoid it. I planted 20
a lawn in the garden, bought huge pots and planted tomatoes, pollinating
the blossoms with a water-color brush. But I can see now that a conspiracy was going on, of which I was not even aware. I walked miles through
the streets for exercise, and began to know the butcher and the newsdealer
and the liquor man, not as props or as enemies but as people.

I have talked to many people about this and it seems to be a kind of
mystical experience. The preparation is unconscious, the realization happens in a flaming second. It was on Third Avenue. The trains were grind-
ing over my head. The snow was nearly waist-high in the gutters and
uncollected garbage was scattered in a dirty mess. The wind was cold,
and frozen pieces of paper went scraping along the pavement. I stopped
to look in a drug-store window where a latex dancing doll was undulat-
ing by a concealed motor—and something burst in my head, a kind of
light and a kind of feeling blended into an emotion which if it had spoken
would have said, "My God! I belong here. Isn't this wonderful?"

Everything fell into place. I saw every face I passed. I noticed every
door-way and the stairways to apartments. I looked across the street at the
windows, lace curtains and potted geraniums through sooty glass. It was
beautiful—but most important, I was part of it. I was no longer a stranger.
I had become a New Yorker.

Now there may be people who move easily into New York without tra-
vail, but most I have talked to about it have had some kind of trial by torture before acceptance. And the acceptance is a double thing. It seems to
me that the city finally accepts you just as you finally accept the city.

A young man in a small town, a frog in a small puddle, if he kicks his
feet is able to make waves, get mud in his neighbor's eyes—make some
impression. He is known. His family is known. People watch him with
some interest, whether kindly or maliciously. He comes to New York and
no matter what he does, no one is impressed. He challenges the city to
fight and it licks him without being aware of him. This is a dreadful blow
to a small-town ego. He hates the organism that ignores him. He hates the
people who look through him.

And then one day he falls into place, accepts the city and does not fight it 25
any more. It is too huge to notice him and suddenly the fact that it does-
n't notice him becomes the most delightful thing in the world. His self-
consciousness evaporates. If he is dressed superbly well—there are half
a million people dressed equally well. If he is in rags—there are a million
ragged people. If he is tall, it is a city of tall people. If he is short the
streets are full of dwarfs; if ugly, ten perfect horrors pass him in one
block; if beautiful, the competition is overwhelming. If he is talented,
talent is a dime a dozen. If he tries to make an impression by wearing

a toga—there's a man down the street in a leopard skin. Whatever he does or says or wears or thinks he is not unique. Once accepted this gives him perfect freedom to be himself, but unaccepted it horrifies him.

I don't think New York City is like other cities. It does not have character like Los Angeles or New Orleans. It is all characters—in fact, it is everything. It can destroy a man, but if his eyes are open it cannot bore him.

New York is an ugly city, a dirty city. Its climate is a scandal, its politics are used to frighten children, its traffic is madness, its competition is murderous. But there is one thing about it—once you have lived in New York and it has become your home, no place else is good enough. All of everything is concentrated here, population, theatre, art, writing, publishing, importing, business, murder, mugging, luxury, poverty. It is all of everything. It goes all right. It is tireless and its air is charged with energy. I can work longer and harder without weariness in New York than any-place else. . . .

I live in a small house on the East Side in the Seventies. It has a pretty little south garden. My neighborhood is my village. I know all of the storekeepers and some of the neighbors. Sometimes I don't go out of my village for weeks at a time. It has every quality of a village except nosiness. No one interferes with our business—no one by chance visits us without first telephoning, certainly a most civilized practice. When we close the front door, the city and the world are shut out and we are more private than any country man below the Arctic Circle has ever been. We have many friends—good friends in the city. Sometimes we don't see them for six or eight months and this in no way interferes with our friendship. Any place else this would be resented as neglect. . . .

Everyone at one time or another tries to explain to himself why he likes New York better than any place else. A man who worked for me liked it because if he couldn't sleep he could go to an all-night movie. That's as good a reason as any.

Every once and a while we go away for several months and we always   30
come back with a "Thank God I'm home" feeling. For New York is the world with every vice and blemish and beauty and there's privacy thrown in. What more could you ask?

Discussion Questions

1. What were Steinbeck's early impressions of New York? Why does the author claim that his first job "nearly killed me and it probably saved my life"?

2. Why does Steinbeck make such a poor reporter at first? What does this say about his personality?

3. Why didn't the author accept his girlfriend's suggestion to work in advertising?

4. What were the challenges the author faced as "the city crept in"?

5. What is different about Steinbeck's status upon his return to the city after living out West? What are the new challenges he faces and how does he react to them?

6. Why does the author use the word "assault" to describe his two New York experiences?

7. When the author finally settles in New York, where does he live? How does he approach life in the city?

8. What do you think the author implies in the description of "two triumphant Brooklyn trees called ailanthus" which "not only survived but thumbed their noses at the soft coal dust and nitric acid which passed for air in New York"?

9. When does Steinbeck realize he has become a New Yorker?

Writing Tasks

1. Write your own "Thank God I'm home" experience.

2. Compare and contrast New York with another city you have visited or lived in.

Subway Rush Hour

Langston Hughes

James Langston Hughes was born February 1, 1902, in Joplin, Missouri. His parents divorced when he was a small child, and his father moved to Mexico. He graduated from Central High School in Cleveland and then went on to New York where he studied, for one year, at Columbia University. He lived in Harlem for much of his life. Hughes's first book of poetry, *The Weary Blues*, was published in 1926. In addition to leaving us a large body of poetic work, Hughes wrote eleven plays and countless works of prose, including the well-known "Simple" books such as *Simple Speaks His Mind*. Hughes died on May 22, 1967, in New York. In his memory, his residence at 20 East 127th Street in Harlem, New York City, has been given landmark status by the New York City Preservation Commission, and East 127th Street has been renamed "Langston Hughes Place."

Pre-reading

What makes subway riding so enjoyable or, at times, so miserable?

SUBWAY RUSH HOUR

Mingled   1
breath and smell
so close
mingled
black and white   5
so near
no room for fear.

Discussion Questions

1. Hughes is legendary for being able to say so much in very few lines. How does he accomplish this in this poem?

Writing Task

1. Write a paper in which you discuss all of Hughes' poems found in this anthology.

New York, 1936

Ralph Ellison

Born in Oklahoma in 1914 and educated at the Tuskegee Institute in Alabama, Ralph Ellison established his literary reputation with his first and only novel, *Invisible Man,* first published in 1947 and reprinted numerous times since. His collections of essays include *Shadow and Act* (1964) and *Going to the Territory* (1986). This essay is excerpted from his memoir entitled "An Extravagance of Laughter" (1986). Ellison died in 1994.

Pre-reading

How does New York compare to other places you know?

In 1936, a few weeks after my arrival in New York City, I was lucky enough to be invited by an old hero and newfound friend, Langston Hughes, to be his guest at what would be my introduction to Broadway theater. I was so delighted and grateful for the invitation that I failed to ask my host the title of the play, and it was not until we arrived at the theater that I learned that it would be Jack Kirkland's dramatization of Erskine Caldwell's famous novel *Tobacco Road*. . . . I failed to note the irony of circumstance that would have as my introduction to New York theater a play with a southern setting and characters that were based upon a type and class of whites whom I had spent the last three years trying to avoid. Had I been more alert, it might have occurred to me that somehow a group of white Alabama farm folk had learned of my presence in New York, thrown together a theatrical troupe, and flown north to haunt me. . . . And yet that irony arose precisely from the mixture of motives—practical, educational, and romantic—that had brought me to the North in the first place.

1

Among these was my desire to enjoy a summer free of the South and its problems while meeting the challenge of being on my own for the first time in a great northern city. Fresh out of Alabama, with my junior year at Tuskegee Institute behind me, I was also in New York seeking funds with which to complete my final year as a music major—a goal at which I was having less success than I had hoped. However, there had been compensations. For between working in the Harlem YMCA cafeteria as a substitute for vacationing waiters and countermen and searching for a more profitable job, I had used my free time exploring the city, making new acquaintances, and enjoying the many forms of social freedom that were unavailable to me in Alabama. The very idea of being in New York was dreamlike, for like many young Negroes of the time, I thought of it as the freest of American cities and considered Harlem as the site and symbol of Afro-American progress and hope. Indeed, I was both young and bookish enough to think of Manhattan as my substitute for Paris and of Harlem as a place of Left Bank excitement.

And yet I soon discovered, much to my chagrin, that while I was physically out of the South, I was restrained—sometimes consciously, sometimes not—by certain internalized thou-shalt-nots that had structured my public conduct in Alabama. It was as though I had come to the Eden of American culture and found myself indecisive as to which of its fruits were free for my picking. Beyond the borders of Harlem's briar patch—which seemed familiar because of my racial and cultural identification with the majority of its people and the lingering spell that had been cast nationwide by the music, dance, and literature of the so-called Harlem Renaissance— I viewed New Yorkers through the overlay of my Alabama experience. Contrasting the whites I encountered with those I had observed in the South, I weighed class against class and compared southern styles with their northern counterparts. I listened to diction and noted dress, and searched for attitudes in inflections, carriage, and manners. And in pursuing this aspect of my extracurricular education, I explored the landscape.

I crossed Manhattan back and forth from river to river and up, down, and around again, from Spuyten Duyvil Creek to the Battery, looking and listening and gadding about; rode streetcar and el, subway and bus; took a hint from Edna Millay* and spent an evening riding back and forth on the Staten Island Ferry. From the elevated trains I saw my first penthouses with green trees growing atop tall buildings, caught remote glimpses of homes, businesses, and factories while moving above the teeming streets, and felt a sense of quiet tranquillity despite the bang and clatter. Yes, but the subways were something else again.

In fact, the subways were utterly confusing to my southern-bred idea   5
of good manners, and especially the absence of a certain gallantry that

---

*Edna St. Vincent Millay is a Greenwich Village poet famous for her poem "Recuerdo," which appears in the Literary NY section.

men were expected to extend toward women. Subway cars appeared to be underground arenas where northern social equality took the form of an endless shoving match in which the usual rules of etiquette were turned upside down—or so I concluded after watching a 5:00 footrace in a crowded car.

The contest was between a huge white woman who carried an armful of bundles, and a small Negro man who lugged a large suitcase. At the time I was standing against the track-side door, and when the train stopped at a downtown station I saw the two come charging through the opening doors like racehorses leaving the starting gate at Belmont. And as they spied and dashed for the single empty seat, the outcome appeared up for grabs, but it was the woman, thanks to a bustling, more ruthless stride (and more subway know-how) who won—though but by a hip and a hair. For just as they reached the seat she swung a well-padded hip and knocked the man off stride, thus causing him to lose his balance as she turned, slipped beneath his reeling body, and plopped into the seat. It was a maneuver that produced a startling effect—at least on me.

For as she banged into the seat it caused the man to spin and land smack-dab in her lap—in which massive and heaving center of gravity he froze, stared into her face nose-tip to nose, and then performed a spring like leap to his feet as from a red-hot stove. It was but the briefest conjunction, and then, as he reached down and fumbled for his suitcase, the woman began adjusting her bundles, and with an elegant toss of her head she then looked up into his face with the most ladylike and triumphant of smiles.

I had no idea of what to expect next, but to her sign of good sports-womanship the man let out with an exasperated "Hell, you can have it, I don't want it!" A response that evoked a phrase from an old forgotten ditty to which my startled mind added the unstated line—"Sleeping in the bed with your hand right on it"—and shook me with visions of the train screeching to a stop and a race riot beginning. . . .

But not at all. For while the defeated man pushed his way to another part of the car, the crowd of passengers simply looked on and laughed.   10

Still, for all their noise and tension, it was not the subways that most intrigued me, but the buses. In the South you occupied the back of the bus, and nowhere *but* the back, or so help you God. Being in the North and en-couraged by my anonymity, I experimented by riding all *over* New York buses, excluding only the driver's seat—front end, back end, right side, left side, sitting or standing as the route and flow of passengers de-manded. *And,* since those were the glorious days of double-deckers, both enclosed and open, I even rode *top*side.

Thus having convinced myself that no questions of racial status would be raised by where I chose to ride, I asked myself whether a seat at the back of the bus wasn't actually more desirable than one at the front. For not only did it provide more legroom, it offered a more inclusive perspective on both the interior and exterior scenes. I found the answer obvious and quite amusing. But now that I was no longer forced by law and compelled by custom to ride at the back, what was more desirable—the possibility of exercising what was routinely accepted in the North as an abstract, highly symbolic (even trivial) form of democratic freedom, or the creature comfort that was to be had by occupying a spot from which more of the passing scene could be observed? And in my own personal terms, what was more important— my individual comfort, or the exercise of the democratic right to be squeezed and jostled by strangers? Such questions were akin to that of whether you lived in a Negro neighborhood because you were forced to do so, or because you preferred living among those of your own background. Having experienced life in mixed neighborhoods as a child, I preferred to live where people spoke my own version of the American language, and where misreading of tone or gesture was less likely to ignite lethal conflict.

Discussion Questions

1. Why does Ellison come to New York in 1936? What do you think was his most urgent reason?

2. How does Ellison utilize his free time?

3. How do his experiences help explain the appeal of New York for African-Americans during the 1930s?

4. Why does the author call Harlem "the site and symbol of Afro-American progress and hope"? Does this still hold true?

5. Why doesn't Ellison feel entirely "out of the South" while in New York?

6. Describe the humor in Ellison's "subway story." What does he learn from this incident about New York and himself?

7. Why is Ellison so intrigued with buses in New York?

Writing Tasks

1. Write an essay in which you compare New York to another part of the country.

2. Write an essay which analyzes the many ways New York offers its inhabitants exceptional freedom. Try to include ways in which the city also limits people.

3. Describe something about New York that you particularly enjoy.

Pregnant in New York

Anna Quindlen

Anna Quindlen (b. 1952) is the best-selling author of novels and nonfiction books. Her *New York Times* column, "Public and Private," won the Pulitzer Prize in 1992.

Pre-reading

Have you ever given up your seat to someone in the subway?
Under what circumstances?

I have two enduring memories of the hours just before I gave birth to my   1
first child. One is of finding a legal parking space on Seventy-eighth Street between Lexington and Park, which made my husband and me believe that we were going inside the hospital to have a child who would always lead a charmed life. The other is of walking down Lexington Avenue, stopping every couple of steps to find myself a visual focal point—a stop sign, a red light, a pair of $200 shoes in a store window—and doing what the Lamaze[1] books call first-stage breathing. It was 3:00 A.M. and coming toward me through a magenta haze of what the Lamaze books call discomfort were a couple in evening clothes whose eyes were popping out of their perfect faces. "Wow," said the man when I was at least two steps past them. "She looks like she's ready to burst."

I love New York, but it's a tough place to be pregnant. It's a great place for half sour pickles, chopped liver, millionaires, actors, dancers, akita dogs, nice leather goods, fur coats, and baseball, but it is a difficult place to have any kind of disability and, as anyone who has filled out the forms for a maternity leave lately will tell you, pregnancy is considered a disability. There's no privacy in New York; everyone is right up against everyone else and they all feel compelled to say what they think. When you look like a hot-air balloon with insufficient ballast, that's not good.

New York has no pity: it's every man for himself, and since you are yourself-and-a-half, you fall behind. There's a rumor afoot that if you are

---

[1]Lamaze *adj.* Relating to or being a method of childbirth in which the expectant mother is prepared psychologically and physically to give birth without the use of drugs.

pregnant you can get a seat on the A train at rush hour, but it's totally false. There are, in fact, parts of the world in which pregnancy can get you a seat on public transportation, but none of them are within the boundaries of the city—with the possible exception of some unreconstructed parts of Staten Island.

What you get instead are rude comments, unwarranted intrusions and deli countermen. It is a little-known fact that New York deli countermen can predict the sex of an unborn child. (This is providing that you order, of course. For a counterman to provide this service requires a minimum order of seventy-five cents.) This is how it works: You walk into a deli and say, "Large fruit salad, turkey on rye with Russian, a large Perrier and a tea with lemon." The deli counterman says, "Who you buying for, the Rangers?" and all the other deli countermen laugh.

This is where many pregnant women make their mistake. If it is wintertime and you are wearing a loose coat, the preferred answer to this question is, "I'm buying for all the women in my office." If it is summer and you are visibly pregnant, you are sunk. The deli counterman will lean over the counter and say, studying your contours, "It's a boy." He will then tell a tedious story about sex determination, his Aunt Olga, and a clove of garlic, while behind you people waiting on line shift and sigh and begin to make Zero Population Growth and fat people comments. (I once dealt with an East Side counterman who argued with me about the tea because he said it was bad for the baby, but he was an actor waiting for his big break, not a professional.) Deli countermen do not believe in amniocentesis. Friends who have had amniocentesis tell me that once or twice they tried to argue: "I already know it's a girl." "You are wrong." They gave up: "Don't forget the napkins."

There are also cabdrivers. One promptly pulled over in the middle of Central Park when I told him I had that queasy feeling. When I turned to get back into the cab, it was gone. The driver had taken the $1.80 on the meter as a loss. Luckily, I never had this problem again, because as I grew larger, nine out of ten cabdrivers refused to pick me up. They had read the tabloids. They knew about all those babies christened Checker (actually, I suppose now most of them are Plymouths) because they're born in the back seat in the Midtown Tunnel. The only way I could get a cabdriver to pick me up after the sixth month was to hide my stomach by having a friend walk in front of me. The exception was a really tiresome young cabdriver whose wife's due date was a week after mine and who wanted to practice panting with me for that evening's childbirth class. Most of the time I wound up taking public transportation.

And so it came down to the subways: men looking at their feet, reading their newspapers, working hard to keep from noticing me. One day on the

IRT I was sitting down—it was a spot left unoccupied because the rainwater had spilled in the window from an elevated station—when I noticed a woman standing who was or should have been on her way to the hospital.

"When are you due?" I asked her. "Thursday," she gasped. "I'm September," I said. "Take my seat." She slumped down and said, with feeling, "You are the first person to give me a seat on the subway since I've been pregnant." Being New Yorkers, with no sense of personal privacy, we began to exchange subway, taxi, and deli counterman stories. When a man sitting nearby got up to leave, he snarled, "You wanted women's lib, now you got it."

Well, I'm here to say that I did get women's lib, and it is my only fond memory of being pregnant in New York. (Actually, I did find pregnancy useful on opening day at Yankee Stadium, when great swarms of people parted at the sight of me as though I were Charlton Heston in *The Ten Commandments*. But it had a pariah quality that was not totally soothing.)

One evening rush hour during my eighth month I was waiting for a   10
train at Columbus Circle. The loudspeaker was crackling unintelligibly and ominously and there were as many people on the platform as currently live in Santa Barbara, Calif. Suddenly I had the dreadful feeling that I was being surrounded. "To get mugged at a time like this," I thought ruefully. "And this being New York, they'll probably try to take the baby, too." But as I looked around I saw that the people surrounding me were four women, some armed with shoulder bags. "You need protection," one said, and being New Yorkers, they ignored the fact that they did not know one another and joined forces to form a kind of phalanx around me, not unlike those that offensive linemen build around a quarterback.

When the train arrived and the doors opened, they moved forward, with purpose, and I was swept inside, not the least bit bruised. "Looks like a boy," said one with a grin, and as the train began to move, we all grabbed the silver overhead handles and turned away from one another.

Discussion Questions

1. Why is it difficult to be pregnant or "have any kind of disability" in New York?

2. What two enduring memories does Quindlen include in the opening paragraph? How do these details frame the rest of the essay?

3. Quindlen writes that "There's no privacy in New York" and "New York has no pity." How does she demonstrate this? Do you agree with her general assessment?

4. How do New York cabdrivers react to pregnant passengers?

5. What metaphor does the author use to describe the helpful women on the platform? How does this scene illustrate the general attitude towards privacy amongst New Yorkers?

Writing Tasks

1. Narrate a subway moment of your own that you consider to be typically New York.

2. Write a short essay in which you discuss at least three qualities that make a New Yorker. Be sure to provide examples.

3. Write an essay that describes three types of New Yorkers.

My First Address, Seared in Memory

Angie Cruz

Angie Cruz was born in 1972 in New York City's Washington Heights. She went to La Guardia High School and Fashion Design at Fashion Institute of Technology. She graduated from the NYU's, MFA program in 1999. Cruz has contributed shorter works to numerous periodicals including *Latina Magazine, Callaloo* and the *New York Times*. She has published two novels, *Soledad* and *Let It Rain Coffee*.

Pre-reading

What do you like or dislike about your neighborhood?

In 1997, I returned to the city from college upstate to study creative writing at New York University and found a sublet in my old neighborhood, Washington Heights. It was a steal, $600 a month for an L-shaped one-bedroom in a prewar building at 615 West 164th Street. All the apartments faced the courtyard, and as if watching a stage from a production booth, I saw my relatives and longtime neighbors across the way from my second-floor window.

Because I wanted color and to hide the defects on the walls, I painted the bedroom an oceanic blue, the living room the color of a mango, the bathroom a leaf green. The apartment bore signs of its past and wasn't perfect. The dumbwaiter had been turned into a pantry. The kitchen cabinets didn't close all the way, and the wooden floors were hidden by beige industrial tiles. Then there were the plumbing ghosts. My toilet flushed randomly, all by itself, and the sink in the kitchen filled up with bubbles when the lady upstairs did her wash.

I woke up in the morning with the sunlight, and from my kitchen window I often greeted my grandmother, who lived across the courtyard, her asking me, "Are you still studying up there?" That had been my explanation when she asked me why didn't I have a job with good benefits. "Estudiando" is the one word that magically answered all the questions from my relatives when I locked myself up and didn't pick up the phone, even when they saw that my light was on. "Estudiando" was the excuse I gave when my relatives saw male friends visiting. They wondered why men would visit a young woman living alone. "We are estudiando," I said, when my relatives stood at my front door holding Tupperware containers filled with dinner, and saw a group of women crowded in the living room plotting an event, discussing politics, sharing their writing.

Although my apartment was a snug 500 square feet, filled with books, museum posters and my very bad but honest figurative paintings, remnants of an earlier stint at the Fashion Institute of Technology, the rooms seemed to swell in size when other writers needed a place to stay. And so my apartment was often full of people coming and going, crammed with additional desks and beds for short-term stays. There was always a fresh batch of iced tea in the fridge, an answering machine to answer my calls, photographs on my desk of all the people I love.

The wooden and ceramic dolls I collected from different parts of the world watched over my laptop. My desk faced the courtyard, a neglected garden overgrown with weeds. In the late afternoon I could see if my sassy grandmother was home from her job at the lamp factory in New Jersey, and when the radio next door wasn't at full blast, I could hear my aunt, who also lived across the courtyard, yelling after my teenage nephew from her window.

There were also moments when it was quiet, when kids were at school, people were at work, and the merengue-loving neighbors were taking their afternoon siesta. In one of those rare quiet moments, I remember having a revelation while staring' at a draft of my first novel on my desk, that if I had waited to tell my story until I had a room of my own, as opposed to a place that always brimmed with people, I would never have finished that novel.

But even more so, without all the family members, who showed up with Tupperware and slipped $20 in my hand when I looked tired from long nights at freelance jobs teaching, editing and even window-designing while "estudiando" for my master's degree, I wouldn't have had the confidence that I was right to continue to live my life as a writer. It was the spirit of all that collective activity inside that apartment with elastic walls that gave birth to my first novel.

Discussion Questions

1. What are the defects of the writer's first apartment?
2. How do you describe the writer's living environment? What makes her apartment favorable to her writing?

3. In paragraph 5, the writer explains that the word "estudiando" magically answered all the questions from her relatives. What do you think the writer is trying to convey about her cultural tradition?

4. Cruz once waited for an ideal space to start writing. Have you ever waited for ideal conditions to start doing something you long to do? If so, what was the outcome?

Writing Tasks

1. Pay attention to your apartment and the environment surrounding it. Write an essay that describes your living space and how you relate to its details.

2. Write an essay in which you explain how your immediate and extended families help shape your goal.

Take the F

Ian Frazier

Ian Frazier (b. 1951) grew up in Ohio, lived for years in Brooklyn, and now lives in Montana. He is the author of three collections of humorous essays, *Dating Your Mom* (1986), *Nobody Better, Better than Nobody* (1987), and *Coyote v. Acme* (1996). His essays appear regularly in *The New Yorker, The Atlantic Monthly,* and elsewhere. "Take the F" was selected for the anthology, *Best American Essays* 1996.

Pre-reading

Do you recall any vivid moments on the subway?
What made those moments memorable?

B rooklyn, New York, has the undefined, hard-to-remember shape of a   1
stain. I never know what to tell people when they ask me where in it
I live. It sits at the western tip of Long Island at a diagonal that does not
conform neatly to the points of the compass. People in Brooklyn do not
describe where they live in terms of north or west or south. They refer instead to their neighborhoods, and to the nearest subway lines. I live on the
edge of Park Slope, a neighborhood by the crest of a low ridge that runs
through the borough. Prospect Park is across the street. Airplanes in the
landing pattern for LaGuardia Airport sometimes fly right over my building; every few minutes, on certain sunny days, perfectly detailed airplane
shadows slide down my building and up the building opposite in a blink.
You can see my building from the plane—it's on the left-hand side of
Prospect Park, the longer patch of green you cross after the expanse of
Green-Wood Cemetery.

We moved to a co-op apartment in a four-story building a week before
our daughter was born. She is now six. I grew up in the country and would
not have expected ever to live in Brooklyn. My daughter is a city kid, with
less sympathy for certain other parts of the country. When we visited
Montana, she was disappointed by the scarcity of pizza places. I over-
heard her explaining—she was three or four then—to a Montana kid

about Brooklyn. She said, "In Brooklyn, there is a lot of broken glass, so you have to wear shoes. And, there is good pizza." She is stern in her judgment of pizza. At the very low end of the pizza-ranking scale is some pizza she once had in New Hampshire, a category now called New Hampshire pizza. In the middle is some O.K. pizza she once had at the Bronx Zoo, which she calls zoo pizza. At the very top is the pizza at the pizza place where the big kids go, about two blocks from our house.

Our subway is the F train. It runs under our building and shakes the floor. The F is generally a reliable train, but one spring as I walked in the park I saw emergency vehicles gathered by a concrete-sheathed hole in the lawn. Firemen lifted a metal lid from the hole and descended into it. After a while, they reappeared, followed by a few people, then dozens of people, then a whole lot of people—passengers from the disabled F train, climbing one at a time out an exit shaft. On the F, I sometimes see large women in straw hats reading a newspaper called the *Caribbean Sunrise,* and Orthodox Jews bent over Talmudic texts in which the footnotes have footnotes, and groups of teenagers wearing identical red bandannas with identical red plastic baby pacifiers in the corners of their mouths, and female couples in porkpie hats, and young men with the silhouettes of the Manhattan skyline razored into their short side hair from one temple around to the other, and Russian-speaking men with thick wrists and big wristwatches, and a hefty, tall woman with long, straight blond hair who hums and closes her eyes and absently practices cello fingerings on the metal subway pole. As I watched the F-train passengers emerge among the grass and trees of Prospect Park, the faces were as varied as usual, but the expressions of indignant surprise were all about the same.

Just past my stop, Seventh Avenue, Manhattan-bound F trains rise from underground to cross the Gowanus Canal. The train sounds different—lighter, quieter—in the open air. From the elevated tracks, you can see the roofs of many houses stretching back up the hill to Park Slope, and a bumper crop of rooftop graffiti, and neon signs for Eagle Clothes and Kentile Floors, and flat expanses of factory roofs where seagulls stand on one leg around puddles in the sagging spots. There are fuel-storage tanks surrounded by earthen barriers, and slag piles, and conveyor belts leading down to the oil-slicked waters of the canal. On certain days, the sludge at the bottom of the canal causes it to bubble. Two men fleeing the police jumped in the canal a while ago; one made it across, the other quickly died. When the subway doors open at the Smith–Ninth Street stop, you can see the bay, and sometimes smell the ocean breeze. This stretch of elevated is the highest point of the New York subway system. To the south you can see the Verrazano-Narrows

Bridge, to the north the World Trade towers. For just a few moments, the Statue of Liberty appears between passing buildings. Pieces of a neighborhood—laundry on clotheslines, a standup swimming pool, a plaster saint, a satellite dish, a rectangle of lawn—slide by like quickly dealt cards. Then the train descends again; growing over the wall just before the tunnel is a wisteria bush, which blooms pale blue every May.

I have spent days, weeks on the F train. The trip from Seventh Avenue   5
to midtown Manhattan is long enough so that every ride can produce its own minisociety of riders, its own forty-minute Ship of Fools. Once a woman an arm's length from me on a crowded train pulled a knife on a man who threatened her. I remember the argument and the principals, but mostly I remember the knife—its flat, curved wood-grain handle inlaid with brass fittings at each end, its long, tapered blade. Once a man sang the words of the Lord's Prayer to a mournful, syncopated tune, and he fitted the mood of the morning so exactly that when he asked for money at the end the riders reached for their wallets and purses as if he'd pulled a gun. Once a big white kid with some friends was teasing a small old Hispanic lady, and when he got off the train I looked at him through the window and he slugged it hard next to my face. Once a thin woman and a fat woman sitting side by side had a long and loud conversation about someone they intended to slap silly: "Her butt be in the *hospital!*" Bring out the ar-*tillery!*" The terminus of the F in Brooklyn is at Coney Island, not far from the beach. At an off hour, I boarded the train and found two or three passengers and, walking around on the floor, a crab. The passengers were looking at the crab. Its legs clicked on the floor like varnished fingernails. It moved in this direction, then that, trying to get comfortable. It backed itself under a seat, against the wall. Then it scooted out just after some new passengers had sat down there, and they really screamed. Passengers at the next stop saw it and laughed. When a boy lifted his foot as if to stomp it, everybody cried, "Noooh!" By the time we reached Jay Street-Borough Hall, there were maybe a dozen of us in the car, all absorbed in watching the crab. The car doors opened and a heavyset woman with good posture entered. She looked at the crab; then, sternly, at all of us. She let a moment pass. Then she demanded, "*Whose is that?*" A few stops later, a short man with a mustache took a manila envelope, bent down, scooped the crab into it, closed it, and put it in his coat pocket.

The smells in Brooklyn: coffee, fingernail polish, eucalyptus, the breath from laundry rooms, pot roast, Tater Tots. A woman I know who grew up here says she moved away because she could not stand the smell of cooking food in the hallway of her parents' building. I feel just the opposite. I used to live in a converted factory above an Army-Navy store, and I like being in a place that smells like people live there. In the mornings, I sometimes wake to the smell of toast, and I still don't know exactly whose toast it is. And I prefer living in a borough of two and a half million inhabitants, the most of any borough in the city. I think of all the rural places, the pine-timbered canyons and within-commuting-distance farmland, that we are preserving by not living there. I like the immensities of the borough, the unrolling miles of Eastern Parkway and Ocean Parkway and Linden Boulevard, and the dishevelled outlying parks strewn with tree limbs and with shards of glass held together by liquor-bottle labels, and the tough bridges—the Williamsburg and the Manhattan—and the gentle Brooklyn Bridge. And I like the way the people talk; some really do have Brooklyn accents, really do say "dese" and "dose." A week or two ago, a group of neighbors stood on a street corner watching a peregrine falcon on a building cornice contentedly eating a pigeon it had caught, and the sunlight came through its tail feathers, and a woman said to a man, "Look at the tail," "it's so ah-range," and the man replied, "Yeah, I soar it." Like many Americans, I fear living in a nowhere, in a place that is no-place; in Brooklyn, that doesn't trouble me at all.

Everybody, it seems, is here. At Grand Army Plaza, I have seen traffic tieups caused by Haitians and others rallying in support of President Aristide, and by St. Patrick's Day parades, and by Jews of the Lubavitcher sect celebrating the birthday of their Grand Rebbe with a slow procession of ninety-three motor homes—one for each year of his life. Local taxis have bumper stickers that say "Allah Is Great": one of the men who made the bomb that blew up the World Trade Center used an apartment just a few blocks from me. When an election is held in Russia, crowds line up to cast ballots at a Russian polling place in Brighton Beach. A while ago, I volunteer-taught reading at a public elementary school across the park. One of my students, a girl, was part Puerto Rican, part Greek, and part Welsh. Her looks were a lively combination, set off by sea-green eyes. I went to a map store in Manhattan and bought maps of Puerto Rico, Greece, and Wales to read with her, but they didn't interest her. A teacher at the school was directing a group of students to set up chairs for a program in the auditorium, and she said to me, "We have a problem here—each of these kids speaks a different language." She asked the kids to tell me where they were from. One was from Korea, one from Brazil, one from Poland, one from Guyana, one from Taiwan. In the program that followed, a chorus of fourth and fifth graders sang "God Bless America," "You're a Grand Old Flag," and "I'm a Yankee-Doodle Dandy." . . .

Discussion Questions

1. How do people in Brooklyn describe where they are from? Do you yourself find this to be true?

2. What does the comment of Frazier's daughter, "In Brooklyn, there is a lot of broken glass," imply about urban life? Can you think of other features that also represent the city?

3. Focus on Frazier's use of topic sentences. How do they work to organize the essay?

4. What is the effect of Frazier's close attention to details throughout his essay? Focus on specific examples.

5. How does the final scene connect with the overall theme of the essay?

Writing Tasks

1. Write about what you miss the most when you are away from New York.

2. Take a subway ride and get off at a stop you are not familiar with. With pen in hand, explore and observe the environment. Compare and contrast this neighborhood with your own.

Here Is New York

E. B. White

E. B. White was born in 1899 in Mount Vernon, New York and graduated from Cornell University. He joined *The New Yorker* magazine in 1925 and wrote columns in "Talk of the Town." It was while living in Brooklyn that he wrote two famous children's books: *Stuart Little* (1945) and *Charlotte's Web* (1952). White died in 1985.

Pre-reading

What do you believe makes New York unlike any other city?

On any person who desires such queer prizes, New York will bestow the gift of loneliness and the gift of privacy. It is this largess that accounts for the presence within the city's walls of a considerable section of the population; for the residents of Manhattan are to a large extent strangers who have pulled up stakes somewhere and come to town, seeking sanctuary or fulfillment or some greater or lesser grail. The capacity to make such dubious gifts is a mysterious quality of New York. It can destroy an individual, or it can fulfill him, depending a good deal on luck. No one should come to New York to live unless he is willing to be lucky.

New York is the concentrate of art and commerce and sport and religion and entertainment and finance, bringing to a single compact arena the gladiator, the evangelist, the promoter, the actor, the trader and the merchant. It carries on its lapel the unexpungeable odor of the long past, so that no matter where you sit in New York you feel the vibrations of great times and tall deeds, of queer people and events and undertakings. I am sitting at the moment in a stifling hotel room in 90-degree heat, halfway down an air shaft, in midtown. No air moves in or out of the room, yet I am curiously affected by emanations from the immediate surroundings. I am twenty-two blocks from where Rudolph Valentino lay in state, eight blocks from where Nathan Hale was executed, five blocks from the publisher's office where Ernest Hemingway hit Max Eastman on the nose, four miles from where Walt Whitman sat sweating out

5

editorials for the Brooklyn Eagle, thirty-four blocks from the street Willa Cather lived in when she came to New York to write books about Nebraska. . . . (I could continue this list indefinitely); and for that matter I am probably occupying the very room that any number of exalted and some wise memorable characters sat in, some of them on hot, breathless afternoons, lonely and private and full of their own sense of emanations from without.

New York blends the gift of privacy with the excitement of participation; and better than most dense communities it succeeds in insulating the individual (if he wants it, and almost everybody wants or needs it) against all enormous and violent and wonderful events that are taking place every minute. Since I have been sitting in this miasmic air shaft, a good many rather splashy events have occurred in town. A man shot and killed his wife in a fit of jealousy. It caused no stir outside his block and got only small mention in the papers. I did not attend. Since my arrival, the greatest air show ever staged in all the world took place in town. I didn't attend and neither did most of the eight million other inhabitants, although they say there was quite a crowd. I didn't even hear any planes except a couple of westbound commercial airliners that habitually use this air shaft to fly over. . . .

I mention these merely to show that New York is peculiarly constructed to absorb almost anything that comes along (whether a thousand-foot liner out of the East or a twenty-thousand-man convention out of the West) without inflicting the event on its inhabitants; so that every event is, in a sense, optional, and the inhabitant is in the happy position of being able to choose his spectacle and so conserve his soul. In most metropolises, small and large, the choice is often not with the individual at all. . . .

The quality in New York that insulates its inhabitants from life may simply weaken them as individuals. Perhaps it is healthier to live in a community where, when a cornice falls, you feel the blow; where, when the governor passes, you see at any rate his hat.   5

I am not defending New York in this regard. Many of its settlers are probably here merely to escape, not face, reality. But whatever it means, it is a rather rare gift, and I believe it has a positive effect on the creative capacities of New Yorkers—for creation is in part merely the business of forgoing the great and small distractions.

Although New York often imparts a feeling of great forlornness or forsakeness, it seldom seems dead or unresourceful; and you always feel that either by shifting your location ten blocks or by reducing your fortune by five dollars you can experience rejuvenation. Many people who have no real independence of spirit depend on the city's tremendous variety and sources of excitement for spiritual sustenance and maintenance of morale. In the country there are a few chances of sudden rejuvenation—a shift in weather, perhaps, or something arriving in the mail. But in New York the chances are endless. I think that although many persons are here from some excess of spirit (which caused them to break away from their small town), some, too, are here from a deficiency of spirit, who find in New York a protection, or an easy substitution.

There are roughly three New Yorks. There is, first, the New York of the man or woman who was born here, who takes the city for granted and accepts its size and its turbulence as natural and inevitable. Second, there is the New York of the commuter—the city that is devoured by locusts each day and spat out each night. Third, there is the New York of the person who was born somewhere else and came to New York in quest of something. Of these three trembling cities the greatest is the last—the city of final destination, the city that is a goal. It is this third city that accounts for New York's high-strung disposition, its poetical deportment, its dedication to the arts, and its incomparable achievements. Commuters give the city its tidal restlessness; natives give it solidity and continuity; but the settlers give it passion. And whether it is a farmer arriving from Italy to set up a small grocery store in a slum, or a young girl arriving from a small town in Mississippi to escape the indignity of being observed by her neighbors, or a boy arriving from the Corn Belt with a manuscript in his suitcase and a pain in his heart, it makes no difference: each embraces New York with the intense excitement of first love, each absorbs New York with the fresh eyes of an adventurer, each generates heat and light to dwarf the Consolidated Edison Company. . . .

A poem compresses much in a small space and adds music, thus heightening its meaning. The city is like poetry: it compresses all life, all races and breeds, into a small island and adds music and the accompaniment of internal engines. The island of Manhattan is without any doubt the greatest human concentrate on earth, the poem whose magic is comprehensible to millions of permanent residents but whose full meaning will always remain illusive. At the feet of the tallest and plushiest offices lie the crummiest slums. The genteel mysteries housed in the Riverside Church are only a few blocks from the voodoo charms of Harlem. The merchant princes, riding to Wall Street in their limousines down the East River Drive, pass within a few hundred yards of the gypsy kings; but the princes do not know they are passing kings, and the kings are not up yet anyway—they live a more leisurely life than the princes and get drunk more consistently.

New York is nothing like Paris; it is nothing like London; and it is not   10
Spokane multiplied by sixty, or Detroit multiplied by four. It is by all odds

the loftiest of cities. It even managed to reach the highest point in the sky at the lowest moment of the depression. The Empire State Building shot twelve hundred and fifty feet into the air when it was madness to put out as much as six inches of new growth. (The building has a mooring mast that no dirigible has ever tied to; it employs a man to flush toilets in slack times; it has been hit by an airplane in a fog, struck countless times by lightning, and been jumped off of by so many unhappy people that pedestrians instinctively quicken step when passing Fifth Avenue and 34th Street.)

Manhattan has been compelled to expand skyward because of the absence of any other direction in which to grow. This, more than any other thing, is responsible for its physical majesty. It is to the nation what the white church spire is to the village—the visible symbol of aspiration and faith, the white plume saying that the way is up. . . .

It is a miracle that New York works at all. The whole thing is implausible. Every time the residents brush their teeth, millions of gallons of water must be drawn from the Catskills and the hills of Westchester. When a young man in Manhattan writes a letter to his girl in Brooklyn, the love message gets blown to her through a pneumatic tube—pfft—just like that. The subterranean system of telephone cables, power lines, steam pipes, gas mains and sewer pipes is reason enough to abandon the island to the gods and the weevils. Every time an incision is made in the pavement, the noisy surgeons expose ganglia that are tangled beyond belief. By rights New York should have destroyed itself long ago, from panic or fire or rioting or failure of some vital supply line in its circulatory system or from some deep labyrinthine short circuit. Long ago the city should have experienced an insoluble traffic snarl at some impossible bottleneck. It should have perished of hunger when food lines failed for a few days. It should have been wiped out by a plague starting in its slums or carried in by ships' rats. It should have been overwhelmed by the sea that licks at it on every side. The workers in its myriad cells should have succumbed to nerves, from the fearful pall of smoke-fog that drifts over every few days from Jersey, blotting out all light at noon and leaving the high offices suspended, men groping and depressed, and the sense of world's end. It should have been touched in the head by the August heat and gone off its rocker.

Mass hysteria is a terrible force, yet New Yorkers seem always to escape it by some tiny margin: they sit in stalled subways without claustrophobia, they extricate themselves from panic situations by some lucky wisecrack, they meet confusion and congestion with patience and grit— a sort of perpetual muddling through. Every facility is inadequate—the hospitals and schools and playgrounds are overcrowded, the express highways are feverish, the unimproved highways and bridges are bottle-necks; there is not enough air and not enough light, and there is usually either too much heat or too little. But the city makes up for its hazards and its deficiencies by supplying its citizens with massive doses of a supplementary vitamin—the sense of belonging to something unique, cosmopolitan, mighty and unparalleled. . . .

The oft-quoted thumbnail sketch of New York is, of course: "It's a wonderful place, but I'd hate to live there." I have an idea that people from villages and small towns, people accustomed to the convenience and the friendliness of neighborhood over-the-fence living, are unaware that life in New York follows the neighborhood pattern. The city is literally a composite of tens of thousands of tiny neighborhood units. There are, of course, the big districts and big units: Chelsea and Murray Hill and Gramercy (which are residential units), Harlem (a racial unit), Greenwich Village (a unit dedicated to the arts and other matters), and there is Radio City (a commercial development), Peter Cooper Village (a housing unit), the Medical Center (a sickness unit) and many other sections each of which has some distinguishing characteristic. But the curious thing about New York is that each large geographical unit is composed of countless small neighborhoods. Each neighborhood is virtually self-sufficient. Usually it is no more than two or three blocks long and a couple of blocks wide. Each area is a city within a city within a city. Thus, no matter where you live in New York, you will find within a block or two a grocery store, a barbershop, a newsstand and shoeshine shack, an ice-coal-and-wood cellar (where you write your order on a pad outside as you walk by), a dry cleaner, a laundry, a delicatessen (beer and sandwiches delivered at any hour to your door), a flower shop, an undertaker's parlor, a movie house, a radio-repair shop, a stationer, a haberdasher, a tailor, a drugstore, a garage, a tearoom, a saloon, a hardware store, a liquor store, a shoe-repair shop. Every block or two, in most residential sections of New York, is a little main street. A man starts for work in the morning and before he has gone two hundred yards he has completed half a dozen missions: bought a paper, left a pair of shoes to be soled, picked up a pack of cigarettes, ordered a bottle of whiskey to be dispatched in the opposite direction against his home-coming, written a message to the unseen forces of the wood cellar, and notified the dry cleaner that a pair of trousers awaits call. Homeward bound eight hours later, he buys a bunch of pussy willows, a Mazda bulb, a drink, a shine—all between the corner where he steps off the bus and his apartment. So complete is each neighborhood, and so strong the sense of neighborhood, that many a New Yorker spends a lifetime within the confines of an area smaller than a country village. Let him walk two blocks from his corner and he is in a strange land and will feel uneasy till he gets back.

Storekeepers are particularly conscious of neighborhood boundary
lines. A woman friend of mine moved recently from one apartment to another, a distance of three blocks. When she turned up, the day after the
move, at the same grocer's that she had patronized for years, the propri-
etor was in ecstasy—almost in tears—at seeing her. "I was afraid," he said,
"now that you've moved away I wouldn't be seeing you any more." To
him, *away* was three blocks, or about seven hundred and fifty feet. . . .

I've been remembering what it felt like as a young man to live in the
same town with giants. When I first arrived in New York my personal giants were a dozen or so columnists and critics and poets whose names appeared regularly in the papers. . . . The city is always full of young
worshipful beginners—young actors, young aspiring poets, ballerinas,
painters, reporters, singers—each depending on his own brand of tonic to
stay alive, each with his own stable of giants.

New York provides not only a continuing excitation but also a spectacle that is continuing. I wander around, re-examining this spectacle, hoping that I can put it on paper. It is Saturday, toward the end of the
afternoon. I turn through West 48th Street. From the open windows of the
drum and saxophone parlors come the listless sounds of musical instruction, monstrous insect noises in the brooding field of summer. The Cort
Theater is disgorging its matinee audience. Suddenly the whole block is
filled with the mighty voice of a street singer. He approaches, looking for
an audience, a large, cheerful Negro with grand-opera contours, strolling
with head thrown back, filling the canyon with uninhibited song. He carries a long cane as his sole prop, and is tidily but casually dressed—
slacks, seersucker jacket, a book showing in his pocket. . . .

In the café of the Lafayette, the regulars sit and talk. It is busy yet peaceful. Nursing a drink, I stare through the west windows at the Manufacturers
Trust Company and at the red brick fronts on the north side of Ninth Street,
watching the red turning slowly to purple as the light dwindles. Brick buildings have a way of turning color at the end of the day, the way a red rose
turns bluish as it wilts. The café is a sanctuary. The waiters are ageless and
they change not. Nothing has been modernized. Notre Dame stands guard
in its travel poster. The coffee is strong and full of chicory, and good.

Walk the Bowery under the El at night and all you feel is a sort of cold
guilt. Touched for a dime, you try to drop the coin and not touch the hand,
because the hand is dirty; you try to avoid the glance, because the glance
accuses. This is not so much personal menace as universal—the cold
menace of unresolved human suffering and poverty and the advanced
stages of the disease alcoholism. On a summer night the drunks sleep in
the open. The sidewalk is a free bed, and there are no lice. Pedestrians
step along and over and around the still forms as though walking on a

battlefield among the dead. In doorways, on the steps of the savings bank, the bums lie sleeping it off. Standing sentinel at each sleeper's head is the empty bottle from which he drained his release. Wedged in the crook of his arm is the paper bag containing his things. The glib barker on the sight-seeing bus tells his passengers that this is the "street of lost souls," but the Bowery does not think of itself as lost; it meets its peculiar problem in its own way—plenty of gin mills, plenty of flop-houses, plenty of indifference, and always, at the end of the line, Bellevue. . . .

The Consolidated Edison Company says there are eight million people in   20
the five boroughs of New York, and the company is in a position to know. Of these eight million, two million are Jews—or one person in every four. Among this two million who are Jewish are, of course, a great many nationalities—Russian, German, Polish, Rumanian, Austrian, a long list. The Urban League of Greater New York estimates that the number of Negroes in New York is about 700,000. Of these, about 500,000 live in Harlem, a district that extends northward from 110th Street. The Negro population has increased rapidly in the last few years. There are half again as many Negroes in New York today as there were in 1940. There are about 230,000 Puerto Ricans living in New York. There are half a million Irish, half a million Germans. There are 900,000 Russians, 150,000 English, 400,000 Poles, and there are quantities of Finns and Czechs and Swedes and Danes and Norwegians and Latvians and Belgians and Welsh and Greeks, and even Dutch, who have been here from away back. It is very hard to say how many Chinese there are. Officially there are 12,000, but there are many Chinese who are in New York illegally and who don't like census takers.

The collision and the intermingling of these millions of foreign-born people representing so many races and creeds make New York a permanent exhibit of the phenomenon of one world. The citizens of New York are tolerant not only from disposition but from necessity. The city has to be tolerant, otherwise it would explode in a radioactive cloud of hate and rancor and bigotry. If the people were to depart even briefly from the peace of cosmopolitan intercourse, the town would blow up higher than a kite. . . .

To a New Yorker the city is both changeless and changing. In many respects it neither looks nor feels the way it did twenty-five years ago. . . . The slums are gradually giving way to the lofty housing projects—high in stature, high in purpose, low in rent. There are a couple of dozens of these new developments scattered around; each is a city in itself (one of them in the Bronx accommodates twelve thousand families), sky acreage hitherto untilled, lifting people far above the street, standardizing their sanitary life, giving them some place to sit other than an orange crate. Federal money, state money, city money and private money have flowed into these projects. Banks and insurance companies are in back of some of them. Architects have turned the buildings slightly on their bases, to catch more light. In some of them, rents are as low as eight dollars a room. Thousands of new units are still needed and will eventually be built, but New York never quite catches up with itself, is never in equilibrium. In flush times the population mushrooms and the new dwellings sprout from the rock. Come bad times and the population scatters and the lofts are abandoned and the landlord withers and dies.

New York has changed in tempo and in temper during the years I have known it. There is greater tension, increased irritability. You encounter it in many places, in many faces. The normal frustrations of modern life are here multiplied and amplified—a single run of a crosstown bus contains, for the driver, enough frustration and annoyance to carry him over the edge of sanity: the light that changes always an instant too soon, the passenger that bangs on the shut door, the truck that blocks the only opening, the coin that slips to the floor, the question asked at the wrong moment. There is greater tension and there is greater speed. Taxis roll faster than they rolled ten years ago—and they were rolling fast then. Hackmen used to drive with verve; now they sometimes seem to drive with desperation, toward the ultimate tip. On the West Side Highway, approaching the city, the motorist is swept along in a trance—a sort of fever of inescapable motion, goaded from behind, hemmed in on either side, a mere chip in a millrace. . . .

The subtlest change in New York is something people don't speak much about but that is in everyone's mind. The city, for the first time in its long history, is destructible. A single flight of planes no bigger than a wedge of geese can quickly end this island fantasy, burn the towers, crumble the bridges, turn the underground passages into lethal chambers, cremate the millions. The intimation of mortality is part of New York now: in the sound of jets overhead, in the black headlines of the latest edition.

All dwellers in cities must live with the stubborn fact of annihilation;   25 in New York the fact is somewhat more concentrated because of the concentration of the city itself, and because, of all targets, New York has a certain clear priority. In the mind of whatever perverted dreamer might loose the lightning, New York must hold a steady, irresistible charm. . . .

A block or two west of the new City of Man in Turtle Bay there is an old willow tree that presides over an interior garden. It is a battered tree, long suffering and much climbed, held together by strands of wire but beloved of those who know it. In a way it symbolizes the city: life under difficulties, growth against odds, sap-rise in the midst of concrete, and the steady reaching for the sun. Whenever I look at it nowadays, and feel the cold shadow of the planes, I think: "This must be saved, this particular thing, this very tree." If it were to go, all would go—this city, this mischievous and marvelous monument which not to look upon would be like death.

Discussion Questions

1. What are the two "dubious gifts" New York presents its citizens? What can they do to an individual?

2. According to White, what are the three types of New Yorkers? What conclusion does he draw from his divisions?

3. What does the author mean when he says that in New York "every event is, in a sense, optional"?

4. Why does White say: "It is a miracle that New York works at all"?

5. How does White define the city in relation to its neighborhoods?

6. What thoughts cross White's mind when he walks past a homeless person? Discuss his ambivalence.

7. What function does the metaphor of an old willow tree in the concluding paragraph serve? Can you think of another metaphor to describe New York?

8. This essay was written in 1948. How have things changed? In what ways are they the same?

Writing Tasks

1. Choose your favorite passage. Summarize and respond to it according to your personal experience.

2. Write an essay that encapsulates the characteristics of "your" New York.

3. Look up White's many references to people, places, and things. Share with your classmates what you discover.

Making Connections

1. Write an essay on the traits that make a New Yorker that incorporates and elaborates on the reflections made in two or more of the readings in this section.

2. Write an essay that discusses the elements that define your neighborhood (or your favorite place in the city). Consider the following possibilities, utilized by the writers you have read, for developing your essay. You may discuss a personal memory, describe the people and the highlights of the neighborhood (bridges, buildings, parks, restaurants, etc.), and/or document its sights and sounds. Consider also themes such as privacy, community, tensions, neighborhood transformations, and/or your relationship to the place where you dwell.

CHAPTER 2

Crossings

"Chinatown in New York"
Bob Krist/CORBIS

How far my little grass-roofed, hill-wrapped village from this gigantic rebellion which was New York! And New York's rebellion called to me excitedly, this savagery which piled great concrete block on concrete block, topping at the last moment as in an afterthought, with crowns as delicate as pinnacled ice; this lavishness which, without a prayer, pillaged coal mines and waterfalls for light, festooning the great nature-severed city with diamonds of frozen electrical phenomena—it fascinated me . . . .

Younghill Kang
From *East Meets West* (1937)

Crossings

"Give me your poor, your tired, your huddled masses yearning to breathe free . . ." Since the inscription of these words at the foot of the Statue of Liberty over a century ago, many have responded and made their passage to New York, their land of promise. This chapter presents a historical and cultural cross section of these numerous crossings, each of which depicts a unique experience and an extravagant vision that perpetuate the greatness of New York. The readings chronicle the dreams and sacrifices, struggles and fulfillment of individuals in their process of becoming New Yorkers.

Emma Lazarus' "The New Colossus" is a welcoming invitation that echoes the promise of the American Dream. Her poem speaks of hope and a power that transforms and delivers new lives. And Anzia Yezierska, a Jewish immigrant from Russia, is one of them. "America and I" is an intimate account of her personal journey from a sweatshop worker on the Lower East Side to a notable writer. The invaluable lesson she learns from the first Pilgrims inspires and empowers her to create her own America.

In "New York: Science Fiction," Junot Diaz sees the City from across the Hudson River. Somewhat different from the experience of his father, a first-generation immigrant from the Dominican Republic, New York, for him, represents a vision that is both distant and within reach. Articulating a similar vision of New York is Edwidge Danticat's "New York Was My City on the Hill." In her essay Danticat traces the footsteps of her parents from Haiti to New York and recounts their labor and sacrifices that have inspired her own intellectual pilgrimage in what used to be her "city on the hill." Similarly, June Jordan's "For My American Family" celebrates those who have paved the way for her and her generation to live a life of freedom and respect. She redefines the term "family" to include those who, regardless of their race, have inspired and nurtured her intellectually through their faith, courage, and contribution to the making of this nation.

Suki Kim's "Facing Poverty with a poor Girl's Habit" speaks about the challenges new young immigrants face today. Her experience illustrates that prejudice exists not only among different races, but is also pertinent in the same ethnic group. She also exposes her dilemmas in the areas of cultural identity, class difference, and generational prejudice growing up as a young Korean in New York. In "My Name Is Not Cool Anymore" Mohammed Naseehu Ali, a Muslim immigrant from Nigeria, faces another kind of dilemma. His experience brings the latent vice of cultural stereotyping to the surface. After the 9/11 terrorist attacks, Ali's name takes on a new connotation and induces paranoiac reactions among many New Yorkers.

The New Colossus

Emma Lazarus

Emma Lazarus (1849–1887) was of German-Jewish descent. In 1883 a committee was formed to raise funds for a pedestal for "Liberty Enlightening the People," a gift from the French to be installed on Ellis Island. "The New Colossus" was written as part of this fund-raising effort.

Pre-reading

What does the Statue of Liberty mean to you?

Not like the brazen giant of Greek fame,   1
With conquering limbs astride from land to land;
Here at our sea-washed, sunset gates shall stand
A mighty woman with a torch, whose flame
Is the imprisoned lightning, and her name   5
Mother of Exiles. From her beacon-hand
Glows world-wide welcome; her mild eyes command
The air-bridged harbor that twin cities frame.
"Keep, ancient lands, your storied pomp!" cries she   10
With silent lips. "Give me your tired, your poor,
Your huddled masses yearning to breathe free,
The wretched refuse of your teeming shore.
Send these, the homeless, tempest-tost to me,
I lift my lamp beside the golden door!"

Emma Lazarus, THE POEMS OF EMMA LAZARUS, *Vol. 1, 1889.*

Discussion Questions

1. What is the significance of the title?
2. What distinguishes Lady Liberty from her Greek predecessor?
3. Can you determine what the "twin cities" refers to? What bridge is referred to in the poem?
4. What do you think Lazarus and the committee who commissioned her work wanted to communicate? Do you think her promise still holds true?

Writing Tasks

1. Write a response that compares the message of the poem to your own experiences or observations.
2. Write a line-by-line explication of this poem that fully analyzes the meaning of each verse.

"Nineteenth-Century immigrants arriving in New York City harbor"
© Stefans Bianchetti/CORBIS

Good Morning

Langston Hughes

Pre-reading

Can you think of any significant lessons you have learned from your parent(s) about the history and heritage of your people?

GOOD MORNING

Good morning daddy!	1
I was born here, he said,	
watched Harlem grow	
until colored folks spread	
from river to river	
across the middle of Manhattan	5
out of Penn Station	
dark tenth of a nation,	
planes from Puerto Rico,	
and holds of boats, chico,	10
up from Cuba Haiti Jamaica,	
in buses marked New York	
from Georgia Florida Louisiana	
to Harlem Brooklyn the Bronx	15
but most of all to Harlem	
dusky sash across Manhattan	
I've seen them come dark	
wondering	
wide-eyed	
dreaming	20
out of Penn Station-	
but the trains are late.	
The gates open-	
Yet there're bars	
at each gate.	
What happens	
to a dream deferred?	
Daddy, ain't you heard?	

From *The Collected Poems of Langston Hughes* by Langston Hughes, edited by Arnold Rampersad with David Roessel, Associate Editor, copyright © 1994 by The Estate of Langston Hughes. Used by permission of Alfred A. Knopf, a division of Random House, Inc.

Discussion Questions

1. In the time when the poem was written, what ethnic groups comprised the population in Harlem?
2. Why do you think Hughes titled the poem "Good Morning"?
3. What is the main idea of the poem?
4. What does Hughes imply in lines 20–25. "out of Penn station—/ but the trains are late./ The gates open—/ Yet there are bars/ at each gate"?
5. What do you think the phrase "a dream deferred" in line 26 means?

Writing Tasks

1. Analyze the literary elements of this poem that help convey its theme and power. Consider, for example, the author's use of rhythm, tone, imagery, and/or irony.
2. The key to understanding poetry is in listening to the unspoken words and reading hidden details in between. Try to transform this poem into a short story, focusing on probable dialogue, description, and actions that are beneath the surface of the poem.

America and I

Anzia Yezierska

Anzia Yezierska (1881–1970) was born in the Russian-Polish ghetto of Plotsk, and emigrated to New York City with her family in 1890. She worked as a servant, a laundress, and a button sewer in sweatshops on the Lower East Side. She also attended night school and in 1904 graduated from Columbia Teachers College. She is the author of five novels and two volumes of short stories, *Hungry Hearts* (1920) and *Children of Loneliness* (1923).

Pre-reading

What is required for success in America?

As one of the dumb, voiceless ones I speak. One of the millions of im-   1
migrants beating, beating out their hearts at your gates for a breath of understanding.

Ach! America! From the other end of the earth from where I came, America was a land of living hope, woven of dreams, aflame with longing and desire.

Choked for ages in the airless oppression of Russia, the Promised Land rose up—wings for my stifled spirit—sunlight burning through my darkness—freedom singing to me in my prison—deathless songs tuning prison-bars into strings of a beautiful violin.

I arrived in America. My young, strong body, my heart and soul pregnant with the unlived lives of generations clamoring for expression.

What my mother and father and their mother and father never had a   5
chance to give out in Russia, I would give out in America. The hidden sap of centuries would find release; colors that never saw light—songs that died unvoiced—romance that never had a chance to blossom in the black life of the Old World.

In the golden land of flowing opportunity I was to find my work that was denied me in the sterile village of my forefathers. Here I was to be free from the dead drudgery for bread that held me down in Russia. For the first time in America, I'd cease to be a slave of the belly. I'd be a creator, a giver, a human being! My work would be the living job of fullest self-expression.

Originally appeared in *CHILDREN OF LONELINESS,* 1923.

But from my high visions, my golden hopes, I had to put my feet down on   10
earth. I had to have food and shelter. I had to have the money to pay for it.

I was in America, among the Americans, but not *of* them. No speech,
no common language, no way to win a smile of understanding from them,
only my young, strong body and my untried faith. Only my eager, empty
hands, and my full heart shining from my eyes!

God from the world! Here I was with so much richness in me, but my
mind was not wanted without the language. And my body, unskilled, un-
trained, was not even wanted in the factory. Only one of two chances was
left open to me: the kitchen, or minding babies.

My first job was as a servant in an Americanized family. Once, long
ago, they came from the same village from where I came. But they were
so well-dressed, so well-fed, so successful in America, that they were
ashamed to remember their mother tongue.

"What were to be my wages?" I ventured timidly, as I looked up to the
well-fed, well-dressed "American" man and woman.

They looked at me with a sudden coldness. What have I said to draw
away from me their warmth? Was it so low from me to talk of wages? I
shrank back into myself like a low-down bargainer. Maybe they're so
high up in well-being they can't any more understand my low thoughts
for money.

From his rich height the man preached down to me that I must not be so
grabbing for wages. Only just landed from the ship and already thinking
about money when I should be thankful to associate with "Americans."

The woman, out of her smooth, smiling fatness assured me that this
was my chance for a summer vacation in the country with her two lovely
children. My great chance to learn to be a civilized being, to become an
American by living with them.

So, made to feel that I was in the hands of American friends, invited to   15
share with them their home, their plenty, their happiness, I pushed out
from my head the worry for wages. Here was my first chance to begin my
life in the sunshine, after my long darkness. My laugh was all over my
face as I said to them: "I'll trust myself to you. What I'm worth you'll
give me." And I entered their house like a child by the hand.

The best of me I gave them. Their house cares were my house cares. I
got up early. I worked till late. All that my soul hungered to give I put into
the passion with which I scrubbed floors, scoured pots, and washed
clothes. I was so grateful to mingle with the American people, to hear the
music of the American language, that I never knew tiredness.

There was such a freshness in my brains and such a willingness in my
heart that I could go on and on—not only with the work of the house, but
work with my head—learning new words from the children, the grocer,
the butcher, the iceman. I was not even afraid to ask for words from

the policeman on the street. And every new word made me see new American things with American eyes. I felt like a Columbus, finding new worlds through every new word.

But words alone were only for the inside of me. The outside of me still branded me for a steerage immigrant. I had to have clothes to forget myself that I'm a stranger yet. And so I had to have money to buy these clothes.

The month was up. I was so happy! Now I'd have money. *My own, earned* money. Money to buy a new shirt on my back—shoes on my feet. Maybe yet an American dress and hat!

Ach! How high rose my dreams! How plainly I saw all that I would do   20
with my visionary wages shining like a light over my head!

In my imagination I already walked in my new American clothes. How beautiful I looked as I saw myself like a picture before my eyes! I saw how I would throw away my immigrant rags tied up in my immigrant shawl. With money to buy—free money in my hands—I'd show them that I could look like an American in a day.

Like a prisoner in his last night in prison, counting the seconds that will free him from his chains, I trembled breathlessly for the minute I'd get the wages in my hand.

Before dawn I rose.

I shined up the house like a jewel-box.

I prepared breakfast and waited with my heart in my mouth for my lady   25
and gentleman to rise. At last I heard them stirring. My eyes were jumping out of my head to them when I saw them coming in and seating themselves by the table.

Like a hungry cat rubbing up to its boss for meat, so I edged and simpered around them as I passed them the food. Without my will, like a beggar, my hand reached out to them.

The breakfast was over. And no word yet from my wages.

"*Gottuniu!*" I thought to myself. "Maybe they're so busy with their own things they forgot it's the day for my wages. Could they who have everything know what I was to do with my first American dollars? How could they, soaking in plenty, how could they feel the longing and the fierce hunger in me, pressing up through each visionary dollar? How could they know the gnawing ache of my avid fingers for the feel of my own, earned dollars? My dollars that I could spend like a free person. *My dollars that would make me feel with everybody alike!*"

Lunch came. Lunch past.

Oi-i weh! Not a word yet about my money.   30

It was near dinner. And not a word yet about my wages.

I began to set the table. But my head—it swam away from me. I broke a glass. The silver dropped from my nervous fingers. I couldn't stand it any longer. I dropped everything and rushed over to my American lady and gentleman.

"*Oi weh!* The money—my money—my wages!" I cried breathlessly.

Four cold eyes turned on me.

"Wages? Money?" The four eyes turned into hard stone as they looked 35
me up and down. "Haven't you a comfortable bed to sleep, and three good meals a day? You're only a month here. Just came to America. And you already think about money. Wait till you're worth any money. What use are you without knowing English? You should be glad we keep you here. It's like a vacation for you. Other girls pay money yet to be in the country."

It went black for my eyes. I was so chocked no words came to my lips. Even the tears went dry in my throat.

I left. Not a dollar for all my work.

For a long, long time my heart ached and ached like a sore wound. If murderers would have robbed me and killed me it wouldn't have hurt me so much. I couldn't think through my pain. The minute I'd see before me how they looked at me, the words they said to me—then everything began to bleed in me. And I was helpless.

For a long, long time the thought of ever working in an "American" family made me tremble with fear, like the fear of wild wolves. No— never again would I trust myself to an "American" family, no matter how fine their language and how sweet their smile.

It was blotted out in me all trust in friendship from "Americans." But 40
the life in me still burned to live. The hope in me still craved to hope. In darkness, in dirt, in hunger and want, but only to live on!

There had been no end to my day—working for the "American" family.

Now rejecting false friendships from higher-ups in America, I turned back to the Ghetto. I worked on a hard bench with my own kind on either side of me. I knew before I began what my wages were to be. I knew what my hours were to be. And I knew the feeling of the end of the day.

From the outside my second job seemed worse than the first. It was in a sweat-shop of a Delancey Street basement, kept up by an old, wrinkled woman that looked like a black witch of greed. My work was sewing on buttons. While the morning was still dark I walked into a dark basement. And darkness met me when I turned out of the basement.

Day after day, week after week, all the contact I got with America was handling dead buttons. The money I earned was hardly enough to pay for bread and rent. I didn't have a room to myself. I didn't even have a bed. I slept on a mattress on the floor in a rat-hole of a room occupied by a dozen other immigrants. I was always hungry—oh, so hungry! The scant meals I could afford only sharpened my appetite for real food. But I felt myself better off than working in the "American" family, where I had three good meals a day and a bed to myself. With all the hunger and darkness of the sweat-shop, I had at least the evening to myself. And all night was mine. When all were asleep, I used to creep up on the roof of the tenement and talk out my heart in silence to the stars in the sky.

"Who am I? What am I? What do I want with my life? Where is   45
America? Is there an America? What is this wilderness in which I'm lost?"

I'd hurl my questions and then think and think. And I could not tear it out of me, the feeling that America must be somewhere, somehow—only I couldn't find it—*My America,* where I would work for love and not for a living. I was like a thing following blindly after something far off in the dark!

"*Oi weh!*" I'd stretch out my hand up in the air. "My head is so lost in America! What's the use of all my working if I'm not in it? Dead buttons is not me."

Then the busy season started in the shop. The mounds of buttons grew and grew. The long day stretched out longer. I had to begin with the buttons earlier and stay with them till later in the night. The old witch turned into a huge greedy maw for wanting more and more buttons.

For a glass of tea, for a slice of herring over black bread, she would buy us up to stay another and another hour, till there seemed no end to her demands.

One day, the light of self-assertion broke into my cellar darkness.   50

"I don't want the tea. I don't want your herring," I said with terrible boldness. "I only want to go home. I only want the evening to myself!"

"You fresh mouth, you!" cried the old witch. "You learned already too much in America. I want no clock-watchers in my shop. Out you go!"

I was driven out to cold and hunger. I could no longer pay for my mattress on the floor. I no longer could buy the bite in my mouth. I walked the streets. I knew what it is to be alone in a strange city, among strangers.

But I laughed through my tears. So I learned too much already in America because I wanted the whole evening to myself? Well America has yet to teach me still more: how to get not only the whole evening to myself, but a whole day a week like the American workers.   55

That sweat-shop was a bitter memory but a good school. It fitted me for a regular factory. I could walk in boldly and say I could work at something, even if it was only sewing on buttons.

Gradually, I became a trained worker. I worked in a light, airy factory, only eight hours a day. My boss was no longer a sweater and a blood-squeezer. The first freshness of the morning was mine. And the whole evening was mine. All day Sunday was mine.

Now I had better food to eat. I slept on a better bed. Now, I even looked dressed up like the American-born. But inside of me I knew that I was not yet an American. I choked with longing when I met an American-born, and I could say nothing.

Something cried dumb in me. I couldn't help it. I didn't know what it was I wanted. I only knew I wanted. I wanted. Like the hunger in the heart that never gets food.

An English class for foreigners started in our factory. The teacher had such a good, friendly face, her eyes looked so understanding, as if she could see right into my heart. So I went to her one day for advice:

"I don't know what is with me the matter," I began. "I have no rest in   60
me. I never yet done what I want."

"What is it you want to do, child?" she asked me.

"I want to do something with my head, my feelings. All day long, only with my hands I work."

"First you must learn English." She patted me as if I was not yet grown up. "Put your mind on that, and then we'll see."

So for a time I learned the language. I could almost begin to think with English words in my head. But in my heart the emptiness still hurt. I burned to give, to give something, to do something, to be something. The dead work with my hands was killing me. My work left only hard stones on my heart.

Again I went to our factory teacher and cried out to her: "I know al-   65
ready to read and write the English language, but I can't put it into words what I want. What is it in me so different that can't come out?"

She smiled at me down from her calmness as if I were a little bit out of my head. "What *do you want* to do?"

"I feel. I see. I hear. And I want to think it out. But I'm like dumb in me. I only feel I'm different—different from everybody."

She looked at me close and said nothing for a minute. "You ought to join one of the social clubs of the Women's Association," she advised.

"What's the Women's Association?" I implored greedily.

"A group of American women who are trying to help the working-girl   70
find herself. They have a special department for immigrant girls like you."

I joined the Women's Association. On my first evening there they announced a lecture: "The Happy Worker and His Work," by the Welfare director of the United Mills Corporation.

"Is there such a thing as a happy worker at his work?" I wondered. Happiness is only by working at what you love. And what poor girl can ever find it to work at what she loves? My old dreams about my America rushed through my mind. Once I thought that in America everybody works for love. Nobody has to worry for a living. Maybe this welfare man came to show me the *real* America that till now I sought in vain.

With a lot of polite words the head lady of the Women's Association introduced a higher-up that looked like the king of kings of business. Never before in my life did I ever see a man with such a sureness in his step, such power in his face, such friendly positiveness in his eye as when he smiled upon us.

"Efficiency is the new religion of business," he began. "In big business houses, even in up-to-date factories, they no longer take the first comer and give him any job that happens to stand empty. Efficiency begins at the employment office. Experts are hired for the one purpose, to find out how best to fit the worker to his work. It's economy for the boss to make the worker happy." And then he talked a lot more on efficiency in educated language that was over my head.

I didn't know exactly what it meant—efficiency—but if it was to make   75
the worker happy at his work, then that's what I had been looking for since I came to America. I only felt from watching him that he was happy by his job. And as I looked on this clean, well-dressed, successful one, who wasn't ashamed to say he rose from an office-boy, it made me feel that I, too, could lift myself up for a person.

He finished his lecture, telling us about the Vocational-Guidance Center that the Women's Association started.

The very next evening I was at the Vocational-Guidance Center. There I found a young, college-looking woman. Smartness and health shining from her eyes! She, too, looked as if she knew her way in America. I could tell at the first glance: here is a person that is happy by what she does.

"I feel you'll understand me," I said right away.

She leaned over with pleasure in her face: "I hope I can."

"I want to work by what's in me. Only, I don't know what's in me. I   80
only feel I'm different."

She gave me a quick, puzzled look from the corner of her eyes. "What are you doing now?"

"I'm the quickest shirtwaist hand on the floor. But my heart wastes away by such work. I think and think, and my thoughts can't come out."

"Why don't you think out your thoughts in shirtwaists? You could learn to be a designer. Earn more money."

"I don't want to look on waists. If my hands are sick from waists, how could my head learn to put beauty into them?"

"But you must earn your living at what you know, and rise slowly from   85
job to job."

I looked at her office sign: "Vocational Guidance." "What's your vocational guidance?" I asked, "How to rise from job to job—how to earn more money?"

The smile went out from her eyes. But she tried to be kind yet. "What *do* you want?" she asked, with a sigh of last patience.

"I want America to want me."

She fell back in her chair, thunderstruck with my boldness. But yet, in a low voice of educated self-control, she tried to reason with me:

"You have to *show* that you have something special for America before America has need of you." 90

"But I never had a chance to find out what's in me, because I always had to work for a living. Only, I feel it's efficiency for America to find out what's in me so different, so I could give it out by my work."

Her eyes half closed as they bored through me. Her mouth opened to speak, but no words came from her lips. So I flamed up with all that was choking in me like a house on fire:

"America gives free bread and rent to criminals in prison. They got grand houses with sunshine, fresh air, doctors and teachers, even for the crazy ones. Why don't they have free boarding-schools for immigrants— strong people—willing people? Here you see us burning up with something different, and America turns her head away from us."

Her brows lifted and dropped down. She shrugged her shoulders away from me with the look of pity we give to cripples and hopeless lunatics.

"America is no Utopia. First you must become efficient in earning a living before you can indulge in your poetic dreams." 95

I went away from the vocational-guidance office with all the air out of my lungs. All the light out of my eyes. My feet dragged after me like dead wood.

Till now there had always lingered a rosy veil of hope over my emptiness, a hope that a miracle would happen. I would open up my eyes some day and suddenly find the America of my dreams. As a young girl hungry for love sees always before her eyes the picture of lover's arms around her, so I saw always in my heart the vision of Utopian America.

But now I felt that the America of my dreams never was and never could be. Reality had hit me on the head as with a club. I felt that the America that I sought was nothing but a shadow—an echo—a chimera of lunatics and crazy immigrants.

Stripped of all illusion, I looked about me. The long desert of wasting days of drudgery stared me in the face. The drudgery that I had lived through, and the endless drudgery still ahead of me rose over me like a withering wilderness of sand. In vain were all my cryings, in vain were all frantic efforts of my spirit to find the living waters of understanding for my perishing lips. Sand, sand was everywhere. With every seeking, every reaching out I only lost myself deeper and deeper in a vast sea of sand.

I knew now the American language. And I knew now, if I talked to the Americans from morning till night, they could not understand what the Russian soul of me wanted. They could not understand *me* any more than if I talked to them in Chinese. Between my soul and the American soul 100 were worlds of difference that no words could bridge over. What was that difference? What made the Americans so far apart from me?

I began to read the American history. I found from the first pages that America started with a band of Courageous Pilgrims. They had left their native country as I had left mine. They had crossed an unknown ocean and landed in an unknown country, as I.

But the great difference between the first Pilgrims and me was that they expected to make America, build America, create their own world of liberty. I wanted to find it ready made.

I read on. I delved deeper down into the American history. I saw how the Pilgrim Fathers came to a rocky desert country, surrounded by Indian savages on all sides. But undaunted, they pressed on—through danger—through famine, pestilence, and want—they pressed on. They did not ask the Indians for sympathy, for understanding. They made no demands on anybody, but on their own indomitable spirit of persistence.

And I—I was forever begging a crumb of sympathy, a gleam of understanding from strangers who could not understand.

I, when I encountered a few savage Indian scalpers, like the old witch   105
of the sweat-shop, like my "Americanized" countryman, who cheated me of my wages—I, when I found myself on the lonely, untrodden path through which all seekers of the new world must pass, I lost heart and said: "There is no America!"

Then came a light—a great revelation! I saw America—a big idea—a deathless hope—a world still in the making. I saw that it was the glory of America that it was not yet finished. And I, the last comer, had her share to give, small or great, to the making of America, like those Pilgrims who came in the *Mayflower.*

Fired up by this revealing light, I began to build a bridge of understanding between the American-born and myself. Since their life was shut out from such as me, I began to open up my life and the lives of my people to them. And life draws life. In only writing about the Ghetto I found America.

Great chances have come to me. But in my heart is always a deep sadness. I feel like a man who is sitting down to a secret table of plenty, while his near ones and dear ones are perishing before his eyes. My very joy in doing the work I love hurts me like secret guilt, because all about me I see so many with my longings, my burning eagerness, to do and to be, wasting their days in drudgery they hate, merely to buy bread and pay rent. And America is losing all that richness of the soul.

The Americans of tomorrow, the America that is every day nearer coming to be, will be too wise, too open-hearted, too friendly-handed, to let the least lastcomer at their gates knock in vain with his gifts unwanted.

Discussion Questions

1. What is Yezierska's initial impression of America? How does she compare it to her life in Russia?

2. What does she aspire to do when she first arrives in America? What must she do first?

3. Do you think her "Americanized family" treats her fairly? Why or why not?

4. What was the best part of her second job on Delancey Street? Why did she end up quitting it?

5. What kind of work does Anzia prefer to do? What is stopping her?

6. Do you agree with the author's argument that immigrants should receive free room and board? Why or why not?

7. What lessons did she learn from the Pilgrims? How did this knowledge transform her idea of what it takes to succeed in America? Do you agree with her assessment?

8. How does the author utilize the concepts of "hunger" and "appetite" to bring out her thesis?

Writing Tasks

1. Write an essay arguing whether immigrants should have the right to receive preferential treatments. Give examples from Yezierska's essay and your own experience to support your argument.

2. Write an essay explaining your dreams and expectations of living in New York. What obstacles do you foresee in your pursuit of the American Dream?

3. Write an essay in which you explain how living in New York has transformed you. Provide examples of specific learning experiences.

New York: Science Fiction

Junot Diaz

Junot Diaz was born in Santo Domingo, Dominican Republic, in 1968 and came to the United States in 1975 at the age of seven. He graduated from Rutgers University, received an M.F.A. from Cornell University, and presently teaches at Syracuse University. In 1999, *The New Yorker* magazine named Diaz one of the twenty best fiction writers in America.

Pre-reading

Have you ever had an experience that turned out to be radically different from what you expected?

My father was first; he reached Nueva York at the start of the Seventies, in the Years of the Puerto Rican Obituary. This was the decade of "benign neglect" and "planned shrinkage," when New York City—specifically the poor colored neighborhoods in which my father was attempting to live—was being burned to the ground by the "cost-effective" policies of Roger Starr and his Rand Corporation cronies.

He had the "usual" Caribbean immigrant experience: he worked crap jobs, he slept in unheated buildings, he starved his ass off. All around him buildings exploded into fire. Fortunately he wasn't in them, but it didn't help his sleep any knowing that a family of seven had been roasted to death the week before. The stench of the smoke, of those destroyed lives, seeped into his dreams.

Who's surprised that after five unhappy years in Nueva York my father decided that he'd had enough? Right before he brought the rest of us over from Santo Domingo my father abandoned New York City, where he had friends, where he had a life, and relocated to New Jersey, where he knew no one. He said it was for our sake—we didn't hear about this move until after we arrived—but I think it was also for his peace of mind. He settled in a Section 8 apartment complex that was bounded on one side by Old Bridge (where Vitamin C is from) and on the other by Sayreville (BonJoviLand). This is where me and my

1

Reprinted by permission of Junot Diaz and Aragi Inc. First published in *The New York Times Magazine*.

siblings lived when we reached the States, where I spent my Ghetto-American childhood, marooned in the middle of suburbs white as a gringo's ass.

New York went from the Oz I dreamed about in the Dominican Republic to the distant sight of the Verrazano Bridge (visible from the entrance of my development). Transformed from the City of Everything to the ruined boroughs we visited on weekends. A future that had been promised but never arrived.

Eventually I would move to Nueva York, at twenty-six gaining the life I always thought should have been mine to begin with. I didn't arrive in the Years of the Puerto Rican Obituary; it was, by then, the Years of the Nightstick. I had the "usual" Caribbean college-graduate New York experience. I worked temp jobs, I lived in an unwinterized apartment in Brooklyn, I smoked cheap hydro and was too broke for anything but activism. Nothing burned, thank God, not even bread. Often I found myself in Washington Heights, the Capital of the Dominican Diaspora, visiting friends, visiting relatives; sometimes I would stand on the street corners with my writer's notebook, trying to imagine what-could-have-been.

Certain nights, when I was restless and nothing was working out, I'd take the D over the Manhattan Bridge. As the train left the tunnel and began to cross the East River I'd step between the cars. This, for some reason, made me happy. It wasn't really dangerous and the view it afforded of New York was beyond words. A city ablaze, suspended between black-sky and river. Our first night in the States my old man wanted us to see a similar city, on our drive from JFK. I remember our silence, the cold of the windows against our faces. The city looked like science fiction. Like an incubator for stars, where suns are made. This was before we realized that we were actually bound for New Jersey, when we thought one of those lights was going to be our home.

Discussion Questions

1. What was the immigrant experience of Diaz's father like?

2. Where did Junot think he was going to live? Where in fact did the family move? Why?

3. What is Junot's experience in New York like? Why does he repeat the term "usual"?

4. In what way does the city look like "science fiction?" What is the irony of this image?

Writing Tasks

1. The father and son in this piece are immigrants from different generations, but they share many similar experiences as well as different ones. Discuss whether you think the issues and challenges facing immigrants today have changed, either for the better or for the worse.

2. Discuss this essay as it relates to Piedro Pietri's "Puerto Rican Obituary" (available on-line). How does Pietri extend and complicate the concerns raised by Diaz?

3. Do you think living in a community outside their own culture is beneficial or detrimental to immigrants (or anybody for that matter)? Carefully explain your answer.

The Tropics in New York

Claude Mckay

Claude Mckay (1890-1948) grew up in Jamaica, and his poems often express nostalgia for life there. After leaving Jamaica in 1912, he studied at Tuskegee Institute and then came to New York, where he established himself as a poet, novelist, and radical spokesman. He is the author of the poetry collection, *Harlem Shadows,* and the novel, *Home to Harlem.*

Pre-reading

Recall a time when something or someone you saw brought back past memories.

THE TROPICS IN NEW YORK

Bananas ripe and green, and ginger-root,
Cocoa in pods and alligator pears,   1
And tangerines and mangoes and grape fruit,
Fit for the highest prize at parish fairs,
Set in the window, bringing memories
Of fruit-trees laden by low-singing rills,   5
And dewy dawns, and mystical blue skies
In benediction over nun-like hills.
My eyes grew dim, and I could no more gaze;
A wave of longing through my body swept,
And, hungry for the old, familiar ways,   10
I turned aside and bowed my head and wept.

From *Harlem Shadows: The Poems of Claude McKay,*
Harcourt Brace, 1922.

Discussion Questions

1. What does the title of the poem imply?
2. Read the visual imagery in the poem carefully and explain how the author's emotions shift from one stanza to another.
3. Are there any shift in tones and perspectives in the poem? What effects do they create?

Writing Tasks

1. Write an essay that focuses on the ethnic characteristics of a neighborhood in New York. Make sure you include as many sensory details as you can.

2. Write an essay that discusses the unique challenges that immigrants face coming to a new land and culture.

Riding the Subway Is an Adventure

Frances Chung

Frances Chung (1950–1990) published her poetry in several anthologies and journals, including *The Portable Lower East Side and IKON*. Chung's poetry stands alone as the most perceptive, aesthetically accomplished, and compassionate depiction of New York's Chinatown and Lower East Side. Chung incorporates Spanish and Chinese into her English in deft evocations of these neighborhoods' streets, fantasies, commerce, and toil. Her work is published in *Crazy Melon and Chinese Apple* (2000).

Pre-reading

Have you ever been in a foreign country where you couldn't understand the language? How did you get around?

RIDING THE SUBWAY IS AN ADVENTURE

Riding the subway is an adventure	
especially if you cannot read the signs.	1
One gets lost. One becomes anxious and	
does not know whether to get off when	
the other Chinese person in your car	5
does. (Your crazy logic tells you that	
the both of you must be headed for the	
same stop.) One woman has discovered the	
secret of one-to-one correspondence.	
She keeps the right amount of pennies	10
in one pocket and upon arriving in each	
new station along the way she shifts one	
penny to her other pocket. When all the	
pennies in the first pocket have disappeared,	
she knows that she is home.	15

Discussion Questions

1. Why does the woman in the poem have such difficulties in the subway? What other challenges do you anticipate she faces when she ventures out into the city?
2. What is the tone of the poem?
3. What do you think the poet wants to show us in line 3–5?

Writing Task

1. Write an essay that captures an adventure you have recently experienced on the subway.
2. Write an essay in which you suggest ways with which the MTA can improve travel in the subway system for all New Yorkers.

Yo Vivo En El Barrio Chino

Frances Chung

Pre-reading

What is your impression of the Chinatown in New York?

Yo Vivo En El Barrio Chino

Yo vivo en el barrio chino   1
de Neuva York . . . I live in
New York's Chinatown. Some
call it a ghetto, some call it
a slum, some call it home.
Little Italy or Northern
Chinatown, to my mind, the   5
boundaries have become fluid.
I have two Chinatown moods.
Time when Chinatown is a
terrible place to live in.
Time when Chinatown is
the *only* place to live . . .   10

Discussion Questions

1. Why does the author write in two languages in this poem?
2. What does the author hope to convey about places some people refer to as slums?
3. Elaborate on the two Chinatown moods the author feels in the poem.

Writing Task

1. Take a walk through Chinatown or another ethnic enclave and record your experiences.

New York Was Our City on the Hill

Edwidge Danticat

Edwidge Danticat was born in Port-au-Prince Haiti in 1969. Her father immigrated to the United States just two years later looking for work. Her mother followed him in 1973. Danticat remained in Haiti eight more years, raised by her Aunt. At age twelve she reunited with her parents in a predominantly Haitian-American neighborhood in Brooklyn, New York City. Two short years later, Danticat published an article that inspired her first novel, *Breath, Eyes Memory.* She has also published a collection of stories, *Krik? Krak!* and *The Farming of the Bones.*

Pre-reading

Have you ever been disillusioned by a place before?

If you are an immigrant in New York, there are some things you   1
inevitably share. For one, if you're a new immigrant, you probably left
behind someone you love in the country of your birth. In my case, I was
the person left in Haiti when my mother and father escaped the brutal
regimes of François and Jean-Claude Duvalier in the early 1970's and
fled the extreme poverty caused by the Duvaliers' mismanagement and
excesses.

The plan was for my parents to send for me and my younger brother,
André, who were 4 and 2 years old at the time of their departure, when
they found jobs and got settled in New York. But because of United
States immigration red tape, our family separation lasted eight years.
The near decade we were apart was filled with long letters, lengthy
voice messages on cassette tapes and tearful phone calls, all brimming
with the promise that one day my brother and I would be united not only
with our parents but with our two Brooklyn-born brothers whom we
didn't know at all.

Still André and I were constantly reminded by our Aunt Denise and
Uncle Joseph, who were caring for us in an impoverished and politically
volatile neighborhood in the Haitian capital, Port-au-Prince, that we were
lucky our parents were in New York. If we dared to disagree with that
idea, the Faustian bargain our parents had faced would be clearly laid out

for us. They could have stayed behind with us and we could have all gone without a great many necessary things, or they could have gone to New York to work so that we could have not only clothes and food and school fees but also a future.

As my Uncle Joseph liked to say, for people like us, the malere, the poor, the future was not a given. It was something to be clawed from the edge of despair with sweat and blood. At least in New York, our parents would be rewarded for their efforts.

If living in one of the richest cities in the world did not guarantee a   5
struggle-free life, my brother and I didn't realize it. New York was our city on the hill, the imaginary haven of our lives. When we fantasized, we saw ourselves walking the penny-gilded streets and buying all the candies we could stuff into ourselves. Eventually we grew to embrace the idea that New York was where we were meant to be, as soon as the all-powerful gatekeepers saw fit to let us in, and if we could help it, we would never leave once we were again at our parents' side.

Our parents might have had utopian fantasies of their own when they sold most of their belongings to pay for passports, visas and plane fares to New York. I can't imagine making the choices they made without being forced, mapping out a whole life in a place that they'd seen only in one picture, a snow-covered street taken by my mother's brother, who lived there.

Later my parents would tell me that what kept them trudging through that snow to their factory jobs was their visions of their two New York-born children playing with the children they'd left in Haiti and the future that we might all forge as individuals and as a family.

When I finally joined my parents in Brooklyn, in 1981, at age 12, I became acutely aware of something else that New York immigrants shared. If they were poor, they were likely to be working more hours than anyone else, for less money, and with few if any benefits.

For years my father had worked two minimum-wage jobs to support two households in two countries. One job was in a textile factory, where my mother also worked, and another in a night car wash. Tired of intermittent layoffs and humiliating immigration raids, my father finally quit both jobs when André and I arrived so he could accompany my brothers and me to and from school.

That same year, our family car also became a gypsy cab, a term that, when I first heard and researched it, led me to think that we were part of   10
a small clan of nomads whose leader, my father, chauffeured other people around when he was not driving us.

Though my brothers and I weren't aware of it at the time, our financial situation was precarious at best. Once my parents paid the rent and utility bills and bought a week's worth of groceries, there was little left for much else. My father never knew from day to day or week to week how much he would collect in fares.

Winter mornings were more profitable than summer afternoons. But in the winter, our needs were greater: coats and boots for four growing children, and regular hospital trips for my youngest brother, Karl, who was prone to ear infections and, as one doctor pointed out to us, might have suffered through 25 different colds one long winter.

We had no health insurance, of course, and each of Karl's visits to the doctor, or those for my brother Kelly—the only child I knew who got migraines, which we later discovered were a result of some kind of pressure on his optic nerve—were negotiated down at Cumberland Hospital's payment services department when my father took in my parents' joint tax return.

I remember going to the same hospital's women's clinic with my mother for one of her regular checkups when I was 16. She had a headache, her blood pressure was high, and the doctor told her that she'd have to be hospitalized that day if she wanted to avoid a stroke.

"Doctor, I have children at home and work tomorrow," my mother said, 15 before signing papers declaring that she'd been advised of the treatment for her condition but had refused it. On the bus home, I watched her carefully, fearful that she would keel over and die for our sake, but she made it home, and despite the persistent headache, she went to work the next day.

I don't know what a catastrophic illness might have cost our family financially. But it was something my parents always had in mind. My father tried to pay all his bills religiously so that if we ever needed a bank loan for a sudden emergency, we would have no trouble getting it.

What we would eventually need a loan for was our house, which my parents purchased 18 years ago in East Flatbush. The day we moved in was one of the scariest and most exhilarating of our lives. My parents invited groups of church friends over to celebrate and bless our new home, but at the same time, they warned my brothers and me that the biggest battle they'd face from then on would be to try to keep it. The mortgage was nearly double the amount they'd paid in rent, and some months my father drove his cab both at night and during the day to make the payment, which he then took to the bank, in person, during the final hours of the grace period.

It is the burden of each generation to embrace or reject the dreams set out by those who came before.

In my family it was no different. My parents wanted me to be a doctor, and when I wasn't accepted by a Brooklyn high school specializing in the health professions, my father met with the principal and persuaded him to reverse the decision.

When I decided, after a brief school-sponsored internship at Kings   20
County Hospital Center, that medicine was not for me, my parents
were disappointed, but accepted my decision. My brother André has
never forgotten the day he turned 14 and my father took him to the post
office to buy a money order for the application fee for his first summer
job. And over time we have all nearly wept when tallying small loans
and advances from Mom and Dad on salaries spent way before they
were collected.

Over the years, I have also come to understand my parents' intense desire to see my brothers and me financially stable. They had sacrificed so
much that to watch us struggle as they had would have been, to quote a
Creole expression, like lave men siye atè—washing one's hands only to
dry them in the dirt.

These days, if you're an immigrant in New York, you might not consider yourself an immigrant at all, but a transnational, someone with vot-
ing privileges and living quarters not just in one country but in two. This
was my parents' dream until they reached middle age and realized that
with their decade-long friendships and community ties in Brooklyn, they
didn't want to live anywhere else.

Last year, when my father became ill with pulmonary fibrosis—a result, some doctors say, of environmental pollution, to which he was especially vulnerable from working such long hours in his cab—he began
to have long talks with my brothers and me, fearing that as the disease
progressed, it might become harder and harder for him to speak. While I
was writing this, we talked a little about how New York had changed from
the time he arrived.

The most striking difference, he observed, is that these days, like
most New Yorkers, he has to worry about terrorism, both becoming a
victim and being blamed for it. He also worries about the high cost of
everything from food to housing, about doors closing behind him, and
thousands of families never having the kind of opportunities that
we've enjoyed. When he first got to New York, all he did was work
nonstop and pray to see his children and grandchildren grow up. Looking back, it feels like a simpler time, but maybe it wasn't. Then and
now, he whispered wistfully, one can only hope that the journey was
worthwhile.

On Nov. 3, after this essay was submitted, my Uncle Joseph died at age   25
81. More formally known as the Rev. Joseph N. Dantica, he died in
Miami after fleeing gang violence and death threats in Haiti. He was de-
tained by Department of Homeland Security officials after requesting
asylum in the United States and died in their custody. The department said
the cause was pancreatitis.

Discussion Questions

1. Why was life so hard in America for Danticat's parents at first?

2. Explain the "Faustian bargain" offered to the children. Do you think it was a fair offer?

3. How did Uncle Joseph and the children differ in their views of America? What contributes to their respective points of view?

4. What is the first lesson that Danticat learns about life in New York? Do you think this lesson is commonly shared by immigrants? Is it fair?

5. Discuss the quote: "it is the burden of each generation to embrace or reject the dreams set out by those who came before." What do children owe their parents when many sacrifices have been made?

6. What is the difference between an immigrant and a "transnational"? What are the advantages and disadvantages of each? Which label do Danticat's parents ultimately choose? Why?

7. How does the American experience of Danticat's father worsen after 9/11? Why do you think this treatment of him occurred?

8. What is the connection of Uncle Joseph's death to the beginning of the essay?

9. Why do you think the past tense is used in the title of the essay?

Writing Task

1. Write an essay in which you discuss the many challenges someone you know has gone through to achieve a particular goal. Address the lessons that the experiences of this person teach.

For My American Family: A Belated Tribute to a Legacy of Gifted Intelligence and Guts

June Jordan

June Jordan (1936–2002) was born in Harlem, New York of Jamaican parents, and attended Barnard College and the University of Chicago. A significant poet, Jordan was also an educator, essayist, novelist, and writer of children's books, lyrics, and librettos.

Pre-reading

Who has been your greatest role model?

I would love to see pictures of the Statue of Liberty taken by my father. They would tell me so much about him that I wish I knew. He couldn't very well ask that lady to "hold that smile" or "put on a little something with red to brighten it up." He'd have to take her "as is," using a choice of angles or focus or distance as the means to his statement. And I imagine that my father would choose a long-shot, soft-focus, wide-angle lens: that would place Miss Liberty in her full formal setting, and yet suggest the tears that easily spilled from his eyes whenever he spoke about "this great country of ours: America."

A camera buff, not averse to wandering around the city with both a Rolleiflex and a Rolleicord at the ready, my father thought nothing of a two or three hours' "setup" for a couple of shots of anything he found beautiful. I remember one Saturday, late morning, when I watched my father push the "best" table in the house under the dining-room windows, fidget the venetian blinds in order to gain the most interesting, slatted light, and then bring the antique Chinese vase downstairs from the parlor, fill that with fresh roses from the backyard, and then run out to the corner store for several pieces of fruit to complete his still-life composition.

All of this took place in the 1940s. We lived in the Bedford-Stuyvesant neighborhood of Brooklyn, one of the largest urban Black communities in the world. Besides the fruit and the flowers of my father's aesthetic pre-occupation, and just beyond those narrow brownstone dining-room windows, there was a burly mix of unpredictable street life that he could not control, despite incessant telephone calls, for example, to the Department of Sanitation: "Hello. This is a man by the name of Granville Ivanhoe Jordan, and I'm calling about garbage collection. What happened? Did you forget?!"

The unlikely elements of my father's name may summarize his history and character rather well. Jordan is a fairly common surname on the island of Jamaica where he was born, one of perhaps twelve or thirteen children who foraged for food, and who never forgot, or forgave, the ridicule his ragged clothing provoked in school. Leaving the classroom long before the normal conclusion to an elementary education, my father later taught himself to read and, after that, he never stopped reading and reading everything he could find, from Burpee seed catalogues to Shakespeare to the *National Geographic* magazines to "Negro" poetry to linear notes for the record albums of classical music that he devoured. But he was also "the little bull"—someone who loved a good rough fight and who even volunteered to teach boxing to other young "Negroes" at the Harlem YMCA, where he frequently participated in political and militant "uplifting-the-race" meetings, on West 135th Street.

Except for weekends, my father pursued all of his studies in the long early hours of the night, 3 or 4 A.M., after eight hours' standing up at the post office where he speed-sorted mail quite without the assistance of computers and zip codes which, of course, had yet to be invented. Exceptionally handsome and exceptionally vain, Mr. G. I. Jordan, immaculate in one of his innumerable, rooster-elegant suits, would readily hack open a coconut with a machete, or slice a grapefruit in half, throw his head back, and squeeze the juice into his mouth—carefully held a tricky foot away—all to my mother's head-shaking dismay: "Why now you have to act up like a monkey chaser, eh?"

It is a sad thing to consider that this country has given its least to those who have loved it the most. I am the daughter of West Indian immigrants. And perhaps there are other Americans as believing and as grateful and as loyal, but I doubt it. In general, the very word *immigrant* connotes somebody white, while *alien* denotes everybody else. But hundreds and hundreds of thousands of Americans are hardworking, naturalized Black citizens whose trust in the democratic promise of the mainland has never been reckoned with, fully, or truly reciprocated. For instance, I know that my parents would have wanted to say, "Thanks, America!" if only there had been some way, some public recognition and

5

welcome of their presence, here, and then some really big shot to whom their gratitude might matter.

I have seen family snapshots of my mother pushing me in a baby carriage decorated with the single decal F.D.R., and I have listened to endless tall stories about what I did or didn't do when my father placed me in the lap of New York's mayor, Fiorello La Guardia, and, on top of the ornate wallpaper of our parlor floor there was a large color photograph of the archbishop of the Episcopal diocese of Long Island; my parents lived in America, full of faith.

When I visited the birthplace of my mother, twelve years ago, I was embarrassed by the shiny rented car that brought me there: even in 1974, there were no paved roads in Clonmel, a delicate dot of a mountain village in Jamaica. And despite the breathtaking altitude, you could not poke or peer yourself into a decent position for "a view": the vegetation was that dense, that lush, and that chaotic. On or close to the site of my mother's childhood home, I found a neat wood cabin, still without windowpanes or screens, a dirt floor, and a barefoot family of seven, quietly bustling about.

I was stunned. There was neither electricity nor running water. How did my parents even hear about America, more than a half century ago? In the middle of the Roaring Twenties, these eager Black immigrants came, by boat. Did they have to borrow shoes for the journey?

I know that my aunt and my mother buckled into domestic work, once   10
they arrived, barely into their teens. I'm not sure how my father managed to feed himself before that fantastic 1933 afternoon when he simply ran all the way from midtown Manhattan up to our Harlem apartment, shouting out the news: A job! He had found a job!

And throughout my childhood I cannot recall even one utterance of disappointment, or bitterness with America. In fact, my parents hid away any newspaper or magazine article that dealt with "jim crow" or "lynchings" or "discrimination." These were terms of taboo status neither to be spoken nor explained to me. Instead I was given a child's biography of Abraham Lincoln and the Bible stories of Daniel and David, and, from my father, I learned about Marcus Garvey and George Washington Carver and Mary McLeod Bethune. The focus was relentlessly upbeat. Or, as Jimmy Cliff used to sing it, "You can make it if you really try."

My mother's emphasis was more religious, and more consistently race-conscious, and she was equally affirmative: God would take care of me. And, besides, there was ("C'mon, Joe! C'mon!") the Brown Bomber, Joe Louis, and then, incredibly, Jackie Robinson who, by himself, elevated the Brooklyn Dodgers into a sacred cult worshipped by apparently dauntless Black baseball fans.

We had a pretty rich life. Towards the end of the 1960s I was often amazed by facile references to Black communities as "breeding grounds of despair" or "culturally deprived" or "ghettos." That was not the truth. There are grounds for despair in the suburbs, evidently, and I more than suspect greater cultural deprivation in economically and racially and socially homogeneous Long Island commuter towns than anything I ever had to overcome!

In Bedford-Stuyvesant, I learned all about white history and white literature, but I lived and learned about my own, as well. My father marched me to the American Museum of Natural History and to the Planetarium, at least twice a month, while my mother picked up "the slack" by riding me, by trolley car, to public libraries progressively farther and farther away from our house. In the meantime, on our own block of Hancock Street, between Reid and Patchen avenues, we had rice and peas and curried lamb or, upstairs, in my aunt and uncle's apartment, pigs' feet and greens. On the piano in the parlor there was boogie-woogie, blues, and Chopin. Across the street, there were cold-water flats that included the Gumbs family or, more precisely, Donnie Gumbs, whom I saw as the inarguable paragon of masculine cute. There were "American Negroes," and "West Indians." Some rented their housing, and some were buying their homes. There were Baptists, Holy Rollers, and Episcopalians, side by side.

On that same one block, Father Coleman, the minister of our church, lived and worked as the first Black man on New York's Board of Higher Education. There was Mrs. Taylor, whose music studio was actually a torture chamber into which many of us were forced for piano lessons. And a Black policeman. And a mail carrier. And a doctor. And my beloved Uncle Teddy, with a Doctor of Law degree from Fordham University. And the tiny, exquisite arrow of my aunt, who became one of the first Black principals in the entire New York City public school system. And my mother, who had been president of the first Black class to graduate from the Lincoln School of Nursing, and my father, who earned the traditional gold watch as a retiring civil servant, and Nat King Cole and calypso and boyfriends and Sunday School and confirmation and choir and stickball and roller skates and handmade wooden scooters and marbles and make-believe tea parties and I cannot recall feeling underprivileged, or bored, in that "ghetto."

And from such "breeding grounds of despair," Negro men volunteered, in droves, for active duty in an army that did not want or honor them. And from such "limited" communities, Negro women, such as my mother, left their homes in every kind of weather, and at any hour, to tend to the ailing and heal the sick, regardless of their color, or ethnicity. And in such a "culturally deprived" house as that modest home created by my parents, I became an American poet.

And in the name of my mother and my father, I want to say thanks to America. And I want something more:

My aunt has survived the deaths of her husband and my parents in typical, if I may say so, West Indian fashion. Now in her seventies, and no longer principal of a New York City public school, she rises at 5 A.M., every morning, to prepare for another day of complicated duties as the volunteer principal of a small Black private academy. In the front yard of her home in the Crown Heights section of Brooklyn, the tulips and buttercups have begun to bloom already. Soon every passerby will see her azaleas and jonquils and irises blossoming under the Japanese maple tree and around the base of the Colorado blue spruce.

She is in her seventies, and she tells me:

> *I love the United States and I always will uphold it as a place of opportunity. This is not to say that you won't meet prejudice along the way but it's up to you to overcome it. And it can be overcome!*

Well, I think back to Clonmel, Jamaica, and I visualize my aunt skipping along the goat tracks, fast as she can, before the darkness under the banana tree leaves becomes too scary for a nine-year-old. Or I think about her, struggling to fetch water from the river, in a pail. And I jump-cut to Orange High School, New Jersey, U.S.A., where my aunt maintained a 95 average, despite her extracurricular activities as a domestic, and where she was denied the valedictory because, as the English teacher declared, "You have an accent that the parents will not understand." And I stay quiet as my aunt explains, "I could have let that bother me, but I said, 'Naw, I'm not gone let this keep me down!'.

And what I want is to uphold this America, this beckoning and this shelter provided by my parents and my aunt. I want to say thank you to them, my faithful American family.

20

Discussion Questions

1. What is the significance of Jordan beginning the essay with a discussion of her father's favorite hobby?

2. What is Jordan's reaction to the "facile references" that are usually attached to Black communities? How does she establish her argument against these stereotypes?

3. What images of America did the writer have growing up? How did her parents handle the unpleasant reality of racism?

4. Who is the American family Jordan refers to in the title? What do you think is the writer's notion of a "family"?

5. What message does Jordan want to convey by quoting her aunt at the end of the essay?

Writing Tasks

1. Jordan spends a great deal of time exposing stereotypes. Write an essay in which you discuss certain misconceptions and their effects on particular groups of people. Thinking of Jordan's approach, how do you propose such stereotypes can be challenged?

2. Write an essay in which you discuss the role a community can play in raising a child.

Facing Poverty with a Rich Girl's Habits

Suki Kim

Suki Kim (b. 1975) is the author of *The Interpreter,* a novel. She lives in New York.

Pre-reading

When did you first become conscious of your ethnicity or class?

Queens in the early 80's struck me as the Wild West. Our first home there was the upstairs of a two-family brownstone in Woodside. It was a crammed, ugly place, I thought, because in South Korea I had been raised in a hilltop mansion with an orchard and a pond and peacocks until I entered the seventh grade, when my millionaire father lost everything overnight. Gone in an instant was my small world, made possible by my father's shipping company, mining business and hotels. Because bankruptcy was punishable by a jail term, we fled, penniless, to America.

The ugly house was owned by a Korean family that ran a dry cleaner in Harlem. Their sons, Andy and Billy, became my first playmates in America, though playmate was a loose term, largely because they spoke English and I didn't. The first English word I learned at the junior high near Queens Boulevard was F.O.B., short for "fresh off the boat." It was a mystery why some kids called me that when I'd actually flown Korean Air to Kennedy Airport.

At 13, I took public transportation to school for the first time instead of being driven by a chauffeur. I had never done homework without a governess helping me. I also noticed that things became seriously messy if no maids were around. Each week, I found it humiliating to wheel our dirty clothes to a bleak place called Laundromat.

One new fact that took more time to absorb was that I was now Asian, a term that I had heard mentioned only in a social studies class. In Korea, yellow was the color of the forsythia that bloomed every spring along the fence that separated our estate from the houses down the hill. I certainly never thought of my skin as being the same shade.

Unlike students in Korean schools, who were taught to bow to teach- 5
ers at every turn, no one batted an eye when a teacher entered a classroom. Once I saw a teacher struggle to pronounce foreign-sounding
names from the attendance list while a boy in the front row French-kissed
a girl wearing skintight turquoise Jordache jeans. In Korea, we wore slip-
pers to keep the school floor clean, but here the walls were covered with
graffiti, and some mornings, policemen guarded the gate and checked
bags.

My consolation was the English as a Second Language class where I
could speak Korean with others like me. Yet it did not take me long to realize that the other students and I had little in common. The wealthier
Korean immigrants had settled in Westchester or Manhattan, where their
children attended private schools. In Queens, most of my E.S.L. classmates came from poor families who had escaped Korea's rigid class hi-
erarchy, one dictated by education level, family background and financial
status.

Immigration is meant to be the great equalizer, yet it is not easy to eradicate the class divisions of the old country. What I recall, at 13, is an acute
awareness of the distance between me and my fellow F.O.B.'s, and another, more palpable one between those of us in E.S.L. and the occasional
English-speaking Korean-American kids, who avoided us as though we
brought them certain undefined shame.

It was not until years later that I learned that we were, in fact, separated
from them by generations.

We who sat huddled in that E.S.L. class grew up to represent the so-
called 1.5 generation. Many of us came to America in our teens, already
rooted in Korean ways and language. We often clashed with the first generation, whose minimal command of English traps them in a time-warped
immigrant ghetto, but we identified even less with the second generation,
who, with their Asian-American angst and anchorman English, struck us
as even more foreign than the rest of America.

Even today, we, the 1.5 generation, can just about maneuver our 10
anchor. We hip-hop to Usher with as much enthusiasm as we have for
belting out Korean pop songs at a karaoke. We celebrate the lunar Korean
thanksgiving as well as the American one, although our choice of food
would most likely be the moon-shaped rice cake instead of turkey. We appreciate eggs Benedict for brunch, but on hung-over mornings, we cannot do without a bowl of thick ox-bone soup and a plate of fresh kimchi.
We are 100 percent American on paper but not quite in our soul.

In Queens of the early 80's, I did not yet understand the layers of division that existed within an immigrant group. I preferred my Hello Kitty
backpack to the ones with pictures of the Menudo boys, and I cried

for weeks because my parents would not let me get my ears pierced. I watched reruns of "Three's Company" in an attempt to learn English, thinking the whole time that John Ritter was running a firm called Three's. I stayed up until dawn to make sense of "Great Expectations," flipping through the dictionary for the definition of words like "Pip."

More brutal than learning English was facing poverty with a rich girl's habits and memory. In my neighborhood, a girl who grew up with a governess and a chauffeur belonged to a fairy tale. This was no Paris Hilton's "Simple Life," but the beginning of my sobering, often-terrifying, never simple American journey. I soon discovered that I had no choice but to adjust. I had watched my glamorous mother, not long ago a society lady who lunched, taking on a job as a fish filleter at a market.

Before the year was over, my parents moved us out of the neighborhood in search of better jobs, housing and education. As for the family who owned the house in Woodside, I did not see any of them again until the fall of 2001, when Billy walked into the Family Assistance Center at Pier 94, where I was volunteering as an interpreter. He was looking for his brother, Andy, who had been working on the 93rd floor when the first plane crashed into the north tower.

Discussion Questions

1. Why did the author and her family immigrate to America?

2. What was Kim's initial experience as a new immigrant in New York like? Do you think her experience is common among most new immigrants?

3. What does the term "F.O.B." imply?

4. How does the author react to the racial prescriptions imposed on her?

5. Why do you think the English-speaking Korean-American kids avoided their newly immigrated Korean classmates? Do you think this division is typical also in other immigrant communities?

6. How are the schools in New York different from those in Korea?

7. What defines the "1.5 generation" immigrants? What are the challenges they face?

8. What does the author want us to reflect about in the final paragraph?

Writing Task

1. Write an essay exploring the causes of division between different generations of immigrants (or different ethnic groups).

My Name Is Not Cool Anymore

Mohammed Naseehu Ali

Mohammed Naseehu Ali (b. 1972) is the author of *The Prophet of Zongo Street,* a story collection to be published in 2005.

Pre-reading

Do you think names can affect how individuals are perceived?

How I came to possess the name of the boxer who was once the most   1
famous and baddest man on the planet happened by accident.

Well, not quite by accident. By religious default almost every male child born in the predominantly Islamic Zongo section of Kumasi, Ghana, where I grew up, had Mohammed as a first name. The Mohammed would be followed by a defining second name, usually an adjective that described the infinite qualities of the original Muhammad, the Holy Prophet of Islam (the spelling of the name varies). My name, Mohammed Naseehu, means Mohammed the Sincere One. One of my brothers is Mohammed Nazeer, the Overseer, another is Mohammed Nuru Deen, the Light of Islam. So for most of my teens, in Ghana, I was usually addressed by my second name.

But soon after I landed at Kennedy Airport in 1988 at age 16 on my way to Michigan to attend Interlochen, the boarding school for the arts, I noticed how little middle names matter in America. They are like dirty little secrets you share only with people you trust. And mine, Naseehu, is one that many non-Muslims find hard to pronounce.

I also liked the prospect of having the same name as the famed American boxer, so I dropped my second name. I hoped that my new identity would quicken my assimilation into American culture.

For 13 years I enjoyed the way people did a double take when they   5
heard my name. I enjoyed flirting with telephone salespeople when they asked, "Really, is that your name?" or "You kidding me?" or "Get outta here." Before handing me back my credit card, cashiers would say,

"Floats like a butterfly, stings like a bee!" Sometimes they'd shout across the store to their co-workers—"Look who I got here!"—and invite them to check out the puny freak named after the heavyweight champion.

I wasn't always sure if they were making fun of me or were simply fascinated that I shared the name of someone so bad and mean. But I didn't care, any more than I objected when the doorman in my office building started calling me the Legend. After I moved to New York for good in 1995, my name was an icebreaker, not to mention a handle that, at least for those initial few minutes after I met someone, conferred a few degrees of coolness.

My name is not cool anymore. On 9/11, I was one of the PATH train passengers evacuated from the World Trade Center after the first plane hit. Once outside, I called my wife in Brooklyn, and while we were speaking, the second plane hit. My phone died; I ran for my life.

In the days after the attacks, I didn't realize how the actions of the Arab religious zealots who masterminded them would affect my life. Two weeks later, I got a call from a worker at Western Union, which I had used to wire money for many years. The company had frozen the $100 I had sent my younger brother for his school fees in Ghana and were demanding that I fax them copies of my identification to prove that the money wasn't being sent to support terrorists. Verbal attacks were left on our answering machine by people who thought they were getting back at an Arab for Sept. 11.

These were mere inconveniences. What really got me was that my name had lost its cachet. People who had thought of "Ali" or "the Greatest!" when they heard "Mohammed" were now apt to think, "Atta." I am proud of the illustrious name of my grandfather, Ali, named for the Prophet's son-in-law. My grandfather himself became an immigrant at the turn of the 20th century when his father migrated with his family on horseback from Zamfara Kingdom, in what is now Nigeria, to the Gold Coast, which is now Ghana. Still I have considered changing my name, not only to fend off wary looks and offensive phone calls but also to restore the coolness I had lost.

Sometimes I think I'd be better off as Cassius Clay.   10

As I weigh the pros and cons of such a move—the effect on my work, my identity; the legal hurdles; the cognitive dissonance it would create in the minds of friends and relatives who would surely think I am losing it altogether—one benefit is clear. I could still enjoy the morale boost I get from the doorman at my office, who could still shout "the Legend" each time I flash my security badge.

Discussion Questions

1. What is the origin of the author's name? Why did he drop his middle name after coming to America? Would you choose to do the same if you were in his position?

2. What initial advantages did the writer enjoy by adopting the new version of his name?

3. Why does he say that his name is not cool anymore? What was lost in his name after 9/11?

4. How does the essay end? What is the author's tone in his conclusion? How well do you think he handles his name issue?

5. What cultural assumptions of Americans does this essay reflect? What do you think causes the hostility and inconveniences Mohammed faces?

Writing Task

1. Do you think that profiling a particular group can ever be justified? Use examples to support your argument.

Making Connections

1. Several of the essays and fiction in this chapter deal, more or less directly, with the different aspects of cultivating and living the American Dream. Discuss what America has meant to one or more of these authors and the disparity with what they experienced here. Connect these episodes to your own aspirations and experiences of living in New York.

2. Review the works in this chapter and discuss with classmates the broad issues they raise (longing, struggle, family, freedom, work, language, education, disillusionment, generational conflict, etc.). Choose one or more of these themes and examine how they are presented in two of the selections. Write a paper in which you compare, contrast, and evaluate the pieces and how you feel about the issues they raise. Feel free to bring in your personal experience and/or observations.

3. Do you think immigrants are treated fairly in America? Write an essay that draws from the readings in this section, other sources, and/or your own experiences.

4. Read Danticat's "New York Day Women" in the literary New York section. Discuss the theme of inter-generational relationships among immigrant families in New York.

CHAPTER 3

Class Matters

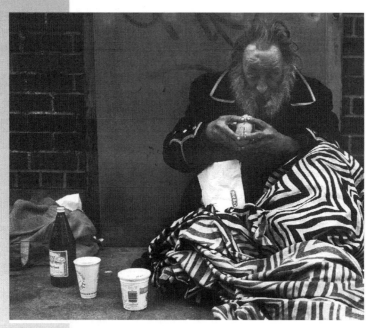

"Homeless Man"
Andrew Holbrooke/CORBIS

The city presents in microcosm all the contrasts of our modern life—its worst and its best aspects. Here are the broad avenues . . . the beautiful parks where landscape gardening has done its best, and here the fetid streets whose festering filth pollutes the atmosphere; here palaces on which selfish extravagance has lavished every artifice for luxury and display, and here tenements where, in defiance of every law, moral and sanitary, men, women, and children are crowded together like maggots in a cheese. Here are the greatest universities, equipping men for the noblest intellectual work, and here the grossest illiteracy and the most absolute ignorance of the simplest and plainest laws of life. . . . Here are the noblest men and women putting forth the most consecrated energies in self-sacrificing labors for the redemption of their fellow-men, appalled, but not discouraged, by the immensity of the problem which confronts them; and here the most hopeless specimens of degraded humanity, in whom, so far as human sight can see, the last spark of divinity has been quenched forever. What shall we do with our great cities? What will our great cities do with us? These are the two problems which confront every thoughtful American.

**The Reverend Lyman Abbot
Plymouth Church, Brooklyn (1898)**

Class Matters

By the end of the nineteenth century, New York City was at the center of America's new industrial age. Everywhere one looked, buildings—that literally seemed to "scrape the sky"—began sprouting from the granite below. Set against the mighty Brooklyn Bridge that was finished in 1883, downtown commerce was flourishing, most notably on Wall Street. As Marina Van Rensselaer wrote in 1892, "New York is steadily attracting . . . the best business ability in the country, not only as a matter of convenience, but . . . because of the exceptional opportunity it offers its favored inhabitants of making and spending money." Evidence of growing riches amongst the "favored" classes was the parade of ornate mansions stretching for two and half miles along Fifth Avenue. But for every Andrew Carnegie, Henry Frick, or John D. Rockefeller living in splendor were hundreds of thousands of freshly arrived immigrants and native New Yorkers living in tenement housing or shanty-towns. Clearly, industrial progress had brought with it great problems. In 1890 a Danish immigrant by the name of Jacob Riis decided to write of the grueling poverty affecting nearly two-thirds of the city's 1.5 million residents. Armed with the latest invention, flash photography, Riis documented in text and images "sights that gripped his heart" in his influential best-seller *How the Other Half Lives.*

This section asks you to think about the chasm between rich and poor in this country, and New York specifically. In "Wealth" Andrew Carnegie claims that such contrasts are a necessary evil, though the wealthy do have an obligation to provide for the common good in a prescribed fashion. Janny Scott and David Leonhardt, on the other hand, questions some of Carnegie's beliefs. Their essay attempts to explain how it is possible that in a land promising endless opportunities, the reality often lies far from the myth. They also ask why it is that the "great divide" continues to grow . . . and continues to be ignored.

Whereas Riis' book sought to spur people to address the plight of the poor, the problem remains unsolved even in our present generation. Today, the situation is most acute in the population known as "the homeless" as discussed in the essay "Helping and Hating the Homeless" by Peter Marin. Marin explains what should and can be done and ultimately indicts America for its short-sightedness and lack of compassion.

"The Gospel of Wealth"
(1889)

Andrew Carnegie

Andrew Carnegie (1835–1919) was born in Scotland in 1835, but moved with his family to Pittsburgh in 1848. After working a variety of jobs, Carnegie invested in the steel business, and his company, U.S. Steel, grew into the largest steel and iron works in America. Carnegie felt it was important to give his wealth back to the public. When he retired, he dedicated much of his fortune to establishing institutions for the public good, including Carnegie-Mellon University, Carnegie Hall, the Carnegie Foundation, and municipal libraries.

Pre-reading

Do you feel that the wealthy have an obligation to "give back" to society?

The problem of our age is the proper administration of wealth, so that   1
the ties of brotherhood may still bind together the rich and poor in harmonious relationship. The conditions of human life have not only been changed, but revolutionized, within the past few hundred years. In former days there was little difference between the "dwelling," dress, food, and environment of the Indian chief and those of his subjects. . . . The contrast between the palace of the millionaire and the cottage of the laborer with us to-day measures the change which has come with civilization.

This change, however, is not to be deplored, but welcomed as highly beneficial. It is well, nay, essential for the progress of the race, that the houses of some should be homes for all that is highest and best in literature and the arts, and for all the refinements of civilization, rather than that none should be so. Much better this great irregularity than universal squalor. Without wealth there can be no great houses or cities.

The price which society pays for the law of competition, like the price it pays for cheap comforts and luxuries, is also great; but the advantages of this law are also greater still, for it is to this law that we owe our wonderful material development, which brings improved conditions in its train. But, whether the law be benign or not, we must say of it: It is here; we cannot evade it; no substitutes for it have been found; and while the law may be sometimes hard for the individual, it is best for the race,

From *The Gospel of Wealth* by Andrew Carnegie, 1889.

because it insures the survival of the fittest in every department. We accept and welcome, therefore, as conditions to which we must accommodate ourselves, great inequality of environment, the concentration of business, industrial and commercial, in the hands of a few, and the law of competition between these, as being not only beneficial, but essential for the future progress of the race.

Having accepted these points, it follows that there must be great scope for the exercise of special ability in the merchant and in the manufacturer who has to conduct affairs upon a great scale. That this talent for organization and management is rare among men is proved by the fact that it invariably secures for its possessor enormous rewards, no matter where or under what laws or conditions. Such men soon create capital; while, without the special talent required, capital soon takes wings.

Objections to the foundations upon which society is based are not in order, because the condition of the race is better with these than it has been with any others which have been tried. Of the effect of any new substitutes proposed we cannot be sure. The Socialist or Anarchist who seeks to overturn present conditions is to be regarded as attacking the foundation upon which civilization itself rests, for civilization took its start from the day that the capable, industrious workman said to his incompetent and lazy fellow, "If thou dost not sow, thou shalt not reap," and thus ended primitive Communism by separating the drones from the bees.

One who studies this subject will soon be brought face to face with the conclusion that upon the sacredness of property civilization itself depends–the right of the laborer to his hundred dollars in the savings bank, and equally the legal right of the millionaire to his millions. To those who propose to substitute Communism for this intense Individualism the answer, therefore, is: The race has tried that. All progress from that barbarous day to the present time has resulted from its displacement. Not evil, but good, has come to the race from the accumulation of wealth by those who have the ability and energy that produce it.

***

We start, then, with a condition of affairs under which the best interests   5
of the race are promoted, but which inevitably gives wealth to the few. Thus far, accepting conditions as they exist, the situation can be surveyed and pronounced good. The question then arises, What is the proper mode of administering wealth after the laws upon which civilization is founded have thrown it into the hands of the few?

There are but three modes in which surplus wealth can be disposed of. It can be left to the families of the decedents; or it can be bequeathed for public purposes; or, finally, it can be administered during their lives by its possessors.

In this last mode we have the true antidote for the temporary unequal distribution of wealth, the reconciliation of the rich and the poor–a reign of harmony–another ideal, differing, indeed, from that of the Communist in requiring only the further evolution of existing conditions, not the total overthrow of our civilization. It is founded upon the present most intense individualism. Under its sway we shall have an ideal state, in which the surplus wealth of the few will become, in the best sense, the property of the many, because administered for the common good, and this wealth, passing through the hands of the few, can be made a much more potent force for the elevation of our race than if it had been distributed in small sums to the people themselves. Even the poorest can be made to see this, and to agree that great sums gathered by some of their fellow-citizens and spent for public purposes, from which the masses reap the principal benefit, are more valuable to them than if scattered among them through the course of many years in trifling amounts.

If we consider what results flow from the Cooper Institute, for instance, and compare these with those which would have arisen for the good of the masses from an equal sum distributed by Mr. Cooper in his lifetime in the form of wages, which is the highest form of distribution, being for work done and not for charity, we can form some estimate of the possibilities for the improvement of the race which lie embedded in the present law of the accumulation of wealth. Much of this sum, if distributed in small quantities among the people, would have been wasted in the indulgence of appetite, some of it in excess, and it may be doubted whether even the part put to the best use, that of adding to the comforts of the home, would have yielded results for the race, as a race, at all comparable to those which are flowing and are to flow from the Cooper Institute from generation to generation. Let the advocate of violent or radical change ponder well this thought.

This, then, is held to be the duty of the man of Wealth: First, to set an example of modest, unostentatious living, shunning display or extravagance; to provide moderately for the legitimate wants of those dependent upon him; and after doing so to consider all surplus revenues which come to him simply as trust funds, which he is called upon to administer so as to produce the most beneficial results for the community. The man of wealth thus becomes the mere agent and trustee for his poorer brethren, bringing to their service his superior wisdom, experience, and ability to administer, doing for them better than they would or could do for themselves. . . .

In Bestowing Charity, the main consideration should be to help those who will help themselves; to provide part of the means by which those who desire to improve may do so; to give those who desire to rise the aids by which they may rise; to assist, but rarely or never to do all. Neither the individual nor the race is improved by almsgiving. Those worthy of assistance, except in rare cases, seldom require assistance.

10

The rich man is thus almost restricted to following the examples of Peter Cooper, Enoch Pratt of Baltimore, Mr. Pratt of Brooklyn, Senator Stanford, and others, who know that the best means of benefiting the community is to place within its reach the ladders upon which the aspiring can rise – parks, and means of recreation, by which men are helped in body and minds; works of art, certain to give pleasure and improve the public taste, and public institutions of various kinds, which will improve the general condition of the people; – in this manner returning their surplus wealth to the mass of their fellows in the forms best calculated to do them lasting good.

Thus is the problem of Rich and Poor to be solved. The laws of accumulation will be left free; the laws of distribution free. Individualism will continue, but the millionaire will be but a trustee for the poor; intrusted for a season with a great part of the increased wealth of the community, but administering it for the community far better than it could or would have done for itself. The best minds will thus have reached a stage in the development of the race in which it is clearly seen that there is no mode of disposing of surplus wealth creditable to thoughtful and earnest men into whose hands it flows save by using it year by year for the general good.

Such, in my opinion, is the true Gospel concerning Wealth, obedience to which is destined some day to solve the problem of the Rich and the Poor, and to bring "Peace on earth, among men Good-Will."

Discussion Questions

1. How does Carnegie support his assertion that the standard of living in his time is higher than it has ever been before? How would you compare the American standard of living today to what Carnegie describes?

2. Do you agree with the author's assertion that other economic systems have been tried and do not work? What in particular makes the capitalistic system appealing to Carnegie?

3. Do you believe that great fortunes are directly related to management talent as Carnegie asserts? Are there exceptions to this rule?

4. What are your views in regards to Carnegie's argument that a great fortune in the hands of a few does society more good than an equal distribution of wealth among many people?

5. Explain what Carnegie means when he assures his readers that "the ties of brotherhood" will bring "the rich and poor in harmonious relationship" if the rich give back to society. Do you find his argument convincing?

6. "How do you get to Carnegie Hall? Practice, Practice, Practice" is a well-known witticism. What does its message imply? Do you believe that making it in America is simply about hard work and perseverance as Carnegie suggests?

Writing Tasks

1. Write an essay in which you explain what you would do for the benefit of humanity if you came into an extremely large sum of money. Would you provide for your family and friends? Would you implement and fund programs in your community? Would you donate money to needy individuals? Be sure to give your reasons for your decisions.

2. Carnegie argues that we pay a social price for the advantages of modern life. Write an essay in which you discuss the price today's society pays for its advances.

3. Write a counter argument to Carnegie's proposal to solve the great divide. What do you propose would be a fair solution to the inequities of wealth distribution?

How the Other Half Lives

Jacob Riis

Jacob Riis (1849–1914) was a Danish immigrant who had experienced home-lessness and poverty on arriving in New York. His famous study of the city's slums, *How the Other Half Lives* (1890), first-hand accounts of the New York housing crisis at the turn of the century and led to new tenement construction laws which required better light and ventilation for tenants.

Pre-reading

Do you feel that the city does enough to ensure adequate affordable housing?

Enough of them [tenements] everywhere. Suppose we look into one? 1
No.—Cherry Street. Be a little careful, please! The hall is dark and you might stumble over the children pitching pennies back there. Not that it would hurt them; kicks and cuffs are their daily diet. They have little else. Here where the hall turns and dives into utter darkness is a step, and another, another. A flight of stairs. You can feel your way, if you cannot see it. Close? Yes! What would you have? All the fresh air that ever enters these stairs comes from the hall door that is forever slamming, and from the windows of dark bedrooms that in turn receive from the stairs their sole supply of the elements God meant to be free, but man deals out with such niggardly hand. That was a woman filling her pail by the hydrant you just bumped against. The sinks are in the hallway, that all the tenants may have access—and all be poisoned alike by their summer stenches. Hear the pump squeak! It is the lullaby of tenement house babes. In summer, when a thousand thirsty throats pant for a cooling drink in this block, it is worked in vain. But the saloon, whose open door you passed in the hall, is always there. The smell of it has followed you up. Here is a door. Listen! That short hacking cough, that tiny, helpless wail—what do they mean?—Oh! a sadly familiar story—before the day is at an end. The child is dying with measles. With half a chance it might have lived; but it had none. That dark bedroom killed it.

"It was took all of a suddint," says the mother, smoothing the throbbing little body with trembling hands. There is no unkindness in the rough voice of the man in the jumper, who sits by the window grimly smoking a clay pipe, with the little life ebbing out in his sight, bitter as his words sound: "Hush, Mary! If we cannot keep the baby, need we complain—such as we?"

Such as we! What if the words ring in your ears as we grope our way up the stairs and down from floor to floor, listening to the sounds behind the closed doors—some of quarrelling, some of coarse songs, more of profanity. They are true. When the summer heats come with their suffering they have meaning more terrible than words can tell. Come over here. Step carefully over this baby—it is a baby, [in] spite of its rags and dirt—under these iron bridges called fire escapes, but loaded down, despite the incessant watchfulness of the firemen, with broken household goods, with washtubs and barrels, over which no man could climb from a fire. This gap between dingy brick walls is the yard. That strip of smoke-colored sky up there is the heaven of these people. What sort of an answer, think you, would come from these tenements to the question "Is life worth living?" were they heard at all in the discussion? It may be that this, cut from the last report but one of the Association for the Improvement of the Condition of the Poor, a long name for a weary task, has a suggestion of it: "In the depth of winter the attention of the Association was called to a Protestant family living in a garret in a miserable tenement in Cherry Street. The family's condition was most deplorable. The man, his wife, and three small children shivering in one room through the roof of which the pitiless winds of winter whistled. The room was almost barren of furniture; the parents slept on the floor, the elder children in boxes, and the baby was swung in an old shawl attached to the rafters by cords by way of a hammock. The father, a seaman, had been obliged to give up that calling because he was in consumption, and was unable to provide either bread or fire for his little ones."

Perhaps this may be put down as an exceptional case, but one that came to my notice some months ago in a Seventh Ward tenement was typical enough to escape that reproach. There were nine in the family: husband, wife, an aged grandmother, and six children; honest, hard-working Germans, scrupulously neat, but poor. All nine lived in two rooms, one about ten feet square that served as parlor, bedroom, and eating room, the other, a small half room made into a kitchen. The rent was seven dollars and a half a month, more than a week's wages for the husband and father, who was the only breadwinner in the family. That day the mother had thrown herself out of the window, and was carried up from the street dead.

She was "discouraged," said some of the other women from the tenement, who had come in to look after the children while a messenger carried the news to the father at the shop. They went stolidly about their task, although they were evidently not without feeling for the dead woman. No doubt she was wrong in not taking life philosophically, as did the four families a city missionary found housekeeping in the four corners of one room. They got along well enough together until one of the families took a boarder and made trouble. Philosophy, according to my optimistic friend, naturally inhabits the tenements. The people who live there come to look upon death in a different way from the rest of us—do not take it as hard.

"A tenement house in 19th-century New York" © Corbis.

Today, what is a tenement? The law defines it as a house "occupied by three or more families, living independently and doing their cooking on the premises; or by more than two families on a floor, so living and cooking and having a common right in the halls, stairways, yards, etc." That is the legal meaning, and includes flats and apartment houses, with which we have nothing to do.[1] In its narrower sense the typical tenement was thus described when last arraigned before the bar of public justice: "It is generally a brick building from four to six stories high on the street, frequently with a store on the first floor which, when used for the sale of liquor, has a side opening for the benefit of the inmates and to evade the Sunday law; four families occupy each floor, and a set of rooms consists of one or two dark closets, used as bedrooms, with a living room twelve feet by ten. The staircase is too often a dark well in the center of the house, and no direct through ventilation is possible, each family being separated from the other by partitions. Frequently the rear of the lot is occupied by another building of three stories high with two families on a floor." The picture is nearly as true today as ten years ago, and will be for a long time to come. The dim light admitted by the air shaft shines upon greater crowds than ever. Tenements are still "good property," and the poverty of the poor man is destruction. A barrack downtown where he *has to live* because he is poor brings in a third more rent than a decent flat house in Harlem. The statement once made a sensation that between seventy and eighty children had been found in one tenement. It no longer excites even passing attention, when the sanitary police report counting 101 adults and 91 children in a Crosby Street house, one of twins, built together. The children in the other, if I am not mistaken, numbered 89, a total of 180 for two tenements! Or when a midnight inspection in Mulberry Street unearths a hundred and fifty "lodgers" sleeping on filthy floors in two buildings. Spite of brownstone trimmings, plate glass and mosaic vestibule floors, the water does not rise in summer to the second story, while the beer flows unchecked to the all-night picnics on the roof. The saloon with the side door and the landlord divide the prosperity of the place between them, and the tenant, in sullen submission, foots the bills.

Where are the tenements of today? Say rather: where are they not? In fifty years they have crept up from the Fourth Ward slums and the Five Points the whole length of the island, and have polluted the Annexed District to the Westchester line. Crowding all the lower wards, wherever business leaves a foot of ground unclaimed; strung along both rivers, like ball and chain tied to the foot of every street, and filling up Harlem with their restless, pent-up multitudes, they hold within their clutch the wealth and business of New York, hold them at their mercy in the day of mob rule and wrath. The bulletproof shutters, the stacks of hand grenades, and the Gatling guns of the Subtreasury are tacit admissions of the fact and of the quality of the mercy expected. The tenements today are New York, harboring three-fourths of its population. When another generation shall have doubled the census of our city, and to that vast army of workers, held captive by poverty, the very name of home shall be as a bitter mockery, what will the harvest be?

Discussion Questions

1. Can you list what makes the tenements such an unhealthy place to live?
2. What is the effect of the many questions that Riis addresses directly to the reader?
3. Why does Riis offer two definitions of the word "tenement"?
4. What does Riis imply when he writes how the "pent-up multitudes" hold the wealthy "at their mercy in the day of mob rule and wrath"?

Writing Tasks

1. Write a persuasive essay in which you discuss the disparity of wealth in the city today and the problems it causes. What solutions could remedy the problem?
2. Find an article on the Internet on housing in New York. Engage the main argument of the piece and take a stand in the debate.

Shadowy Lines That Still Divide

Janny Scott and David Leonhardt

Pre-reading

Do you think this nation pays enough attention to issues of class such as the gap between the rich and the poor?

There was a time when Americans thought they understood class. The upper crust vacationed in Europe and worshiped an Episcopal God. The middle class drove Ford Fairlanes, settled the San Fernando Valley, and enlisted as company men. The working class belonged to the AFL-CIO, voted Democratic, and did not take cruises to the Caribbean.

Today, the country has gone a long way toward an appearance of classlessness. Americans of all sorts are awash in luxuries that would have dazzled their grandparents. Social diversity has erased many of the old markers. It has become harder to read people's status in the clothes they wear, the cars they drive, the votes they cast, the god they worship, the color of their skin. The contours of class have blurred; some say they have disappeared.

But class is still a powerful force in American life. Over the past three decades it has come to play a greater, not lesser, role in important ways. At a time when education matters more than ever, success in school remains linked tightly to class. At a time when the country is increasingly integrated racially, the rich are isolating themselves more and more. At a time of extraordinary advances in medicine, class differences in health and life span are wide and appear to be widening.

And new research on mobility, the movement of families up and down the economic ladder, shows there is far less of it than economists once thought and less than most people believe. In fact, mobility, which once buoyed the working lives of Americans as it rose in the decades after World War II, has lately flattened out or possibly even declined, many researchers say.

Even as mobility seems to have stagnated, the ranks of the elite are opening. Today, anyone may have a shot at becoming a United States Supreme Court justice or a CEO, and there are more and more self-made billionaires. Only thirty-seven members of last year's Forbes 400, a list of the richest Americans, inherited their wealth, down from almost two hundred in the mid-1980s.

So it appears that while it is easier for a few high achievers to scale the summits of wealth, for many others it has become harder to move up from one economic class to another. Americans are arguably more likely than they were thirty years ago to end up in the class into which they were born.

A paradox lies at the heart of this new American meritocracy. Merit has replaced the old system of inherited privilege, in which parents to the manner born handed down the manor to their children. But merit, it turns out, is at least partly class-based. Parents with money, education, and connections cultivate in their children the habits that the meritocracy rewards. When their children then succeed, their success is seen as earned.

The scramble to scoop up a house in the best school district, channel a child into the right preschool program, or land the best medical specialist are all part of a quiet contest among social groups that the affluent and educated are winning in a rout.

"The old system of hereditary barriers and clubby barriers has pretty much vanished," said Eric Wanner, president of the Russell Sage Foundation, a social science research group in New York City that has published a series of studies on the social effects of economic inequality. In place of the old system, Wanner said, have arisen "new ways of transmitting advantage that are beginning to assert themselves."

Faith in the System

Most Americans remain upbeat about their prospects for getting ahead. A recent *New York Times* poll on class found that 40 percent of Americans believed that the chance of moving up from one class to another had risen over the last thirty years, a period in which the new research shows that it has not. Thirty-five percent said it had not changed, and only 23 percent said it had dropped.

More Americans than twenty years ago believe it possible to start out poor, work hard, and become rich. They say hard work and a good education are more important to getting ahead than connections or a wealthy background.

"I think the system is as fair as you can make it," Ernie Frazier, a sixty-five-year-old real estate investor in Houston, said in an interview after participating in the poll. "I don't think life is necessarily fair. But if you persevere, you can overcome adversity. It has to do with a person's willingness to work hard, and I think it's always been that way."

Most say their standard of living is better than their parents' and imagine that their children will do better still. Even families making less than $30,000 a year subscribe to the American dream; more than half say they have achieved it or will do so.

But most do not see a level playing field. They say the very rich have too much power, and they favor the idea of class-based affirmative action to help those at the bottom. Even so, most say they oppose the government's taxing the assets a person leaves at death.

"They call it the land of opportunity, and I don't think that's changed much," said Diana Lackey, a sixty-year-old homemaker and wife of a retired contractor in Fulton, New York, near Syracuse. "Times are much, much harder with all the downsizing, but we're still a wonderful country."

The Attributes of Class

One difficulty in talking about class is that the word means different things to different people. Class is rank, it is tribe, it is culture and taste. It is attitudes and assumptions, a source of identity, a system of exclusion. To some, it is just money. It is an accident of birth that can influence the outcome of a life. Some Americans barely notice it; others feel its weight in powerful ways.

At its most basic, class is one way societies sort themselves out. Even societies built on the idea of eliminating class have had stark differences in rank. Classes are groups of people of similar economic and social position; people who, for that reason, may share political attitudes, lifestyles, consumption patterns, cultural interests, and opportunities to get ahead. Put ten people in a room and a pecking order soon emerges.

When societies were simpler, the class landscape was easier to read. Marx divided nineteenth-century societies into just two classes; Max Weber added a few more. As societies grew increasingly complex, the old classes became more heterogeneous. As some sociologists and marketing consultants see it, the commonly accepted big three—the upper, middle, and working classes—have broken down into dozens of microclasses, defined by occupations or lifestyles.

A few sociologists go so far as to say that social complexity has made the concept of class meaningless. Conventional big classes have become so diverse—in income, lifestyle, political views—that they have ceased to be classes at all, said Paul W. Kingston, a professor of sociology at the University of Virginia. To him, American society is a "ladder with lots and lots of rungs."

THE POLL RESULTS

To discover how Americans regard class and where they place themselves, *The New York Times* conducted a nationwide survey in March 2005. The poll uncovered optimism about social mobility. It found differences in the views of rich and poor in some areas, including the likelihood of achieving the American dream. The poll was followed by interviews with respondents, chosen to represent different economic groups.

A Land of Opportunity

More than ever, Americans cherish the belief that it is possible to become rich. Three-quarters think the chances of moving up to a higher class are the same as or greater than thirty years ago. Still, more than half thought it unlikely that they would become wealthy. A large majority favors programs to help the poor get ahead.

Is it possible to start out poor, work hard, and become rich?

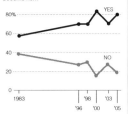

Compared with their social class when growing up, people said their current class was:

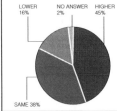

LOWER 16%   NO ANSWER 2%   HIGHER 45%   SAME 38%

How likely is it that you will ever become financially wealthy?

ALREADY RICH 1%   NO ANSWER 1%   SOMEWHAT 34%   VERY 11%   NOT AT ALL 22%   NOT VERY 30%

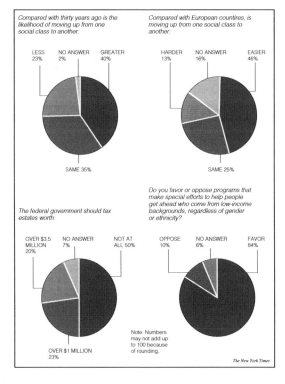

Compared with thirty years ago is the likelihood of moving up from one social class to another:

LESS 23%   NO ANSWER 2%   GREATER 40%   SAME 35%

Compared with European countires, is moving up from one social class to another:

HARDER 13%   NO ANSWER 16%   EASIER 46%   SAME 25%

The federal government should tax estates worth:

OVER $3.5 MILLION 20%   NO ANSWER 7%   NOT AT ALL 50%   OVER $1 MILLION 23%

Do you favor or oppose programs that make special efforts to help people get ahead who come from low-income backgrounds, regardless of gender or ethnicity?

OPPOSE 10%   NO ANSWER 6%   FAVOR 84%

Note: Numbers may not add up to 100 because of rounding.

The New York Times

"There is not one decisive break saying that the people below this all have this common experience," Kingston said. "Each step is equal-sized. Sure, for the people higher up this ladder, their kids are more apt to get more education, better health insurance. But that doesn't mean there are classes."

Many other researchers disagree. "Class awareness and the class language is receding at the very moment that class has reorganized American society," said Michael Hout, a professor of sociology at the University of California, Berkeley. "I find these 'end of class' discussions naïve and ironic, because we are at a time of booming inequality and this massive reorganization of where we live and how we feel, even in the dynamics of our politics. Yet people say, 'Well, the era of class is over.'"

One way to think of a person's position in society is to imagine a hand of cards. Everyone is dealt four cards, one from each suit: education, income, occupation, and wealth, the four commonly used criteria for gauging class. Face cards in a few categories may land a player in the upper middle class. At first, a person's class is his parents' class. Later, he may pick up a new hand of his own; it is likely to resemble that of his parents, but not always.

Bill Clinton traded in a hand of low cards with the help of a college education and a Rhodes scholarship and emerged decades later with four face cards. Bill Gates, who started off squarely in the upper middle class, made a fortune without finishing college, drawing three aces.

Many Americans say that they too have moved up the nation's class ladder. In the *Times* poll, 45 percent of respondents said they were in a higher class than when they grew up, while just 16 percent said they were in a lower one. Overall, 1 percent described themselves as upper class, 15 percent as upper middle class, 42 percent as middle, 35 percent as working, and 7 percent as lower.

"I grew up very poor and so did my husband," said Wanda Brown, the fifty-eight-year-old wife of a retired planner for the Puget Sound Naval Shipyard who lives in Puyallup, Washington, near Tacoma. "We're not rich but we are comfortable and we are middle class and our son is better off than we are."

The American Ideal

The original exemplar of American social mobility was almost certainly Benjamin Franklin, one of seventeen children of a candle maker. About twenty years ago, when researchers first began to study mobility in a rigorous way, Franklin seemed representative of a truly fluid society, in which the rags-to-riches trajectory was the readily achievable ideal, just as the nation's self-image promised.

In a 1987 speech, Gary S. Becker, a University of Chicago economist who would later win a Nobel Prize, summed up the research by saying that mobility in the United States was so high that very little advantage was passed down from one generation to the next. In fact, researchers seemed to agree that the grandchildren of privilege and of poverty would be on nearly equal footing.

If that had been the case, the rise in income inequality beginning in the mid-1970s should not have been all that worrisome. The wealthy might have looked as if they were pulling way ahead, but if families were moving in and out of poverty and prosperity all the time, how much did the gap between the top and bottom matter?

But the initial mobility studies were flawed, economists now say. Some studies relied on children's fuzzy recollections of their parents' income. Others compared single years of income, which fluctuate considerably. Still others misread the normal progress people make as they advance in their careers, like from young lawyer to senior partner, as social mobility.

The new studies of mobility, which methodically track people's earnings over decades, have found far less movement. The economic advantage once believed to last only two or three generations is now believed to last closer to five. Mobility happens, just not as rapidly as was once thought.

"We all know stories of poor families in which the next generation did much better," said Gary Solon, a University of Michigan economist who is a leading mobility researcher. "It isn't that poor families have no chance."

But in the past, Solon added, "people would say, 'Don't worry about inequality. The offspring of the poor have chances as good as the chances of the offspring of the rich.' Well, that's not true. It's not respectable in scholarly circles anymore to make that argument."

One study, by the Federal Reserve Bank of Boston, found that fewer families moved from one quintile, or fifth, of the income ladder to another during the 1980s than during the 1970s and that still fewer moved in the 1990s than in the 1980s. A study by the Bureau of Labor Statistics also found that mobility declined from the 1980s to the 1990s.

The incomes of brothers born around 1960 have followed a more similar path than the incomes of brothers born in the late 1940s, researchers at the Chicago Federal Reserve and the University of California, Berkeley, have found. Whatever children inherit from their parents—habits, skills, genes, contacts, money—seems to matter more today.

Studies on mobility over generations are notoriously difficult, because they require researchers to match the earnings records of parents with those of their children. Some economists consider the findings of the new studies murky; it cannot be definitively shown that mobility has fallen during the last generation, they say, only that it has not risen. The data will probably not be conclusive for years.

Nor do people agree on the implications. Liberals say the findings are evidence of the need for better early-education and antipoverty programs to try to redress an imbalance in opportunities. Conservatives tend to assert that mobility remains quite high, even if it has tailed off a little.

But there is broad consensus about what an optimal range of mobility is. It should be high enough for fluid movement between economic levels but not so high that success is barely tied to achievement and seemingly random, economists on both the right and left say.

As Phillip Swagel, a resident scholar at the American Enterprise Institute, put it, "We want to give people all the opportunities they want. We want to remove the barriers to upward mobility."

Yet there should remain an incentive for parents to cultivate their children. "Most people are working very hard to transmit their advantages to their children," said David I. Levine, a Berkeley economist and mobility researcher. "And that's quite a good thing."

One surprising finding about mobility is that it is not higher in the United States than in Britain or France. It is lower here than in Canada and some Scandinavian countries but not as low as in developing countries like Brazil, where escape from poverty is so difficult that the lower class is all but frozen in place.

Those comparisons may seem hard to believe. Britain and France had hereditary nobilities; Britain still has a queen. The founding document of the

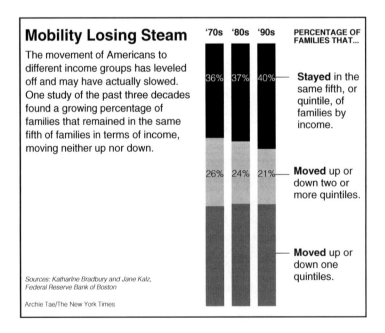

Mobility Losing Steam

The movement of Americans to different income groups has leveled off and may have actually slowed. One study of the past three decades found a growing percentage of families that remained in the same fifth of families in terms of income, moving neither up nor down.

'70s '80s '90s   PERCENTAGE OF FAMILIES THAT...

36% 37% 40% — **Stayed** in the same fifth, or quintile, of families by income.

26% 24% 21% — **Moved** up or down two or more quintiles.

Moved up or down one quintiles.

Sources: Katharine Bradbury and Jane Kalz, Federal Reserve Bank of Boston

Archie Tae/The New York Times

United States proclaims all men to be created equal. The American economy has also grown more quickly than Europe's in recent decades, leaving an impression of boundless opportunity.

But the United States differs from Europe in ways that can gum up the mobility machine. Because income inequality is greater here, there is a wider disparity between what rich and poor parents can invest in their children. Perhaps as a result, a child's economic background is a better predictor of school performance in the United States than in Denmark, the Netherlands, or France, one study found.

"Being born in the elite in the U.S. gives you a constellation of privileges that very few people in the world have ever experienced," Levine said. "Being born poor in the U.S. gives you disadvantages unlike anything in Western Europe and Japan and Canada."

Blurring the Landscape

Why does it appear that class is fading as a force in American life?

For one thing, it is harder to read position in possessions. Factories in China and elsewhere churn out picture-taking cellphones and other luxuries that are now affordable to almost everyone. Federal deregulation has done the same for plane tickets and long-distance phone calls. Banks, more confident about measuring risk, now extend credit to low-income families, so that owning a home or driving a new car is no longer evidence that someone is middle class.

The economic changes making material goods cheaper have forced businesses to seek out new opportunities so that they now market to groups they once ignored. Cruise ships, years ago a symbol of the high life, have become the oceangoing equivalent of the Jersey Shore. BMW produces a cheaper model with the same insignia. Martha Stewart sells chenille jacquard drapery and scallop-embossed ceramic dinnerware at Kmart.

"The level of material comfort in this country is numbing," said Paul Bellew, executive director for market and industry analysis at General Motors. "You can make a case that the upper half lives as well as the upper 5 percent did fifty years ago."

Like consumption patterns, class alignments in politics have become jumbled. In the 1950s, professionals were reliably Republican; today they lean Democratic. Meanwhile, skilled labor has gone from being heavily Democratic to almost evenly split.

People in both parties have attributed the shift to the rise of social issues, like gun control and same-sex marriage, which have tilted many working-class voters rightward and upper-income voters toward the left.

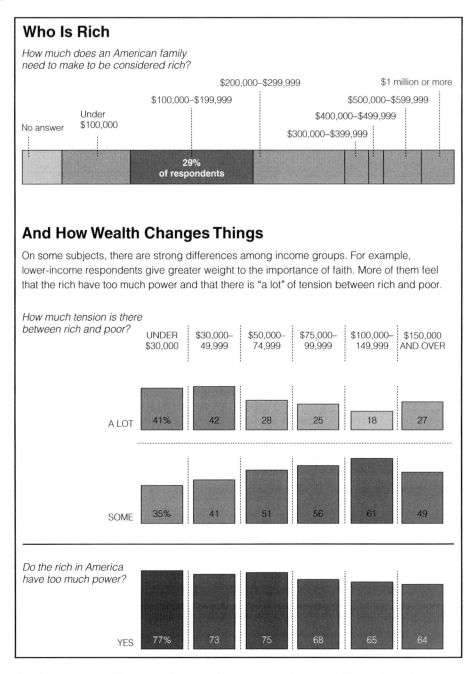

Who Is Rich

*How much does an American family
need to make to be considered rich?*

$200,000–$299,999

$100,000–$199,999

$1 million or more

$500,000–$599,999

Under
$100,000

$400,000–$499,999

No answer

$300,000–$399,999

**29%
of respondents**

And How Wealth Changes Things

On some subjects, there are strong differences among income groups. For example,
lower-income respondents give greater weight to the importance of faith. More of them feel
that the rich have too much power and that there is "a lot" of tension between rich and poor.

*How much tension is there
between rich and poor?*

UNDER $30,000	$30,000–49,999	$50,000–74,999	$75,000–99,999	$100,000–149,999	$150,000 AND OVER

A LOT

| 41% | 42 | 28 | 25 | 18 | 27 |

SOME

| 35% | 41 | 51 | 56 | 61 | 49 |

*Do the rich in America
have too much power?*

YES

| 77% | 73 | 75 | 68 | 65 | 64 |

But increasing affluence plays an important role, too. When there is not
only a chicken, but an organic, free-range chicken, in every pot, the traditional economic appeal to the working class can sound off-key.

Religious affiliation, too, is no longer the reliable class marker it once
was. The growing economic power of the South has helped lift evangelical

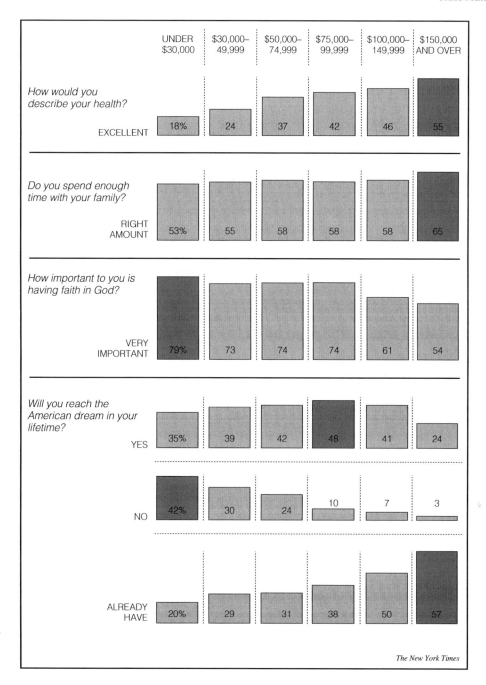

	UNDER $30,000	$30,000–49,999	$50,000–74,999	$75,000–99,999	$100,000–149,999	$150,000 AND OVER
How would you describe your health? EXCELLENT	18%	24	37	42	46	55
Do you spend enough time with your family? RIGHT AMOUNT	53%	55	58	58	58	65
How important to you is having faith in God? VERY IMPORTANT	79%	73	74	74	61	54
Will you reach the American dream in your lifetime? YES	35%	39	42	48	41	24
NO	42%	30	24	10	7	3
ALREADY HAVE	20%	29	31	38	50	57

The New York Times

Christians into the middle and upper middle classes, just as earlier generations of Roman Catholics moved up in the mid-twentieth century. It is no longer necessary to switch one's church membership to Episcopal or Presbyterian as proof that one has arrived.

"You go to Charlotte, North Carolina, and the Baptists are the establishment," said Mark A. Chaves, a sociologist at the University of Arizona. "To imagine that for reasons of respectability, if you lived in North Carolina, you would want to be a Presbyterian rather than a Baptist doesn't play anymore."

The once tight connection between race and class has weakened, too, as many African-Americans have moved into the middle and upper middle classes. Diversity of all sorts—racial, ethnic, and gender—has complicated the class picture. And high rates of immigration and immigrant success stories seem to hammer home the point: The rules of advancement have changed.

The American elite, too, is more diverse than it was. The number of corporate chief executives who went to Ivy League colleges has dropped over the past fifteen years. There are many more Catholics, Jews, and Mormons in the Senate than there were a generation or two ago. Because of the economic earthquakes of the last few decades, a small but growing number of people have shot to the top.

"Anything that creates turbulence creates the opportunity for people to get rich," said Christopher S. Jencks, a professor of social policy at Harvard. "But that isn't necessarily a big influence on the 99 percent of people who are not entrepreneurs."

These success stories reinforce perceptions of mobility, as does cultural mythmaking in the form of television programs like *American Idol* and *The Apprentice*.

But beneath all that murkiness and flux, some of the same forces have deepened the hidden divisions of class. Globalization and technological change have shuttered factories, killing jobs that were once stepping-stones to the middle class. Now that manual labor can be done in developing countries for two dollars a day, skills and education have become more essential than ever.

This has helped produce the extraordinary jump in income inequality. The after-tax income of the top 1 percent of American households jumped 139 percent, to more than $700,000, from 1979 to 2001, according to the Congressional Budget Office, which adjusted its numbers to account for inflation. The income of the middle fifth rose by just 17 percent, to $43,700, and the income of the poorest fifth rose only 9 percent.

For most workers, the only time in the last three decades when the rise in hourly pay beat inflation was during the speculative bubble of the 1990s. Reduced pensions have made retirement less secure.

Clearly, a degree from a four-year college makes even more difference than it once did. More people are getting those degrees than did a generation ago, but class still plays a big role in determining who does or does not. At 250 of the most selective colleges in the country, the proportion of students from upper-income families has grown, not shrunk.

What it Takes to Get Ahead . . .

Hard work—more than education, natural ability, or the right connections—is regarded as crucial for getting ahead in life. While other factors can help a person's advancement, most Americans, regardless of income level, regard the individual's efforts as critical.

Percent in income group who said each was essential to get ahead in life:	UNDER $30,000	$30,000– 49,999	$50,000– 74,999	$75,000– 99,999	$100,000– 149,999	$150,000 AND OVER
COMING FROM A WEALTHY FAMILY	14%	13	9	5	10	5
KNOWING THE RIGHT PEOPLE	17%	18	15	15	16	12
NATURAL ABILITY	22%	25	23	15	19	28
GOOD EDUCATION	38%	37	42	39	38	42
HARD WORK	35%	49	55	47	55	51

How much education does a person need to get ahead in life?

NO ANSWER 3%

DON'T NEED A HIGH SCHOOL DIPLOMA 2%

COLLEGE DEGREE 51%

HIGH SCHOOL DIPLOMA 7%

POSTGRADUATE DEGREE 17%

SOME COLLEGE 20%

Some colleges, worried about the trend, are adopting programs to enroll more lower-income students. One is Amherst, whose president, Anthony W. Marx, explained: "If economic mobility continues to shut down, not only will we be losing the talent and leadership we need, but we will face a risk of a society of alienation and unhappiness. Even the most privileged among us will suffer the consequences of people not believing in the American dream."

Class differences in health, too, are widening, recent research shows. Life expectancy has increased overall; but upper-middle-class Americans live longer and in better health than middle-class Americans, who live longer and in better health than those at the bottom.

Class plays an increased role, too, in determining where and with whom affluent Americans live. More than in the past, they tend to live apart from everyone else, cocooned in their exurban châteaus. Researchers who have studied census data from 1980, 1990, and 2000 say the isolation of the affluent has increased.

Family structure, too, differs increasingly along class lines. The educated and affluent are more likely than others to have their children while married. They have fewer children and have them later, when their earning power is high. On average, according to one study, college-educated women have their first child at age thirty, up from twenty-five in the early 1970s. The average age among women who have never gone to college has stayed at about twenty-two.

Those widening differences have left the educated and affluent in a superior position when it comes to investing in their children. "There is no reason to doubt the old saw that the most important decision you make is choosing your parents," said David Levine, the Berkeley economist and mobility researcher. "While it's always been important, it's probably a little more important now."

The benefits of the new meritocracy do come at a price. It once seemed that people worked hard and got rich in order to relax, but a new class marker in upper-income families is having at least one parent who works extremely long hours (and often boasts about it). In 1973, one study found, the highest-paid tenth of the country worked fewer hours than the bottom tenth. Today, those at the top work more.

In downtown Manhattan, black cars line up outside Goldman Sachs's headquarters every weeknight around nine. Employees who work that late get a free ride home, and there are plenty of them. Until 1976, a limousine waited at 4:30 p.m. to ferry partners to Grand Central Terminal. But a new management team eliminated the late-afternoon limo to send a message: four thirty is the middle of the workday, not the end.

A RAGS-TO-RICHES FAITH

Will the trends that have reinforced class lines while papering over the distinctions persist?

The economic forces that caused jobs to migrate to low-wage countries are still active. The gaps in pay, education, and health have not become a major political issue. The slicing of society's pie is more unequal than it used to be, but most Americans have a bigger piece than they or their parents once did. They appear to accept the trade-offs.

Faith in mobility, after all, has been consciously woven into the national self-image. Horatio Alger's books have made his name synonymous with rags-to-riches success, but that was not his personal story. He was a second-generation Harvard man, who became a writer only after losing his Unitarian ministry because of allegations of sexual misconduct. Ben Franklin's autobiography was punched up after his death to underscore his rise from obscurity.

The idea of fixed class positions, on the other hand, rubs many the wrong way. Americans have never been comfortable with the notion of a pecking order based on anything other than talent and hard work. Class contradicts their assumptions about the American dream, equal opportunity, and the reasons for their own successes and even failures. Americans, constitutionally optimistic, are disinclined to see themselves as stuck.

Blind optimism has its pitfalls. If opportunity is taken for granted, as something that will be there no matter what, then the country is less likely to do the hard work to make it happen. But defiant optimism has its strengths. Without confidence in the possibility of moving up, there would almost certainly be fewer success stories.

Discussion Questions

1. Why is it now so hard to understand and define class? Why was it easier in previous decades?

2. According to the authors, why is it still important to address class issues though many consider the topic irrelevant?

3. What does new research on economic mobility show? What's the significance of this trend?

4. What does the author suggest about America's much revered meritocracy? What are the "new ways of transmitting advantage"?

5. What do most Americans believe about their prospects for moving up the economic ladder? What does actual economic data suggest?

6. Discuss the competing claims sociologists have regarding the concept of class? Whose argument do you find to be most convincing?

7. Explain the quote: "Being born poor in the U.S. gives you disadvantages unlike anything in Western Europe and Japan and Canada."

Writing Tasks

1. Using some of the arguments that Scott and Leonhardt provide, discuss how having or not having enough money has helped or hindered the choices you or somebody you know has made. If you can, try to compare two or more different case scenarios.

2. Watch the media tonight (the news or an entertainment program such as *The Apprentice* or *American Idol*). Discuss how class issues and/or other American values are presented. In your view, are these programs accurate indicators of the "real" world everyday Americans live in?

3. Write an essay that argues the secret to success in America. Consider the following possibilities: inherited wealth, knowing the right people, natural ability, good education, hard work. Include in your essays clear-cut examples.

4. Write a review of Michael Moore's recent film *"Sicko,"* which deals with the state of America's health care system. Where does class come into play in regards to quality health care?

A Chinaman's Chance: Reflections on the American Dream

Eric Liu

Eric Liu is a fellow at the New America Foundation and a contributor to *Slate* and MSNBC. A former speechwriter for President Clinton, he founded *The Next Progressive,* an acclaimed journal of opinion and edited the anthology *Next: Young American Writers on the New Generation.* He is the author of *The Accidental Asian: Notes of a Native Speaker* published in 1999.

Pre-reading

Do you personally know of any "rags-to-riches" success stories?

A lot of people my age seem to think that the American Dream is dead. I think they're dead wrong. 1

Or at least only partly right. It is true that for those of us in our twenties and early thirties, job opportunities are scarce. There looms a real threat that we will be the first American generation to have a lower standard of living than our parents.

But what is it that we mean when we invoke the American Dream?

In the past, the American Dream was something that held people of all races, religions, and identities together. As James Comer has written, it represented a shared aspiration among all Americans—black, white, or any other color—"to provide well for themselves and their families as valued members of a democratic society." Now, all too often, it seems the American Dream means merely some guarantee of affluence, a birthright of wealth.

At a basic level, of course, the American Dream is about prosperity 5 and the pursuit of material happiness. But to me, its meaning extends beyond such concerns. To me, the dream is not just about buying a bigger house than the one I grew up in or having shinier stuff now than I had as a kid. It also represents a sense of opportunity that binds generations together in commitment, so that the young inherit not only property but also perseverance, not only money but also a mission to make good on the strivings of their parents and grandparents.

The poet Robert Browning once wrote that "a man's reach must exceed his grasp—else what's a heaven for?" So it is in America. Every generation will strive, and often fail. Every generation will reach for success, and often miss the mark. But Americans rely as much on the next generation as on the next life to prove that such struggles and frustrations are not in vain. There may be temporary setbacks, cutbacks, recessions, depressions. But this is a nation of second chances. So long as there are young Americans who do not take what they have—or what they can do—for granted, progress is always possible.

My conception of the American Dream does not take progress for granted. But it does demand the *opportunity* to achieve progress—and values the opportunity as much as the achievement. I come at this question as the son of immigrants. I see just as clearly as anyone else the cracks in the idealist vision of fulfillment for all. But because my parents came here with virtually nothing, because they did build something, I see the enormous potential inherent in the ideal.

I happen still to believe in our national creed: freedom and opportunity, and our common responsibility to uphold them. This creed is what makes America unique. More than any demographic statistic or economic indicator, it animates the American Dream. It infuses our mundane struggles—to plan a career, do good work, get ahead—with purpose and possibility. It makes America the only country that could produce heroes like Colin Powell—heroes who rise from nothing, who overcome the odds.

I think of the sacrifices made by my own parents. I appreciate the hardship of the long road traveled by my father—one of whose first jobs in America was painting the yellow line down a South Dakota interstate—and by my mother—whose first job here was filing pay stubs for a New York restaurant. From such beginnings, they were able to build a comfortable life and provide me with a breadth of resources—through arts, travel, and an Ivy League education. It was an unspoken obligation for them to do so.

I think of my boss in my first job after college, on Capitol Hill. George   10
is a smart, feisty, cigar-chomping, take-no-shit Greek-American. He is about fifteen years older than I, has different interests, a very different personality. But like me, he is the son of immigrants, and he would joke with me that the Greek-Chinese mafia was going to take over one day. He was only half joking. We'd worked harder, our parents doubly harder, than almost anyone else we knew. To people like George, talk of the withering of the American Dream seems foreign.

It's undeniable that principles like freedom and opportunity, no matter how dearly held, are not enough. They can inspire a multiracial March on Washington, but they can not bring black salaries in alignment with white salaries. They can draw wave after wave of immigrants here, but they can not provide them the means to get out of our ghettos and barrios and Chinatowns. They are not sufficient for fulfillment of the American Dream.

But they are necessary. They are vital. And not just to the children of immigrants. These ideals form the durable thread that weaves us all in union. Put another way, they are one of the few things that keep America from disintegrating into a loose confederation of zip codes and walled-in communities.

Discussion Questions

1. What does Liu mean when he claims "the dream is not just about buying a bigger house that the one I grew up in . . ."?

2. How does Liu handle the counterargument that racial and class injustice continue to affect people?

3. What is Liu's thinking about the idea of community in connection with the American Dream?

4. According to Liv, what qualities are required for achieving success? Do you agree with his optimism?

Writing Tasks

1. To what extent is it true that achieving success in America depends on assimilation and one's ability to conform to the dominant culture? Use specific examples to illustrate your point.

Bricklayer's Boy

Alfred Lubrano

Alfred Lubrano is a reporter for the *Philadelphia Enquirer* and is a contributor to *Gentleman's Quarterly,* where this essay originally appeared. Lubrano frequently writes about personal relationships and family life.

Pre-reading

Do you totally agree with your parents' values?

My father and I were college buddies back in the mid 1970s. While I was in class at Columbia, struggling with the esoterica du jour, he was on a bricklayer's scaffold not far up the street, working on a campus building.

Sometimes we'd hook up on the subway going home, he with his tools, I with my books. We didn't chat much about what went on during the day. My father wasn't interested in Dante, I wasn't up on arches. We'd share a *New York Post* and talk about the Mets.

My dad has built lots of places in New York City he can't get into: colleges, condos, office towers. He makes his living on the outside. Once the walls are up, a place takes on a different feel for him, as if he's not welcome anymore. It doesn't bother him, though. For my father, earning the dough that paid for my entrée into a fancy, bricked-in institution was satisfaction enough, a vicarious access.

We didn't know it then, but those days were the start of a branching off, a redefining of what it means to be a workingman in our family. Related by blood, we're separated by class, my father and I. Being the white-collar son of a blue-collar man means being the hinge on the door between two ways of life.

It's not so smooth jumping from Italian old-world style to U.S. yuppie   5 in a single generation. Despite the myth of mobility in America, the true rule, experts say, is rags to rags, riches to riches. According to Bucknell University economist and author Charles Sackrey, maybe 10 percent climb from the working to the professional class. My father has had a tough time accepting my decision to become a mere newspaper reporter, a field that pays just a little more than construction does. He wonders why I haven't cashed in on that multi-brick education and taken on some lawyer-lucrative job. After bricklaying for thirty years, my father promised himself I'd never pile bricks and blocks into walls for a living. He figured an education—genielike and benevolent—would somehow rocket me into the consecrated trajectory of the upwardly mobile, and load some serious loot into my pockets. What he didn't count on was his eldest son breaking blue-collar rule No. 1: Make as much money as you can, to pay for as good a life as you can get.

He'd tell me about it when I was nineteen, my collar already fading to white. I was the college boy who handed him the wrong wrench on help-around-the-house Saturdays. "You better make a lot of money," my blue-collar handy dad wryly warned me as we huddled in front of a disassembled dishwasher I had neither the inclination nor the aptitude to fix. "You're gonna need to hire someone to hammer a nail into a wall for you."

In 1980, after college and graduate school, I was offered my first job, on a now-dead daily paper in Columbus, Ohio. I broke the news in the kitchen, where all the family business is discussed. My mother wept as if it were Vietnam. My father had a few questions: "Ohio? Where the hell is Ohio?"

I said it's somewhere west of New York City, that it was like Pennsylvania, only more so. I told him I wanted to write, and these were the only people who'd take me.

"Why can't you get a good job that pays something, like in advertising in the city, and write on the side?"

"Advertising is lying," I said, smug and sanctimonious, ever the unctuous undergraduate. "I wanna tell the truth."   10

"The truth?" the old man exploded, his face reddening as it does when he's up twenty stories in high wind. "What's truth?" I said it's real life, and writing about it would make me happy. "You're happy with your family," my father said, spilling blue-collar rule No. 2. "That's what makes you happy. After that, it all comes down to dollars and cents. What gives you comfort besides your family? Money, only money."

During the two weeks before I moved, he reminded me that newspaper journalism is a dying field, and I could do better. Then he pressed advertising again, though neither of us knew anything about it, except that you could work in Manhattan, the borough with the water-beading high gloss, the island polished clean by money. I couldn't explain myself, so I packed, unpopular and confused. No longer was I the good son who studied hard and fumbled endearingly with tools. I was hacking people off.

One night, though, my father brought home some heavy tape and that clear, plastic bubble stuff you pack your mother's second-string dishes in.

"You probably couldn't do this right," my father said to me before he sealed the boxes and helped me take them to UPS. "This is what he wants," my father told my mother the day I left for Columbus in my grandfather's eleven-year-old gray Cadillac. "What are you gonna do?" After I said my good-byes, my father took me aside and pressed five $100 bills into my hands. "It's okay," he said over my weak protests. "Don't tell your mother."

When I broke the news about what the paper was paying me, my father suggested I get a part-time job to augment the income. "Maybe you could drive a cab." Once, after I was chewed out by the city editor for something trivial, I made the mistake of telling my father during a visit home. "They pay you nothin', and they push you around too much in that business," he told me, the rage building. "Next time, you gotta grab the guy by the throat and tell him he's a big jerk."

"Dad, I can't talk to the boss like that."   15

"Tell him. You get results that way. Never take any shit." A few years before, a guy didn't like the retaining wall my father and his partner had built. They tore it down and did it again, but the guy still bitched. My father's partner shoved the guy into the freshly laid bricks. "Pay me off," my father said, and he and his partner took the money and walked. Blue-collar guys have no patience for office politics and corporate bile-swallowing. Just pay me off and I'm gone. Eventually, I moved on to a job in Cleveland, on a paper my father has heard of. I think he looks on it as a sign of progress, because he hasn't mentioned advertising for a while.

When he was my age, my father was already dug in with a trade, a wife, two sons and a house in a neighborhood in Brooklyn not far from where he was born. His workaday, family-centered life has been very much in step with his immigrant father's. I sublet what the real-estate people call a junior one-bedroom in a dormlike condo in a Cleveland suburb. Unmarried and unconnected in an insouciant, perpetual student kind of way, I rent movies during the week and feed single women in restaurants on Saturday nights. My dad asks me about my dates, but he goes crazy over the word "woman." "A girl," he corrects. "You went out with a girl. Don't say 'woman.' It sounds like you're takin' out your grandmother."

I've often believed blue-collaring is the more genuine of lives, in greater proximity to primordial manhood. My father is provider and protector, concerned only with the basics: food and home, love and progeny. He's also a generation closer to the heritage, a warmer spot nearer the fire that forged and defined us. Does heat dissipate and light fade further from the source? I live for my career, and frequently feel lost and codeless, devoid of the blue-collar rules my father grew up with. With no baby-boomer groomer to show me the way, I've been choreographing my own tentative shuffle across the wax-shined dance floor on the edge of the Great Middle Class, a different rhythm in a whole new ballroom.

I'm sure it's tough on my father, too, because I don't know much about bricklaying, either, except that it's hell on the body, a daily sacrifice. I idealized my dad as a kind of dawn-rising priest of labor, engaged in holy ritual. Up at five every day, my father has made a religion of responsibility. My younger brother, a Wall Street white-collar guy with the sense to make a decent salary, says he always felt safe when he heard Dad stir before him, as if Pop were taming the day for us. My father, fifty-five years old, but expected to put out as if he were three decades stronger, slips on machine-washable vestments of khaki cotton without waking my mother. He goes into the kitchen and turns on the radio to catch the temperature. Bricklayers have an occupational need to know the weather. And because I am my father's son, I can recite the five-day forecast at any given moment.

My father isn't crazy about this life. He wanted to be a singer and actor   20 when he was young, but that was frivolous doodling to his Italian family, who expected money to be coming in, stoking the stove that kept hearth fires ablaze. Dreams simply were not energy-efficient. My dad learned a trade, as he was supposed to, and settled into a life of pre-scripted routing. He says he can't find the black-and-white publicity glossies he once had made.

Although I see my dad infrequently, my brother, who lives at home, is with the old man every day. Chris has a lot more blue-collar in him than I do, despite his management-level career; for a short time, he wanted to be a construction worker, but my parents persuaded him to go to Columbia. Once in a while he'll bag a lunch and, in a nice wool suit, meet my father at a construction site and share sandwiches of egg salad on semolina bread.

It was Chris who helped my dad most when my father tried to change his life several months ago. My dad wanted a civil-service bricklayer foreman's job that wouldn't be so physically demanding. There was a written test that included essay questions about construction work. My father hadn't done anything like it in forty years. Why the hell they needed bricklayers to write essays I have no idea, but my father sweated it out. Every morning before sunrise, Chris would be ironing a shirt, bleary-eyed, and my father would sit at the kitchen table and read aloud his practice essays on how to wash down a wall, or how to build a tricky corner. Chris would suggest words and approaches.

It was so hard for my dad. He had to take a Stanley Kaplan-like prep course in a junior high school three nights a week after work for six weeks. At class time, the outside men would come in, twenty-five construction workers squeezing themselves into little desks. Tough blue-collar guys armed with No. 2 pencils leaning over and scratching out their practice essays, cement in their hair, tar on their pants, their work boots too big and clumsy to fit under the desks.

"Is this what finals felt like?" my father would ask me on the phone when I pitched in to help long-distance. "Were you always this nervous?" I told him yes. I told him writing's always difficult. He thanked Chris and me for the coaching, for putting him through school this time. My father thinks he did okay, but he's still awaiting the test results. In the meantime, he takes life the blue-collar way, one brick at a time.

When we see each other these days, my father still asks how the money is. Sometimes he reads my stories; usually he likes them, although he recently criticized one piece as being a bit sentimental: "Too schmaltzy," he said. Some psychologists say that the blue-white-collar gap between fathers and sons leads to alienation, but I tend to agree with Dr. Al Baraff, a clinical psychologist and director of the Men-Center in Washington, D.C. "The core of the relationship is based on emotional and hereditary traits," Baraff says. "Class [distinctions] just get added on. If it's a healthful relationship from when you're a kid, there's a respect back and forth that'll continue."

Nice of the doctor to explain, but I suppose I already knew that. Whatever is between my father and me, whatever keeps us talking and keeps us close, has nothing to do with work and economic class.

During one of my visits to Brooklyn not long ago, he and I were in the car, on our way to buy toiletries, one of my father's weekly routines. "You know, you're not as successful as you could be," he began, blue-collar blunt as usual. "You paid your dues in school. You deserve better restaurants, better clothes." Here we go, I thought, the same old stuff. I'm sure every family has five or six similar big issues that are replayed like well-worn videotapes. I wanted to fast-forward this thing when we stopped at a red light.

Just then my father turned to me, solemn and intense. His knees were aching and his back muscles were throbbing in clockable intervals that registered in his eyes. It was the end of a week of lifting fifty-pound blocks. "I envy you," he said quietly. "For a man to do something he likes and get paid for it—that's fantastic." He smiled at me before the light changed, and we drove on. To thank him for the understanding, I sprang for the deodorant and shampoo. For once, my father let me pay.

25

Discussion Questions

1. According to what you have read, describe the author's relationship with his father.

2. What are the blue-collar rules mentioned in the story? What do they imply? Do you think they are significant in and represent the values of only one particular class?

3. What does the writer's father mean when he says that his son's collar is "fading into white"? What typifies a white-collar lifestyle?

4. What differences can you see between the writer's and his father's values? How do they resolve the differences?

5. What insight did the writer's father gain when he was preparing for his test? How does it affect his relationship with his sons?

6. What is the significance of the conclusion in which the writer's father let him pay for the first time?

Writing Tasks

1. Write an essay in which you discuss the differences and similarities between your values and beliefs and those of your parents'.

2. Is personal interest or money more important to you when choosing a career? Write an essay explaining your answer.

Helping and Hating the Homeless

Peter Marin

Peter Marin is a poet, novelist, and essayist in southern California, where he is a longtime advocate for homeless people. He is the author of *Freedom and Its Discontents: Reflections on Four Decades of American Moral Experience* (1995) and contributor to *Harper's Magazine,* where this essay was published in 1987 to wide acclaim.

Pre-reading

What are your attitudes towards the homeless?
Why do you believe they are in this condition?

The trouble begins with the word "homeless." It has become such an   1
abstraction, and is applied to so many different kinds of people, with
so many different histories and problems, that it is almost meaningless.

Homelessness, in itself, is nothing more than a condition visited upon
men and women (and, increasingly, children) as the final stage of a variety of problems about which the word "homelessness" tells us almost
nothing. Or, to put it another way, it is a catch basin into which pour all
of the people disenfranchised or marginalized or scared off by processes
beyond their control, those which lie close to the heart of American life.
Here are the groups packed into the single category of "the homeless":

- Veterans, mainly from the war in Vietnam. In many American cities, vets
  make up close to 50 percent of all homeless males.

- The mentally ill. In some parts of the country, roughly a quarter of the
  homeless would, a couple of decades ago, have been institutionalized.

- The physically disabled or chronically ill, who do not receive any benefits
  or whose benefits do not enable them to afford permanent shelter.

- The elderly on fixed incomes whose funds are no longer sufficient for
  their needs.

- Men, women, and whole families pauperized by the loss of a job.

- Single parents, usually women, without the resources or skills to establish new lives.

- Runaway children, many of whom have been abused.

- Alcoholics and those in trouble with drugs (whose troubles often begin with one of the other conditions listed here).

- Immigrants, both legal and illegal, who often are not counted among the homeless because they constitute a "problem" in their own right.

- Traditional tramps, hobos, and transients, who have taken to the road or the streets for a variety of reasons and who prefer to be there.

You can quickly learn two things about the homeless from this list. First, you can learn that many of the homeless, before they were homeless, were people more or less like ourselves: members of the working or middle class. And you can learn that the world of the homeless has its roots in various policies, events, and ways of life for which some of us are responsible and from which some of us actually prosper.

We decide, as a people, to go to war, we ask our children to kill and to   5
die, and the result, years later, is grown men homeless on the street.

We change, with the best intentions, the laws pertaining to the mentally ill, and then, without intention, neglect to provide them with services; and the result, in our streets, drives some of us crazy with rage.

We cut taxes and prune budgets, we modernize industry and shift the balance of trade, and the result of all these actions and errors can be read, sleeping form by sleeping form, on our city streets.

The liberals cannot blame the conservatives. The conservatives cannot   10
blame the liberals. Homelessness is the *sum total* of our dreams, policies, intentions, errors, omissions, cruelties, kindnesses, all of it recorded, in flesh, in the life of the streets.

You can also learn from this list one of the most important things there is to know about the homeless—that they can be roughly divided into two groups: those who have had homelessness forced upon them and want nothing more than to escape it; and those who have at least in part *chosen* it for themselves, and now accept, or in some cases, embrace it.

I understand how dangerous it is to introduce the idea of choice into a discussion of homelessness. It can all too easily be used to justify indifference or brutality toward the homeless, or to argue that they are only getting what they "deserve." And yet it seems to me that it is only by taking choice into account, in all of the intricacies of its various forms and expressions, that one can really understand certain kinds of homelessness.

The fact is, many of the homeless are not only hapless victims but voluntary exiles, "domestic refugees," people who have turned not against life itself but against us, our life, American life. Look for a moment at the vets. The price of returning to America was to forget what they had seen or learned in Vietnam, to "put it behind them." But some could not do that, and the stress of trying showed up as alcoholism, broken marriages, drug addiction, crime. And it showed up too as life on the street, which was for some vets a desperate choice made in the name of life—the best they could manage. It was a way of avoiding what might have occurred had they stayed where they were: suicide, or violence done to others.

We must learn to accept that there may indeed be people, and not only vets, who have seen so much of our world, or seen it so clearly, that to live in it becomes impossible. Here, for example, is the story of Alice, a homeless middle-aged woman in Los Angeles, where there are, perhaps, 50,000 homeless people. It was set down a few months ago by one of my students at the University of California, Santa Barbara, where I taught for a semester. I had encouraged them to go find the homeless and listen to their stories. And so, one day, when this student saw Alice foraging in a dumpster outside a McDonald's, he stopped and talked to her:

> *She told me she had led a pretty normal life as she grew up and eventually went to college. From there she went on to Chicago to teach school. She was single and lived in a small apartment.*
>
> *One night, after she got off the train after school, a man began to follow her to her apartment building. When she got to her door she saw a knife and the man hovering behind her. She had no choice but to let him in. The man raped her.*
>
> *After that, things got steadily worse. She had a nervous breakdown. She went to a mental institution for three months, and when she went back to her apartment she found her belongings gone. The landlord had sold them to cover the rent she hadn't paid.*
>
> *She had no place to go and no job because the school had terminated her employment. She slipped into depression. She lived with friends until she could muster enough money for a ticket to Los Angeles. She said she no longer wanted to burden her friends, and that if she had to live outside, at least Los Angeles was warmer than Chicago.*
>
> *It is as if she began back then to take on the mentality of a street person. She resolved herself to homelessness. She's been out West since 1980, without a home or job. She seems happy, with her best friend being her cat. But the scars of memories still haunt her, and she is running from them, or should I say him.*

This is, in essence, the same story one hears over and over again on the street. You begin with an ordinary life; then an event occurs—traumatic, catastrophic; smaller events follow, each one deepening the original wound; finally, homelessness becomes inevitable, or begins to *seem* inevitable to the person involved—the only way out of an intolerable situation. You are struck continually, hearing these stories, by something seemingly unique in American life, the absolute isolation involved. In what other culture would there be such an absence or failure of support from familial, social, or institutional sources? Even more disturbing is the fact that it is often our supposed sources of support—family, friends, government organizations—that have caused the problem in the first place.

Everything that happened to Alice—the rape, the loss of job and apartment, the breakdown—was part and parcel of a world gone radically wrong, a world, for Alice, no longer to be counted on, no longer worth living in. Her homelessness can be seen as flight, as failure of will or nerve, even, perhaps, as *disease.* But it can also be seen as a mute, furious refusal, a self-imposed exile far less appealing to the rest of us than ordinary life, but *better,* in Alice's terms.

We like to think, in America, that everything is redeemable, that everything broken can be magically made whole again, and that what has been "dirtied" can be cleansed. Recently I saw on television that one of the soaps had introduced the character of a homeless old woman. A woman in her thirties discovers that her long-lost mother has appeared in town, on the streets. After much searching the mother is located and identified and embraced; and then she is scrubbed and dressed in style, restored in a matter of days to her former upper-class habits and role.

A triumph—but one more likely to occur on television than in real life. Yes, many of those on the streets could be transformed, rehabilitated. But there are others whose lives have been irrevocably changed, damaged beyond repair, and who no longer want help, who no longer recognize the *need* for help, and whose experience in our world has made them want only to be left alone. How, for instance, would one restore Alice's life, or reshape it in a way that would satisfy *our* notion of what a life should be? What would it take to return her to the fold? How to erase the four years of homelessness, which have become as familiar to her, and as much a home, as her "normal" life once was? Whatever we think of the way in which she has resolved her difficulties, it constitutes a sad peace made with the world. Intruding ourselves upon it in the name of redemption is by no means as simple a task—or as justifiable a task—as one might think.

It is important to understand too that however disorderly and dirty and unmanageable the world of homeless men and women like Alice appears to us, it is not without its significance, and its rules and rituals. The homeless in our cities mark out for themselves particular neighborhoods, blocks, buildings, doorways. They impose on themselves often obsessively strict

15

routines. They reduce their world to a small area, and thereby protect themselves from a world that might otherwise be too much to bear.

Daily the city eddies around the homeless. The crowds flowing past leave a few feet, a gap. We do not touch the homeless world. Perhaps we cannot touch it. It remains separate even as the city surrounds it.

The homeless, simply because they are homeless, are strangers, alien—and therefore a threat. Their presence, in itself, comes to constitute a kind of violence; it deprives us of our sense of safety. Let me use myself as an example. I know, and respect, many of those now homeless on the streets of Santa Barbara. Twenty years ago, some of them would have been my companions and friends. And yet, these days, if I walk through the park near my home and see strangers bedding down for the night, my first reaction, if not fear, is a sense of annoyance and intrusion, of worry and alarm. I think of my teenage daughter, who often walks through the park, and then of my house, a hundred yards away, and I am tempted—only tempted, but tempted, still—to call the "proper" authorities to have the strangers moved on. Out of sight, out of mind.

Notice: I do not bring them food. I do not offer them shelter or a shower in the morning. I do not even stop to talk. Instead, I think: my daughter, my house, my privacy. What moves me is not the threat of *danger*—nothing as animal as that. Instead there pops up inside of me, neatly in a row, a set of anxieties, ones you might arrange in a dollhouse living room and label: Family of bourgeois fears. The point is this: Our response to the homeless is fed by a complex set of cultural attitudes, habits of thought, and fantasies and fears so familiar to us, so common, that they have become a *second* nature and might as well be instinctive, for all the control we have over them. And it is by no means easy to untangle this snarl of responses. What does seem clear is that the homeless embody all that bourgeois culture has for centuries tried to eradicate and destroy.

If you look to the history of Europe you find that homelessness first appeared (or is first acknowledged) at the very same moment that bourgeois culture begins to appear. The same processes produced them both: the breakup of feudalism, the rise of commerce and cities, the combined triumphs of capitalism, industrialism, and individualism. The historian Fernand Braudel, in *The Wheels of Commerce,* describes, for instance, the armies of impoverished men and women who began to haunt Europe as far back as the eleventh century. And the make up of these masses? Essentially the same then as it is now: the unfortunates, the throwaways, the misfits, the deviants.

> *In the eighteenth century, all sorts and conditions were to be found in this human dross . . . widows, orphans, cripples, . . . journeymen who had broken their contracts, out-of-work*

20

*labourers, homeless priests with no living, old men, fire victims,
. . . war victims, deserters, discharged soldiers, would-be ven-
dors of useless articles, vagrant preachers with or without li-
censes, "pregnant servant-girls and unmarried mothers driven
from home," children sent out "to find bread or to maraud."*

Then, as now, distinctions were made between the "homeless" and the
supposedly "deserving" poor, those who knew their place and willingly
sustained, with their labors, the emergent bourgeois world.

*The good paupers were accepted, lined up and registered on the
official list; they had a right to public charity and were sometimes allowed to solicit it outside churches in prosperous districts, when the congregation came out, or in market places. . . .*

*When it comes to beggars and vagrants, it is a very different
story, and different pictures meet the eye: crowds, mobs, proces-
sions, sometimes mass emigrations, "along the country highways or the streets of the Towns and Villages," by beggars
"whom hunger and nakedness has driven from home." . . . The
towns dreaded these alarming visitors and drove them out as
soon as they appeared on the horizon.*

And just as the distinctions made about these masses were the same
then as they are now, so too was the way society saw them. They seemed
to bourgeois eyes (as they still do) the one segment of society that remained resistant to progress, unassimilable and incorrigible, inimical to
all order.

It is in the nineteenth century, in the Victorian era, that you can find the
beginnings of our modern strategies for dealing with the homeless: the
notion that they should be controlled and perhaps eliminated through
"help." With the Victorians we begin to see the entangling of self-protection
with social obligation, the strategy of masking self-interest and the urge
to control as *moral duty*. Michel Foucault has spelled this out in his books
on madness and punishment: the zeal with which the overseers of early
bourgeois culture tried to purge, improve, and purify all of urban civilization—whether through schools and prisons, or, quite literally, with
public baths and massive new water and sewage systems. Order, or-
dure—this is, in essence, the tension at the heart of bourgeois culture, and
it was the singular genius of the Victorians to make it the main compo-
nent of their medical, aesthetic, *and* moral systems. It was not a sense of
justice or even empathy which called for charity or new attitudes toward
the poor; it was *hygiene*. The very same attitudes appear in nineteenth-
century America. Charles Loring Brace, in an essay on homeless and
vagrant children written in 1876, described the treatment of delinquents

in this way: "Many of their vices drop from them like the old and verminous clothing they left behind. . . . The entire change of circumstances seems to cleanse them of bad habits." Here you have it all: *vices, verminous clothing, cleansing them of bad habits*—the triple association of poverty with vice with dirt, an equation in which each term comes to stand for all of them.

These attitudes are with us still; that is the point. In our own century the person who has written most revealingly about such things is George Orwell, who tried to analyze his own middle-class attitudes toward the poor. In 1933, in *Down and Out in Paris and London,* he wrote about tramps:

> *In childhood we are taught that tramps are blackguards, . . . a repulsive, rather dangerous creature, who would rather die than work or wash, and wants nothing but to beg, drink or rob hen-houses. The tramp monster is no truer to life than the sinister Chinaman of the magazines, but he is very hard to get rid of. The very word "tramp" evokes his image.*

All of this is still true in America, though now it is not the word   25 "tramp" but the word "homeless" that evokes the images we fear. It is the homeless who smell. Here, for instance, is part of a paper a student of mine wrote about her first visit to a Rescue Mission on skid row.

> *The sermon began. The room was stuffy and smelly. The mixture of body odors and cooking was nauseating. I remember thinking: How can these people share this facility? They must be repulsed by each other. They had strange habits and dispositions. They were a group of dirty, dishonored, weird people to me.*
>
> *When it was over I ran to my car, went home, and took a shower. I felt extremely dirty. Through the day I would get flashes of that disgusting smell.*

To put it as bluntly as I can, for many of us the homeless are *shit.* And our policies toward them, our spontaneous sense of disgust and horror, our wish to be rid of them—all of this has hidden in it, close to its heart, our feelings about excrement. Even Marx, that most bourgeois of revolutionaries, described the deviant *lumpen* in *The Eighteenth Brumaire of Louis Bonaparte* as "scum, offal, refuse of all classes." These days, in puritanical Marxist nations, they are called "parasites"—a word, perhaps not incidentally, one also associates with human waste.

What I am getting at here is the *nature* of the desire to help the homeless—what is hidden behind it and why it so often does harm. Every government program, almost every private project, is geared as much to the needs of those giving help as it is to the needs of the homeless. Go to any government agency, or, for that matter, to most private charities, and you will find yourself enmeshed, at once, in a bureaucracy so tangled and oppressive, or confronted with so much moral arrogance and contempt, that you will be driven back out into the streets for relief.

Santa Barbara, where I live, is as good an example as any. There are three main shelters in the city—all of them private. Between them they provide fewer than a hundred beds a night for the homeless. Two of the three shelters are religious in nature: the Rescue Mission and the Salvation Army. In the mission, as in most places in the country, there are elaborate and stringent rules. Beds go first to those who have not been there for two months, and you can stay for only two nights in any two-month period. No shelter is given to those who are not sober. Even if you go to the mission only for a meal, you are required to listen to sermons and participate in prayer, and you are regularly proselytized—sometimes overtly, sometimes subtly. There are obligatory, regimented showers. You go to bed precisely at ten: lights out, no reading, no talking. After the lights go out you will find fifteen men in a room with double-decker bunks. As the night progresses the room grows stuffier and hotter. Men toss, turn, cough, and moan. In the morning you are awakened precisely at five forty-five. Then breakfast. At seven-thirty you are back on the street.

The town's newest shelter was opened almost a year ago by a consortium of local churches. Families and those who are employed have first call on the beds—a policy which excludes the congenitally homeless. Alcohol is not simply forbidden *in* the shelter; those with a history of alcoholism must sign a "contract" pledging to remain sober and chemical-free. Finally, in a paroxysm of therapeutic bullying, the shelter has added a new wrinkle: If you stay more than two days you are required to fill out and then discuss with a social worker a complex form listing what you perceive as your personal failings, goals, and strategies—all of this for men and women who simply want a place to lie down out of the rain!

It is these attitudes, in various forms and permutations, that you find   30
repeated endlessly in America. We are moved either to "redeem" the homeless or to punish them. Perhaps there is nothing consciously hostile about it. Perhaps it is simply that as the machinery of bureaucracy cranks itself up to deal with these problems, attitudes assert themselves automatically. But whatever the case, the fact remains that almost every one of our strategies for helping the homeless is simply an attempt to rearrange the world *cosmetically,* in terms of how it looks and smells to *us.* Compassion is little more than the passion for control.

The central question emerging from all this is, What does a society owe to its members in trouble, and *how* is that debt to be paid? It is a question which must be answered in two parts: first, in relation to the men and women who have been marginalized against their will, and then, in a slightly different way, in relation to those who have chosen (or accept or even prize) their marginality.

As for those who have been marginalized against their wills, I think the general answer is obvious: A society owes its members whatever it takes for them to regain their places in the social order. And when it comes to specific remedies, one need only read backward the various processes which have created homelessness and then figure out where help is likely to do the most good. But the real point here is not the specific remedies required—affordable housing, say—but the basis upon which they must be offered, the necessary underlying ethical notion we seem in this nation unable to grasp: that those who are the inevitable casualties of modern industrial capitalism and the free-market system are entitled, *by right,* and by the simple virtue of their participation in that system, to whatever help they need. They are entitled to help to find and hold their places in the society whose social contract they have, in effect, signed and observed.

Look at that for just a moment: the notion of a contract. The majority of homeless Americans have kept, insofar as they could, to the terms of that contract. In any shelter these days you can find men and women who have worked ten, twenty, forty years, and whose lives have nonetheless come to nothing. These are people who cannot afford a place in the world they helped create. And in return? Is it life on the street they have earned? Or the cruel charity we so grudgingly grant them?

But those marginalized against their will are only half the problem. There remains, still, the question of whether we owe anything to those who are voluntarily marginal. What about them: the street people, the rebels, and the recalcitrants, those who have torn up their social contracts or returned them unsigned?

I was in Las Vegas last fall, and I went out to the Rescue Mission at the   35
lower end of town, on the edge of the black ghetto, where I first stayed years ago on my way west. It was twilight, still hot; in the vacant lot next-door to the mission 200 men were lining up for supper. A warm wind blew along the street lined with small houses and salvage yards, and in the distance I could see the desert's edge and the smudge of low hills in the fading light. There were elderly alcoholics in line, and derelicts, but mainly the men were the same sort I had seen here years ago: youngish, out of work, restless and talkative, the drifters and wanderers for whom the word "wanderlust" was invented.

At supper—long communal tables, thin gruel, stale sweet rolls, ice water—a huge black man in his twenties, fierce and muscular, sat across from me. "I'm from the Coast, man," he said. "Never been away from home before. Ain't sure I like it. Sure don't like *this* place. But I lost my job back home a couple of weeks ago and figured, why wait around for another. I thought I'd come out here, see me something of the world."

After supper, a squat Portuguese man in his mid-thirties, hunkered down against the mission wall, offered me a smoke and told me: "Been sleeping in my car, up the street, for a week. Had my own business back in Omaha. But I got bored, man. Sold everything, got a little dough, came out here. Thought I'd work construction. Let me tell you, this is one tough town."

In a world better than ours, I suppose, men (or women) like this might not exist. Conservatives seem to have no trouble imagining a society so well disciplined and moral that deviance of this kind would disappear. And leftists envision a world so just, so generous, that deviance would vanish along with inequity. But I suspect that there will always be something at work in some men and women to make them restless with the systems others devise for them, and to move them outward toward the edges of the world, where life is always riskier, less organized, and easier going.

Do we owe anything to these men and women, who reject our company and what we offer and yet nonetheless seem to demand *something* from us?

We owe them, I think, at least a place to exist, a way to exist. That may   40
not be a *moral* obligation, in the sense that our obligation to the involuntarily marginal is clearly a moral one, but it is an obligation nevertheless, one you might call an existential obligation.

Of course, it may be that I think we owe these men something because I have liked men like them, and because I want their world to be there always, as a place to hide or rest. But there is more to it than that. I think we as a society need men like these. A society needs its margins as much as it needs art and literature. It needs holes and gaps, *breathing spaces,* let us say, into which men and women can escape and live, when necessary, in ways otherwise denied them. Margins guarantee to society a flexibility, an elasticity, and allow it to accommodate itself to the natures and needs of its members. When margins vanish, society becomes too rigid, too oppressive by far, and therefore inimical to life.

Let me put it as simply as I can: What we see on the streets of our cities are two dramas, both of which cut to the troubled heart of the culture and demand from us a response we may not be able to make. There is the drama of those struggling to survive by regaining their place in the social order. And there is the drama of those struggling to survive outside of it.

The resolution of both struggles depends on a third drama occurring at the heart of the culture: the tension and contention between the magnanimity we owe to life and the darker tendings of the human psyche: our fear of strangeness, our hatred of deviance, our love of order and control. How we mediate by default or design between those contrary forces will determine not only the destinies of the homeless, but also something crucial about the nation, and perhaps—let me say it—about our own souls.

Discussion Questions

1. What is Marin's concern about the general perception of the term "homeless"?
2. What does the author imply in the line: "Homelessness is the sum total of our dreams, policies, intentions, errors, omissions, cruelties, kindnesses, all of it recorded, in flesh, in the life of the streets"?
3. What is Marin's central point in discussing the two types of homeless people?
4. What was the Victorian manner of dealing with the homeless? Does Marin feel that modern society has advanced in its views?
5. Do you think society's contending dramas of "magnanimity" and "hatred of deviance" will ever be resolved? If so, how?

Writing Tasks

1. Address Marin's point about the need for margins in society. To what extent do you agree or disagree with him? Write an essay which explores margins you know of, that are available to people who wish to live alternatively (artistically, socially, politically, etc.).
2. Write an essay in which you discuss the advantages and difficulties of going against society's expectations. In your essay try to address where you feel America fails to meet the needs of its citizens.

Making Connections

1. Write an essay in which you discuss the first time you became conscious of the issue of class. Be sure to incorporate some of the ideas from your readings.
2. Compare and contrast the differing views of Carnegie and that of Scott and Leonhardt regarding the accumulation and distribution of wealth. Whose position do you find to be more convincing?
3. With Jacob Riis "How the Other Half Lives" and Peter Marin's "Helping and Hating the Homeless" in mind, write an essay in which you discuss society's commitment to those who live on the margins. In addition to summarizing and analyzing the readings, discuss your own knowledge or observations of the needy and suggest ways society might change to help those in need.

4. With Scott and Leonhardt's "Shadowy Lines that Still Divide" and Liu's "A Chinaman's Chance: Reflections on the American Dream" in mind, write an essay in which you discuss class mobility in America. In your essay, summarize Scott and Leonhardt's thinking about the uneven distribution of wealth and its effects. Draw a relationship between these authors' views on the possibility of transcending class boundaries. In light of the readings, discuss your own knowledge or observations of class mobility and the degree to which your experience does or does not reflect the ideas of either or both writers. Make specific references to the readings to support your ideas.

5. Compare the different ways Liu and Lubrano define the American dream in relation to class.

CHAPTER 4

Urban Education

"An early American urban public school"
Museum of the City of New York, The Jacob A. Riis Collection.

The basic purpose of a liberal arts education is to liberate the human being to exercise his or her potential to the fullest.

Barbara M. White

The mind is a mansion, but most of the time we are content to live in the lobby.

William Michaels

Urban Education

This chapter engages the issues of urban education at different levels. The selected readings offer various perspectives and answers to the central questions about the goals and purposes of public education. Our main focus in this chapter is to lead you to explore some of the issues raised by the readings and to consider such questions yourselves, to think and evaluate critically what education is for and what it should be in your generation and beyond.

The mission of the government in education, according to Dewitt Clinton, a former mayor of New York, is to make it free and accessible to all children. His essay "Free Schools," written in 1809, asserts that free education promotes equality and is essential for a stable and peaceful civil society. But over a century later, for Jonathan Kozol, equality is not always attainable by virtue of free education. After spending two years investigating the subject and visiting schools in New York, Kozol concludes that there exists a huge disparity in the treatments and quality of education students receive in the city's public high school system. He uses Morris High School, a severely under-funded high school in the Bronx, as an example of, as the title of his essay suggests, "Savage Inequalities." Contrary to Kozol's essay both in tone and purpose is "My American Journey" by Former Secretary of State Colin Powell. A graduate of Morris High School and City College several decades ago, Powell attributes his success to his solid education in the City's public education system.

John Taylor Gatto's "Against School" is a thorough and sobering reflection on the public school system in America. He argues that formal schooling is detrimental rather than beneficial in educating young minds. Public education, having its primary goal to fabricate conforming and obedient citizens, in his opinion, not only produces mediocrity and childishness, but also stifles creativity and character development. To a certain extent, his view is illustrated by Esmeralda Santiago's initial experience in a New York public school. In "When I was Puerto Rican," Santiago challenges her school's placement system, which is based on students' language ability, and wins her first battle as a young immigrant student.

This section concludes with essays by Claudia Wall is and Sonja Steptoe who offer solutions for improving the public school system as it enters the 21st century.

Free Schools

DeWitt Clinton

DeWitt Clinton (1769–1828) was the mayor of New York between 1803 and 1815, during which time he spearheaded the founding of the New York Historical Society, the Literary and Philosophical Society, the American Bible Society, the African Free School, the New York Institution for the Deaf and Dumb, and the Orphan Asylum. Clinton's view of the government's role was founded on a belief in education for the entire population.

Pre-reading

What do you think are the goals of public education?

In casting a view over the civilized world, we find universal agreement   1
on the benefits of education; unfortunately, this opinion has not been put into practice. While magnificent Colleges and Universities are erected, we behold few liberal appropriations for diffusing the blessings of knowledge among all descriptions of people. The fundamental error of Europe has been to confine the light of knowledge to the wealthy, while the humble and the depressed have been excluded from its participation. . . The consequence of this has been that ignorance, the prolific parent of every crime and vice, has predominated over the great body of the people, and a corresponding moral debasement has prevailed. "Man differs more from man, than man from beast," says Montaigne, a once celebrated writer. This remark, however generally false, will certainly apply with great force to a man in a state of high mental cultivation, and man in a state of extreme ignorance.

Ignorance is the cause as well as the effect of bad governments, and without the cultivation of our rational powers, we can entertain no just ideas of the obligations of morality or the excellencies of religion. Although England is justly renowned for its cultivation of the arts and sciences, yet there is no Protestant country where the education of the poor has been so grossly and infamously neglected. If a fair sum had been applied to the education of the poor, the blessings of order, knowledge, and innocence would have been diffused among them, and a total revolution

From *THE LIFE AND WRITINGS OF DEWITT CLINTON*. Address of DeWitt Clinton, 1809.

would have taken place in the habits and lives of the people, favorable to the cause of industry, good morals, good order, and rational religion.

More just and rational views have been entertained on this subject in the United States. Here, no privileged orders—no distinctions in society—no hereditary nobility—exist, to interpose barriers between the people, and to create distinct classifications in society. All men being considered as enjoying an equality of rights, the propriety and necessity of dispensing, without distinction, the blessings of education, followed of course. In New England the greatest attention has been invariably given to this important object. In Connecticut, particularly, the schools are supported at least three-fourths of the year by the interest of a very large fund created for that purpose, and a small tax on the people. The result of this beneficial arrangement is obvious and striking. Our Eastern brethren are a well-informed and moral people. In those States it is as uncommon to find a poor man who cannot read and write, as it is rare to see one in Europe who can.

New York has proceeded in the same career, but on a different, and perhaps more eligible plan. For a few years back, a fund has been accumulating appropriated to the support of common schools. This fund consists at present of near four hundred thousand dollars in bank stock, mortgages, and bonds. The capital will be increased by the accumulating interest and the sale of three hundred and thirty-six thousand acres of land. It is highly probable that the whole fund will, in a few years, amount to one million two hundred and fifty thousand dollars, a sum more than sufficient to accommodate all our poor with a gratuitous education.

We have every reason to believe, that this great fund, established for   5
sinking vice and ignorance, will never be diverted or destroyed, but that it will remain unimpaired across the years, as an illustrious establishment, erected by the benevolence of the State for the propagation of knowledge, and the diffusion of virtue among the people.

A number of benevolent persons had seen, with concern, the increasing vices of this city, arising in a great degree from the neglected education of the poor. Great cities are at all times the nurseries and hot-beds of crime. Bad men from all quarters repair to them, in order to obtain the benefit of concealment, and to enjoy in a superior degree the advantages of rapine and fraud. And the dreadful examples of vice, which are presented to youth, and the alluring forms in which it is arrayed, cannot fail to increase the mass of moral depravity. "In London," it is reported, "above twenty thousand individuals rise every morning, without knowing how, or by what means they are to be supported through the passing day, and in many instances even where they are to lodge on the ensuing night." There can be no doubt that hundreds are in the same situation in this city, prowling about our streets for prey, the victims of intemperance [alcohol abuse], the slaves of idleness, and ready to fall into any vice, rather than to cultivate industry and good order.

After a full view of the case, those persons of whom I have spoken agreed that the evil must be corrected at its source, and that education was the sovereign prescription.

Discussion Questions

1. According to Clinton, what was the fundamental error of Europe? How can it be rectified?

2. What point does Clinton want to make in this quote: "Man differs more from man, than man from beast"? What constitutes this view?

3. What was the author's view of the educational system in New England?

4. What was the cause for the increased crime rate of New York City during Clinton's time? Do you think Clinton's view still holds true today?

5. How do you evaluate the impact of Clinton's educational reform? Do you think his vision has been enacted in our city today?

Writing Task

1. DeWitt Clinton believed that free education for the entire population would create equality among people from different classes. Do you agree with him? Write an essay in support of or arguing against the point of view that free education guarantees equal opportunities.

Savage Inequalities

Jonathan Kozol

Jonathan Kozol (b.1936) is a well-known educator and writer. A Rhodes Scholar and recipient of Guggenheim and Rockefeller fellowships, Kozol won the National Book Award in 1968. *Savage Inequalities* (1991) was the result of his spending two years visiting schools and talking with children in thirty city neighborhoods all over the United States.

Pre-reading

To what extent do you think family background affects a child's academic achievement?

From the street, the school looks like a medieval castle; its turreted tower   1
rises high above the devastated lots below. A plaque in the principal's office tells a visitor that this is the oldest high school in the Bronx.

The first things that one senses in the building are the sweetness, the real innocence, of many of the children, the patience and determination of the teachers, and the shameful disrepair of the surroundings. The principal is unsparing in her honesty. "The first floor," she tells me as we head off to the stairwell, "isn't bad—unless you go into the gym or auditorium." It's the top two floors, she says, the fourth and fifth floors, that reveal the full extent of Morris High's neglect by New York City's Board of Education.

Despite her warning, I am somewhat stunned to see a huge hole in the ceiling of the stairwell on the school's fourth floor. The plaster is gone, exposing rusted metal bars embedded in the outside wall. It will cost as much as $50 million to restore the school to an acceptable condition, she reports.

Jack Forman, the head of the English department, is a scholarly and handsome gray-haired man whose academic specialty is British literature. Sitting in his office in a pinstripe shirt and red suspenders, his feet up on the table, he is interrupted by a stream of kids. A tiny ninth grade student seems to hesitate outside the office door. Forman invites her to come in and, after she has given him a message ("Carmen had to leave—for an emergency") and gone to her next class, his face breaks out into a smile. "She's a lovely little kid. These students live in a tough neighborhood, but they are children and I speak to them as children."

Forman says that freshman English students get a solid diet of good   5
reading: *A Tale of Two Cities, Manchild in the Promised Land,* Steinbeck's *The Pearl,* some African fiction, a number of Greek tragedies. "We're implementing an AP course ["advanced placement"—for pre-college students] for the first time. We don't know how many children will succeed in it, but we intend to try. Our mission is to stretch their minds, to give them every chance to grow beyond their present expectations.

"I have strong feelings about getting past the basics. Too many schools are stripping down curriculum to meet the pressure for success on tests that measure only minimal skills. That's why I teach a theater course. Students who don't respond to ordinary classes may surprise us, and surprise themselves, when they are asked to step out on a stage."

"I have a student, Carlos, who had dropped out once and then returned. He had no confidence in his ability. Then he began to act. He memorized the part of Pyramus. Then he played Sebastian in *The Tempest.* He had a photographic memory. Amazing! He will graduate, I hope, this June."

"Now, if we didn't have that theater program, you have got to ask if Carlos would have stayed in school."

In a sun-drenched corner room on the top floor, a female teacher and some 25 black and Hispanic children are reading a poem by Paul Laurence Dunbar. Holes in the walls and ceiling leave exposed the structural brick. The sun appears to blind the teacher. There are no shades. Sheets of torn construction paper have been taped to windowpanes, but the glare is quite relentless. The children look forlorn and sleepy.

> *I know why the caged bird sings. . . .*

> *It is not a carol of joy. . . .*

"This is your homework," says the teacher. "Let's get on with it."   10
But the children cannot seem to wake up to the words. A 15-year-old boy, wearing a floppy purple hat, white jersey and striped baggy pants, is asked to read the lines.

> *I know what the caged bird feels. . .*
> *When the wind stirs soft through the springing grass,*
> *And the river flows like a stream of glass. . . .*

A 15-year-old girl with curly long red hair and many freckles reads the lines. Her T-shirt hangs down almost to her knees.

I know why the caged bird beats his wing
Till its blood is red on the cruel bars.

A boy named Victor, sitting at my side, whispers the words: "I know why the caged bird beats his wing. . . its blood is red. He wants to spread his wings."

The teacher asks the children what the poet means or what the imagery conveys. There is no response at first. Then Victor lifts his hand. "The poem is about ancient days of slavery," he says. "The bird destroys himself because he can't escape the cage."

"Why does he sing?" the teacher asks.   15

"He sings out of the longing to be free."

At the end of class the teacher tells me, "Forty, maybe 45 percent out of this group will graduate."

The counseling office is the worst room I have seen. There is a large blue barrel by the window.

"When it rains," one of the counselors says, "that barrel will be full." I ask her how the kids react. "They would like to see the rain stop in the office," she replies.

The counselor seems to like the kids and points to three young women   20
sitting at a table in the middle of the room. One of them, an elegant tall girl with long dark hair, is studying her homework. She's wearing jeans, a long black coat, a black turtleneck, a black hat with a bright red band. "I love the style of these kids," the counselor says.

A very shy light-skinned girl waits by the desk. A transfer from another school, she's with her father. They fill out certain transfer forms and ask the counselor some questions. The father's earnestness, his faith in the importance of these details, and the child's almost painful shyness stay in my mind later.

At eleven o'clock, about 200 children in a top-floor room are watching Forman's theater class performing *The Creation* by James Weldon Johnson. Next, a gospel choir sings—"I once was lost and now am found"—and then a tall black student gives a powerful delivery of a much-recited speech of Martin Luther King while another student does an agonizing, slow-paced slave ballet. The students seem mesmerized. The speaker's voice is strong and filled with longing.

"One day, the sons of former slaves and the sons of former slave-owners will be able to sit down together at the table of brotherhood."

But the register of enrollment given to me by the principal reflects the demographics of continued racial segregation: Of the students in this school, 38 percent are black, 62 percent Hispanic. There are no white children in the building.

The session ends with a terrific fast jazz concert by a band composed of   25
students dressed in black ties, crimson jackets and white shirts. A student
with a small trimmed beard and mustache stands to do a solo on the saxophone. The pianist is the same young man who read the words of Martin
Luther King. His solo, on a battered Baldwin, brings the students to their feet.

Victor Acosta and eight other boys and girls meet with me in the freshman counselors' office. They talk about "the table of brotherhood"—the
words of Dr. King that we have heard recited by the theater class upstairs.

"We are not yet seated at that table," Victor says.

"The table is set but no one's in the chairs," says a black student who,
I later learn, is named Carissa.

Alexander, a 16-year-old student who was brought here by his parents
from Jamaica just a year ago, says this: "You can understand things better when you go among the wealthy. You look around you at their school,
although it's impolite to do that, and you take a deep breath at the sight
of all those beautiful surroundings. Then you come back home and see
that these are things you do not have. You think of the difference. Not at
first. It takes a while to settle in."

I ask him why these differences exist.   30

"Let me answer that," says Israel, a small, wiry Puerto Rican boy. "If
you threw us all into some different place, some ugly land, and put white
children in this building in our place, this school would start to shine. No
question. The parents would say: This building sucks. It's ugly. Fix it up.
They'd fix it fast—no question.

"People on the outside," he goes on, "may think that we don't know
what it is like for other students, but we *visit* other schools and we have
eyes and we have brains. You cannot hide the differences. You see it and
compare. . . .

"Most of the students in this school won't go to college. Many of them
will join the military. If there's war, we have to fight. Why should I go to
war and fight for opportunities I can't enjoy—for things rich people
value, for their freedom, but I do not *have* that freedom and I can't go to
their schools?"

"You tell your friends, 'I go to Morris High,'" Carissa says. "They
make a face. How does that make you feel?" She points to the floor beside the water barrel. "I found wild mushrooms growing in that corner."

"Big fat ugly things with hairs," says Victor.   35

Alexander then begins an explanation of the way that inequality becomes ensconced. "See," he says, "the parents of rich children have the
money to get into better schools. Then, after a while, they begin to say,
Well, I have this. Why not keep it for my children? In other words, it locks
them into the idea of always having something more. After that, these

things—the extra things they have—are seen like an *inheritance.* They feel it's theirs and they don't understand why we should question it.

"See, that's where the trouble starts. They get used to what they have. They think it's theirs by rights because they had it from the start. So it leaves those children with a legacy of greed. I don't think most people understand this."

One of the counselors, who sits nearby, looks at me and then at Alexander. Later he says, "It's quite remarkable how much these children see. You wouldn't know it from their academic work. Most of them write poorly. There is a tremendous gulf between their skills and capabilities. This gulf, this dissonance, is frightening. I mean, it says so much about the squandering of human worth. . . ."

I ask the students if they can explain the reasons for the physical condition of the school.

"Hey, it's like a welfare hospital! You're getting it for free," says   40
Alexander. "You have no power to complain."

"Is money really everything?" I ask.

"It's a nice fraction of everything," he says.

Janice, who is soft-spoken and black, speaks about the overcrowding of the school. "I make it my business," she says, "to know my fellow students. But it isn't easy when the classes are so large. I had 45 children in my fifth grade class. The teacher sometimes didn't know you. She would ask you, 'What's your name?' "

"You *want* the teacher to know your name," says Rosie, who is Puerto Rican. "The teacher asks me, 'Are you really in this class?' 'Yes, I've been here all semester.' But she doesn't know my name."

All the students hope to go to college. After college they have ambitious   45
plans. One of them hopes to be a doctor. Two want to be lawyers. Alexander wants to be an architect. Carissa hopes to be a businesswoman. What is the likelihood that they will live up to these dreams? Five years ago, I'm told, there were approximately 500 freshman students in the school. Of these, only 180 survived four grades and made it through twelfth grade to graduation; only 82 were skilled enough to take the SATs. The projection I have heard for this year's ninth grade class is that 150 or so may graduate four years from now. Which of the kids before me will survive?

Rosie speaks of sixth grade classmates who had babies and left school. Victor speaks of boys who left school during eighth grade. Only one of the children in this group has ever been a student in a racially desegregated school.

"How long will it be," I ask, "before white children and black and Hispanic children in New York will go to the same schools?"

"How long has the United States existed?" Alexander asks.

Janice says, "Two hundred years."

"Give it another two hundred years," says Alexander.

"Thank you," says Carissa.   50

At the end of school, Jack Forman takes me down to see the ground floor auditorium. The room resembles an Elizabethan theater. Above the proscenium arch there is a mural, circa 1910, that must have been impressive long ago. The ceiling is crossed by wooden ribs; there are stained-glass windows in the back. But it is all in ruins. Two thirds of the stained-glass panes are missing and replaced by Plexiglas. Next to each of eight tall windows is a huge black number scrawled across the wall by a contractor who began but never finished the repairs. Chunks of wall and sections of the arches and supporting pillars have been blasted out by rot. Lights are falling from the ceiling. Chunks of plaster also hang from underneath the balcony above my head. The floor is filled with lumber, broken and upended desks, potato-chip bags, Styrofoam coffee cups and other trash. There is a bank of organ pipes, gold-colored within a frame of dark-stained wood, but there is no organ. Spilled on the floor beside my feet are several boxes that contain a "Regents Action Plan" for New York City's schools. Scattered across the floor amid the trash: "English Instructional Worksheets: 1984."

"Think what we could do with this," says Forman. "This kind of room was meant for theater and to hold commencements. Parents could enter directly from outside. The mural above the proscenium arch could be restored.

"This could be the soul of the school," he says. "Hopefully, three years from now, when Victor is a senior, we will have this auditorium restored. That's my dream: to see him stand and graduate beneath this arch, his parents out there under the stained glass."

From my notes: "Morris High could be a wonderful place, a center-   55
piece of education, theater, music, every kind of richness for poor children. The teachers I've met are good and energized. They seem to love the children, and the kids deserve it. The building mocks their goodness."

Like Chicago, New York City has a number of selective high schools that have special programs and impressive up-to-date facilities. Schools like Morris High, in contrast, says the *New York Times,* tend to be "most overcrowded" and have "the highest dropout rates" and "lowest scores." In addition, we read, they receive "less money" per pupil.

The selective schools, according to the *Times,* "compete for the brightest students, but some students who might qualify lose out for lack of information and counseling." Other families, says the paper, "win admission through political influence."

The *Times* writes that these better-funded schools should not be "the preserve of an unfairly chosen elite." Yet, if the experience of other cities holds in New York City, this is what these special schools are meant to be. They are *intended* to be enclaves of superior education, private schools essentially, within the public system.

New York City's selective admissions program, says the principal of nonselective Jackson High, "has had the effect of making Jackson a racially segregated high school. . . . Simultaneously, the most 'difficult' and 'challenging' black students [have been] *encouraged* to select Jackson. . . ." The plan, she says, has had the effect of "placing a disproportionate number" of nonachieving children in one school. Moreover, she observes, students who do not meet "acceptable standards" in their chosen schools are sent back to schools like Jackson, making it effectively a dumping ground for children who are unsuccessful elsewhere.

"The gerrymandered zoning and the high school selection processes,"   60
according to a resident of the Jackson district, "create a citywide skimming policy that we compare to orange juice — our black youngsters are being treated like the sediment." The city, she says, is "not shaking the juice right." But she may be wrong. In the minds of those who have their eyes on an effective triage process — selective betterment of the most fortunate — this may be exactly the right way to shake the juice.

Unfairness on this scale is hard to contemplate in any setting. In the case of New York City and particularly Riverdale, however, it takes on a special poignance. Riverdale, after all, is not a redneck neighborhood. It has been home for many years to some of the most progressive people in the nation. Dozens of college students from this neighborhood went south during the civil rights campaigns to fight for the desegregation of the schools and restaurants and stores. The parents of those students often made large contributions to support the work of SNCC and CORE. One generation passes, and the cruelties they fought in Mississippi have come north to New York City. Suddenly, no doubt unwittingly, they find themselves opposed to simple things they would have died for 20 years before. Perhaps it isn't fair to say they are "opposed." A better word, more accurate, might be "oblivious." They do not want poor children to be harmed. They simply want the best for their own children. To the children of the South Bronx, it is all the same.

The system of selective schools in New York City has its passionate defenders. There are those who argue that these schools *deserve* the preferential treatment they receive in fiscal areas and faculty assignment because of the remarkable success that they have had with those whom they enroll. One such argument is made by the sociologist and writer Nathan Glazer.

Noting that excellent math and science teachers are in short supply in New York City, Glazer asks, "If they are scarce, is their effectiveness maximized by scattering them" to serve all children "or by their concentration" so that they can serve the high-achieving? "I think there is a good argument to be made that their effectiveness is maximized by concentration. They, like their students, have peers to talk to and work with and to motivate them." While recognizing the potential for inequity, Glazer nonetheless goes on, "I would argue that nowhere do we get so much for so little . . . than where we bring together the gifted and competent. They teach each other. They create an institution which provides them with an advantageous . . . label."

The points that Glazer makes here seem persuasive, though I think he contemplates too comfortably the virtually inevitable fact that "concentration" of the better teachers in the schools that serve the "high-achieving" necessarily requires a dilution of such teachers in the schools that serve the poorest children. While disagreeing with him on the fairness of this policy, I am not in disagreement on the question of the value of selective schools and am not proposing that such schools should simply not exist. Certain of these schools—New York's Bronx High School of Science, for instance, Boston's Latin School, and others—have distinguished histories and have made important contributions to American society.

If there were a multitude of schools *almost* as good as these in every city, so that applicants for high school could select from dozens of good options—so that even parents who did not have the sophistication or connections to assist their children in obtaining entrance to selective schools would not see their kids attending truly *bad* schools, since there would be none—then it would do little harm if certain of these schools were even better than the rest. In such a situation, kids who couldn't be admitted to a famous school such as Bronx Science might be jealous of the ones who did get in, but would not, for this reason, be condemned to third-rate education and would not be written off by the society. 65

But that is not the situation that exists. In the present situation, which is less a field of education options than a battlefield on which a class and racial war is being acted out, the better schools function, effectively, as siphons which draw off not only the most high-achieving and the best-connected students but their parents too; and this, in turn, leads to a rather cruel, if easily predictable, scenario: Once these students win admission to the places where, in Glazer's words, the "competent" and "gifted" "teach each other" and win "advantageous" labels, there is no incentive for their parents to be vocal on the issues that concern the students who have been excluded. Having obtained what they desired, they secede, to a degree, from the political arena. The political effectiveness of those who have been left behind is thus depleted. Soon enough, the failure of their children and the chaos, overcrowding and low funding of the schools that they attend confirm the wisdom of those families who have fled to the selective schools. This is, of course, exactly what a private school makes possible; but public schools in a democracy should not be allowed to fill this role.

Discussion Questions

1. What is the significance of the title?
2. According to Jack Forman, what is the mission of the English Department in Morris High? What attempts have they made to achieve their goal?
3. What does Kozol want to emphasize in the episode of reading Dunbar's poem? How does it set the tone for the rest of his essay?
4. Given their experience in Morris High School, how did the students respond to the words of Dr. Martin Luther King, Jr. "One day, the sons of former slaves and the sons of former slave-owners will be able to sit down together at the table of brotherhood"?
5. How does the author describe the teachers and the students in Morris High?
6. What are the difficulties the teachers and the students in Morris High are facing?
7. What are selective high schools? Do you think they should continue to receive preferential treatment in fiscal areas and faculty assignment?

Writing Tasks

1. Write an essay in which you discuss the reasons for the disparity in quality amongst different schools and ways to mend the gap.
2. Imagine yourself as one of the students in Morris High, and write a letter to the Mayor demanding reform in the City's education system.

My American Journey

Colin Powell

Colin Powell (b. 1937) was the 65th United States Secretary of State, serving from 2001 to 2005 under President George W. Bush. When appointed, Powell became the highest ranking African American government official in the history of the United States. As a general in the United States Army, Powell also served as National Security Advisor (1987–89) and Chairman of the Joint Chiefs of Staff (1989–93).

Pre-reading

Do you believe that private education is better than public education?

Following my sister's example and Mom and Pop's wishes, I applied   1
to two colleges, the City College of New York and New York University. I must have been better than I thought, since I was accepted at both. Choosing between the two was a matter of simple arithmetic; tuition at NYU, a private school, was $750 a year; at CCNY, a public school, it was $10. I chose CCNY. My mother turned out to be my guidance counselor. She had consulted with the family. My two Jamaican cousins, Vernon and Roy, were studying engineering. "That's where the money is," Mom advised. And she was not far wrong. In the boom years of the fifties, demand for consumer goods and for engineers to design the refrigerators, automobiles, and hi-fi sets was strong. And so I was to be an engineering major, despite my allergy to science and math.

The Bronx can be a cold, harsh place in February, and it was frigid the day I set out for college. After two bus rides, I was finally deposited, shivering, at the corner of 156th Street and Convent Avenue in Harlem. I got out and craned my neck like a bumpkin in from the sticks, gazing at handsome brownstones and apartment houses. This was the best of Harlem, where blacks with educations and good jobs lived, the Gold Coast.

I stopped at the corner of Convent and 141st and looked into the campus of the City College of New York. I was about to enter a college established in the previous century "to provide higher education for the children of the working class." Ever since then, New York's poorest and brightest have seized that opportunity. Those who preceded me at CCNY include the polio vaccine discoverer, Dr. Jonas Salk, Supreme Court Justice Felix Frankfurter, the muckraker novelist Upton Sinclair, the actor Edward G. Robinson, the playwright Paddy Chayefsky, the *New York Times* editor Abe Rosenthal, the novelist Bernard Malamud, the labor leader A. Philip Randolph, New York City mayors Abraham Beame and Edward Koch, U.S. Senator Robert Wagner, and eight Nobel Prize winners: As I took in the grand Gothic structures, a C-average student out of middling Morris High School, I felt overwhelmed. And then I heard a friendly voice: "Hey, kid, you new?"

He was a short, red-faced, weather-beaten man with gnarled hands, and he stood behind a steaming cart of those giant pretzels that New Yorkers are addicted to. I had met a CCNY fixture called, for some unaccountable reason, "Raymond the Bagel Man," though he sold pretzels. I bought a warm, salty pretzel from Raymond, and we shot the breeze for a few minutes. That broke the ice for me. CCNY was somehow less intimidating. I was to become a regular of Raymond's over the next four and a half years. And it either speaks well of his character or poorly of my scholarship that while my memory of most of my professors has faded, the memory of Raymond the Bagel Man remains undimmed.

As I headed toward the main building, Sheppard Hall, towering like a 5
prop out of a horror movie, I passed by an undistinguished old building. I do not remember paying any attention to it at the time. It was, however, to become the focus of my life for the next four years, the ROTC drill hall.

My first semester as an engineering major went surprisingly well, mainly because I had not yet taken any engineering courses. I decided to prepare myself that summer with a course in mechanical drawing. One hot afternoon, the instructor asked us to draw "a cone intersecting a plane in space." The other students went at it; I just sat there. After a while, the instructor came to my desk and looked over my shoulder at a blank page. For the life of me, I could not visualize a cone intersecting a plane in space. If this was engineering, the game was over.

My parents were disappointed when I told them that I was changing my major. There goes Colin again, nice boy, but no direction. When I announced my new major, a hurried family council was held. Phone calls flew between aunts and uncles. Had anybody ever heard of anyone studying geology? What did you do with geology? Where did you go with it? Prospecting for oil? A novel pursuit for a black kid from the South Bronx. And, most critical to these security-haunted people, could geology lead to a pension? That was the magic word in our world. I remember coming home after I had been in the Army for five years and visiting my well-meaning, occasionally meddling Aunt Laurice. What kind of career was this Army? she asked, like a cross-examiner. What was I doing with my life? Snatching at the nearest defense, I mentioned that after twenty years I would get a half-pay pension. And I would only be forty-one. Her eyes widened. A pension? At forty-one? The discussion was over. I had made it.

During my first semester at CCNY, something had caught my eye—young guys on campus in uniform. CCNY was a hotbed of liberalism, radicalism, even some leftover communism from the thirties; it was not a place where you would expect much of a military presence. When I returned to school in the fall of 1954, I inquired about the Reserve Officers Training Corps, and I enrolled in ROTC. I am not sure why. Maybe it was growing up in World War II and coming of age during the Korean conflict: the little banners in windows with a blue star, meaning someone from the family was in the service, or a gold star, meaning someone was not coming back. *Back to Bataan, Thirty Seconds over Tokyo, Guadalcanal Diary,* Colin Kelly, Audie Murphy, the five Sullivan brothers who went down with the cruiser U.S.S. *Juneau, Pork Chop Hill,* and *The Bridges at Toko-Ri.* All these images were burned into my consciousness during my most impressionable years. Or maybe it was the common refrain of that era—you are going to be drafted anyway, you might as well go in as an officer. I was not alone. CCNY might not have been West Point, but during the fifties it had the largest voluntary ROTC contingent in America, fifteen hundred cadets at the height of the Korean War.

There came a day when I stood in line in the drill hall to be issued olive-drab pants and jacket, brown shirt, brown tie, brown shoes, a belt with a brass buckle, and an overseas cap. As soon as I got home, I put the uniform on and looked in the mirror. I liked what I saw. At this point, not a single Kelly Street friend of mine was going to college. I was seventeen. I felt cut off and lonely. The uniform gave me a sense of belonging, and something I had never experienced all the while I was growing up; I felt distinctive.

In class, I stumbled through math, fumbled through physics, and did   10 reasonably well in, and even enjoyed, geology. All I ever looked forward to was ROTC. Colonel Harold C. Brookhart, Professor of Military Science and Tactics, was our commanding officer. The colonel was a West Pointer and regular Army to his fingertips. He was about fifty years old, with thinning hair, of only medium height, yet he seemed imposing because of his bearing, impeccable dress, and no-nonsense manner. His assignment could not have been a coveted one for a career officer. I am sure he would have preferred commanding a regiment to teaching ROTC to a bunch of smart-aleck city kids on a liberal New

York campus. But the Korean War had ended the year before. The Army was overloaded with officers, and Brookhart was probably grateful to land anywhere. Whatever he felt, he never let us sense that what we were doing was anything less than deadly serious.

That fall, I experienced the novel pleasure of being courted by the three military societies on campus, the Webb Patrol, Scabbard and Blade, and the Pershing Rifles, ROTC counterparts of fraternities. Rushing consisted mostly of inviting potential pledges to smokers where we drank beer and watched pornographic movies. The movies, in the sexually repressed fifties, were supposed to be a draw. I hooted and hollered with the rest of the college boys through these grainy 8-millimeter films, in which the male star usually wore socks. But they were not what drew me to the Pershing Rifles. I pledged the PRs because they were the elite of the three groups.

The pledge period involved typical ritualistie bowing and scraping before upperclassmen, and some hazing that aped West Point traditions. A junior would stand you at attention and demand the definition of certain words. To this day I can parrot the response for milk: "She walks, she talks, she's made of chalk, the lactile fluid extracted from the female of the bovine species . . ." and on and on. I can spout half a dozen similar daffy definitions. When we finished the pledge period, we were allowed crests on our uniforms. I found that I was much attracted by forms and symbols.

One Pershing Rifles member impressed me from the start. Ronald Brooks was a young black man, tall, trim, handsome, the son of a Harlem Baptist preacher and possessed of a maturity beyond most college students. Ronnie was only two years older than I, but something in him commanded deference. And unlike me, Ronnie, a chemistry major, was a brilliant student. He was a cadet leader in the ROTC and an officer in the Pershing Rifles. He could drill men so that they moved like parts of a watch. Ronnie was sharp, quick, disciplined, organized, qualities then invisible in Colin Powell. I had found a model and a mentor. I set out to remake myself in the Ronnie Brooks mold.

My experience in high school, on basketball and track teams, and briefly in Boy Scouting had never produced a sense of belonging or many permanent friends. The Pershing Rifles did. For the first time in my life I was a member of a brotherhood. The PRs were in the CCNY tradition only in that we were ethnically diverse and so many of us were the sons of immigrants. Otherwise, we were out of sync with both the student radicals and the conservative engineering majors, the latter easy to spot by the slide rules hanging from their belts. PRs drilled together. We partied together. We cut classes together. We chased girls together. We had a fraternity office on campus from which we occasionally sortied out to class or, just as often, to the student lounge, where we tried to master the mambo. I served as an unlikely academic advisor, steering other Pershing Rifles into geology as an easy yet respectable route to a degree.

The discipline, the structure, the camaraderie, the sense of belonging were what I craved. I became a leader almost immediately. I found a selflessness within our ranks that reminded me of the caring atmosphere within my family. Race, color, background, income meant nothing. The PRs would go the limit for each other and for the group. If this was what soldering was all about, then maybe I wanted to be a soldier.

15

***

I returned to college in the fall of 1955, commuting from Kelly Street. I did not have to be an urbanologist to see that the old neighborhood was deteriorating. The decline was just the latest chapter in the oldest story in New York, people moving up and out as their fortunes improved, and poorer people moving in to take their places. The Jewish families who had escaped Lower East Side tenements for the South Bronx were now moving to the suburbs. Poor Puerto Ricans were moving into their old apartments. Hunts Point had never been verandas and wisteria. And now it was getting worse, from gang fights to gang wars, from jackknives to switchblades, from zip guns to real guns, from marijuana to heroin. One day, I came home from CCNY to find that a kid I knew had been found in a hallway, dead of a heroin overdose. He would not be the last. I had managed to steer clear of the drug scene. I never smoked marijuana, never got high, in fact never experimented with any drugs. And for a simple reason: my folks would have killed me.

As better-off families continued to flee, properties began to decay, even to be abandoned. Landlords cut their losses short and walked away from their buildings. In years to come, my own 952 Kelly Street would be abandoned, then burned out and finally demolished. But that was all in the future. For now, conversation among my relatives typically began, "When you getting out?" Aunt Laurice moved to the northern edge of the Bronx. So did Godmother Brash. Aunt Dot was already in Queens. When were Luther and Arie going to leave?

The secret dream of these tenement dwellers had always been to own their own home. And so the Powell family began heading for the upper Bronx or Queens, Sunday after Sunday, house hunting in desirable black neighborhoods. But the prices were outrageous—$15,000, $20,000, with my parents' combined income totaling about $100 a week. Weekends often ended with the real estate agent sick to death of us and my sister embarrassed to tears.

My father also dreamed about numbers. He bought numbers books at the newsstands to work out winning combinations. And he still went in every day with Aunt Beryl. They usually played quarters. Then, one Saturday night, my father dreamed a number, and the next morning at St. Margaret's the *same* number appeared on the hymn board. This, surely, was God taking Luther Powell by the hand and leading him to the Promised Land. Somehow, Pop and Aunt Beryl managed to scrape up $25 to put on the number. And they hit it, straight.

I still remember the atmosphere of joy, disbelief, and anxiety when the   20 numbers runner delivered the brown paper bags to our house. Pop took them to his room and dumped the money on his bed, $10,000 in tens and twenties, more than three years' pay. He let me help him count it. The money was not going into any bank. This strike was nobody's business. The bills were stashed all over the house, with my mother terrified that the tax man or thieves would be coming through the door any minute.

And that was how the Powells managed to buy 183–68 Elmira Avenue, in the community of Hollis in the borough of Queens—for $17,500. The house was a three-bedroom bungalow in a neighborhood in transition; the whites were moving out and the blacks moving in. My folks bought from a Jewish family named Wiener, one of the few white families left. The neighborhood looked beautiful to us, and the Hollis address carried a certain cachet, a cut above Jamaica, Queens, and just below St. Albans, then another gold coast for middle-class blacks. Our new home was ivy-covered, well kept, and comfortable, and had a family room and a bar in the finished basement. Pop was now a property holder, eager to mow his postage-stamp lawn and prune his fruit trees. Luther Powell had joined the gentry. . . .

I now began commuting from Queens to CCNY via the subway, which led to my first serious romance, with a CCNY student. We began riding the A train from the campus downtown, where we would transfer, I out to Queens and the girl out to Brooklyn. I took her to meet my parents. They were perfectly polite to her, but reserved.

My main college interest remained ROTC and the Pershing Rifles. Geology continued to be secondary, though I did enjoy the field trips. We went upstate and clambered over formations of synclines and anticlines. We had to diagram them and figure out their mirror images. If you had an anticline here, you should be able to predict a complementing syncline bulging out somewhere else. Very satisfying when I got it right. Geology allowed me to display my brilliance to my noncollege friends. "You know, the Hudson really isn't a river." "What are you talking about? College kid. Schmuck. Everybody knows the Hudson River's a river." I would then explain that the Hudson was a "drowned" river, up to about

Poughkeepsie. The Ice Age had depressed the riverbed to a depth that allowed the Atlantic Ocean to flood inland. Consequently, the lower Hudson was really a saltwater estuary. I proudly pinpointed the farthest advance of the Ice Age. It stopped at Hillside Avenue running through Queens. You can see the ground sloping down along that line into St. Albans and Jamaica. I was startled to earn an A in one of my geology courses and wound up with three A's in my major by graduation.

In my junior year, I enrolled in advanced ROTC, which paid a princely $27.90 a month. My idol was still Ronnie Brooks. In his first two years at CCNY, Ronnie had become a cadet sergeant. I became a cadet sergeant. In advanced ROTC, Ronnie became a battalion commander. I became a battalion commander. Ronnie was a drillmaster. I became a drillmaster. Ronnie had been the PRs' pledge officer, and in my junior year I became pledge officer, which allowed me to do something about the way we went after pledges. I told the brothers there was something wrong if the only way we could attract members was with dirty movies. Besides, I said, all the fraternities are doing the same thing. So what's our edge? Let's use a little imagination. Let's show movies of what we do, like drill competitions. Let's show them what we're all about.

The Pershing Rifles had a basement room in one of the houses along Amsterdam Avenue, provided by the CCNY administration to give this largely commuter campus a touch of college social life. I told the brothers to go out on the street, corral kids after they had gotten their jollies from porn movies at other houses, and bring them over to our place to see movies about what the PRs did. I was taking a risk. Success as a pledge officer was easy to measure. Pledges were either up or down from previous years. I anxiously awaited the day the rushees made their choice. When it was over, the Pershing Rifles had attracted the largest pledge class in years. This was a defining moment for me, the first small indication that I might be able to influence the outcome of events.

25

I have a desk set that I have carried with me for over thirty-five years, two Schaeffer pens and pen holders mounted on a marble base. I kept the set on my desk in the White House when I was National Security Advisor and at the Pentagon when I was Chairman of the Joint Chiefs of Staff. I cherish it for what it says on a small attached plaque, a story that begins on a day in the summer of 1957.

It was an anxious moment for my father. Pop had taken me to lunch with two ROTC pals, Tony DePace and George Urcioli, and then to the Greyhound bus terminal in Manhattan. He was fidgeting, full of dire warnings, convinced he was never going to see his son again. My friends and I were off to Fort Bragg, North Carolina, for ROTC summer training, my first venture into the South. Pop told me that he had asked our priest, Father Weeden, to find some black Episcopalians in Fayetteville, near Fort Bragg, to look after me. I was embarrassed and told him to stop fussing.

As it turned out, we were picked up by the Army at the bus depot immediately and whisked off to Fort Bragg, where I spent the next six weeks isolated from Southern life. If Fort Bragg was an ethnic awakening for me, it was in meeting whites who were not Poles, Jews, or Greeks. Here I met virtually my first WASPs. We spent our days training on the rifle range, firing 81mm mortars, learning how to camouflage and how to set up roadblocks, and I loved every minute of it. I also got off to a running start. My reputation for drilling troops had preceded me, and I was named acting company commander.

At the end of our six weeks, we fell out on the parade ground for presentation of honors. We were judged on course grades, rifle range scores, physical fitness, and demonstrated leadership. I was named "Best Cadet, Company D." These are the words engraved on the desk set that was presented to me that day and that I still treasure. A student from Cornell, Adin B. Capron, was selected Best Cadet for the entire encampment. I came in second in that category.

I was feeling marvelous about my honor. And then, the night before we left, as we were turning in our gear, a while supply sergeant took me aside. "You want to know why you didn't get best cadet in camp?" he said. I had not given it a thought. "You think these Southern ROTC instructors are going to go back to their colleges and say the best kid here was a Negro?" I was stunned more than angered by what he said. I came from a melting-pot community. I did not want to believe that my worth could be diminished by the color of my skin. Wasn't it possible that Cadet Capron was simply better than Cadet Powell?   30

I got a more elemental taste of racism while driving home. I left Fort Bragg with two white noncommissioned officers from the CCNY ROTC unit. We drove straight through the night, occasionally stopping at gas stations that had three rest rooms, men, women, and colored, the one I had to use. Blacks were apparently ahead of their time, already unisex. I did not start to relax until we reached Washington, didn't feel safe until we were north of Baltimore. I was reminded of that old routine from the Apollo Theater: "Hey, brother, where you from?" "Alabama." "I'd like to welcome you to the United States and hope you had a pleasant crossing."

These brief episodes apart, the summer of '57 was a triumph for me. I was returning home to my girl. I was bringing my parents something they had never had from me—proof, with my desk set, that I had at last excelled. And I had found something that I did well. I could lead. The discovery was no small gift for a young man at age twenty.

Back in college, I continued doing just enough to get by, my other mediocre grades pulled up by straight A's in ROTC. The previous spring, Colonel Brookhart had informed me that I was going to succeed Ronnie Brooks. I was to be cadet colonel, running the entire CCNY regiment, then one thousand strong. I was also elected company commander of the Pershing Rifles. I was intent on winning both the regular and trick drill competitions for the PRs at that year's regional meet, as Ronnie had done before me. I led the regular drill team and delegated the trick drill team to an imposing fellow named John Pardo, a fine leader.

I sensed early on, however, that the drill team was losing its edge. John was distracted by girlfriend problems. Other members came to me complaining that his mind was not on the upcoming competition. I wanted to take the team away from John and give it to somebody else. The best solution was probably to take it over myself, since I had led the winning team the year before. But John kept saying, "I can do it." We competed that year, as I recall, at the 369th Regiment Armory. We won the regular competition, which I led, but lost the trick competition. Overall, we came in second. I was angry, mostly at myself. I had failed the trick drill team, and I had failed John Pardo too, by letting him go on that floor unprepared, when I knew better.

That day, I started absorbing a lesson as valid for a cadet in a musty   35 college drill hall as for a four-star general in the Pentagon. I learned that being in charge means making decisions, no matter how unpleasant. If it's broke, fix it. When you do, you win the gratitude of the people who have been suffering under the bad situation. I learned in a college drill competition that you cannot let the mission suffer, or make the majority pay to spare the feelings of an individual. Long years afterward, I kept a saying under the glass on my desk at the Pentagon that made the point succinctly if inelegantly: "Being responsible sometimes means pissing people off."

On June 9, 1958, at 8:00 P.M., I entered CCNY's Aronowitz Auditorium. A few weeks before, my father had come into my room, sat on the edge of the bed, and, with a twinkling eye, handed me an envelope. He had cleaned out a savings account that he and my mother had been keeping for me since I was a child. Six hundred dollars. I was rich! The first thing I did was to head downtown to Morry Luxenberg's, regarded as the best military haberdasher in New York, to be outfitted.

The First Army band was playing and I was wearing Morry's uniform when I strode past my parents onto the Aronowitz Auditorium stage. "I, Colin Luther Powell, do solemnly swear that I will support and defend the Constitution of the United States against all enemies foreign and domestic," I repeated with my classmates. "and that I will well and faithfully discharge the duties of the office upon which I am about to enter, so help me God." We live in a more cynical age today. We are embarrassed by expressions of patriotism. But when I said those words almost four decades ago, they sent a shiver down my spine. They still do.

Because I was a "Distinguished Military Graduate," I was offered a regular rather than a reserve commission, which meant that I would have to serve three rather than two years on active duty. I eagerly accepted.

For me, graduation from college the next day was anticlimactic. The night before, after our commissioning, I had gone out celebrating with the boys. We had resumed the revelry the following noon at a college hangout called the Emerald Bar. My mother, knowing where to find me, had to send a cousin to haul me over to my graduation, which in her mind had been the whole point of the previous four and a half years. I tended to look on my B.S. in geology as an incidental dividend.

For much of our growing up, Marilyn and I had been "latchkey kids,"   40
left by ourselves or with neighbors and relatives after school. This situation is supposed to be a prescription for trouble. But that day, Luther and Arie Powell, Jamaican immigrants, garment-district workers, were the parents of two college graduates, with their son now an Army officer as well. Small achievements as the world measures success, but mountaintops in their lives. Thirty-five years later, I was asked by *Parade* magazine to talk about those two people. "My parents," I said, "did not recognize their own strengths." It was nothing they ever said that taught us, I recalled. "It was the way they lived their lives," I said. "If the values seem correct or relevant, the children will follow the values." I had been shaped not by preaching, but by example, by moral osmosis. Banana Kelly, the embracing warmth of an extended family, St. Margaret's Church, and let's weave in the Jamaican roots and a little calypso—all provided an enviable send-off on life's journey.

I also owe an unpayable debt to the New York City public education system. I typified the students that CCNY was created to serve, the sons and daughters of the inner city, the poor, the immigrant. Many of my college classmates had the brainpower to attend Harvard, Yale, or Princeton. What they lacked was money and influential connections. Yet they have gone on to compete with and often surpass alumni of the most prestigious private campuses in this country.

I have made clear that I was no great shakes as a scholar. I have joked over the years that the CCNY faculty handed me a diploma, uttering a sigh of relief, and were happy to pass me along to the military. Yet, even this C-average student emerged from CCNY prepared to write, think, and communicate effectively and equipped to compete against students from colleges that I could never have dreamed of attending. If the Statue of Liberty opened the gateway to this country, public education opened the door to attainment here. Schools like my sister's Buffalo State Teachers College and CCNY have served as the Harvards and Princetons of the poor. And they served us well. I am, consequently, a champion of public secondary and higher education. I will speak out for them and support them for as long as I have the good sense to remember where I came from. . . .

Discussion Questions

1. Why does Powell ultimately decide to go to CUNY? Do you think he made the wise decision?

2. How does Powell feel upon arriving at City College? What is causing him to feel this way?

3. What qualities does Powell admire about Ronnie Brooks? How important do you think role models are for new students?

4. According to Powell, what does the ROTC (Reserve Officers Training Corp.) offer young men like him?

5. What lessons does Powell learn as a drill master? Are these lessons applicable to situations you have known?

6. Why does Powell spend so much time discussing the involvement of his parents and extended family in *his* American journey? Cite specific examples in the text to make your point.

7. According to the author, what specific skills did CUNY provide him that allowed him to compete with anybody from anywhere later in life? Do you agree with his assessment?

Writing Tasks

1. Discuss the value for you of an extracurricular activity that your college offers.

2. Research the life of a well-known New Yorker and write an essay discussing the key elements that led to his or her success.

3. Discuss an important role model you have had in comparison to the ones Powell had during his young adult life.

Against School

John Taylor Gatto

John Taylor Gatto is a former New York State and New York City Teacher of the Year and the author, most recently, of *The Underground History of American Education.* This essay appeared in *Harper's Magazine* in September 2003.

Pre-reading

What was the most interesting class you have ever had?

I taught for thirty years in some of the worst schools in Manhattan, and in some of the best, and during that time I became an expert in boredom. Boredom was everywhere in my world, and if you asked the kids, as I often did, *why* they felt so bored, they always gave the same answers: They said the work was stupid, that it made no sense, that they already knew it. They said they wanted to be doing something real, not just sitting around. They said teachers didn't seem to know much about their subjects and clearly weren't interested in learning more. And the kids were right: their teachers were every bit as bored as they were.

Boredom is the common condition of schoolteachers, and anyone who has spent time in a teachers' lounge can vouch for the low energy, the whining, the dispirited attitudes, to be found there. When asked why *they* feel bored, the teachers tend to blame the kids, as you might expect. Who wouldn't get bored teaching students who are rude and interested only in grades? If even that. Of course, teachers are themselves products of the same twelve-year compulsory school programs that so thoroughly bore their students, and as school personnel they are trapped inside structures even more rigid than those imposed upon the children. Who, then, is to blame?

We all are. My grandfather taught me that. One afternoon when I was seven I complained to him of boredom, and he batted me hard on the head. He told me that I was never to use that term in his presence again, that if I was bored it was my fault and no one else's. The obligation to amuse and instruct myself was entirely my own, and people who didn't

1

know that were childish people, to be avoided if possible. Certainly not to be trusted. That episode cured me of boredom forever, and here and there over the years I was able to pass on the lesson to some remarkable student. For the most part, however, I found it futile to challenge the official notion that boredom and childishness were the natural state of affairs in the classroom. Often I had to defy custom, and even bend the law, to help kids break out of this trap.

The empire struck back, of course; childish adults regularly conflate opposition with disloyalty. I once returned from a medical leave to discover that all evidence of my having been granted the leave had been purposely destroyed, that my job had been terminated, and that I no longer possessed even a teaching license. After nine months of tormented effort I was able to retrieve the license when a school secretary testified to witnessing the plot unfold. In the meantime my family suffered more than I care to remember. By the time I finally retired in 1991, I had more than enough reason to think of our schools—with their long-term, cell-block-style, forced confinement of both students and teachers—as virtual factories of childishness. Yet I honestly could not see *why* they had to be that way. My own experience had revealed to me what many other teachers must learn along the way, too, yet keep to themselves for fear of reprisal: if we wanted to we could easily and inexpensively jettison the old, stupid structures and help kids *take* an education rather than merely *receive* a schooling. We could encourage the best qualities of youthfulness—curiosity, adventure, resilience, the capacity for surprising insight—simply by being more flexible about time, texts, and tests, by introducing kids to truly competent adults, and by giving each student what autonomy he or she needs in order to take a risk every now and then.

But we don't do that. And the more I asked why not, and persisted in   5
thinking about the "problem" of schooling as an engineer might, the more I missed the point: What if there is no "problem" with our schools? What if they are the way they are, so expensively flying in the face of common sense and long experience in how children learn things, not because they are doing something wrong but because they are doing something right? Is it possible that George W. Bush accidentally spoke the truth when he said we would "leave no child behind"? Could it be that our schools are designed to make sure not one of them ever really grows up?

Do we really need school? I don't mean education, just forced schooling: six classes a day, five days a week, nine months a year, for twelve years. Is this deadly routine really necessary? And if so, for what? Don't hide behind reading, writing, and arithmetic as a rationale, because 2 million happy homeschoolers have surely put that banal justification to rest. Even if they hadn't, a considerable number of well-known Americans never went through the twelve-year wringer our kids currently go through, and they turned out all right. George Washington, Benjamin Franklin, Thomas Jefferson, Abraham Lincoln? Someone taught them, to be sure, but they were not products of a school *system,* and not one of them was ever "graduated" from a secondary school. Throughout most of American history, kids generally didn't go to high school, yet the unschooled rose to be admirals, like Farragut; inventors, like Edison; captains of industry, like Carnegie and Rockefeller; writers, like Melville and Twain and Conrad; and even scholars, like Margaret Mead. In fact, until pretty recently people who reached the age of thirteen weren't looked upon as children at all. Ariel Durant, who co-wrote an enormous, and very good, multivolume history of the world with her husband, Will, was happily married at fifteen, and who could reasonably claim that Ariel Durant was an uneducated person? Unschooled, perhaps, but not uneducated.

We have been taught (that is, schooled) in this country to think of "success" as synonymous with, or at least dependent upon, "schooling," but historically that isn't true in either an intellectual or a financial sense. And plenty of people throughout the world today find a way to educate themselves without resorting to a system of compulsory secondary schools that all too often resemble prisons. Why, then, do Americans confuse education with just such a system? What exactly is the purpose of our public schools?

Mass schooling of a compulsory nature really got its teeth into the United States between 1905 and 1915, though it was conceived of much earlier and pushed for throughout most of the nineteenth century. The reason given for this enormous upheaval of family life and cultural traditions was, roughly speaking, threefold:

1) To make good people.

2) To make good citizens.

3) To make each person his or her personal best.

These goals are still trotted out today on a regular basis, and most of us accept them in one form or another as a decent definition of public education's mission, however short schools actually fall in achieving them. But we are dead wrong. Compounding our error is the fact that the national literature holds numerous and surprisingly consistent statements of compulsory schooling's true purpose. We have, for example, the great H. L. Mencken, who wrote in *The American Mercury* for April 1924 that the aim of public education is not

> *to fill the young of the species with knowledge and awaken their intelligence. . . . Nothing could be further from the truth. The*

aim . . . is simply to reduce as many individuals as possible to the same safe level, to breed and train a standardized citizenry, to put down dissent and originality. That is its aim in the United States . . . and that is its aim everywhere else.

Because of Mencken's reputation as a satirist, we might be tempted to   10
dismiss this passage as a bit of hyperbolic sarcasm. His article, however, goes on to trace the template for our own educational system back to the now vanished, though never to be forgotten, military state of Prussia. And although he was certainly aware of the irony that we had recently been at war with Germany, the heir to Prussian thought and culture, Mencken was being perfectly serious here. Our educational system really is Prussian in origin, and that really is cause for concern.

The odd fact of a Prussian provenance for our schools pops up again and again once you know to look for it. William James alluded to it many times at the turn of the century. Orestes Brownson, the hero of Christopher Lasch's 1991 book, *The True and Only Heaven,* was publicly denouncing the Prussianization of American schools back in the 1840s. Horace Mann's "Seventh Annual Report" to the Massachusetts State Board of Education in 1843 is essentially a paean to the land of Frederick the Great and a call for its schooling to be brought here. That Prussian culture loomed large in America is hardly surprising, given our early association with that utopian state. A Prussian served as Washington's aide during the Revolutionary War, and so many German-speaking people had settled here by 1795 that Congress considered publishing a German-language edition of the federal laws. But what shocks is that we should so eagerly have adopted one of the very worst aspects of Prussian culture: an educational system deliberately designed to produce mediocre intellects, to hamstring the inner life, to deny students appreciable leadership skills, and to ensure docile and incomplete citizens—all in order to render the populace "manageable."

It was from James Bryant Conant—president of Harvard for twenty years, WWI poison-gas specialist, WWII executive on the atomic-bomb project, high commissioner of the American zone in Germany after WWII, and truly one of the most influential figures of the twentieth century—that I first got wind of the real purposes of American schooling. Without Conant, we would probably not have the same style and degree of standardized testing that we enjoy today, nor would we be blessed with gargantuan high schools that warehouse 2,000 to 4,000 students at a time like the famous Columbine High in Littleton, Colorado. Shortly after I retired from teaching I picked up Conant's 1959 book-length essay, *The Child, the Parent, and the State,* and was more than a little intrigued to see him mention in passing that the modern schools we attend were the result of a "revolution" engineered between 1905 and 1930. A revolution? He declines to elaborate, but he does direct the curious and the un-informed to Alexander Inglis's 1918 book, *Principles of Secondary Education,* in which "one saw this revolution through the eyes of a revolutionary."

Inglis, for whom a lecture in education at Harvard is named, makes it perfectly clear that compulsory schooling on this continent was in-tended to be, just what it had been for Prussia in the 1820s: a fifth col-umn into the burgeoning democratic movement that threatened to give the peasants and the proletarians a voice at the bargaining table. Mod-ern, industrialized, compulsory schooling was to make a sort of surgi-cal incision into the prospective unity of these underclasses. Divide children by subject, by age-grading, by constant rankings on tests, and by many other more subtle means, and it was unlikely that the ignorant mass of mankind, separated in childhood, would ever re-integrate into a dangerous whole.

Inglis breaks down the purpose—the *actual* purpose—of modern schooling into six basic functions, any one of which is enough to curl the hair of those innocent enough to believe the three traditional goals listed earlier:

1) The *adjustive* or *adaptive* function. Schools are to establish fixed habits of reaction to authority. This, of course, precludes critical judg-ment completely. It also pretty much destroys the idea that useful or in-teresting material should be taught, because you can't test for *reflexive* obedience until you know whether you can make kids learn, and do, fool-ish and boring things.

2) The *integrating* function. This might well be called "the conform-ity function," because its intention is to make children as alike as possi-ble. People who conform are predictable, and this is of great use to those who wish to harness and manipulate a large labor force.

3) The *diagnostic and directive* function. School is meant to deter-mine each student's proper social role. This is done by logging evidence mathematically and anecdotally on cumulative records. As in "your per-manent record." Yes, you do have one.

4) The *differentiating* function. Once their social role has been "diag-nosed," children are to be sorted by role and trained only so far as their destination in the social machine merits—and not one step further. So much for making kids their personal best.

5) The *selective* function. This refers not to human choice at all but to Darwin's theory of natural selection as applied to what he called "the favored races." In short, the idea is to help things along by consciously

attempting to improve the breeding stock. Schools are meant to tag the unfit—with poor grades, remedial placement, and other punishments—clearly enough that their peers will accept them as inferior and effectively bar them from the reproductive sweepstakes. That's what all those little humiliations from first grade onward were intended to do: wash the dirt down the drain.

6) The *propaedeutic* function. The social system implied by these rules will require an elite group of caretakers. To that end, a small fraction of the kids will quietly be taught how to manage this continuing project, how to watch over and control a population deliberately dumbed down and declawed in order that government might proceed unchallenged and corporations might never want for obedient labor.

15

That, unfortunately, is the purpose of mandatory public education in this country. And lest you take Inglis for an isolated crank with a rather too cynical take on the educational enterprise, you should know that he was hardly alone in championing these ideas. Conant himself, building on the ideas of Horace Mann and others, campaigned tirelessly for an American school system designed along the same lines. Men like George Peabody, who funded the cause of mandatory schooling throughout the South, surely understood that the Prussian system was useful in creating not only a harmless electorate and a servile labor force but also a virtual herd of mindless consumers. In time a great number of industrial titans came to recognize the enormous profits to be had by cultivating and tending just such a herd via public education, among them Andrew Carnegie and John D. Rockefeller.

There you have it. Now you know. We don't need Karl Marx's conception of a grand warfare between the classes to see that it is in the interest of complex management, economic or political, to dumb people down, to demoralize them, to divide them from one another, and to discard them if they don't conform. Class may frame the proposition, as when Woodrow Wilson, then president of Princeton University, said the following to the New York City School Teachers Association in 1909: "We want one class of persons to have a liberal education, and we want another class of persons, a very much larger class, of necessity, in every society, to forgo the privileges of a liberal education and fit themselves to perform specific difficult manual tasks." But the motives behind the disgusting decisions that bring about these ends need not be class-based at all. They can stem purely from fear, or from the by now familiar belief that "efficiency" is the paramount virtue, rather than love, liberty, laughter, or hope. Above all, they can stem from simple greed.

There were vast fortunes to be made, after all, in an economy based on mass production and organized to favor the large corporation rather than the small business or the family farm. But mass production required mass consumption, and at the turn of the twentieth century most Americans considered it both unnatural and unwise to buy things they didn't actually need. Mandatory schooling was a godsend on that count. School didn't have to train kids in any direct sense to think they should consume non-stop, because it did something even better: it encouraged them not to think at all. And that left them sitting ducks for another great invention of the modern era—marketing.

Now, you needn't have studied marketing to know that there are two groups of people who can always be convinced to consume more than they need to: addicts and children. School has done a pretty good job of turning our children into addicts, but it has done a spectacular job of turning our children into children. Again, this is no accident. Theorists from Plato to Rousseau to our own Dr. Inglis knew that if children could be cloistered with other children, stripped of responsibility and independence, encouraged to develop only the trivializing emotions of greed, envy, jealousy, and fear, they would grow older but never truly grow up. In the 1934 edition of his once well-known book *Public Education in the United States,* Ellwood P. Cubberley detailed and praised the way the strategy of successive school enlargements had extended childhood by two to six years, and forced schooling was at that point still quite new. This same Cubberley— who was dean of Stanford's School of Education, a textbook editor at Houghton Mifflin, and Conant's friend and correspondent at Harvard—had written the following in the 1922 edition of his book *Public School Administration:* "Our schools are . . . factories in which the raw products (children) are to be shaped and fashioned. . . . And it is the business of the school to build its pupils according to the specifications laid down."

It's perfectly obvious from our society today what those specifications were. Maturity has by now been banished from nearly every aspect of our lives. Easy divorce laws have removed the need to work at relationships; easy credit has removed the need for fiscal self-control; easy entertainment has removed the need to learn to entertain oneself; easy answers have removed the need to ask questions. We have become a nation of children, happy to surrender our judgments and our wills to political exhortations and commercial blandishments that would insult actual adults. We buy televisions, and then we buy the things we see on the television. We buy computers, and then we buy the things we see on the computer. We buy $150 sneakers whether we need them or not, and when they fall apart too soon we buy another pair. We drive SUVs and believe the lie that they constitute a kind of life insurance, even when we're upside-down in them. And, worst of all, we don't bat an eye when Ari Fleischer tells us to "be careful what you say," even if we remember having been told somewhere back in school that America is the land of the free. We simply buy that one too. Our schooling, as intended, has seen to it.

20

Now for the good news. Once you understand the logic behind modern schooling, its tricks and traps are fairly easy to avoid. School trains children to be employees and consumers; teach your own to be leaders and adventurers. School trains children to obey reflexively; teach your own to think critically and independently. Well-schooled kids have a low threshold for boredom; help your own to develop an inner life so that they'll never be bored. Urge them to take on the serious material, the *grown-up* material, in history, literature, philosophy, music, art, economics, theology—all the stuff schoolteachers know well enough to avoid. Challenge your kids with plenty of solitude so that they can learn to enjoy their own company, to conduct inner dialogues. Well-schooled people are conditioned to dread being alone, and they seek constant companionship through the TV, the computer, the cell phone, and through shallow friendships quickly acquired and quickly abandoned. Your children should have a more meaningful life, and they can.

First, though, we must wake up to what our schools really are: laboratories of experimentation on young minds, drill centers for the habits and attitudes that corporate society demands. Mandatory education serves children only incidentally; its real purpose is to turn them into servants. Don't let your own have their childhoods extended, not even for a day. If David Farragut could take command of a captured British warship as a preteen, if Thomas Edison could publish a broadsheet at the age of twelve, if Ben Franklin could apprentice himself to a printer at the same age (then put himself through a course of study that would choke a Yale senior today), there's no telling what your own kids could do. After a long life, and thirty years in the public school trenches, I've concluded that genius is as common as dirt. We suppress our genius only because we haven't yet figured out how to manage a population of educated men and women. The solution, I think, is simple and glorious. Let them manage themselves.

Discussion Questions

1. In Gatto's opinion, what are the major reasons for boredom in classrooms? Do you agree with him?

2. Do you also experience boredom in class? What do you think can be some possible solutions?

3. What was his grandfather's comment when Gatto complained to him of boredom? Do you think it was a good advice? How did it affect Gatto's perspective?

4. What did Gatto have to do to help his students break out of the trap of boredom? How was he treated by the school officials? What term did Gatto use to describe them? And why do you think he was treated that way?

5. What are the ways the writer suggests that could help kids "take an education rather than merely receiving a schooling"?

6. What does Gatto want to illustrate by bringing out examples of some well-known Americans? Do you share his point of view?

7. What were the initial goals of public education? Does Gatto think they are realistic and achievable?

8. According to Gatto, what was one of the worst aspects of the Prussian educational model that was adopted here? To what extent do you think it still defines today's American educational system?

9. What is the effect of mass education, according to Gatto, on the modern-day economy?

10. Do you agree with Gatto that our educational system has been successful in "turning our children into children"? What exactly is he trying to say?

Writing Tasks

1. While DeWitt Clinton believes that public education is beneficial to all people because it is essential to societal equality and stability, John Taylor Gatto exposes the vices of public education. To what extent do you share their views? Write an essay stating the reasons why you agree or disagree with either of the authors.

2. What advice does Gatto offer to parents in educating their children? If you were a parent, would you take his advice? Write an essay in which you discuss whether his suggestions are sound and feasible.

When I Was Puerto Rican

Esmeralda Santiago

Esmeralda Santiago (b.1948) came to this country from a poor village in Puerto Rico as an adolescent, one of eleven children. She won scholarships to the High School of Performing Arts in New York City, then to Harvard.

Pre-reading

Have you ever stood up for your rights?

The first day of school Mami walked me to a stone building that loomed over Graham Avenue, its concrete yard enclosed by an iron fence with spikes at the top. The front steps were wide but shallow and led up to a set of heavy double doors that slammed shut behind us as we walked down the shiny corridor. I clutched my eighth-grade report card filled with A's and B's, and Mami had my birth certificate. At the front office we were met by Mr. Grant, a droopy gentleman with thick glasses and a kind smile who spoke no Spanish. He gave Mami a form to fill out. I knew most of the words in the squares we were to fill in: NAME, ADDRESS (CITY, STATE), and OCCUPATION. We gave it to Mr. Grant, who reviewed it, looked at my birth certificate, studied my report card, then wrote on the top of the form "7–18."   1

Don Julio had told me that if students didn't speak English, the schools in Brooklyn would keep them back one grade until they learned it.

"Seven gray?" I asked Mr. Grant, pointing at his big numbers, and he nodded.

"Ino guan seven gray. I eight gray. I teeneyer."

"You don't speak English," he said. "You have to go to the seventh grade while you're learning."   5

"I have A's in school Puerto Rico. I lern good. I no seven gray girl."

Mami stared at me, not understanding but knowing I was being rude to an adult.

"What's going on?" she asked me in Spanish. I told her they wanted to send me back one grade and I would not have it. This was probably the first rebellious act she had seen from me outside my usual mouthiness within the family.

"Negi, leave it alone. Those are the rules," she said, a warning in her voice.

"I don't care what their rules say," I answered. "I'm not going back to   10
seventh grade. I can do the work. I'm not stupid."

Mami looked at Mr. Grant, who stared at her as if expecting her to do something about me. She smiled and shrugged her shoulders.

"Meester Grant," I said, seizing the moment, "I go eight gray six mons. Eef I no lern inglish, I go seven gray. Okay?"

"That's not the way we do things here," he said hesitating.

"I good studen. I lern queek. You see notes." I pointed to the A's on my report card. "I pass seven gray."

So we made a deal.   15

"You have until Christmas," he said. "I'll be checking on your progress." He scratched out "7–18" and wrote in "8–23." He wrote something on a piece of paper, sealed it inside an envelope, and gave it to me. "Your teacher is Miss Brown. Take this note upstairs to her. Your mother can go," he said and disappeared into his office.

"Wow!" Mami said, "You can speak English!"

I was so proud of myself, I almost burst. In Puerto Rico, if I'd been that pushy, I would have been called *mal educada* by the Mr. Grant equivalent and sent home with a note to my mother. But here it was my teacher who was getting the note, I got what I wanted and my mother was sent home.

"I can find my way after school," I said to Mami. "You don't have to come get me."

"Are you sure?"   20

"Don't worry," I said. "I'll be all right."

I walked down the black-tiled hallway, past many doors that were half glass, each one labeled with a room number in neat black lettering. Other students stared at me, tried to get my attention, or pointedly ignored me. I kept walking as if I knew where I was going, heading for the sign that said STAIRS with an arrow pointing up. When I reached the end of the hall and looked back, Mami was still standing at the front door watching me, a worried expression on her face. I waved and she waved back. I started up the stairs, my stomach churning into tight knots. All of a sudden, I was afraid that I was about to make a fool of myself and end up in seventh grade in the middle of the school year. Having to fall back would be worse than just accepting my fate now and hopping forward if I proved to be as good a student as I had convinced Mr. Grant I was. "What have I done?" I kicked myself with the back of my right shoe, much to the surprise of the fellow walking behind me, who laughed uproariously, as if I had meant it as a joke.

Miss Brown's was the learning disabled class, where the administration sent kids with all sort of problems, none of which, from what I could see, had anything to do with their ability to learn but more with their willingness to do so. They were an unruly group. Those who came to class, anyway. Half of them never showed up, or, when they did, they slept through the lesson or nodded off in the middle of Miss Brown's carefully parsed sentences.

We were outcasts in a school where the smartest eighth graders were in the 8-1 homeroom, each subsequent drop in number indicating one notch less smarts. If your class was in the low double digits (8-10 for instance), you were smart, but not a pinhead. Once you got into the teens, your intelligence was in question, especially as the numbers rose to the high teens. And then there were the twenties. I was in 8-23, where the dumbest most undesirable people were placed. My class was, in some ways, the equivalent of seventh grade, perhaps even sixth or fifth.

Miss Brown, the homeroom teacher, who also taught English composition, was a young black woman who wore sweat pads under her arms. The strings holding them in place sometimes slipped outside the short sleeves of her well-pressed white shirts, and she had to turn her back to us in order to adjust them. She was very pretty, with almond eyes and a hairdo that was flat and straight at the top of her head then dipped into tight curls at the ends. Her fingers were well manicured, the nails painted pale pink with white tips. She taught English composition as if everyone cared about it, which I found appealing.

25

After the first week she moved me from the back of the room to the front seat by her desk, and after that, it felt as if she were teaching me alone. We never spoke except when I went up to the blackboard.

"Esmeralda," she called in a musical voice, "would you please come up and mark the prepositional phrase?"

In her class, I learned to recognize the structure of the English language, and to draft the parts of a sentence by the position of words relative to pronouns and prepositions without knowing exactly what the whole thing meant.

Every day after school I went to the library and took out as many children's books as I was allowed. I figured that if American children learned English through books, so could I, even if I was starting later. I studied the bright illustrations and learned the words for the unfamiliar objects of our new life in the United States: A for Apple, B for Bear, C for Cabbage.

As my vocabulary grew, I moved to large-print chapter books. Mami bought me an English-English dictionary because that way, when I looked up a word I would be learning others.

By my fourth month in Brooklyn, I could read and write English much   30
better than I could speak it, and at midterms I stunned the teachers by scoring high in English, History, and Social Studies. During the January assembly, Mr. Grant announced the names of the kids who had received high marks in each class. My name was called out three times. I became a different person to the other eighth graders. I was still in 8-23, but they knew, and I knew, that I didn't belong there.

Discussion Questions

1. Based on what criteria does the principal place Esmeralda? Do you think his decision is reasonable?

2. What is the writer's reaction to her initial placement? Would you do the same if you were in her situation?

3. Why was her mother worried about her daughters outspokenness?

4. How could her placement have been handled differently?

5. How Esmeralda and Miss Brown relate to one another?

6. What lesson does Esmeralda learn when she persuades the principal to put her in the eighth grade?

7. Do you think placement affects later academic performance?

Writing Tasks

1. Drawing reference from Esmeralda's story, write an essay in support of or against bilingual education for immigrant children.

2. Write an essay that either defends or criticizes the way schools categorize students on the basis of academic and/or language skills.

How to Bring Our Schools
Into the 21st Century

Claudia Wallis and Sonja Steptoe

Pre-reading

Can you think of ways new technologies could be used to improve your current educational experience?

There's a dark little joke exchanged by educators with a dissident streak: Rip Van Winkle awakens in the 21st century after a hundred-year snooze and is, of course, utterly bewildered by what he sees. Men and women dash about, talking to small metal devices pinned to their ears. Young people sit at home on sofas, moving miniature athletes around on electronic screens. Older folk defy death and disability with metronomes in their chests and with hips made of metal and plastic. Airports, hospitals, shopping malls—every place Rip goes just baffles him. But when he finally walks into a schoolroom, the old man knows exactly where he is. "This is a school," he declares. "We used to have these back in 1906. Only now the blackboards are green."

American schools aren't exactly frozen in time, but considering the pace of change in other areas of life, our public schools tend to feel like throwbacks. Kids spend much of the day as their great-grandparents once did: sitting in rows, listening to teachers lecture, scribbling notes by hand, reading from textbooks that are out of date by the time they are printed. A yawning chasm (with an emphasis on yawning) separates the world inside the schoolhouse from the world outside.

For the past five years, the national conversation on education has focused on reading scores, math tests and closing the "achievement gap" between social classes. This is not a story about that conversation. This is a story about the big public conversation the nation is *not* having about education, the one that will ultimately determine not merely whether some fraction of our children get "left behind" but also whether an entire generation of kids will fail to make the grade in the global economy because they can't think their way through abstract problems, work in teams, distinguish good information from bad or speak a language other than English.

This week the conversation will burst onto the front page, when the New Commission on the Skills of the American Workforce, a high-powered, bipartisan

From *Time Magazine*, December 9, 2006. Permission conveyed through Rightslink.

assembly of Education Secretaries and business, government and other education leaders releases a blueprint for rethinking American education from pre-K to 12 and beyond to better prepare students to thrive in the global economy. While that report includes some controversial proposals, there is nonetheless a remarkable consensus among educators and business and policy leaders on one key conclusion: we need to bring what we teach and how we teach into the 21st century.

Right now we're aiming too low. Competency in reading and math—the focus of so much No Child Left Behind (NCLB) testing—is the meager minimum. Scientific and technical skills are, likewise, utterly necessary but insufficient. Today's economy demands not only a high-level competence in the traditional academic disciplines but also what might be called 21st century skills. Here's what they are:

Knowing More About the World

Kids are global citizens now, even in small-town America, and they must learn to act that way. Mike Eskew, CEO of UPS, talks about needing workers who are "global trade literate, sensitive to foreign cultures, conversant in different languages"—not exactly strong points in the U.S., where fewer than half of high school students are enrolled in a foreign-language class and where the social-studies curriculum tends to fixate on U.S. history.

Thinking Outside the Box

Jobs in the new economy—the ones that won't get outsourced or automated—"put an enormous premium on creative and innovative skills, seeing patterns where other people see only chaos," says Marc Tucker, an author of the skills-commission report and president of the National Center on Education and the Economy. Traditionally that's been an American strength, but schools have become less daring in the back-to-basics climate of NCLB. Kids also must learn to think across disciplines, since that's where most new breakthroughs are made. It's interdisciplinary combinations—design and technology, mathematics and art—"that produce You-Tube and Google," says Thomas Friedman, the best-selling author of *The World Is Flat*.

Becoming Smarter About New Sources of Information

In an age of overflowing information and proliferating media, kids need to rapidly process what's coming at them and distinguish between what's reliable and what isn't. "It's important that students know how to manage it, interpret it, validate it, and how to act on it," says Dell executive Karen Bruett, who serves on the board of the Partnership for 21st Century Skills, a group of corporate and education leaders focused on upgrading American education.

Developing Good People Skills

EQ, or emotional intelligence, is as important as IQ for success in today's workplace. "Most innovations today involve large teams of people," says former Lockheed Martin CEO Norman Augustine. "We have to emphasize communication skills, the ability to work in teams and with people from different cultures."

Can our public schools, originally designed to educate workers for agrarian life and industrial-age factories, make the necessary shifts? The skills commission will argue that it's possible only if we add new depth and rigor to our curriculum and standardized exams, redeploy the dollars we spend on education, reshape the teaching force and reorganize who runs the schools. But without waiting for such a revolution, enterprising administrators around the country have begun to update their schools, often with ideas and support from local businesses. The state of Michigan, conceding that it can no longer count on the ailing auto industry to absorb its poorly educated and low-skilled workers, is retooling its high schools, instituting what are among the most rigorous graduation requirements in the nation. Elsewhere, organizations like the Bill and Melinda Gates Foundation, the Carnegie Foundation for the Advancement of Teaching and the Asia Society are pouring money and expertise into model programs to show the way.

What It Means to Be a Global Student

Quick! How many ways can you combine nickels, dimes and pennies to get $2.04? That's the challenge for students in a second-grade math class at Seattle's John Stanford International School, and hands are flying up with answers. The students sit at tables of four manipulating play money. One boy shouts "10 plus 10"; a girl offers "10 plus 5 plus 5," only it sounds like this: "*Ju, tasu, go, tasu, go.*" Down the hall, third-graders are learning to interpret charts and graphs showing how many hours of sleep people need at different ages. "*¿Cuantas horas duerme un bebe?*" asks the teacher Sabrina Storlie.

This public elementary school has taken the idea of global education and run with it. All students take some classes in either Japanese or Spanish. Other subjects are taught in English, but the content has an international flavor. The school pulls its 393 students from the surrounding highly diverse neighborhood and by lottery from other parts of the city. Generally, its scores on state tests are at or above average, although those exams barely scratch the surface of what Stanford students learn.

Before opening the school seven years ago, principal Karen Kodama surveyed 1,500 business leaders on which languages to teach (plans for Mandarin were dropped for lack of classroom space) and which skills and disciplines. "No. 1 was technology," she recalls. Even first-graders at Stanford begin to use PowerPoint and Internet tools. "Exposure to world cultures was also an important trait cited by the executives," says Kodama, so that instead of circling back to the Pilgrims and Indians every autumn, children at Stanford do social-studies units on Asia, Africa, Australia, Mexico and South America. Students actively apply the lessons in foreign language and culture by videoconferencing with sister schools in Japan, Africa and Mexico, by exchanging messages, gifts and joining in charity projects.

Stanford International shows what's possible for a public elementary school, although it has the rare advantage of support from corporations like Nintendo and Starbucks, which contribute to its $1.7 million-a-year budget. Still, dozens of U.S. school districts have found ways to orient some of their students toward the global economy. Many have opened schools that offer the international baccalaureate (I.B.) program, a rigorous, off-the-shelf curriculum recognized by universities around the world and first introduced in 1968—well before globalization became a buzzword.

To earn an I.B. diploma, students must prove written and spoken proficiency in a second language, write a 4,000-word college-level research paper, complete a real-world service project and pass rigorous oral and written subject exams. Courses offer an international perspective, so even a lesson on the American Revolution will interweave sources from Britain and France with views from the Founding Fathers. "We try to build something we call international mindedness," says Jeffrey Beard, director general of the International Baccalaureate Organization in Geneva, Switzerland. "These are students who can grasp issues across national borders. They have an understanding of nuances and complexity and a balanced approach to problem solving." Despite stringent certification requirements, I.B. schools are growing in the U.S.—from about 350 in 2000 to 682 today. The U.S. Department of Education has a pilot effort to bring the program to more low-income students.

Real Knowledge in the Google Era

Learn the names of all the rivers in South America. That was the assignment given to Deborah Stipek's daughter Meredith in school, and her mom, who's dean of the Stanford University School of Education, was not impressed. "That's silly," Stipek told her daughter. "Tell your teacher that if you need to know anything besides the Amazon, you can look it up on Google." Any number of old-school assignments—memorizing the battles of the Civil War or the periodic table of the elements—now seem faintly absurd. That kind of information, which is poorly retained unless you routinely use it, is available at a keystroke. Still, few would argue that an American child shouldn't learn the causes of the Civil War or understand how the periodic table reflects the atomic structure and properties of the elements. As school critic E.D. Hirsch Jr. points out in his book, *The Knowledge Deficit*, kids need a substantial fund of information just to make sense of reading materials beyond the grade-school level. Without mastering the fundamental building blocks of math, science or history, complex concepts are impossible.

Many analysts believe that to achieve the right balance between such core knowledge and what educators call "portable skills"—critical thinking, making connections between ideas and knowing how to keep on learning—the U.S. curriculum needs to become more like that of Singapore, Belgium and Sweden, whose students outperform American students on math and science tests. Classes in these countries dwell on key concepts that are taught in depth and in careful sequence, as opposed to a succession of forgettable details so often served in U.S. classrooms. Textbooks and tests support this approach. "Countries from Germany to Singapore have extremely small textbooks that focus on the most powerful and generative ideas," says Roy Pea, co-director of the Stanford Center for Innovations in Learning. These might be the key theorems in math, the laws of thermodynamics in science or the relationship between supply and demand in economics. America's bloated textbooks, by contrast, tend to gallop through a mind-numbing stream of topics and subtopics in an attempt to address a vast range of state standards.

Depth over breadth and the ability to leap across disciplines are exactly what teachers aim for at the Henry Ford Academy, a public charter school in Dearborn, Mich. This fall, 10th-graders in Charles Dershimer's science class began a project that combines concepts from earth science, chemistry, business and design. After reading about Nike's efforts to develop a more environmentally friendly sneaker, students had to choose a consumer product, analyze and explain its environmental impact and then develop a plan for re-engineering it to reduce pollution costs without sacrificing its commercial appeal. Says Dershimer: "It's a challenge for them and for me."

A New Kind of Literacy

The juniors in Bill Stroud's class are riveted by a documentary called *Loose Change* unspooling on a small TV screen at the Baccalaureate School for Global Education, in urban Astoria, N.Y. The film uses 9/11 footage and interviews with building engineers and Twin Towers survivors to make an oddly compelling if paranoid case that interior explosions unrelated to the impact of the airplanes brought down the World Trade Center on that fateful day. Afterward, the students—an ethnic mix of New Yorkers with their own 9/11 memories—dive into a discussion about the elusive nature of truth.

Raya Harris finds the video more convincing than the official version of the facts. Marisa Reichel objects. "Because of a movie, you are going to change your beliefs?" she demands. "Just because people heard explosions doesn't mean there were explosions. You can say you feel the room spinning, but it isn't." This kind of discussion about what we know and how we know it is typical of a theory of knowledge class, a required element for an international-baccalaureate diploma. Stroud has posed this question to his class on the blackboard: "If truth is difficult to prove in history, does it follow that all versions are equally acceptable?"

Throughout the year, the class will examine news reports, websites, propaganda, history books, blogs, even pop songs. The goal is to teach kids to be discerning consumers of information and to research, formulate and defend their own views, says Stroud, who is founder and principal of the four-year-old public school, which is located in a repurposed handbag factory.

Classes like this, which teach key aspects of information literacy, remain rare in public education, but more and more universities and employers say they are needed as the world grows ever more deluged with information of variable quality. Last year, in response to demand from colleges, the Educational Testing Service unveiled a new, computer-based exam designed to measure information-and-communication-technology literacy. A pilot study of the test with 6,200 high school seniors and college freshmen found that only half could correctly judge the objectivity of a website. "Kids tend to go to Google and cut and paste a research report together," says Terry Egan, who led the team that developed the new test. "We kind of assumed this generation was so comfortable with technology that they know how to use it for research and deeper thinking," says Egan. "But if they're not taught these skills, they don't necessarily pick them up."

Learning 2.0

The chairman of Sun Microsystems was up against one of the most vexing challenges of modern life: a third-grade science project. Scott McNealy had spent hours searching the Web for a lively explanation of electricity that his son could understand. "Finally I found a very nice, animated, educational website showing electrons zooming around and tests after each section. We did this for about an hour and a half and had a ball—a great father-son moment of learning. All of a sudden we ran out of runway because it was a site to help welders, and it then got into welding." For McNealy the experience, three years ago, provided one of life's *aha!* moments: "It made me wonder why there isn't a website where I can just go and have anything I want to learn, K to 12, online, browser based and free."

His solution: draw on the Wikipedia model to create a collection of online courses that can be updated, improved, vetted and built upon by innovative teachers, who, he notes, "are always developing new materials and methods of instruction because they aren't happy with what they have." And who better to create such a site than McNealy, whose company has led the way in designing open-source computer software? He quickly raised some money, created a non-profit and—*voila!*—Curriki.org made its debut January 2006, and has been growing fast. Some 450 courses are in the works, and about 3,000 people have joined as members. McNealy reports that a teenager in Kuwait has already completed the introductory physics and calculus classes in 18 days.

Curriki, however, isn't meant to replace going to school but to supplement it and offer courses that may not be available locally. It aims to give teachers classroom-tested content materials and assessments that are livelier and more current and multimedia-based than printed textbooks. Ultimately, it could take the Web 2.0 revolution to school, closing that yawning gap between how kids learn at school and how they do everything else. Educators around the country and overseas are already discussing ways to certify Curriki's online course work for credit.

Some states are creating their own online courses. "In the 21st century, the ability to be a lifelong learner will, for many people, be dependent on their ability to access and benefit from online learning," says Michael Flanagan, Michigan's superintendent of public instruction, which is why Michigan's new high school graduation requirements, which roll out next year, include completing at least one course online.

A Dose of Reality

Teachers need not fear that they will be made obsolete. They will, however, feel increasing pressure to bring their methods—along with the curriculum—into line with the way the modern world works. That means putting a greater emphasis on teaching kids to collaborate and solve problems in small groups and apply what they've learned in the real world. Besides, research shows that kids learn better that way than with the old chalk-and-talk approach.

At suburban Farmington High in Michigan, the engineering-technology department functions like an engineering firm, with teachers as project managers, a Ford Motor Co. engineer as a consultant and students working in teams. The principles of calculus, physics, chemistry and engineering are taught through activities that fill the hallways with a cacophony of nailing, sawing and chattering. The result the kids learn to apply academic principles to the real world, think strategically and solve problems.

Such lessons also teach students to show respect for others as well as to be punctual, responsible and work well in teams. Those skills were badly missing in recently hired high school graduates, according to a survey of over 400 human-resource professionals conducted by the Partnership for 21st Century Skills. "Kids don't know how to shake your hand at graduation," says Rudolph Crew, superintendent of the Miami-Dade school system. Deportment, he notes, used to be on the report card. Some of the nation's more forward-thinking schools are bringing it back. It's one part of 21st century education that sleepy old Rip would recognize.

Discussion Questions

1. Discuss the reference to Rip Van Winkle. In what ways do you see school as "frozen in time"?

2. What skills do the authors believe American students need to learn to excel in the modern world? Can you give examples where these skills are taught?

3. What do the authors mean by "thinking outside the box"? Can you give examples where education is way behind technology?

4. Why is it important nowadays for students to know more about the world? Can you give specific examples where such knowledge would be particularly helpful.

5. Why is it more important than ever to be able to distinguish the quality and credibility of new sources of information?

6. Define what Jeffrey Beard means by "international mindedness."

7. Discuss the difference between "core" knowledge and "portable skills." How should they work together?

8. In your view, what's a better method of learning: amassing a large supply of details about lots of topic or concentrating on key ideas and events?

9. Do you agree that on-line learning ought to be the wave of the future in education? What are its advantages and disadvantages?

Writing Tasks

1. Discuss the advantages of on-line education as compared to the traditional model.

2. Write an essay that takes on an issue debated on a web log or blog. Be sure to incorporate and evaluate the diverse opinions expressed in the blog discussion.

Making Connections

1. Consider the points Gatto raises in "Against School." Do you think that Claudia Wallis and Sonja Steptoe's discussion of the evolution of education in a global context in "How to Build a Student for the 21st Century" addresses any of his concerns? Explain.

2. Drawing from the ideas in your readings, discuss the ways the educational system misserves its students. Suggest solutions.

3. Write an argumentative essay in which you offer your own reflections on what makes a high performance school. Be sure to address some of the issues raised in at least two of the articles in this chapter. Feel free to offer your own experiences to support and develop your positions.

CHAPTER 5

Violence and Resistance

"A Car Explodes during the Harlem Race Riot of 1943" © Bettmann/CORBIS

WHAT HAPPENS TO A DREAM DEFERRED?

Does it dry up
like a raisin in the sun?
Or fester like a sore—
And then run?
Does it stink like rotten meat?
Or crust and sugar over—
like a syrupy sweet?
Maybe it just sags
like a heavy load.
Or does it explode?

"Harlem" (1951) by Langston Hughes

Violence and Resistance

As the recent film *Gangs of New York* (2002) directed by Martin Scorsese shows, intense intergroup conflicts have marked New York City throughout its history. The source of much of this tension is the very fact of the city's unrivaled population density and diversity. Despite such conflagrations as the Draft Riots of 1863 and, more recently, the Crown Heights riots of 1991, it is perhaps more amazing the level of tolerance New Yorkers manage to have in getting along with one another. Nonetheless, cultural violence—prejudice, inequality, and social and economic injustice—has been and continues to be the rudimentary cause of much physical violence throughout urban America.

The challenge of confronting cultural violence before it leads to actual physical violence is the focus of the readings in this chapter. In Langston Hughes' "Harlem" and Ralph Ellison's "Prologue to the *Invisible Man,*" two leading African-American writers give due warning to a society that in the first half of the twentieth century was steeped in, yet blind to, social and racial injustice. Nicky Cruz in "Into the Pit", on the other hand, indicts society for failing to nurture its youth and provide them with viable alternatives to achieve themselves, a theme given a historical overview in "Youth Gangs." Monique Ferrell's "Tu Sabes?" and Michael T. Kaufman's "Of My Friend Hector and My Achilles' Heel" look at the source of cultural violence from yet another angle: the failure to overcome stereotyped thinking. As Kaufman admits in his opening line: "This story is about prejudice and stupidity. My own." In "From Doo Wop to Hip Hop" Mark Naison takes an original look at the origins of hip hop music, an often brilliant art form that came out of the breakdown of local communities that had once flourished. Due to widespread societal neglect, the inner city came in the 1970s to be associated with the lines of Grandmaster Flash in "The Message": "Broken glass everywhere, people pissing on the street, you know they just don't care." Out of the ashes of despair emerged a youth movement known as hip hop culture that sought to both care and entertain, but, according to Naison, more and more threatens to reenact the cultural violence that it once rejected.

Prologue to "Invisible Man"

Ralph Ellison

Born in Oklahoma in 1914 and educated at the Tuskegee Institute in Alabama, Ralph Ellison established his literary reputation with his first and only novel, *Invisible Man,* first published in 1947 and reprinted numerous times since. Ellison lectured at Yale, Columbia, and New York Universities, and remains a dominant figure on the American literary landscape even after his death in 1994.

Pre-reading

Are there groups whose concerns you feel are overlooked or misunderstood?

I am an invisible man. No, I am not a spook like those who haunted Edgar Allan Poe; nor am I one of your Hollywood-movie ectoplasms. I am a man of substance, of flesh and bone, fiber and liquids—and I might even be said to possess a mind. I am invisible, understand, simply because people refuse to see me. Like the bodiless heads you see sometimes in circus sideshows, it is as though I have been surrounded by mirrors of hard, distorting glass. When they approach me they see only my surroundings, themselves, or figments of their imagination—indeed, everything and anything except me.

Nor is my invisibility exactly a matter of a biochemical accident to my epidermis. That invisibility to which I refer occurs because of a peculiar disposition of the eyes of those with whom I come in contact. A matter of the construction of their *inner* eyes, those eyes with which they look through their physical eyes upon reality. I am not complaining, nor am I protesting either. It is sometimes advantageous to be unseen, although it is most often rather wearing on the nerves. Then too, you're constantly being bumped against by those of poor vision. Or again, you often doubt if you really exist. You wonder whether you aren't simply a phantom in other people's minds. Say, a figure in a nightmare which the sleeper tries with all his strength to destroy. It's when you feel like this that, out of resentment, you begin to bump people back. And, let me confess, you feel that way most of the time. You ache with the need to convince yourself that you do exist in the real world, that you're a part of all the sound and

1

anguish, and you strike out with your fists, you curse and you swear to make them recognize you. And, alas, it's seldom successful.

One night I accidentally bumped into a man, and perhaps because of the near darkness he saw me and called me an insulting name. I sprang at him, seized his coat lapels and demanded that he apologize. He was a tall blond man, and as my face came close to his he looked insolently out of his blue eyes and cursed me, his breath hot in my face as he struggled. I pulled his chin down sharp upon the crown of my head, butting him as I had seen the West Indians do, and I felt his flesh tear and the blood gush out, and I yelled, "Apologize! Apologize!" But he continued to curse and struggle, and I butted him again and again until he went down heavily, on his knees, profusely bleeding. I kicked him repeatedly, in a frenzy because he still uttered insults though his lips were frothy with blood. Oh yes, I kicked him! And in my outrage I got out my knife and prepared to slit his throat, right there beneath the lamplight in the deserted street, holding him in the collar with one hand, and opening the knife with my teeth—when it occurred to me that the man had not *seen* me, actually; that he, as far as he knew, was in the midst of a walking nightmare! And I stopped the blade, slicing the air as I pushed him away, letting him fall back to the street. I stared at him hard as the lights of a car stabbed through the darkness. He lay there, moaning on the asphalt; a man almost killed by a phantom. It unnerved me. I was both disgusted and ashamed. I was like a drunken man myself, wavering about on weakened legs. Then I was amused: Something in this man's thick head had sprung out and beaten him within an inch of his life. I began to laugh at this crazy discovery. Would he have awakened at the point of death? Would Death himself have freed him for wakeful living? But I didn't linger. I ran away into the dark, laughing so hard I feared I might rupture myself. The next day I saw his picture in the *Daily News,* beneath a caption stating that he had been "mugged." Poor fool, poor blind fool, I thought with sincere compassion, mugged by an invisible man!

Most of the time (although I do not choose as I once did to deny the violence of my days by ignoring it) I am not so overtly violent. I remember that I am invisible and walk softly so as not to awaken the sleeping ones. Sometimes it is best not to awaken them; there are few things in the world as dangerous as sleepwalkers. I learned in time though that it is possible to carry on a fight against them without their realizing it. For instance, I have been carrying on a fight with Monopolated Light & Power for some time now. I use their service and pay them nothing at all, and they don't know it. Oh, they suspect that power is being drained off, but they don't know where. All they know is that according to the master meter back there in their power station a hell of a lot of free current is disappearing somewhere into the jungle of Harlem. The joke, of course, is that I don't live in Harlem but in a border area. Several years ago (before I discovered the advantages of being invisible) I went through the routine process of buying service and paying their outrageous rates. But no more. I gave up all that, along with my apartment, and my old way of life: That way based upon the fallacious assumption that I, like other men, was visible. Now, aware of my invisibility, I live rent-free in a building rented strictly to whites, in a section of the basement that was shut off and forgotten during the nineteenth century, which I discovered when I was trying to escape in the night from Ras the Destroyer. But that's getting too far ahead of the story, almost to the end, although the end is in the beginning and lies far ahead.

The point now is that I found a home—or a hole in the ground, as you will. Now don't jump to any conclusion that because I call my home a "hole" it is damp and cold like a grave; there are cold holes and warm holes. Mine is a warm hole. And remember, a bear retires to his hole for the winter and lives until spring; then he comes strolling out like the Easter chick breaking from its shell. I say all this to assure you that it is incorrect to assume that, because I'm invisible and live in a hole, I am dead. I am neither dead nor in a state of suspended animation. Call me Jack-the-Bear, for I am in a state of hibernation.

My hole is warm and full of light. Yes, *full* of light. I doubt if there is a brighter spot in all New York than this hole of mine, and I do not exclude Broadway. Or the Empire State Building on a photographer's dream night. But that is taking advantage of you. Those two spots are among the darkest of our whole civilization—pardon me, our whole *culture* (an important distinction, I've heard)—which might sound like a hoax, or a contradiction, but that (by contradiction, I mean) is how the world moves: Not like an arrow, but a boomerang. (Beware of those who speak of the *spiral* of history; they are preparing a boomerang. Keep a steel helmet handy.) I know; I have been boomeranged across my head so much that I now can see the darkness of lightness. And I love light. Perhaps you'll think it strange that an invisible man should need light, desire light, love light. But maybe it is exactly because I *am* invisible. Light confirms my reality, gives birth to my form. A beautiful girl once told me of a recurring nightmare in which she lay in the center of a large dark room and felt her face expand until it filled the whole room, becoming a formless mass while her eyes ran in bilious jelly up the chimney. And so it is with me. Without light I am not only invisible, but formless as well; and to be unaware of one's form is to live a death. I myself, after existing some twenty years, did not become alive until I discovered my invisibility.

Discussion Questions

1. How does the narrator explain his invisibility in this selection? Who actually is to blame for his not being seen?
2. In what ways is invisibility a disadvantage? How is it an advantage?
3. What does the Invisible Man mean when he claims that the world moves "not like an arrow but a boomerang"? How does knowing this help him?
4. What does the narrator hope to accomplish by remaining in "a state of hibernation"? What do you think will happen to the narrator once he leaves his hole in the ground?

Writing Tasks

1. Write an essay discussing the role of others' perceptions and expectations in the shaping of one's identity. Or, alternately, write an essay in which you prejudged someone, only to find out your assessments were mistaken.
2. Write an essay which analyzes the Invisible Man's problems and propose a solution to his existential dilemma.

Into the Pit

Nicky Cruz

Nicky Cruz was born in Puerto Rico in 1941. As a teenager, he was sent to New York to live with his brother because his family could not cope with his rebellion. He joined the "Mau Maus," the most feared and vicious gang in New York City, and later became their leader. After serving time for crime and violence, Cruz dedicated his life to helping others avoid his mistakes. The following selection is excerpted from his autobiography, *Run, Baby, Run.* His story is also chronicled in the book and full-length film, *The Cross and the Switchblade.* Nicky lives in Colorado and runs an organization named T.R.U.C.E. (To Reach Urban Children Everywhere).

Pre-reading

Have you ever had a life-changing experience?

Three days before Easter four of us were on the corner of Auburn and   1
St. Edward in front of St. Edward-St. Michael Church. We knew that the priests collected a lot of money during the Easter week special services and we were making plans to break into the church.

A policeman came out of the Housing Precinct Station across the street and saw us leaning up against the iron spike fence around the church. He crossed the street and said, "Get out of here, you Puerto Rican pigs." We just stood there with our arms draped across the top of the fence and looked at him with blank stares.

He said it again. "You Spics, I said clear out of here." The other boys scattered but I held my ground. The cop glared at me, "I said move, you dirty Spic, move." He drew back his billy club as if to hit me.

I spit on him. He swung at me with his club and I ducked as it smashed into the fence. I charged into him and he grabbed me around the neck. He was twice as big as I, but I was going to kill him if I could. I was reaching for my knife when I felt him unbuckle his holster and reach for his revolver. He was calling for help at the same time.

I quickly backed away and put my hands up. "I surrender! I surrender!"   5

Police poured out the door of the Housing Precinct and rushed across the street. They grabbed hold of me and dragged me back across the street, up the steps and into the station.

The cop who had struggled with me slapped my face hard. I could taste the blood from my lips.

"You're a big man with a gun, but inside you're a coward just like all the rest of these filthy cops," I said.

He hit me again and I pretended to faint and fell to the floor.

"Get up, you dirty pig. This time we're going to send you away for   10
good."

As they dragged me into the other room I heard the desk sergeant mutter. "That kid must be out of his mind. Man, they ought to put him away for good before he kills somebody."

I had been picked up by the police many times before, but they never had been able to hold me. No one would ever testify against me because they knew when I got out I would kill them, or the Mau Maus would kill them for me.

This time they took me across town and put me in a cell. The jailer pushed me as I went into the cell and I turned and charged at him with both fists. He pulled me out in the corridor and another cop held me while he beat me with his fists.

"The only way to handle these S.O.B.'s is to beat the hell out of 'em," he said. "They're all a bunch of stinking, filthy pigs. We got a jail full of niggers, wops, and spics. You're just like all the rest and if you get out of line, we'll make you wish you were dead."

They pushed me back into the cell and I lay on the hard floor cursing   15
them. "Okay, punk," the turnkey said as he closed the cell door, "Why don't you get up and jitterbug for us now? Not so tough are you?" I bit my lips and didn't reply. But I knew I would kill him when I got out.

The next day the jailer came back to my cell. When he opened the door, I charged him again knocking him back across the corridor. He slapped me in the head with his keys. I felt the blood running from a cut over my eye.

"Go ahead, hit me," I screamed. "But one day I'm gonna come to your house and kill your wife and children. Just you wait and see."

I was only being booked on a minor offense of resisting arrest and failing to obey an officer. But I was making it worse. The jailer knocked me back in the cell and locked the door.

"Alright, Spic, you can stay there and rot!"

My hearing came up the following week. I was handcuffed and   20
marched into the courtroom. I sat in a chair while the policeman began reading off the charges.

The judge, a stern faced man in his 50's with rimless glasses, said, "Wait a minute, haven't I had this boy before in this court?"

"Yes, your honor," the policeman answered, "this is his third appearance in this court. Besides this, he has 21 arrests in his record and has been charged with everything from robbery to assault with intent to kill."

The judge turned and looked at me.

"How old are you, young man?"

I slouched down in my chair and looked at the floor.   25

"Stand up when I speak to you!" the judge snapped.

I stood to my feet and looked at him.

"I said, how old are you?" he repeated firmly.

"Eighteen," I answered.

"You're eighteen and you've been arrested 21 times and have been in   30
this court three times. Why aren't your parents with you?"

"They're in Puerto Rico," I answered.

"Who do you live with?"

"With nobody. I don't need nobody. I live with myself."

"How long have you lived by yourself?"

"Ever since I came to New York 3 years ago."   35

"Your honor," the officer interrupted, "he's no good. He's the President of the Mau Maus. He's the heart of all the trouble we've had in the housing project. I've never seen a kid as mean and vicious as this one. He's like an animal and the only thing to do with a mad dog is to pen him up. I'd like to recommend, your honor, that you put him in prison until he's 21. Maybe by then we can restore some order in Ft. Greene."

The judge turned and looked at the officer. "You say he's like an animal, eh? A mad dog, you say,"

"That's right, your honor. And if you turned him loose he'd kill someone before dark."

"Yes, I believe you're right," the judge said, looking back at me. "But I think we need at least to try to find out what makes him like an animal. Why is he so vicious? Why does he want to hate and steal and fight and kill? We have hundreds just like him coming through our courts every day and I think the state has something of an obligation to try to salvage some of these boys—not just lock them up for the rest of their lives. And I believe, that deep down in the heart of this vicious 'mad dog' there's a soul that can be saved."

He turned to the officer, "Do you think we ought to try?"   40

"I don't know, your honor," said the policeman. "These kids have killed three officers in the last two years and we've had almost 50 murders down there since I've been on that beat. The only thing they respond to is force. And I know if you turn him loose we'll just have to lock him back up again—only the next time it will probably be for murder."

The judge glanced down at the sheet of paper in front of him.

"Cruz, is it? Come up here Nicky Cruz and stand before the bench."

I got up and walked to the front of the courtroom. I could feel my knees beginning to shake.

The judge leaned over the desk and looked straight at me.   45

"Nicky, I've got a boy just about your age. He goes to school. He lives in a good house in a nice neighborhood. He doesn't get into trouble. He plays baseball on the school team and makes good grades. He's not a mad dog like you are. And the reason he isn't a mad dog is because he has someone to love him. Obviously, you don't have anyone to love you — and you don't love anyone either. You don't have the capacity to love. You're sick, Nicky, and I want to know why. I want to know what it is that makes you hate so much. You're not normal like other boys. The officer is right. You're an animal. You live like an animal and you act like an animal. I ought to treat you like an animal, but I'm going to find out why you're so abnormal. I'm going to put you under the custody of our court psychologist, Dr. John Goodman. I'm not qualified to determine whether or not you're psychotic. He will examine you and make the final decision."

I nodded. I didn't know whether he was going to turn me loose or keep me in jail, but I did understand that he wasn't going to send me to prison, at least not right then.

"One more thing, Nicky," the judge said, "if you get into any more trouble, if I get a single complaint about you, if you misbehave at all, then I'm going to assume that you are entirely incapable of understanding directions and responding to responsibility and I will send you immediately to Elmira to the work farm. Understand?"

"Yes, sir," I answered. And I was surprised at myself. It was the first time I had ever said "sir" to any man. But it just seemed the right thing to do in this case.

The next morning the court psychologist, Dr. John Goodman, came to   50 my cell. He was a big man with premature gray temples and a deep scar on his face. His shirt collar was frayed and his shoes unshined.

"I've been assigned to review your case," he said, sitting down on my bunk and crossing his legs. "This means we'll have to spend some time together."

"Sure, big man, anything you say."

"Listen, punk, I talk to 20 kids a day like you. You smart your mouth off at me and you'll wish you hadn't."

I was taken aback by his abrupt manner but sneered arrogantly, "You talk mighty big for a headshrinker. Maybe you like to have a visit from the Mau Maus one of these nights."

Before I could move the doctor had hold of the front of my shirt and   55 almost lifted me off the floor. "Let me tell you something, squirt. I spent

4 years in the gangs and three years in the Marines before going to college. See this scar?" He twisted his head so I could see the deep scar running from the point of his cheekbone into his collar. "I got that in the gangs, but not until I had almost killed 6 other punks with a baseball bat. Now if you want to play rough, you've got the right man."

He shoved me backward and I stumbled against the cot and sat down.

I spat on the floor, but said no more.

His voice returned to its matter-of-fact tone as he said, "Tomorrow morning I have to make a trip up to Bear Mountain. You can ride along and we'll talk."

All the next day I was under the informal examination of the psychologist. We drove out of the city into upper New York state. It was my first trip out of the asphalt jungle since I had landed from Puerto Rico three years before. I felt a tinge of excitement but remained sullen and arrogant when he asked me questions.

After a brief stop at the clinic he took me by the zoo in the public park.   60
We walked down the path in front of the cages. I stopped and looked at the wild animals pacing back and forth behind bars.

"Do you like zoos, Nicky?" he asked.

"I hate 'em," I answered, turning away from the cages and walking back down the path.

"Oh? Why's that?"

"I hate them stinking animals. Always pacing. Always wanting out."

We sat on a park bench and talked. Dr. John pulled some notebooks out   65
of his brief case and asked me to draw some pictures. Horses. Cows. Houses. I drew a picture of a house with a huge door in the front.

"Why did you put such a big door on the house?" he asked.

"So the stupid headshrinker can get in," I answered.

"I won't accept that. Give me another answer."

"Alright, so I can get out in a hurry in case someone's chasing me."

"Most people draw doors to get in."   70

"Not me, I'm trying to get out."

"Now draw me a picture of a tree," he said.

I drew a tree. Then I thought it wasn't right to have a tree without a bird, so I drew a bird in the top of the tree.

Dr. Goodman looked at the picture and said, "Do you like birds, Nicky?"

"I hate 'em."   75

"It seems to me you hate everything."

"Yeah. Maybe I do. But I hate birds most of all."

"Why?" he asked, "because they're free?"

In the distance I could hear the dark rumbling of thunder.

This man was beginning to scare me with his questions. I took my pen- 80
cil and bored a hole through the picture of the bird. "So, forget about the
bird. I just killed him."

"You think you can get rid of everything you're afraid of by killing
them, don't you."

"Who the hell do you think you are, you stupid quack?" I screamed.
"You think you can get me to draw a stupid picture and ask me some
dumb questions and know all about me? I ain't afraid of nobody. Everybody's afraid of me. Just ask the Bishops, they'll tell you about me. There
ain't no gang in New York that wants to rumble with the Mau Maus. I
ain't afraid of nobody." My voice had reached a fever pitch as I stood to
my feet in front of him.

Dr. Goodman kept making notes in his pad. "Sit down, Nicky," he said,
glancing up, "you don't have to impress me."

"Listen, man, you keep picking on me and you'll wind up a dead man."

The rumbling on the horizon grew louder as I stood shaking in front of 85
him. Dr. Goodman looked up at me and started to say something, but rain
drops began to splatter on the path beside us. He shook his head. "We'd
better go before we get wet," he said.

We slammed the car doors just as the first huge drops of heavy rain
splashed on the windshield. Dr. John sat silently for a long time before
starting the car and pulling out on the road. "I don't know, Nicky," he
said, "I just don't know."

The trip back was misery. The rain was pelting the car without mercy.
Dr. John drove silently. I was lost in thought. I hated going back to the
city. I dreaded the thought of going back to jail. I couldn't stand to be
caged like a wild animal.

The rain quit but the sun had already gone down as we drove past the
hundreds of blocks of towering, grimy apartments. I felt like I was sinking into a pit. I wanted to get out and run. But instead of turning toward
the jail, Dr. John slowed down and turned on Lafayette toward the Ft.
Greene project.

"Ain't you taking me to jail?" I asked, puzzled.

"No, I have the prerogative of locking you up or turning you loose. I 90
don't think jail will do you any good."

"Yeah man, now you're on my beam," I grinned.

"No, you don't understand what I mean. I don't think anything will do
you any good."

"What do you mean, Doc, you think I'm hopeless?" I laughed.

He pulled his car up at the corner of Lafayette and Ft. Greene Place.
"That's exactly right, Nicky. I've worked with kids like you for years. I
used to live in the ghetto. But I've never seen a kid as hard, cold, and

savage as you. You haven't responded to a thing I've said. You hate everyone and you're afraid of anyone that threatens your security."

I opened the door and got out. "Well, you can go to hell, Doc. I don't   95
need you or nobody."

"Nicky," he said, as I started to walk away from the car. "I'll give it to you straight. You're doomed. There's no hope for you. And unless you change you're on a one way street to jail, the electric chair, and hell."

"Yeah? Well, I'll see you there," I said.

"Where?" he said.

"In hell, man," I said laughing.

He shook his head and drove off into the night. I tried to keep laugh-   100
ing but the sound died in my throat.

I stood on the street corner with my hands in the pockets of my raincoat. It was 7 P.M. and the streets were full of nameless faces with hurrying legs . . . moving, moving, moving. I felt like a leaf on the sea of humanity, being blown in every direction by my own senseless passions. I looked at the people. Everyone was moving. Some were running. It was May but the wind was cold. It whipped my legs and made me cold inside.

The words of the psychologist kept running through my mind like a stuck record, "You're on a one way street to jail, the electric chair, and hell."

I had never looked at myself before. Not really. Oh, I liked to look at myself in the mirror. I had always been a clean boy, which is a bit unusual for most Puerto Ricans in my section. Unlike most of the guys in the gang, I took pride in the way I dressed. I liked to wear a tie and colored shirt. I always tried to keep my slacks pressed and used lots of lotion on my face. I never did like to smoke too much because it made my breath smell bad.

But inside I suddenly felt dirty. The Nicky I saw in the mirror wasn't the real Nicky. And the Nicky I was looking at now was dirty . . . filthy . . . lost.

The juke box in Papa John's was blaring forth with a loud bebop tune.   105
The traffic in the street was bumper-to-bumper. Horns were blowing, whistles shrilling, people shouting. I looked at their blank nameless faces. No one was smiling. Everyone was in a hurry. Some of the creeps were drunk. Most of the goofeys in front of the bar were hopped up. This was the real Brooklyn. This was the real Nicky.

I started up the street toward my room on Ft. Greene. The newspapers were whipping against the iron fence and the iron grates in front of the stores. There were broken bottles and empty beer cans along the sidewalk. The smell of greasy food drifted down the street and made me sick to my stomach. The sidewalks shook beneath my feet as the subways rattled and faded into the dark unknown.

I caught up with an old wretch of a woman. I say "old" but from the rear I couldn't tell her age. She was short, shorter than I. And she had a black scarf pulled tight around her head. Her reddish yellow hair that had been dyed and dyed some more, stuck out around the edges. She had on an old Navy peajacket that was about six sizes too large for her. Her scrawny legs covered with black slacks stuck out like toothpicks below the hemline of the peajacket. She had on men's shoes without any socks.

I hated her. She symbolized all the dirt and filth in my life. I reached in my pocket for my blade. I wasn't kidding this time. I kept wondering to myself how hard I would have to shove it to get the blade to go through the hard felt of the peajacket and into her back. It gave me a warm sticky feeling inside to imagine the blood dripping out from under the edge of the jacket and pudding on the street.

Just then a small dog came running down the street toward us and swerved to miss her. She turned and stared at him with empty ageless eyes. I recognized her as one of the burned out whores who used to live on my block. From the look on her face, the droopy eyelids, and the blank stare in her eyes, I could tell she was high.

I turned loose of the blade, my mind now back on myself, and started to pass her. As I did, I saw her vacant eyes watching a bright red balloon as it bounced before the wind down the middle of the street.   110

A balloon. My first instinct was to dash into the street and step on it. I hated it. Damn, I hated it! It was free.

Suddenly, a huge wave of compassion swept over me. I identified with that stupid bouncing balloon. It's a strange thing that the first time I was to feel pity in all my life it was to be for an inanimate object being blown before the wind, going nowhere.

So, instead of stepping into the street and stomping on it, I passed the old woman by and speeded up to keep up with the balloon as it bounced and rolled down the dirty street.

It seemed to be strangely out of place in that filthy setting. All around it were papers and trash being blown by the cold wind also. On the sidewalk were the broken wine bottles and crushed beer cans. Towering up on each side were the dark dismal concrete and stone walls of the inescapable prison where I lived. And here, in the midst of all this was a free, red balloon, being blown before the invisible forces of the winds of nature.

What was it about that stupid balloon that interested me? I quickened   115
my pace to keep up with it. I found myself hoping it wouldn't hit a piece of broken glass and explode. And yet knowing it could not possibly last. It was too delicate. It was too clean. It was too tender and pure to continue to exist in the midst of all this hell.

I held my breath each time it bounced in the air and came back down in the street. Waiting for that final, irrevocable explosion. And yet it continued on its merry course in the middle of the street. I kept thinking, "Maybe it will make it. Maybe it can get all the way down the block and be blown free into the park. Maybe it has a chance after all."

I was almost praying for it. But then the dejection returned as I thought of the park. That stinking, stupid park. What if it does make it to the park? What then? There's nothing for it there. It will bounce against that rusty fence and explode. Or even if it makes it over the fence and gets inside, it will fall on some of those stickers in the grass and weeds and be gone.

"Or," I thought to myself, "even if somebody picks it up, all they'll do is carry it to their filthy apartment and it will be imprisoned the rest of its life. There is no hope. No hope for it—or for me."

Suddenly, without warning, a police van rolled down the street. Before I could break away from my chain of thought it was on top of the balloon and I heard the pitiful "pop" as the van mercilessly ground it into the pavement. The van was gone—down the street and around the block. It didn't even know what it had done, and even had it known it wouldn't have cared. I wanted to run after the van and shout, "You dirty coppers. Don't you care?" I wanted to kill them for crushing me into the street.

But the life was gone out of me. I stood on the curb and looked into the   120
dark street but there was no sign of the balloon. It had been ground into the trash and rubble in the middle of Ft. Greene and had become like all the other dirt in Brooklyn.

I turned back to my steps and sat down. The old whore shuffled on down the street into the darkness. The wind still whistled and the papers and trash kept blowing down the street and sticking on the fence around the park. Another subway rattled by underneath and rumbled into the darkness. I was afraid. Me, Nicky. I was afraid. I was shaking not with the cold, but from the inside out. I put my head in my hands and thought, "It's useless. I'm doomed. It's just like Dr. John said. There's no hope for Nicky except jail, the electric chair, and hell."

After that I didn't seem to care any more. I turned the presidency of the gang back over to Israel. I was in the pit as deep as I could get. There was no hope any more. I might as well become like all the others in the ghetto and turn to the needle. And I was tired of running. What was it the judge said I needed? Love! But where can you find love in the pit?

Discussion Questions

1. What does the text suggest to be the sources of Nicky's anger?

2. How are the police portrayed in the story? Why do you think the police, and the justice system generally, failed to solve the gang problem in Cruz's time?

3. Why does Nicky hate caged animals and birds so much?

4. What is the court psychologist's conclusion after examining Nicky? Do you think he makes a sound decision in letting the young gangster go?

5. Why does Nicky want to kill the "old wretch of a woman" he encounters after being freed?

6. What is the metaphorical significance of the red balloon? How does Cruz's tone change when he follows and describes the journey of the balloon?

Writing Task

1. Write an essay in which you discuss the possible causes for youth violence and possible solutions.

Youth Gangs

Mark Berkey-Gerard

Mark Berkey-Gerard is a reporter for the *Gotham Gazette.* This article appeared there on March 5, 2001.

Pre-reading

Why do young people join gangs?

At a recent public forum at City Council, police, school officials,   1
politicians, and other experts offered their best guesses as to why the number of gang members in the city has risen over 30 percent in the last year. "We live in a criminal environment," said one expert. "There are cops in our schools, the mayor is obsessed with crime, innocent people are being shot 41 times. It creates a mentality of crime in young people." This particular expert has first-hand experience with the question. She is 19 years old and a member of the Latin Queens, complete with the tattoo of a crown on her ankle. The city has spent increased amount of money and energy in recent years trying to crack down on gangs that recruit young people like her.

In 1997, the mayor stepped up his effort to combat gangs, focusing on them as criminal enterprises, not just as groups of juvenile delinquents. In 1998, the Board of Education agreed to give school security over to the police department with officers patrolling some hallways. And last year, a bill was introduced that would give police the power to arrest suspected gang members loitering on street corners.

Despite such efforts, gangs and their crimes are a routine part of news headlines. Recently 18 members of The Mexican Boys gang were arrested for carrying knives and guns on their way to a party of a rival gang in Brooklyn. The Albany County jail had the highest rate of violence in its history this year, with many of the incidents occurring between New York City and upstate gangs. And last month, three teenagers were arrested in connection with the shooting death of a man in Central Park, the first homicide there in two years. The teens claimed affiliation with both the Bloods and the Crips, though police later determined that they were lying. Clearly, gangs still hold some appeal.

The 19-year-old member of the Latin Queens, who asked that only her last name, Vargas, be used, suggested some reasons why. "There are no jobs, no programs for youth, our schools are falling apart," Vargas said. "Our youth bond together for protection and opportunity." While not everybody would agree with her — New York offers more cultural opportunities and youth programs, some say, than many other cities with gang problems — Councilmember Ken Fisher, chair of the Youth Services Committee, seemed to agree with Vargas at least in part. "I find it troubling that the same day we hear the police testify to an increase in gang members the mayor proposes a 20 million dollar cut in funding for youth services," said Fisher. Youth gangs have been a part of New York City life as long as young people have been hanging out on the streets looking for something to do. Unlike adult crimes, most juvenile crime is committed in groups. And gangs offer a sense of identity, camaraderie, and financial payoff for their loyalty.

The difference is that today's gangs are more widespread and more   5
dangerous. It is estimated that 94 percent of medium and large-cities in the U.S. have gang activity. And with easy access to guns and the drugs market, gangs present a more substantial criminal force. "These kids are not afraid of death or jail," said Robert DeSena who has worked with Brooklyn gangs since 1975. "Once a kid reaches that mindset, you've got a hard-core challenge."

Defining Image

Popular images of gang members range from Tony, who fell in love with a rival gang member's sister in *West Side Story,* to the violent gang-bangers who run the Los Angeles streets in the movie *Boyz 'N the Hood.* There are a wide range of perceptions, and misperceptions, of what youth gangs do and who is a part of them.

The New York Police Department defines a gang as a group that engages in criminal behavior and has a formal organizational structure, identifiable leadership, and territory. The U.S. Department of Justice estimates that there are approximately 750,000 gang members in 28,000 gangs in the U.S., although no one really knows how many there are because accurate counts are nearly impossible to make. It is estimated that females make up approximately 20 percent of the national gang population. And while the average age of gang members is 17, nearly half of all gang members range in age from 18 to 25 years.

The New York Police Department recently reported that the known gang members in the city increased from 11,000 to 15,000 in the past year. However, many researchers doubt the validity of such numbers.

"I've stayed away from New York statistics for years," said Malcolm Klein from the Center for Research for Crime and Social Control, who has been studying gangs for over two decades. Prior to 1976, New York City's Youth Services Administration kept more dependable gang statistics in the city, but in the fiscal problems of the city, the administration was disbanded and tracking was handed over to police.

While the ethnic make-up of gangs, the streets they call "turf," and the names they give themselves have changed over time, the common factor is social class. Most gang members come from lower or working-class backgrounds, looking for a way to gain power in the social order.

History of Gotham Streets

Youth gangs have always been part of New York City life.   10

In 1807, members of the African Methodist Episcopal Zion Church in lower Manhattan complained to the city about the gangs of white, working class youths who harassed churchgoers, according to the book, *Gotham* by Edwin G. Burroughs and Mike Wallace. By the 1820's, the authors explain, young men "swaggered about the city after work and on Sundays, staking out territories, picking fights, defending the honor of their street and trade." Until the mid-1900's, a majority of gangs in America were white, composed of boys from various European backgrounds.

The postwar gangs in the 1940's–1960's were primarily "turf" gangs who defended their areas against neighboring ethnic groups and new immigrants. In his recent book, *Vampires, Dragons, and Egyptian Kings,* Eric Schneider presents Postwar gang life as a world of switchblades, zoot suits, slums, and bebop music. Young men took on brash names like Enchanters, Young Lords, Bishops, Greene Avenue Stompers, and the Latin Gents. While youth gangs were often seen as "violent, short-lived, disorganized collections of misfits whose main purpose was thrill seeking and immediate gratification," says Schneider, they provided a social structure for working-class boys that provided a sense of identity, place, and masculinity.

By 1970, about four-fifths of gang members were either African-American or Hispanic. And the late 1980's and early 1990's saw the growth of West Coast gangs like the Crips and the Bloods, although most experts dispute the notion that the gangs actually migrated across the country. Instead they are local, non-centralized gangs that go by the same names and wear the same identifying colors.

Today in New York, the most prominent New York City gangs are the Bloods, Crips, Latin Kings, Nietas, Five Prisoners, Silenciosos, Matatones, Rat Hunters, and Zulu Nation. They are groups that span ethnicity, race, and neighborhoods.

From Turf to Drugs, From Fists to Guns

Two major changes in recent years have transformed the nature of youth   15
gangs. First, the influx of illegal drugs—first heroin, then cocaine, and
then crack cocaine—changed street gangs from social groups to economic enterprises. Instead of fighting over the geography of turf, gangs
began to wage war over corners used to sell drugs. The institution of the
Rockefeller drug laws in 1973 and stiffer prison penalties for adults, had
a bitterly ironic result: Drug dealers began to recruit minors to do much
of their selling on the streets. While gangs have become a significant part
of the drug trade (a recent study that gangs are involved in about a quarter of the drug arrests), most researchers argue that youth gangs are not
major drug traffickers. "Drug gangs separate themselves from street
gangs," said Klein. "Drugs require tight corporate-like structure that
youth do not have."

The second and perhaps the most devastating change is the availability
of guns. It is estimated that gang related homicides increased nearly five
times between 1987 and 1994. "Violence has always been around, usually
concentrated amongst the poor," said Geoffrey Canada, who runs the non-
profit Rheedlin Center for Children and Families in Harlem. "The difference is that we never had so many guns in our inner cities. The nature of
the violent act has changed from the fist, stick, and knife to the gun."

The Riker's Island Gang Museum

To visit the offices of the Gang Unit at Riker's Island is to visit a virtual
museum of gang paraphernalia. The walls are covered with photographs
of gang member tattoos, red and blue bandanas from the Crips and the
Bloods, and rosaries with black and yellow beads used by members of the
Latin Kings. There is a display of home-made weaponry: knives made
from pocket combs, razor blades fashioned from bottle caps, and even a
small gun made from a toilet paper roll and rubber bands. And on the desk
are computers used to enter the information into the city's gang database.
It is all part of the Corrections Department's "zero tolerance" policy on
gangs and the city's attempt to enhance its gang intelligence.

At Riker's Island, gang members are stripped of any kind of identifying clothing or trinkets, forced to live in the same rooms with rival gangs,
and any act of violence automatically adds time to their sentence. The
Correction's Department says it is working. The incidence of violence in
the city's jail is at the lowest in over a decade.

The School Safety and Prevention Service's division of the New
York City operates under a similar notion. If any student exhibits gang

behavior—wearing colors, using hand signals, graffiti, or any criminal activity—they are immediately removed from school. Efforts to pass legislation to control gangs are generally more difficult. Most of the state legislation has to do with graffiti and tougher sentences for assault.

Last year in the city, Councilmembers John Sabini and Michel Abel introduced a bill that would give police the power to arrest suspected gang members loitering on street corners. The legislation drew criticism from civil rights groups and others who thought the law would lead to police abuse. Currently the proposed legislation is still sitting in committee.

20

Finding Solutions

While legislators and police often take the credit for drops in gang related crime, the ebb and flow of gangs are more susceptible to other less tangible factors. There are several theories of why New York City has less of a problem with gangs than cities like Los Angeles and Chicago.

One is that today's gangs operate in an automobile culture that facilitates drive-by-shootings and drug dealing, and enables gangs to travel in greater anonymity. New York's mass transit system makes it more difficult for such activities. Another theory is that New York City has more opportunities for young people that fill the similar needs as a gang. "In New York you can be part of a religious group, an arts club, a cultural group, you can even be part of a doo-wop group," said Councilmember Ken Fisher, who is Chair of the Youth Services Committee. "There are more opportunities for someone to belong to something."

There are also a host of non-profits that work with gang members on a one-to-one basis. The main challenge for these groups is to offer something that replaces the protection, identity, and money young people gain from being part of a gang.

Robert DeSena, a retired schoolteacher and founder of Council for Unity, a group that works to bring rival gangs together, says many of the gang members he meets are looking for a way out. "Violence is exhausting and gangs realize they are unable to exterminate the opposition," said DeSena. DeSena works to build a network of protection and support that replaces gang life. The youth are responsible for running their own cultural events, support meetings, marketing the programs, soliciting members—using skills they had previously used on the street. The members are paired with alumni of the program who work as mentors, often hiring the youth to work at their companies. "You get an ex-gang member who works for Price Waterhouse to take an interest in a kid," said DeSena, "and the kids will take notice."

Discussion Questions

1. What point does Ken Fisher make when he connects increased gang problems with the mayor's proposal to cut 20 million dollars in funding for youth services?

2. According to the article, what contributes to the "criminal mindset" plaguing many young people today?

3. Do you think increased school security is the best way to combat teen violence?

4. According to the article, what is a common factor linking gangs throughout history? What does this say about one of the universal motivations for gang behavior?

5. What two changes have transformed the nature of youth gangs making them more violent than ever before?

6. Why does New York City tend to have fewer gang-related problems than other major cities? Do you agree with this assessment?

7. What can be done to get kids to stay out of gangs?

Writing Task

1. Write an essay in which you analyze the high school you attended and how students treated each other. Were there cliques, gangs, or even violence? Why or why not?

From Doo Wop to Hip Hop: The Bittersweet Odyssey of African-Americans in the South Bronx

Mark Naison

Dr. Mark Naison (b.1946) is Director of Urban Studies and African-American Studies at Fordham University and author of *Communists in Harlem during the Depression* (1983) and co-author of *The Tenant Movement in New York City, 1940–1984* (1986). Dr. Naison has also written articles on African-American culture and contemporary urban issues, including "Outlaw Culture in Black Culture," *Reconstruction* (Fall 1994). This essay originally appeared in the *Bronx County Historical Society Journal* in 2004.

Pre-reading

What is your favorite genre of music?
What message do you believe it strives to get across?

Sometimes, music can be a powerful tool in interpreting historical   1
events. Played side by side, two of the most popular songs ever to come out of The Bronx, the Chantel's "Maybe" and Grandmaster Flash and the Furious Five's "The Message," dramatize an extraordinary shift in the culture, dreams and lived experience of African Americans in the South Bronx between the mid 1950s and the early 1980s. These songs, so different in tone, content and feeling, were produced by artists who lived less than six blocks away from one another in the Morrisania section of The Bronx, an important center of musical creativity in both the rhythm and blues and hip hop eras.[1]

The Chantels, the most successful "doo wop" group ever to come out of The Bronx, and one of the first of the "girl groups" ever to have a hit single, grew up singing together in the choir at St. Anthony of Padua elementary school, located at East 165th Street and Prospect Avenue. Their song "Maybe" appeared in 1957, a time when many African Americans in The Bronx were having a modest taste of postwar prosperity and were optimistic about their futures. Throughout the South Bronx neighborhoods they inhabited, new housing developments were going up at breakneck speed, allowing thousands of black and Latino families to move into clean airy apartments, with ample heat and hot water, which were a step up from the tenements many of them lived in when they first came to New York. They lived in neighborhoods where most families were intact, where children received strong adult guidance in their home, their block, and their school, and where adolescent violence was rarely life threatening.

Grandmaster Flash, one of three pioneering Bronx DJs credited with founding hip hop, also grew up in Morrisania—at 947 Fox Street, right off East 163rd Street—but it was a very different Morrisania than the one the Chantels grew up in. When Mel Melle, the MC for the group sang "Broken glass, everywhere, people pissing on the street, you know they just don't care" to a pounding, rhythmic backdrop, he was talking about a community buffeted by arson, building abandonment, drugs, gang violence, shattered families, the withdrawal of public services and the erosion of legal job opportunities. Surrounded by tenement districts that had been ravaged by fires, housing projects that were once centers of pride and optimism had become dangerous and forbidding. "Rats on the front porch, roaches in the back, junkies in the alley with a baseball bat." This was the world in which hip hop was created, a world where government was distant and remote, families were under stress, adult authority was weak, and young people had to find economic opportunity and creative outlets on their own in the most forbidding of circumstances.

How did this happen? How did the harmonic, optimistic environment evoked by the Chantels, the Chords (who came out of Morris High School), or Little Anthony and the Imperials, give way to the violent, danger filled world described, in clinical detail, by the Furious Five and, several years later by another brilliant South Bronx hip hop lyricist, KRS-1? And how did people respond to these community destroying forces? Did they give in? Leave? Try to resist? If they did resist, how effective was their resistance?

These are some of the issues that I will try to address in this article. Please keep in mind that what I am sharing with you is the product of preliminary research rather than a polished product. A little more than a year ago, The Bronx County Historical Society and the Department of African and African-American Studies at Fordham University came together to launch The Bronx African American History Project, an effort to document the experience of the more than five hundred thousand people of African descent who live in The Bronx. I decided to focus on the generation of African Americans who moved to the South Bronx from Harlem, the American South and the Caribbean during and after World War II, the generation of people Colin Powell has written about in the early chapters of his autobiography, *An American Journey.*[2]

5

I began interviewing members of that pioneering generation and in the process came across a remarkable group of people who grew up in the Patterson Houses, a 17 building development bounded by Morris and Third avenues and East 139th and East 144th streets. These individuals, who come together every July for a Patterson Houses Reunion, are successful professionals in education, business, and the arts. They remember the Patterson Houses as a safe, nurturing place from the time it opened in 1950 until heroin struck in the early 60s. Their story, which challenges so much of what people think about public housing, the South Bronx, and black and Latino neighborhoods, is important not only because of its intrinsic value, but because it helps us understand the events that follow. Based on interviews and long discussions with Victoria Archibald-Good, Nathan "Bubba" Dukes, Adrian Best, Arnold Melrose, Joel Turner, Michael Singletary, Marilyn Russell and Allen Jones, I am going to bring back a time when public housing was a symbol of hope, not failure, and when working class black and Latino families, supported by strong, well-funded government services, helped each other raise their children with love, discipline, respect and a determination to achieve success in school, athletics and the arts. And though this story is about Patterson, the atmosphere it evokes also existed in the Melrose, St. Mary's and Forest Houses, the other large developments that opened in the South Bronx in the late 1940s and early 50s.

One of the first things that grabbed my attention when I began doing interviews was that African American families who moved into the Patterson Houses saw their arrival there as a "step up" from the crowded tenement neighborhoods where they had been living. Vicki Archibald-Good, whose parents moved to Patterson Houses from Harlem, recalled: "There wasn't a lot of affordable housing. I am not sure how long my parents were on the waiting list for public housing, but I do remember my mother saying they were living in one room in my grandmother's apartment before we moved. . . . By the time we moved from Harlem to The Bronx, I was born, my brother Tiny was born and my mother was pregnant with a third child."[3]

Nathan Dukes, whose family moved from a crowded building in the Morrisania section of The Bronx, where his father was superintendent, recalled: "It was basically like a migration, where people moved from the Tinton Avenue/Prospect Avenue area over into the Patterson Houses. . . . The projects were relatively new and they were accommodating." The new residents, Dukes claims, took tremendous pride in their surroundings. "Outsiders could not come into the Patterson Projects if we didn't know them," he remembers. "A lot of the older guys would question anybody who didn't look right who came into the projects late in the evenings. . . . They were basically patrolling. . . . They would walk around the neighborhood . . . making sure things were OK."[4]

When the project first opened, children who lived in Patterson experienced a level of communal supervision that is difficult to imagine today. The families who lived in the development, ninety percent of whom were black and Latino, took responsibility for raising one another's children. Not only did they help one another with babysitting and childcare, they carefully monitored the behavior of young people in hallways, from apartment windows and project benches, making public spaces of the huge development anything but anonymous. "You couldn't get away with anything," Nathan Dukes recalled, "The moms and the pops . . . they'd be out on the benches. . . . If you went in the wrong direction, by the time you came back, everybody in the neighborhood would know. And that was it. . . . You'd get a whooping."[5] Vicki Archibald-Good, who fondly recalled the "camaraderie and supportiveness and nurturing" she got from people who in her building "who weren't blood relatives," also remembered that people were quick to correct one another's children: ". . . they did not hesitate to speak to you about dropping garbage in the hallway or talking too loud or skating in the hallway. And all a neighbor had to do was say 'Don't let me tell your mother.' That's all it took for us to come back to reality . . ." Even childless people got in the act. Vicki remembered a "Miss Cassie" who used to "stand in that hallway, or sit by the window, or on the bench and everybody knew what was going on in 414 . . ."[6]

This communal investment in child rearing was reinforced by publicly funded programs that provided children in the Patterson Houses with a extraordinary array of cultural and recreational opportunities. As Josh Freeman points out in his landmark book *Working Class New York,* residents of communities like Patterson Houses were the beneficiaries of a remarkable campaign by the city's postwar labor movement to have government invest in education, health care, recreation and youth services for working class families.[7] Children growing up in Patterson in 1950s had round the clock supervised activities in a community center housed in the local elementary school, PS 18, had first rate music instruction from teachers at the local junior high school, went on summer field trips to zoos and museums, and got free medical exams, vaccinations, and dental care in schools and in clinics. The experience made children in the projects feel at home in all of the city's major cultural sites. "We had a vacation day camp, every summer, for children in the projects," Vicki Archibald-Good recalled. "We went to . . . every single museum you could think of, to Coney Island, to baseball games, to the planetarium. . . . I knew The Bronx Zoo like the back of my hand. We went to Prospect Park, we went to the Botanical Garden. . . . I don't think there was one spot in the city that we didn't cover."[8]

These programs were headed by teachers and youth workers who took a deep interest in the welfare of Patterson's children and were in regular communication with parents, reinforcing the communal investment in the neighborhood's young people. Nathan Dukes and Adrian Best both speak with reverence of the instruction and guidance they received from "Mr. Eddie Bonamere," the music teacher at Clark Junior High School, who headed the school's band. At that time, Clark, like most New York public schools, allowed students to take instruments home over the weekend, and Bonamere, a talented jazz pianist, used this opportunity to train hundreds of youngsters from the Patterson Houses to play the trumpet, trombone, flute and violin. Bonamere's extraordinary influence on his pupils—Nathan Dukes referred to him as the "love of my life"—was reinforced by his determination to expand the cultural horizons of everyone living in the neighborhood. At the end of every summer, Dukes recalled, Bonamere would sponsor a jazz concert in the schoolyard of PS 18 that included famous musicians like Willie Bobo and "everyone, I mean the entire projects, would be there."[9]

Supervised sports programs in the Patterson Houses, were, if anything, even more visible and influential. The community center at PS 18, which was directed by the former CCNY basketball star Floyd Lane and ex-Knickerbocker center Ray Felix, was kept open on weekends, holidays, and weekday afternoons and evenings. Not only did children have a chance to play knock hockey and checkers, do double dutch and play in organized basketball leagues, they had an opportunity to watch some of the greatest African American basketball players in the nation play in the holiday basketball tournaments that Lane sponsored. Players like Wilt Chamberlain, Meadlowlark Lemon, Tom Thacker, and Happy Hairston showed up the PS 18 court. Similar programs existed in other South Bronx neighborhoods. Nat Dukes joined a community basketball program headed by Hilton White at a public park near Prospect Avenue, and played on a softball team called the Patterson Knights that was coached by a Burns security guard who lived in the Patterson Houses. Because of this array of sports programs, many young people who grew up in Patterson had successful careers in high school, college, and professional athletics, and one of them, Nate Tiny Archibald, became one of the greatest point guards ever to play in the NBA.[10]

This portrait of a time when black and Latino children in the Patterson Houses experienced strong adult leadership in every dimension of their lives so challenges the standard portrait of life in public housing that you might find it hard to believe. Wasn't the South Bronx in the 1950s the home of numerous street gangs, you might ask? Weren't its neighborhoods filled with illegal activities and a strong underground economy?

The answer to both of these questions is yes. Most of the people who lived in the Patterson Houses were poor and gang fighting and the underground economy were part of their lives. But except in rare cases, neither gangs nor illegal activities led to deadly violence. Boys in the Patterson Houses were constantly fighting kids from other neighborhoods and other projects, but most of the fighting was done with fists, and adults in the projects would step in if knives or zip guns became involved. The underground economy was huge, but its primary manifestation was the numbers and the major numbers entrepreneur in Patterson, Mr. Clay, carried himself more like a community banker than a thug. A "major donor in the church" and a sponsor of the community softball team, Mr. Clay dressed formally, did his entire business in his head and never worried about being robbed by his customers, even though he always carried hundreds of dollars in his pocket. Even those who acted outside the law seemed to operate within a powerful communal consensus.[11]

This remarkable period in the life of the Patterson Houses, which lasted less than fifteen years, rested on a number of intersecting factors which would not exist in public housing from the mid 1960s on. First, the presence of intact families. All of the families with children who moved into Patterson in the 1950s had two parents present. Second, the ready availability of jobs in the local economy that men with high school educations and less could work at. Many of the men in the Patterson Houses worked in factories and small shops located in the South Bronx—Dukes' father was a furniture assembler, other men worked in milk bottling plants, or small metal shops. Third, schools and community centers near the Patterson Houses offered an impressive array of day camps, after-school centers and sports and music and arts programs that offered round the clock supervision and activity for young people in the projects. And fourth, and most importantly, most Patterson residents had a sense, reinforced by public policy and lived experience, that life was getting better, that people heading families were living better than their parents had, and that their children were going to do even better than they had.

In the 1960s, the comfort and security of people living in the Patterson Houses was to be cruelly shattered by a number of forces, creating an environment ruled by fear and mistrust in which children were too often forced to raise themselves. What changed? When people who grew up in Patterson try to explain why the environment that nurtured them fell apart, the two things they mention are heroin and the fragmentation of families.

For both Vicki Archibald-Good and Nathan Dukes, it was heroin use, which reached epidemic proportions in the early and mid 1960s, that did the most to erode bonds of community and trust in the Patterson Houses.

All of a sudden, young men who were bright, popular and ambitious, were transformed into dangerous and disoriented individuals who wouldn't hesitate to rob their neighbors or families to get their next fix. Vicki Archibald-Good, whose best friend's brother was the first person she knew to get hooked, saw heroin strike with the force of a "major epidemic." She recalled: "It was so completely different that it felt that I was living in a dream . . . . All of a sudden, everyone in the projects is talking about break-ins . . . people were saying these were inside jobs, that somebody was letting these folks in to burglarize people's apartments. Then I started hearing about folks that I grew up with getting thrown off rooftops because they were dealing. For the first time, I was starting to feel fear, not only for myself, but for the whole community."[12]

Nathan Dukes remembers heroin hitting with the force of a flood: ". . . there was just an abundance, it came out of nowhere . . . people that you thought would not become involved in narcotics became involved on a very heavy level." Dukes recalled being "devastated" during his first year in college by the news that one of his best friends had just gotten shot and killed while robbing a jewelry store.[13] By 1965 and 1966, Archibald-Good recalled, she didn't feel safe walking back from the subway by herself at night. The Patterson dream had become a nightmare: ". . . here I was in this huge housing complex and there was a story every day about somebody who overdosed or who was thrown off a roof . . . . So yes, it was a troublesome time for most of us."[14]

The impact of heroin on the Patterson community was so traumatic that Nathan Dukes remains convinced it was part of a government conspiracy to weaken the civil rights movement. But there were other forces eroding the community in the mid 60s that would have lasting impact on the projects and the neighborhood. The fragmentation of families also contributed to the atmosphere and disorder. During the early and mid 60s, Dukes recalled, more and more fathers began to desert their families, frustrated by their inability to support their wives and children at a time when the factory jobs they worked at were beginning to leave The Bronx.[15] During those same years, housing projects began to relax their admissions standards and open their doors to families on welfare, many of them recent migrants from Puerto Rico or the South, or refugees from urban renewal projects in the rest of the city. As a result of both of these developments, the adult male presence in the projects which had helped keep gang behavior and teenage violence under control, began to diminish sharply, leaving public space in control of drug dealers, junkies and teenage gangs.

The resulting violence and chaos led to a gradual exodus of families 20 that had managed to resist these corrosive forces, most to the West and

North Bronx. As a result, sections of The Bronx which had once been primarily Jewish, Irish and Italian, such as Morris Heights, University Heights, South Fordham, and Williamsbridge, began to experience a rapid increase in their black population, while the housing projects of the South Bronx increasingly became places for those too poor, or troubled, to escape to safer areas. The exodus increased further with the wave of arson and disinvestment that spread through Melrose, Mott Haven, and Morrisania in the early 1970s, and later spread into Highbridge, Morris Heights and Crotona, exacerbated by a city fiscal crisis that led to dramatic cuts in public services. By the late 1970s, when The Bronx had become an international symbol of social decay, it would have been impossible for most people to imagine that housing projects in the South Bronx were once safe and nurturing places where children were watched over in every aspect of their lives and exposed to the best cultural opportunities the city had to offer.

In this moment of decay and despair, an improbable cultural movement would arise among young people in the South, West and East Bronx whose creative impulses were integrally linked to the atmosphere of social breakdown that surrounded them. That movement was hip hop, and its unique styles of dancing, visual arts, and musical expression were created in The Bronx in the face of skepticism, indifference, and occasionally hostility from adults inside and outside the communities they lived in. In fact, a good argument could be made that it was the breakdown of social order and adult authority that made this form of artistic innovation possible, especially in the formative years when hip hop had no commercial viability. The music writer Nelson George offered the following ironic observations of how the music fit the times:

> *The New York that spawned hip hop spit me out, too. I came of age in the 70s. . . . But I'd be lying if I told you the 70s were a time of triumph. . . . It was, at times, a frightful experience to walk the streets, ride the subways, or contemplate the future. . . . But in chaos there is often opportunity, in pain a measure of pleasure and joy is just a stroke or two away from pain. The aesthetic industry now known as hip hop is a product of these blighted times, a child that walked, talked and partied amidst negativity.[16]*

Hip hop developed at a time when the adult presence in the lives of young people in The Bronx had radically diminished. Not only had informal supervision by family members and neighbors become far less significant, but music instruction had disappeared from the public schools, parks and recreation staffing had been cut in half, afternoon and evening programs in the schools had been eliminated, and sports programs had been cut to the bone. More and more, young people had to bring up themselves, and the result was that gangs in The Bronx had become far larger and more violent than their 50s counterparts, rates of violent crime had quadrupled, and the underground economy had come to replace the legal economy as a source of employment for youth.

Along with gang activity came radical politics. In the late 60s and early 70s, more intellectually inclined Bronx youngsters were gravitating to the Black Panther Party and the Young Lords, the Nation of Islam and the Five Percenters, as well as the community action groups seeking to wrest political control of The Bronx from its Irish, Jewish and Italian leadership. These events occurred at the same time that black and Puerto Rican studies courses were being created on the CUNY campuses and elsewhere. Along with the gangs, drugs, disinvestment and crime, race conscious political activism, reinforced by open admissions in the City University system, was part of the unique chemistry that created hip hop as a cultural movement.

The birth of hip hop as a distinctive music form can be traced to the year 1973, when a Jamaican immigrant nicknamed "Cool DJ Herc" began holding parties at the community center in his building, 1520 Sedgwick Avenue in the Morris Heights section of The Bronx. At that time, you could not hold a party in The Bronx without being concerned which of the gangs would show up and how they would respond—particularly the Savage Skulls and the Black Spades. Competition for territory and prestige by gangs dominated public space in many parts of The Bronx, with neither a fiscal crisis-decimated police force, nor local adults, able to control their activity. In addition to fighting, the competition had begun to take the form of graffiti writing and dancing, with gang members at clubs trying to outdo each other in launching acrobatic moves on the dance floors of clubs and parties they attended. 25

The innovation that Herc inaugurated was to take music that was no longer played on mass market radio—particularly heavily rhythmic music by James Brown, Sly and the Family Stone, and George Clinton—and use incredibly powerful speakers to accentuate the base line. In addition, two turntables were used so that the most danceable portions of the record—the break beats—could be played in consecutive order. The result was a sound that drove dancers wild and turned the competition on the floor between gang members into high theater. What soon became known as "break dancing" described the increasingly acrobatic moves that took place at Herc's parties at the Sedgwick community center, which people all over The Bronx flocked to see.

Soon, Herc was moving his events outdoors by hooking up his sound system to streetlights, and thousands of people were starting to attend them. He eventually found a commercial venue for his shows at "Club Hevalo" on Jerome Avenue between Tremont and Burnside avenues. By 1974 and 1975. Herc's style of dee jaying had started to spread through other neighborhoods of The Bronx, connecting with traditions of toasting and boasting, long established in black communities. To add variety to his shows and stir up the audience, Herc began to allow one of his partner DJs, Coke La Rock, "grab the mike and start to throw out his poetry." This innovation was so successful that Herc added other "MCs" to his shows, and they soon began to compete to see how well they could stir up the crowd. This, some people say, is where "rapping" (long a respected art in black communities) became a part of hip hop.

While Herc built a reputation in the West Bronx, even establishing a major venue near Fordham University at PAL (Police Athletic League) center on East 183rd Street and Webster Avenue, a former gang leader from the Bronx River Houses in Soundview who called himself Afrika Bambaataa began holding parties in the community center of his housing project that built on and in some respects expanded Herc's innovations. Influenced by the Nation of Islam and the Black Panthers, Bambaataa created an organization called the Zulu Nation aimed at bringing cooperation among Bronx gangs, using hip hop culture to attract them to his shows. Eclectic in his tastes, Bambaataa added rock and latin and jazz to the funk driven beats he was playing. He encouraged break dancers from all over The Bronx to come to his center, knowing they would be protected from violence by Bambaataa's bodyguards. He also encouraged poets and MCs to work alongside him, creating a more artistically varied product than Herc usually did. Bambaataa was explicitly political in his objectives. As he told Jim Fricke and Charlie Ahearn:

> *I grew up in the southeast Bronx. It was an area where back in the late 60s, early 70s, there was "broken glass everywhere," like Mel Melle said in "The Message." But it was also an area where there was a lot of unity and social awareness going on, at a time when people of color was coming into their own, knowin' that they were black people, hearing records like James Brown's "Say It Loud—I'm Black and Proud," giving us awareness. . . . Seeing all the violence that was going on with the Vietnam War and all the people in Attica and Kent State, and being aware of what was going on in the late 60s, with Woodstock and the Flower Power . . . just being a young person and seeing all this happening around me put a lot of consciousness in my mind*

*to get up and do something; it played a strong role in trying to
say, "We've got to stop this violence with the street gangs."[17]*

The final hip hop innovator was Grandmaster Flash, an electronic wiz-   30
ard who figured out ways of having turntables mingle break beats automatically. Flash, a graduate of Samuel Gompers Vocational High School,
began performing in schoolyards (his biggest events took place outside
PS 163 at East 169th Street and Boston Road), clubs and community centers in Morrisania—a neighborhood which had been devastated by fires,
but was anchored by several large public housing projects. Flash became
the dominant figure in the South Bronx neighborhoods of Melrose, Mott
Haven and Hunts Point, attracting a brilliant group of poets and rappers
led by Mel Melle, the voice which is heard on Flash's signature song,
"The Message."

What makes this entire movement remarkable is that it was created entirely by people under the age of thirty, with little support from parents,
teachers, or the music industry. The music teachers who had once played
a vital role in exposing an earlier generation to instrumental music, and
sponsoring talent shows for vocal groups in after school centers, had been
removed or reassigned during the fiscal crisis. Community center direc-
tors like Arthur Crier in the Tremont section, who sponsored parties and
talent shows at which hip hop pioneers performed, were the only adults
present at hip hop's genesis, but they had little influence on its musical
content.[18]

Because hip hop was about rhythm, rather than harmony, and because
turntables and records had replaced musical instruments and voice, many
people brought up on gospel, blues, jazz and soul had difficulty regarding it as music, just as many people had difficulty regarding graffiti as art.
But because so many young people had grown up in the fractured world
that hip hop became the major form of community entertainment among
young people in The Bronx and soon spread far beyond its borders.

The story of hip hop's rise is a testimony to the vitality of the human
spirit, but it does not give my story a happy ending. Although hip hop has
given young people in the South Bronx (and communities like it throughout the world) a vehicle and a moral compass that helps them describe the
conditions in which they live, and has prevented the media and government from rendering them invisible, it has not been able to turn fractured
neighborhoods into safe supportive communities like the one that Vicki
Archibald-Good and Nathan Dukes grew up in.

The opportunities provided by growing up in The Bronx after World
War II, however, provide us with insights as to how to improve the current situation for its people. We cannot replace the nuclear family and
bring back the industrial jobs that left The Bronx in the 1950s, 60s and

70s, but we can restore music instruction to the public schools, rehire recreation supervisors in parks and playgrounds, and revive the after school programs and evening centers that were once a fixture of every elementary school in the city. Public housing was once a place where dreams of success and achievement were nurtured. There is no reason why public housing cannot play that role again, if we restore the round-the-clock youth programs Patterson children once benefitted from and make a generous investment in child care, education and medical care for working class children and families.

Notes

[1]On rhythm and blues in Morrisania, see Philip Groia, *They All Sang On the Corner: A Second Look at New York City's Rhythm and Blues Vocal Groups* (Port Jefferson, NY: Phillie Dee Enterprises, 1983, 130–132.) PS 99, which sponsored evening talent shows as part of a night center directed by a legendary teacher named Vincent Tibbs, and Morris High School, were centers of musical creativity in the "doo wop" years. Groia writes: "After three o'clock, P.S. 99 and Morris High School became rehearsal halls for the simplest of musical instruments, the human voice. Both schools were major forces in keeping young people off the streets . . ."

[2]Colin Powell, with Joseph E. Persico, *My American Journey* (New York: Ballantine, 1995). Chapter One discusses Powell's experiences growing up in the South Bronx.

[3]Mark Naison, " 'It Take a Village to Raise a Child': Growing Up in the Patterson Houses in the 1950s and Early 1960s, An Interview with Victoria Archibald-Good," *The Bronx County Historical Society Journal,* 40, No. 1 (Spring 2003): 7

[4]Oral history interview with Nathan Dukes by Mark Naison, April 25, 2003. Transcript and videotape at The Bronx County Historical Society and at the Walsh Library of Fordham University.

[5]Ibid.

[6]Naison, "Interview with Victoria Archibald-Good," 8–9.

[7]Joshua B. Freeman *Working Class New York: Life and Labor Since World War II* (New York: New Press, 2000).

[8]Naison, "Interview with Victoria Archibald-Good," 8.

[9]Dukes oral history interview and oral history interview with Adrian Best by Mark Naison, July 1, 2003. Transcripts and videotapes at The Bronx County Historical Society and at the Walsh Library of Fordham University.

[10]Dukes oral history interview.

[11]Ibid.

[12]Naison, "Interview with Victoria Archibald-Good," 17–18.

[13]Dukes oral history interview.

[14]Naison, "Interview with Victoria Archibald-Good," 18.

[15]Dukes oral history interview.

[16]Jim Fricke and Charlie Aheam *"Yes Yes Y'All: The Experience Music Project Oral History of Hip Hop's First Decade* (New York: Da Capo Press, 2002), vii. Nelson George wrote the introduction to this remarkable book, which provides the best portrait of the rise of hip hop in The Bronx in the 1970s. The discussion of hip hop's origins draws on this book and other works documenting hip hop's Bronx years: Raquel Rivera, *New York Ricans In the Hip Hop Zone* (New York: Palgrave, 2003); Tricia Rose, *Black Noise: Rap Music and Black Culture in Contemporary America* (Hanover: Wesleyan University Press, 1994); Alan Light, ed. *The Vibe History of Hip Hop* (New York: Three Rivers Press, 1999); James D. Eure and James Spady, *Nation Conscious Rap* (New York: PC International Press, 1991); James G. Spady, Charles G. Lee, and H. Samy

Alin, *Street Conscious Rap* (Philadelphia: Black History Museum, Umum/Loh Publishers, 1999).

[17]Frick and Ahearn *"Yes Yes Y'All,"* 44.

[18]In an interview with The Bronx African American History Project on January 30, 2004, Crier, a singer, arranger, producer and songwriter who was one of the major figures in the Morrisania rhythm and blues scene in the 1950s and 60s, said that the talent shows at PS 99 in the 1950s were his inspiration when he began organizing talent shows at his community center in the middle and late 1970s.

Discussion Questions

1. Discuss how Naison uses the music of the Chantels and the rap lyrics of Grandmaster Flash to structure his overall argument.

2. What is the effect of interviewing actual people as evidence to support his argument?

3. How did the tenants of the Patterson houses in the 1950s view their new residences?

4. How were children treated at this time? What was available to them? What role did adults play in their lives?

5. What was the economy like for working-class families in the 1950s?

6. What was the effect of heroin use in the mid-1960s?

7. What role did the loss of jobs have? Do you think this is a larger social issue?

8. What was early hip hop like? What social and political agenda did it serve?

9. Why does Naison argue that the story of hip hop's rise "does not have a happy ending"? How did hip hop, according to him, change? Do you agree with his assessment?

10. What solutions does Naison offer to revitalize troubled neighborhoods? Can you suggest any other ones?

Writing Tasks

1. Write an essay that discusses the history of your neighborhood and your own feelings about the current situation. If possible, interview someone who has lived in your neighborhood for quite some time about these changes.

2. Choose a hip hop song and discuss the message it conveys.

3. Research articles that defend and/or attack the value of hip hop as a musical genre & social influence. Take a stance in this debate that considers both perspectives.

Of My Friend Hector and My Achilles' Heel

Michael T. Kaufman

Michael T. Kaufman attended the City College of New York and Columbia University. In 1959, he began work as a copy boy at the *New York Times* and eventually became bureau chief in New Delhi, Ottawa, and Warsaw, Poland. This essay was published in the *New York Times* in 1992.

Pre-reading

Have you ever been falsely stereotyped?

This story is about prejudice and stupidity. My own.   1

It begins in 1945 when I was a seven-year-old living on the fifth floor of a tenement walkup on 107th Street between Columbus and Manhattan Avenues in New York City. The block was almost entirely Irish and Italian, and I believe my family was the only Jewish one around.

One day a Spanish-speaking family moved into one of the four apartments on our landing. They were the first Puerto Ricans I had met. They had a son who was about my age named Hector, and the two of us became friends. We played with toy soldiers and I particularly remember how, using rubber bands and wood from orange crates, we made toy pistols that shot off little squares we cut from old linoleum.

We visited each other's home and I know that at the time I liked Hector and I think he liked me. I may even have eaten my first avocado at his house.

About a year after we met, my family moved to another part of Man-   5
hattan's West Side and I did not see Hector again until I entered Booker T. Washington Junior High School as an eleven-year-old.

The class I was in was called 7SP-1; the SP was for special. Earlier, I recall, I had been in the IGC class, for "intellectually gifted children." The SP class was to complete the seventh, eighth and ninth grades in two years and almost all of us would then go to schools like Bronx Science, Stuyvesant or Music and Art, where admission was based on competitive exams. I knew I was in the SP class and the IGC class. I guess I also knew that other people were not.

Hector was not. He was in some other class, maybe even 7-2, the class that was held to be the next-brightest, or maybe 7-8. I remember I was happy to see him whenever we would meet, and sometimes we played punchball during lunch period. Mostly, of course, I stayed with my own classmates, with other Intellectually Gifted Children.

Sometimes children from other classes, those presumably not so intellectually gifted, would tease and taunt us. At such times I was particularly proud to have Hector as a friend. I assumed that he was tougher than I and my classmates and I guess I thought that if necessary he would come to my defense.

For high school, I went uptown to Bronx Science. Hector, I think, went downtown to Commerce. Sometimes I would see him in Riverside Park, where I played basketball and he worked out on the parallel bars. We would acknowledge each other, but by this time the conversations we held were perfunctory—sports, families, weather.

After I finished college, I would see him around the neighborhood 10 pushing a baby carriage. He was the first of my contemporaries to marry and to have a child.

A few years later, in the 60s, married and with children of my own, I was once more living on the West Side, working until late at night as a reporter. Some nights as I took the train home I would see Hector in the car. A few times we exchanged nods, but more often I would pretend that I didn't see him, and maybe he also pretended he didn't see me. Usually he would be wearing a knitted watch cap, and from that I deduced that he was probably working on the docks as a long-shoreman.

I remember quite distinctly how I would sit on the train and think about how strange and unfair fate had been with regard to the two of us who had once been playmates. Just because I had become an intellectually gifted adult or whatever and he had become a longshoreman or whatever, was that any reason for us to have been left with nothing to say to each other? I thought it was wrong and unfair, but I also thought that conversation would be a chore or a burden. That is pretty much what I thought about Hector, if I thought about him at all, until one Sunday in the mid-70s, when I read in the drama section of this newspaper that my childhood friend, Hector Elizondo, was replacing Peter Falk in the leading role in "The Prisoner of Second Avenue."

Since then, every time I have seen this versatile and acclaimed actor in movies or on television I have blushed for my assumptions. I have replayed the subway rides in my head and tried to fathom why my thoughts had led me where they did.

In retrospect it seems far more logical that the man I saw on the train, the man who had been my friend as a boy, was coming home from an Off Broadway theater or perhaps from a job as a waiter while taking acting classes. So why did I think he was a longshoreman? Was it just the cap? Could it be that his being Puerto Rican had something to do with it? Maybe that reinforced the stereotype I concocted, but it wasn't the root of it.

No, the foundation was laid when I was eleven, when I was in 7SP-1 15 and he was not, when I was in the IGC class and he was not.

I have not seen him since I recognized how I had idiotically kept tracking him for years and decades after the school system had tracked both of us. I wonder now if my experience was that unusual, whether social categories conveyed and absorbed before puberty do not generally tend to linger beyond middle age. And I wonder, too, that if they affected the behavior of someone like myself who had been placed on the upper track, how much more damaging it must have been for someone consigned to the lower.

I have at times thought of calling him, but kept from doing it because how exactly does one apologize for thoughts that were never expressed? And there was still the problem of what to say. "What have you been up to for the last forty years?" Or "Wow, was I wrong about you!" Or maybe just, "Want to come over and help me make a linoleum gun?"

Discussion Questions

1. What is the significance of Kaufman's title (refer to a book on Greek mythology if necessary).

2. Evaluate the effectiveness of Kaufman's opening sentences. Does his essay support his self-judgement?

3. What do you think of the academic "tracking" system Kaufman describes. Do you think this system is a part of a larger "tracking" system society imposes on young people?

4. Why is Kaufman "proud" to have Hector as a friend in Junior High School? What subsequent stereotypes enter Kaufman's mind as the years pass?

5. Why did the possibility that Hector was a professional actor never occur to Kaufman?

6. Can you think of how society stereotypes other groups of people? Who do you feel is responsible? What can be done to change misperceptions?

Writing Task

1. Write an essay in which you stereotyped another person only to find out later that your assumptions had been wrong or, conversely, write an essay in which someone falsely stereotyped you.

Tu Sabes?

Monique Ferrell

Monique Ferrell is a published poet and fiction writer who teaches English at CUNY. She has published her work in *Quarterly West, Puerto del Sol, Antioch Review,* and *North American Review,* among others. Her first volume of poetry, *Black Bloody Parts,* was published by CrossRoads Press in 2002.

¿Tú Sabes? A Story in Three Parts

One

Maybe she had it coming. Maybe she didn't. But for me, it was, quite frankly, the last straw. I had finally lost my ability to curb what I said to White women.   1

I think my anger started as a question mark in the middle of my stomach during my high school years—I wanted to know why White girls talked the way they did? How many times while attending the integrated, overly-populated, multicultural, and diverse McMillian High had I heard a group of fifteen year old young White girls walking by exclaiming at what could only be the very top of their lungs, "Ohmygod" as if it were one word? Hair bobbing at their shoulders, smiling, giggling, I wondered just how many of my great, great, great-grandmothers had waited on theirs. These White girls bothered me. They were intrusions in my neighborhood. They were foreigners and they spread themselves about, without care, fear, or restriction.

My high-school was supposed to be the embodiment of good New York City race relations. It was, on the surface, the culmination of Martin Luther King's dream. It held within its doors and classrooms the best and the brightest Black, White, Puerto Rican, Cuban, Dominican, Chinese, Korean, Jewish, Buddhist, Muslim, Atheist—you name it, we had it, teenage minds.

And it was set right in the middle of Harlem, New York.

Harlem. Struggling to remember itself Harlem. Last vestige of the   5
Harlem Renaissance—Harlem. The place where the Talented Tenth were cultivated and set forth upon the nation—Harlem. Poor, on the verge of gentrification, Harlem.

Reprinted with permission of Monique Ferrell.

My grandmother was ill with the whole concept. She never believed that the races should mix for any reason—especially not in Harlem. Not her home. The place where poor, disenfranchised, hopeful Blacks came to reside in droves, fleeing the segregated south. Harlem, where the streets were once so clean you could eat off the ground. Harlem, a neighborhood that once boasted of some of the most wealthy Black people in the country—whose night clubs were restricted from Black patrons and whose Black acts which played to sold out, standing room only, White audiences every night had to enter through back stage doors or through kitchens past food and garbage.

"Not Harlem," my grandmother said when talk began to spread about the construction of the school.

"First the kids will come, and then their parents will follow. They'll drop their kids off. First it will be quickly, stopping long enough to open the car doors to let the kid out. Then, you mark my words, they'll slow those cars down and start looking at what Black people left behind. Empty brownstones, abandoned store-fronts, vacant lots. They'll shake their heads and laugh at us because we're always leaving things of value behind. And they'll buy up everything in sight and drive up the property values. Pretty soon, those of us who managed to hold on to our houses won't be able to take two breaths without exhaling on someone White. And people who can only afford to rent here will have to move, because their new White landlords will hike up the rents and decent families will have to move to real shit-holes."

My grandmother was right. You'd hardly recognize Harlem now. More and more White faces are among my neighbors. More white faces are coming out of the subways. 125th Street is all lit up like Times Square. Posh hotels are breaking ground.

One day, I actually watched my grandmother chase off a White couple 10 with a mop when they returned a third time to make an offer on her home. Her home, where she and my grandfather had raised three children. They thought it a compliment, she thought it a grave insult. It was, after all, her home. She could mark every pivotal moment of her life and our lives with her by each brick of that house. And they wanted to buy it. It was like buying her, and Nana wasn't for sale.

The major insult was when my parents, her son, sent me to that very high school. She was convinced that my mother had turned my father into what she called a "new breed Negro," a Black man who was more concerned with being an American than with being Black.

Nana tolerated the school because she loved me. And she wanted me to have the best. And if the school was the best then she wanted me to have that. Even if it came with White people. "You watch them," she told me. And I did.

Our lives are so different, Whites and Blacks. It seemed as if the school had only succeeded in fleshing out how different we were from one another. And no where did I feel my *otherness* more sharply than with White girls.

The conversations of my Black contemporaries always seemed less-joyous than that of the White girls around us. I think we laughed, but I don't believe we were ever truly happy. We walked around poking fun at one another. It was like we were always playing some form of the dozens. You had to talk about somebody else's momma before someone got to your momma, your poor house, or your daddy who wasn't living in your house. There were never any racial or cultural biases at our school. All of the colors of the rainbow learned alongside each other. Ate along side of one another but never understood each other.

I left high school with a diploma in one hand and that overpowering   15
question mark centered in my belly.

I wish that I could say my confusion about Whites subsided when I got to college. But, all six years of undergraduate and graduate study in a small Midwestern college-town did was give me a specific face on whom to place my rage.

Once in college the question mark about White people — White women in particular — formed itself into a fisherman's knot, tightly coiled and bloody.

I surveyed my college campus daily and wondered why so many young White women were so interested in dating the Black men at our school — especially if they were on the basketball, baseball, or football teams? And, furthermore, why were these same Black men so interested in dating them right back? My contemporaries and I would gather to-gether on our so-called girl's nights and hate these women with a voodoo intensity.

We young Black women on campus eyed Rodney Clark, our Heisman potential Union State quarterback, through tight pupiled slits when he rode by in Mindy Conner's Lexus. He drove that car through our mid-western town with his chest puffed out. When his homeboys Mark and Paul (and we know their names because unlike Rodney they chased every Black woman on campus) arrived from Detroit, he drove them around in it too. In fact, we never saw Mindy in *her* car. Mindy's parents got wind of it, and Mindy didn't return the following fall semester.

Rodney found another flaxen-haired beauty. It was easy for him to do   20
so because there was another one waiting to take her place. These were the options for Black men on any college campus in America, we outcasts proclaimed. I wondered now about the young Black men I'd gone to high school with. Was this what they wanted? All the time had they been

observing white girls, coveting them, studying, just waiting for the opportunity to draw these women into their beds? Had dating us simply been the prelude to what they really wanted?

The Black women on campus saw ourselves as little more than women who would always have to get perms in order for our hair to lay about our shoulders, provided we were not descended from Blacks with the mythical wandering "Indian" in our families—which always explained our so-called good hair and light skin. We thought of ourselves as second rate, second-class, second best; so, by the time we returned to our respective hometowns and cities, ventured into the honest-to-god working world, we had major attitude problems. I returned home to Harlem after graduate school, moved into the Harlem brownstone that Nana willed me, and settled into my newly integrated Harlem neighborhood.

Although educated, beautiful—according to some—and extremely proficient at my job, behind the doors of my office I believed the world was out to get me. And I made damn sure that no one was going to get to me, get by me, or get over on me without a battle.

I watched out for little comments, looking for the slightest racist overtone. No one was safe. When someone, namely a White woman, admired my braids at work and asked how I cared for them, I launched into a ten minute diatribe about how Black women cared for their hair and person just like any White person, like any human being who cared about their personal grooming.

When I took my braids out, one of the Black women in my office noticed and asked, "Why did you have your hair braided? You have good hair." I shot her a look and motioned her into another part of the office.

"Don't ever ask me that kind of question again," I told her. "Are we on some kind of a plantation, or some backward Jim Crow town in country Bama' still talking about good hair and bad hair? And don't ever say no shit like that in front of White people again." And I left her standing there with her mouth open.

25

When the company policies were handed down about diversity and Affirmative Action, I waited like a lion in the bush for someone to say just one ignorant thing. I was prepared to give them the verbal lynching of a lifetime.

When promotions were given out, I watched to see who got promoted, why they were getting promoted and how many were people of color. I took stellar notes, with dates, saved every memo—waiting for the time I ever felt it necessary to file a class action lawsuit on the grounds of racial discrimination.

Each day I began to resent White women a little bit more. I resented the fact that the majority of them hadn't had to scrape and scuffle to get through college. I resented the fact that the majority of their parents were still married. Never did I hear the phrase, "my baby's daddy" ever exit their thin pouty lips. I hated the way they stood in the bathrooms and regarded the tans they'd achieved during the course of long weekends. I hated their big ass engagement rings. I hated the fact that the majority of the Black men in my office dated White women or had very light skinned girlfriends.

Most of all I hated the contempt these feelings made me feel for my own race and my own body and self worth and that I lived with all of this inside of me—in silence. They never knew how much their presence distracted me. All I could think of was that if the experience of Black people was a road to travel upon—my people still hadn't come very far and the spaces between our strides were getting shorter and shorter, dragging us further and further behind.

But of all the things I detested—I hated the way White women flipped   30
their hair over their shoulders. I began to see it as little more than a passive aggressive way of telling someone to go fuck themselves. Occasionally, I take the subway to work because parking is problematic in a city like New York. Inevitably, once I hit the subway platform—and I've managed to carve out an unobtrusive niche of space for myself—some White woman with a latté in one hand, and an oversized pocket book draped over her shoulders, flicks her damn hair, which always manages to graze my face, my coat, my space. Never once has one of the hussies ever said excuse me or acknowledged my presence.

At work, I ate lunch with women like these subway bandits, worked on projects with these women. I even talked about the pit-falls of dating with these women. While, silently, deep within myself, wanting to grab one of those wenches and shave her bald.

The Fisherman's knot in my stomach grew teeth.

Just as my grandmother had been invaded in her home, her Harlem, I made it my business to invade the spaces where they go. Park and Madison Avenue shops and boutiques became my second homes. These are the places many Black women never even dream of shopping in. I watched these women, with their friends, sisters and daughters, watched their eyes wonder at each other silently signaling each other with the, "I wonder how she can afford to shop here looks."

"Yes bitches," I said in my mind, "I can shop here too. I'm not dating Puff Daddy. My man is not a rapper. I am not financing this shopping excursion with the money Maury Povich pays me to keep coming on his show to find my baby's daddy. I didn't inherit my money, or get it from my husband. It's my money. I work for it. Invest it. And I'm going to stand in line next to you and lay down my platinum, my silver, my gold card—on the counter right next to yours."

Their part of the city became my city. It was my revenge. I felt new and   35
whole. And no other store gave me that sense of fulfillment like Ellington's on Fifth Avenue in Manhattan.

So when that White woman stepped up alongside me while I was paying for my purchases—disregarded my presence and began to ask the
salesperson a series of questions which distracted her from waiting on me
all while flipping her shoulder length strawberry-blond hair, all hell broke
loose: I went off.

"Are you out of your mind?" I said. "Do you not see me standing here?
Have I suddenly become transparent? Am I lacking a solid form? Or are
you seeing what you want to see, what so many of you White women see
when you look at us—nothing?"

"Listen," she said. "I just wanted . . ."

"Yes, I know what you wanted. You just wanted what you wanted and
you wanted it when you wanted it. But maybe, just maybe, what I wanted
was to come into this store, pick out my merchandise without being followed, pay for it and leave without having someone interrupt my process
for ten minutes—which incidentally is how long you've been talking to
the salesperson who was waiting on me—first. But forget me right? All
of you are exactly the same—you have Entitlement Syndrome. I think it's
in your damn blood. You've had so many of my people taking care of
your people's needs hand and foot, serving as your nannies, mammies,
and Aunt Jemimas that a Black woman in a fur coat is just a nigger who
needs a shave on her way to her job as a maid, huh? Well, I'm not a maid,
I am standing here, and if you ask this saleswoman one more question,
both you and I are going to create another milestone in the fight for civil
rights." You funky White bitch. But I thought that to myself because
that's what someone like her would expect me to say. She'd expect me to
be wild, Black, loud, and uncouth.

She just stood there in utter shock and moved aside. The saleswoman   40
continued to ring up my purchases, her eyes as wide as saucers. I could
tell she had mentally recorded the entire conversation for audio playback
with friends tonight. After all, this *was* Ellington's on Fifth Avenue. The
starting rate for any garment was $500 dollars and one simply does not
have this caliber of conversation in *this* store. The saleswoman almost
peed on herself; it was just too good. I turned around after paying for my
purchases and saw that the line was comprised of six other women. They
too were shocked. I interpreted a few of the looks as, "See this is why we
don't like for *you people* to shop here."

Some just avoided me for fear I might say, "And as for you . . ." But what
struck me most was that there was a young Hispanic woman there who just
looked at me as if she pitied me. I thought at least she'd understand. But

since she didn't, "Fuck her too," I thought to myself. Some of them could blend in with White America if they wanted to and, therefore, were viable candidates for the enemy list.

I didn't walk out of the store immediately. I waited for that white woman to finish with her shopping. I wanted to walk out of that store with her — side by side.

Two

I wasn't really scared. She wasn't an animal. I don't think Black people are animals or naturally overly-aggressive. But it did give me pause to see that she'd actually waited around for me to finish my purchases. She just walked out of the store at the same time I did. I thought she'd turn and say something else. But I think the point was that we were equals and to show me her Forrest green BMW.

It was the same make and model as mine and we'd parked not more than two parking meters apart, and as hard as it is to find parking around here, it was a damn weird coincidence. I thought maybe I should try to say something, but I decided against it. I just got in and started the car.

If I had been with any of my White friends they would have given me   45 shit. They would say that I should have ignored her and just continued to ask the sales person what I wanted to. They would have said that Black women are notorious, angry bullies. One might have suggested that I call her a Black bitch and signal security. But I guess I know better than that, because my very best friend in the world of ten years is named Cheryl Matthews and she is a Black woman.

Cheryl and I met at *The Bridal Shop* on Fifth Avenue, a few doors down from Ellington's, the year we both got engaged and were planning our weddings. It turned out that our orders had never been made. The owners of the shop were trying to bend over backwards to accommodate us. But Cheryl, a brilliant attorney, started talking about suing, consumer laws, and breach of contract. I just started to cry, because like Cheryl, my wedding was in three weeks and I had no dress for me or dresses for my wedding party.

The owner said that he could put together a quickly fashioned dress for one of us but not both. Cheryl, God bless her heart, said, "Look girl, you and I are about the same size. Our weddings are a week apart, we'll share the damn dress and then we're going to take this wedding pimp to court — I'll draft the paper work myself. Stop crying."

We've been best friends ever since. We even went to one another's weddings. Our husbands liked each other relatively well, but we, quite frankly, are inseparable.

But I have to admit, while I am not a card carrying racist or separatist, if it had not been for that moment I would never have dared to enter into a friendship with a Black woman. Because while Cheryl is my best friend—she is my *only* Black friend—and my White friends, especially those I've known for years do not often get or appreciate her presence. I see Black women everyday, on trains, in the streets, at work. While they occupy the same city and state I live in, I feel as if they're aliens. As much as this city blends all kinds of people together, our worlds rarely collide. We, all of us, live in the state of New York, but White people live upstate, or in the heart of Manhattan, like myself. I grew up on West 82nd Street. Black people live in places like Harlem and Brooklyn. Asian people live in China Town and Hispanic people live in the Bronx and somewhere called Spanish Harlem, a place I've never even seen.

My family has always lived a different and distinctive life from any   50
people of color. I don't think they see them as lazy louts. I don't think they see them at all. Moreso, they regard them as nonentities and, quite frankly, are uncomfortable in their presence. We summered where there were only other White families. I went to all White prep schools on the East Side of Manhattan and the private college I went to had only a very small population of Black and brown faces. When I look back on it, I have to acknowledge the fact that both of my parents were professional people and they had to have worked with someone who didn't look like us—but never did these so called "others" cross our doorstep. Even our maids were White.

It took years before they began to regard Cheryl's presence—they were shocked to know that I'd wear a dress after she'd worn it. In the second year of our friendship, my father asked me if I'd ever actually seen her law degree from Princeton because, "It's nothing against Cheryl, hon, but people do tend to fudge these things to bolster their own self importance. Especially when they befriend someone who has so much," he said.

You should have seen his face when Cheryl invited my family to share Thanksgiving with her and her husband Eli, who happens to be an investigative reporter. On a tour of their two-story townhouse in Long Island, Cheryl showed my father their den, where, proudly displayed, were both her Princeton Bachelors and Jurist Doctorate, various law journals in which she was published—and a wonderfully framed eight by ten photograph of Cheryl shaking hands with President Bill Clinton. Apparently, she'd done some work for the White House.

"Well, Jesus Christ Cheryl. These are some important accomplishments," my father said surprisingly—almost a little too surprised if you asked me. Like they were all forgeries.

"They're just things, Mr. Dodson. They are moments in my life. They do not solely define me any more than growing up in one the poorest neighborhoods in the country did. How I treat people, well that's all that really matters."

That's how Cheryl handled people. But I think while my parents be-   55
gan to take stock of Cheryl in new way, she began to see them in a new way too—and I have a feeling that it was with the same disdain, that the woman in the Ellington's regarded me with—a huge sweeping brush stroke which etched out the words that all White people were inevitably the same and would rather a world without any color at all—especially if it had arms, legs, a mind, and could talk back.

From time to time I began to share Cheryl's accomplishments with my parents. I thought I'd damn near pass out when my mother said one day, "That Cheryl, she's a good one."

I was too afraid to ask what she'd meant—and I began to fear other things as well. Such as, if I was looking at my parents differently, and Cheryl was looking at my parents differently, how was she looking at me, and could she tell that as much as I loved her, there were some things about her people that I didn't get?

You see, I don't get why that woman just embarrassed the both of us by making a scene. In *my* world, we don't act like that. You keep it to yourself and find ways or people who can deal with the problem or the problematic individual later. A scene is regarded as uncouth, especially in a place of that stature.

While Cheryl never makes a scene, she does not, as she calls it, "bite her tongue." And while Cheryl wasn't a stereotype or a caricature of a Black person in my daily walk with life, I see so many that are. In a sub-way, I once watched a Black woman belittle a booth clerk because she said he was rude and had short-changed her. Whether or not he was rude or had short-changed her was not the point—she was acting like an ass. She went into this prolonged monologue about White people thinking they were smarter than everyone else was. She yelled and screamed, and told the young man she was old enough to be his mother and she would, "break her foot off in his ass." I'd honestly never heard an expression like that before.

Black people are also very loud. Everywhere, all of the time. In the   60
subway, in the streets, on their cell phones, in stores, on television, in their music, even the way they dress. They are always loud and appear to have little sense of boundaries or propriety. There are too many people in this city for them to be so loud and so unobtrusive all of the time. I know this city has five boroughs and there appears to be enough space for everyone, but I half suspect that White people crowd Manhattan and most New York

suburban neighborhoods to get away from Blacks and other people like them.

Cheryl once took me to her old neighborhood in Brooklyn called Bed-Sty. All of the Black women I saw walking the streets looked so angry. Let's not even begin to talk about their gaudy outfits. All of the men were stereotypical homeboys and had nothing but gold in their mouths and something that Cheryl referred to as "plantinum fronts." Why in the hell would anyone want platinum in anything other than a place setting? On every corner we walked to there were groups of young Black men standing there talking—loudly. All I kept thinking was, "Why are they here? Don't they have any other place to be? Don't they understand how intimidating it is to see groups of men standing on a corner, in front of a building or a neighborhood store?"

I looked at the property. Gorgeous hundred-year-old brownstones in   65
disrepair, just ruined. Even if someone managed to take care of their property, it made little difference because the house next to it, or on either side of it, was always in shambles.

Why do they do this to themselves? Everything can't be White people's fault all of the time. This was a Black neighborhood.

Black people are always screaming about being Black, and keeping neighborhoods Black. There wasn't a White person in sight and look what they had done to themselves.

I over-heard some of the most ignorant conversations in my entire life, consisting of the poorest usage of diction and grammar, "know what I'm saying, Nigga?" "Naw man, you know how people be trippin' over shit."

For a brief moment I understood what my mother meant about Cheryl being a "good one." And I hated myself for it. But here I am having encountered the quintessential stereotypical Black woman and I'm wondering why can't I say that the woman was out of line and that I don't get Black people, the same way that Black woman was clearly saying she didn't get White people.

I don't get baby's daddies. I don't get Black people calling each other niggers and then wanting to riot when someone outside of the race uses the word. I don't get so called Black English and I don't think it should be allowed or encouraged. I don't get that poor Black people are too poor to buy food, houses, cars or provide a better education for their children, but they can buy them clothing they cannot pronounce with labels they cannot read—in order to live what Cheryl refers to as Ghetto Fabulous. I don't get Al Sharpton—I think he's a monster and a jerk and Black people can certainly do better in terms of a leader and role model.

But am I a racist?

Can I ever say these things to Cheryl? Will I one day lose my friend whom I love so very much? Can I ask her all of the things that lay on my heart? Like does she trust in our friendship or am I just another White monster waiting to strike?

I know I'll never ask. I pray she's never put in a position where she'll   70
have to tell me. Because I don't want to know.

Three

Who is worse: a White woman with money or a Black woman who was once poor coming into money? I ask myself this question everyday. I am an assistant to Madelyn Murray and Corrin Moore, White and Black respectively, the only female partners at the most prestigious law firm in the country. And after witnessing the foolishness I just saw at Ellington's, namely a Black woman paying for her purchases verbally ripping into the White woman who interrupted her process asking ridiculous question after ridiculous question, all the while inconsiderately holding up the line in Ellington's, the most expensive store to shop in this city, I have come to a few conclusions: (a) I now know how an actual argument might sound like between Madelyn and Corrin, (b) I have come to detest women who have too much education and too much money, and (c) all of this is too much for me to digest and more than I wish to think about during this ride on this hot ass cross-town bus.

This it what people without cars in the city do. We take Mass Transit because there are no alternatives. People like those two, who got into their expensive cars, fail to realize there are other, *other* people living, dying, and barely surviving in New York.

The Black woman *was* in the right though. She *had* been there first and it *was* her turn. The White woman didn't seem to care that the sales person was talking to someone else or that there were six other women in line. And my god, Ms. Dolce and Gabana did flick her blonde hair in the way that White women do as if to say, "Enough about me. What do you think about me?"

I did see the floor workers observing her Royal Blackness as she shopped, because they did the same thing to me—brown people are apparently a hazard in shops that are of the upper echelon. I guess their idea was that the well-to-do Black woman had come in to stuff her twenty thousand dollar flawless mink with silk blouses. Ignorance is bliss, especially when it's an excuse for racism.

But what peeved me was that she had to make a scene. They always   75
do. They always have to launch into a loud, embarrassing, ignorant monologue about the endless abuses that Blacks have suffered at the

hands of Whites—as if nobody else on planet Earth has ever had to deal with White people and the bullshit that sometimes comes with them. What she should have done was simply say, "Excuse me miss, but the sales person was waiting on me. I am nearly done. Can you wait until I have completed my purchase?" And then she should have turned her back and went on with her transaction.

But no—it had to be her way and now all of the White women present will have internal conversations with themselves.

"You see how they act?" They'll say to themselves. "Being able to shop in stores of this quality certainly doesn't imply breeding," they'll say. Tonight and in future conversations this whole process will become an anecdote over dinner at some $100 a plate restaurant. They will remember this moment when they go into their voting booths. They'll click the button for the party who vows to keep the niggers and the spics on the other side of town. They'll use it to continue talking like shit to their maids Esmerelda, Juanita and Luz—women who look just like me.

And then her Royal Blackness looked at me, as if I'm supposed to validate her experience. Well who in the hell is going to validate mine? Or that of the sales woman who I thought was White, who leaned into me once it was time to ring up my purchase, saying in Spanish, "Do you get those two? Rich and richer. And does either one care about the fact that I stand on my feet for ten hours each day having to listen to wealthy people ask me ridiculous questions and harass me about sizes and price tags that I can't change. It is the same everyday. Meanwhile, even with the 30% employee discount I still can't afford to shop here. My co-workers don't even know that I'm Cuban. Do you think that I could work here if they didn't think I was white? It's all of them against you and I. You understand me? Tu Sabes?"

And I did. I shook my head in agreement and let her deal with the Question Queen, who, after all of the foolishness she started by being rude, decided not to shop.

I noticed the Black woman seemed to be waiting for her, my curiosity 80 made me wait to see how this would play out. They walked out of the store, two true ice queens in minks, side by side in silence.

What bums me is that both of these obviously wealthy women both drove off in identical BMWs and I got on a bus, complete with a $450 purchase that I'd made for one of the women that I work for during company time when I've got a stack of paperwork that needs to be done.

One of the great ladies needed this silk blouse for a cocktail party later on this evening and she just had to have it—and I just had to get it for her.

"Don't worry about the paperwork," Corrin said. "Handle it later. Oh come on, you can multi-task. I'd do it myself, but I've got a meeting."

Meanwhile, she's got another meeting tomorrow. I ought to know because the paperwork that needs to be filed is sitting on my desk, and if it's not completed—silk blouse or not, that's my Puerto Rican ass.

They always do this to me—expect more of me than they do of them-   85
selves. It's like I'm paying dues to belong to some future women's club that is only attainable after you've put up with shit from men and shit from women who've gone through the process—attained some form of power.

Madelyn asks me questions and then doesn't wait for a reply. She corrects my mistakes on drafts of legal briefs and says, "Oh don't worry about it. Sometimes that happens with native Spanish speakers." I have told this woman at least thirty times during the two years I've worked for them that English is my first language, that I was born in Queens, New York, have always been an A student and that I speak two other languages in addition to English and neither one of them is Spanish. I am ashamed to say that while I understand Spanish I don't speak it, because my parents, who are native to Puerto Rico, said that it was a vulgar language and was of no importance in America. In our Woodside neighborhood, I marveled at the beautiful ease of the other families calling to one another in Spanish. It felt secretive, warm and embracing. My parents never let me socialize with the children of these families. "You must have White friends because it is a White world," my father said. Each day, he and my mother ushered me off to a nearly all White prep school. They nearly went into hock trying to pay the tuition in order to send me there. I speak the Queens' English, yet it never occurs to Madelyn that the incorrect word on the document was simply a typo.

What Corrin doesn't know is that Madelyn believes she is too aggressive, probably a lesbian, brags too much about what she has and finds her dreadlocks unprofessional and uncomfortable to look at. She also thinks that Corrin is a know-it-all and that her clothes accentuate her ass too much.

And what Madelyn doesn't know is that when she says something Corrin believes to be absurd, Corrin mouths the phrase, "White Women" at me and rolls her eyes. She also believes that Madelyn slept with one of the partners in order to become a partner. In short, she thinks Madelyn is a "blond whore who had better marry a wealthy man who dies quickly."

And what the two of them know about me—could fit in the one cup of a bra for women with small breasts.

For example, neither one of them know that I've been going to law   90
school at night. They do not know that I graduated Magna Cum Laude from an Ivy League university and was the only Hispanic woman to complete the Baccalaureate program in my discipline in ten years.

They do not know that I lived with my parents until I was twenty-five. They do not know that my mother, who still washes clothes by hand on a scrub board in a big tub because only a lazy American woman would let a machine or another woman wash her private things—brought my laundry into my room, opened my draws, and found condoms and my birth control pills among my belongings. Because she is a slave to Catholicism and to my tyrant of a father, she both told and showed him what she'd found. When I returned that evening, my father and mother were waiting for me. My father threw the pills in my face, called me whore, and told me to leave his house. I haven't been back. I haven't spoken to them either. It's been well over a year. And the absurdity of it all is that they wanted their daughter to be smart, Americanized, above and beyond the other Puerto-Ricans, but they still wanted me to be a stereotypical Hispanic virgin, who cooks for her man, and gives him strong sons who grow up not to be homosexuals.

These two women do know that I moved in with my boyfriend as a result of my unfortunate dislocation and that I am engaged. But suddenly, this man, who called my father a "Machismo asshole who needed to step into the 21st century," is now mad at me because I told him I do not wish to take his name when we get married and that any child we have should have both of our names.

He has informed me that I am selfish and destroying the concept of what it means to be a unified family. Moreover, he asked me, "How is anybody going to know whether or not you're a married woman if you don't take my name?"

"The same way someone will know whether or not you're a married man. I'll tell them or they'll look at my ring" I said, incredulously.

"It's not the same," he said. 95

And now we're at an impasse. Because if this is just the tip of his selfish iceberg, I am not marrying this man. I lived with a man like this for 25 years. I watched him insult my mother, and turn her into an enemy of women everywhere. I watched him treat my sisters and me like second class citizens who washed, cooked and cleaned, while my brothers were treated like little Latin kings.

I watched men like him give us confession, and tell us that we must bare the heavy load of our sexist, abrasive men as the virgin bore the weight of her own cross.

These women, women like the two at Ellington's, know nothing of what it means to hear CNN, MSNBC and the like, discuss how Hispanics are now the largest so-called minority in America, but find out that this means so little when it breaks down to equal protection under the law, the availability of jobs, obtaining degrees, or economics.

They don't see that just as men trod White women underfoot, and
White women trod Black women underfoot—I am little more than the
footstool upon which they rest their newly-emancipated feet.

And I have nothing but time to think these thoughts on crowded city   100
buses carrying me and my thoughts, from work to school, on errands for
bosses, and home again. Home, where the rent costs me half of my
monthly salary. A cramped, one bedroom, Manhattan apartment whose
windows I crack each night listening for voices from across rivers—and
maybe even oceans wanting, waiting for someone to understand me.

Discussion Questions

1. Who is the narrator of part one? Why is she "so bothered" by white women?
   How does she think they are different from her own people?

2. What concerns does the first narrator's grandmother have regarding her
   Harlem neighborhood ? What is this neighborhood like today?

3. How does the narrator of part one try to compensate for her racial resentment? What might be a better way of solving her issues?

4. Define "Entitlement Syndrome." In your view, does it actually exist?

5. Is the narrator of part two any more enlightened than the narrator of part
   one? Would you call either one a "racist"?

6. How do the white friends of the narrator in part two view her relationship
   with Cheryl? What is the narrator's concern about her "friend"?

7. What is the third narrator's most prominent complaint about both the white
   and black narrators? How valid are her concerns?

8. How does the fact that the third narrator is Cuban affect how she thinks as
   well as how she is viewed by others? Give examples from the text.

Writing Tasks

1. Do you agree with the statement that "as much as this city blends all
   kinds of people together, [their] worlds rarely collide"?

2. How do you see race relations faring in high school and college today. Is
   segregation/prejudice a thing of the past? If not, what might bring "the culmination of Martin Luther's King's dream" to fruition?

3. Do you think that it's ever acceptable for different ethnic or cultural groups to live part of their lives separate from the mainstream? Explain.

4. This story uses the "N"-word on occasion. Look up the debate regarding the use of this word. Do you feel young people have the right to use it or should it be banned?

5. Hispanics are now the largest so-called minority in America. Is this an advantage or a disadvantage? Explain.

Making Connections

1. Based on your reading of Mark Naison, Nicky Cruz, and Mark Berkey-Gerard, what seems to up the central causes of violence in youth today? How should society address this issue?

2. Compare "Prologue to *Invisible Man*" to "Into the Pit." How is the theme of invisibility developed in each? What solutions and/or warnings does each provide?

3. Compare Michael T. Kaufman's essay to Monique Ferrell's "Tu Sabes?" and Ralph Ellison's "Prologue." How is stereotyping presented in each of the pieces.

4. Watch the recent academy-award winning film *Crash* (2005). What does this film and your readings say about prejudice in America today?

CHAPTER 6

Current Issues

"Pro-immigrant Rally Crossing the Brooklyn Bridge in 2007"
© Seth Wenig/Reuters CORBIS

The experiment is how close can rich and poor live before the fabric completely falls apart? How close can you put ethnic groups that don't like one another much? How much can you promise people about a rich and privileged future, and then not be able to deliver before they rise up and say enough? And the answer here, over and over and over again, has been that the fabric becomes tattered, that sometimes the fabric even becomes torn, but the fabric survives.

Anna Quindlen, from *New York: A Documentary Film*

Current Issues

In an article entitled "Ask Not What They'd Do for Your City" that appeared in the *New York Times* during the 2004 Presidential election campaigns, Joyce Purnick reported on how ten candidates met for a debate in New York City and discussed issues ranging from health care to tax policy to the war on terrorism. To her surprise, Purnick noted that there was no discussion whatsoever about urban America even though the candidates were just blocks from Ground Zero. Not one mention, for example, of federal spending for buses and subways compared to highways. Not one mention of subsidized housing. No discussion of homelessness, welfare, urban education, nor the political rights of immigrants (legal or otherwise), a large percentage of whom settle in urban centers. For Purnick, the lack of discussion of urban issues in our largest city shows just how far they have been pushed onto the margins of America's national consciousness.

Beginning with Mayor Michael Bloomberg's, "State of the City" address, this section redirects attention onto issues currently in the forefront of city life. It allows you to become engaged in debates concerning global warming, gentrification, crime, public transportation, urban development, and other issues and encourages you to further examine causes and solutions. The majority of these selections come from an online website called Gothamgazette.com, which offers numerous articles on a wide array of urban issues. We encourage you to visit this site, which has links to other local and national publications, to explore topics and discussions beyond the scope of this chapter. Following the lead of Aaron Barlow, we also encourage you to visit web logs, or blogs, of thoughtful citizen journalists. Better yet, create your own!

State of the City Address 2007

Mayor Michael Bloomberg

Michael Bloomberg studied at Johns Hopkins Univ. (B.S., 1964) and Harvard Business School (M.B.A., 1966). Rising quickly in the world of finance, he became a partner at Salomon Brothers, but in 1981, after a merger, he was fired. Anticipating growing needs for business information, he used his $10 million severance to start a financial data and communications company, Bloomberg L.P. The company grew rapidly into a huge multifaceted enterprise that provides accurate real-time financial and business data as well as historical data and analysis and electronic communications and produces television and radio programs. Bloomberg himself became a multibillionaire. In 2001, running as a Republican and spending record-breaking amounts of his own money on the campaign, Bloomberg was elected to succeed Rudolph Giuliani as New York's mayor. He was reelected in 2005.

January 17, 2007

The following is the text of Mayor Bloomberg's State of the City Address as prepared at New York City College of Technology in Brooklyn:

Marty Markowitz, and a marching band, as they say in Brooklyn, Fuhgeddaboutit!

How about those Brooklyn Steppers!

Thank you, Marty, for those very kind words, and for welcoming us here to the New York City College of Technology. I also want to thank Dr. Russell Hotzler, the President of City Tech, for hosting us.

Of course, being a gracious host comes naturally at this school, which has one of the finest hospitality management programs in the nation. That includes outstanding training in the culinary arts and and I can vouch for that first hand. One of City Tech's current students happens to be the most important man at Gracie Mansion, the executive chef, Feliberto Estevez.

I think I get to eat his final exam, so I hope he does well.

Speaker Quinn, a true partner in government, members of the Council, Comptroller Thompson, Public Advocate Gotbaum, Borough presidents, distinguished guests, my fellow New Yorkers.

State of the City Address by Mayor Michael Bloomberg January 17, 2007

Last year, we began a new term and promised that we would come out of the gate stronger than ever. I think it's safe to say, we've blazed through the first year at a record pace. Behind me, you see a visual record showing the progress of the year just passed, and the promise of the years ahead.

Much Went Right in 2006

During 2006, so much went right throughout this great city, even if that Subway Series I promised somehow slipped through our grasp. In 2006, unemployment hit an all-time low, while our bond rating hit an all-time high. Our population surged to new heights (8.2 million and counting) and we hosted a record number of visitors (44 million). We drove crime to historic lows and made our streets their cleanest ever. We won our campaign to convince the State to pay its share of our historic school construction plan.

And all across New York from the Freedom Tower rising in Lower Manhattan to the new Yankees and Mets stadiums in the Bronx and Queens, to the new rail link at Howland Hook on Staten Island, to right here in Brooklyn, where from East New York to the East River, new homes are going up and new businesses are opening. The evidence is all around us. This is a great time for New York, an encouraging, optimistic time. And our spirits have been lifted higher still by the special guests whom I'm honored to introduce now.

Heroic New Yorkers

First please join me in recognizing someone whose service to our nation fills us with pride: Marine Captain Ray Lopes. Born on Staten Island now a Manhattan resident and awarded the Purple Heart for his service to our nation in Iraq. Thank you, Ray, on behalf of 8.2 million New Yorkers.

I'm also proud to share the stage with some other exceptionally brave New Yorkers: Two winners of the Sanitation Departments Gold Medal of Honor. They rescued a little Borough Park girl who had been struck by a van by actually lifting the van off of her with their bare hands.

Please welcome men who are truly our Strongest: Ralph Cimmino and John Talmadge. Three weeks ago, our next special guest was off-duty and shopping with his family when a pair of armed bank robbers tried to steal his car for their getaway. They picked the wrong guy. He fought them off and despite being wounded, chased them down. He's definitely one of New York's Finest: Officer John Lopez!

Next, a man who captured the attention of the world last month demonstrating once more the compassion and bravery of New Yorkers. A guy who today barely needs an introduction. The Harlem superhero: Wesley Autrey!

And you know, heroism comes in all forms, as our final guest shows. He gashed a tendon while helping apprehend a criminal here in Brooklyn last week and he is fresh out of the hospital. But he told us he wouldn't miss the State of the City address for anything. Please welcome one great German shepherd Ranger of the NYPD's K-9 unit and his handler, Officer Neal Campbell.

Just take a look at these amazing New Yorkers!

How can you not feel that New York's future is bright with promise and that the State of our City is alive with hope. Now fueled by the energy of New Yorkers like these, we are ready to take the next strong and confident steps forward to reach our goals.

The Year Ahead

In the year ahead, we'll make the long-term investments, and pioneer the innovations, that will ensure New York's future, and our continued national and international leadership. We'll make them in reforming our schools, growing our economy for all New Yorkers, making the safest big city even safer, and improving the efficiency of our government.

All those investments and innovations will mobilize the ideas and energy of the people of New York City empowering everyday New Yorkers to step forward to take fuller control of their destinies and to pass on to our children a city even greater than it is today.

Education

I've always said that our first priority is improving education, so let me start by describing further dramatic reforms to our public schools. Four years ago this week on Martin Luther King Junior's birthday in 2003, we spelled out our plan to uphold a basic and fundamental civil right: The right to a quality education.

Under the old Board of Ed, children were abandoned by people who too often put favoritism and patronage first. We've come a long way in leaving those bad old days behind, and believe me—we're not going back. Not ever!

Because the progress we've made is strong and clear: On-time graduation rates are now the highest they've been in more than 20 years reading and math test scores have risen substantially. Our Black and Hispanic students are closing the racial and ethnic performance gap that has long been the shame of our school system. Those successes are evident in schools like the International High School in Prospect Heights—one of the 332 schools in our Empowerment Schools Initiative.

I'm happy to say we have one special student from that school with us today. Chime Dolma. She fled political persecution in her native Tibet four years ago and started school for the first time ever when she arrived here at age 13.

Now a junior, she is an 'A' student, a school leader and her principal says that she is "as college-bound as it gets." I'd like to ask her to stand, along with her principal, Alexandra Anormaliza, and one of her teachers, Danny Walsh. Congratulations to all of you and keep up the good work!

We've come a long way in our schools but we've still got a long way to go. Because even today more than half of Black and Hispanic students still do not perform at grade-level standards and only one in four Black or Hispanic students now graduates with a Regents degree. If that's not reversed, too many of our children will face dead-end futures in a highly competitive global economy.

We cannot let that happen.

During our first term, we brought stability, accountability, and standards to a school system where they were sorely lacking. With this strong foundation now laid, we can take the next steps forward, creating great schools where all students can succeed. That means encouraging and expecting leadership, accountability, and empowerment to thrive at the school level.

And now, four fundamental reforms that we'll launch this year will take us toward that goal: First, we'll empower school principals to be true leaders. Second, we'll hold schools publicly accountable for student progress. Third, we'll reform our system of teacher tenure. And fourth, we'll bring fairness to our school funding system. Let me briefly discuss each.

As to empowering principals, we've always known that great principals make great schools. But until now, we haven't always given them the full authority they need in order to lead. Today, important decisions about, for example, teacher professional development, get made for principals by regional offices — whether the principals like it or not.

But beginning this year, principals will have the power to make such choices themselves. No one, not outside consultants or the DOE, (Department of Education) will be able to force such decisions on principals. The principals will be in charge of what's best for their students, always.

With this reform, the regional offices that we established four years ago to stabilize a failing system will be eliminated now that their job is done. And the 32 community school district superintendents will report directly to the Chancellor. Each school will be able to pick the path that's best for its students, parents, and teachers. And the money we save by downsizing the bureaucracy will go directly to the schools to help our kids, where it belongs!

As we give principals more autonomy, the second of our four reforms will also hold them more accountable. By next fall, we'll be sending **user-friendly** reports on every school to every public school parent across the city. Each school will receive a grade, from "A" to "F", on its year-to-year progress in helping students advance.

Personally, I can't think of a better way to hold a principal's feet to the fire than arming mom and dad with the facts about how well or poorly, their children's school is performing.

Our third reform focuses on the classrooms. Reforming the tenure process—which we'll undertake with the help of the United Federation of Teachers—will allow us to reward teacher excellence and begin to eliminate mediocrity. The UFT (United Federation of Teachers) shares my view that improving the number of quality teachers is the most critical element of all in driving reform. Too many of our new teachers leave the system after only a few years, frustrated by their inability to make a difference for children.

We must do a better job of keeping new teachers who are effective instructors and we must continue to give them the support they need. But we must also make sure that ineffective teachers are not awarded the privilege of tenure and the near-lifetime job security that comes with it.

Accordingly, we are building a more rigorous review process, one that will assure that tenure decisions are made thoughtfully, and based on the facts. Teachers have been and must continue to be our strong partners, and we look forward to working with the UFT on these important issues.

Fourth and finally, we will overhaul a decades-old school funding system that, solely for political reasons, rewards some schools over others. You won't believe this, but today, funding gaps between comparable schools can top $1 million, or $2,000 per student, year after year.

That's not right and we're going to fix it.

Starting in September, we're going to fund students instead of schools, basing our investment on the number of students enrolled, and their particular needs. The goal is equitable funding among our schools and ensuring that each school has what it needs to teach its students.

We will implement this approach flexibly, and phase it in over time to make sure that important programs and services for our kids are not jeopardized. We may use Campaign for Fiscal Equity funds, or other resources, to achieve this critical goal. But in the end, all kids deserve the same level of commitment from us and they're going to get it.

All four of these reforms have this in common. They're about empowering school leaders, and then holding them accountable. That's the only way we can ensure that the investments we make produce the results we all want. Students who are ready and able to follow their dreams. And to help realize their diverse dreams, we must give them a wider range of schools to choose from. To further empower these students and their parents, we will again demand that the State Legislature expands the number of charter schools this year.

The Economy

Great public schools will prepare our next generation of New Yorkers for jobs in our growing economy. And it's an economy that today is firing on all cylinders. You can see the sparks here in Brooklyn, where we've cut the unemployment rate almost by half over the past four years from 9 percent in 2002 to 4.7 percent today.

In fact, across the city, in the past two years alone we've created nearly 100,000 new private sector jobs. Now it's time to take the next steps forward in growing the economy ensuring New York's position as a global hub of commerce making business districts in all five boroughs stronger and investing in the parks and cultural institutions that make this an exciting destination for visitors from around the world.

We are in an age of information, when technology increasingly makes major financial transactions possible from virtually anywhere and that means that we can't take New York's longstanding leadership in financial services and other industries for granted.

We've got to continue to protect consumers and investors but at the same time, New Yorkers, and the nation, have to balance that objective with the barriers—regulatory, legal, and otherwise—hurting our global competitiveness. Other nations have figured out how to do both, we can, too!

Next week, Senator Chuck Schumer and I will set out the local and national steps needed to ensure New York City's continued leadership in global financial services, including re-opening our nation to the highly skilled workers, from every corner of the globe, who truly make our economy thrive.

As we think globally, we'll also act locally, with policies and investments making all our communities more business-friendly. And because New York's international leadership also depends on our great education and research institutions we will promote projects such as the development of Columbia University's new campus, in a way that also meets the needs of its host West Harlem community.

We'll unveil a master plan to build on the amazing renaissance of the South Bronx and another to transform Willets Point. We'll rezone Jamaica, Coney Island, and 125th Street to catalyze new business development. We'll work with the Downtown Brooklyn Partnership that's doing so much to promote business and the arts in this great borough. And we'll help launch construction of the most exciting private development Brooklyn has ever seen: the Atlantic Yards project!

We'll continue supporting our city's Business Improvement Districts, which bolster the neighborhood businesses that are the backbone of our economy. And to strengthen them even more—this year, we'll launch "NYC Clean Streets" a $1.6 million initiative making commercial corridors in all five boroughs more attractive.

We'll also keep investing in the transportation infrastructure critical to our economy. That means not only extending the Number 7 line, a City-funded project that will spur the historic development of the Far West Side, but also helping Congressman Rangel, Senators Schumer and Clinton, and others, to secure Federal support for Lower Manhattan's rail link to Jamaica, Long Island and Downtown Brooklyn, too. And I also look forward to working with Governor Spitzer to finally create the rail gateway our city deserves, one that will be a lasting monument to the great Daniel Patrick Moynihan.

To foster our city's growth, we'll also continue to invest in the cultural facilities that make us the world's most exciting city. Tell me what other town has 500 art galleries, 375 theater companies, 330 dance companies, 150 museums, 96 orchestras, 24 performing arts centers and one Burmese python named "Fantasia" at the Brooklyn Children's Museum?

Every year, tens of millions of tourists flock here to enjoy our cultural offerings, which generate hundreds of millions of dollars for our economy. In fact, two major art events—the Armory Show and the Art Show—are expected to draw more than 60,000 visitors in one weekend next month. And just last month, the Museum of Natural History set a new attendance record—when more than 31,000 people passed through its doors on one single day. (Maybe some of them wanted to spend "A Night at the Museum" with Ben Stiller and Robin Williams.)

So this year we'll restore that Museum's classic 77th Street façade. We'll also go forward—Marty won't mind hearing—with a major renovation of the great New York Aquarium in Coney Island. And we'll continue work on a project that is close to the heart of Yvette Simmons, who is with us today. Yvette's roots in Central Brooklyn, you should know, run deep. In fact, her great-grandfather, Moses Cobb, was one of the first African American police officers in the community.

By next year, Yvette, family stories like yours will get the showcase they deserve when we complete the new education museum at the expanded Weeksville Historical Society in Bedford-Stuyvesant. Moses Cobb will never be forgotten!

We're also making unprecedented investments in another area crucial to our quality of life: our parks. Just a few blocks from here, for example, we'll proceed with building Brooklyn Bridge Park—the borough's biggest new park in nearly 130 years.

We'll also break ground for the first playing fields in what will become the 2,200-acre Fresh Kills Park on Staten Island—which will be nearly three times the size of Central Park.

Affordable Housing

As we make New York a better place to live, we'll also make it a more affordable place to live. That's why we're engaged in the biggest affordable housing initiative ever undertaken by an American city a $7.5 billion plan that will build and preserve 165,000 units—enough housing to accommodate the entire population of Atlanta.

But big as it is, we can't stop there—not with our city projected to reach nine million people by the year 2030. To meet the demands of that growing population, this year we'll begin taking the next steps forward to create even more affordable housing in our city.

We'll do that with targeted rezonings around town. And, thanks to the leadership of Speaker Quinn and our partners in the City Council the recently enacted changes to the 421—a program will also begin to generate hundreds of millions of dollars for affordable housing investment.

Creating more housing—and making more housing affordable—was one of the key long-term sustainability goals that we outlined last month. And in March—as part of the "PLAN-NYC" process—we will present a detailed agenda for implementing those goals and for solving the problems raised by the bigger, older, and more environmentally challenged city New York will be in the year 2030.

Planning for the future includes setting the right priorities now and that's what the city's budgeting process is all about.

Finances—$1 Billion of Tax Relief

Next week, we will release our preliminary budget for Fiscal Year 2008. It will continue the sound policies that have put New York City on a firm budgetary footing and that permitted us to end Fiscal '06 with a record surplus. But, rather than increasing spending in good times, that needs to be cut in bad times—and thus hurting New Yorkers in the process, I believe that a good portion of the surplus revenues we anticipate in the current fiscal year should go back to the New Yorkers who made sure that the city's recovery from 9/11 exceeded our wildest dreams and who we want to continue living, working, and investing in New York.

So, my preliminary budget will include $1 billion of tax relief. This is a broad-based package of tax cuts, designed to pump money back into our neighborhoods, create jobs, lower the burden on property owners, and make New York an even more attractive place to live and work.

First I will propose to the City Council that we lower the property tax rate— for one year—by roughly five percent, or by $750 million. I've always said I wanted to cut property taxes and this year we can.

It would be great if we can extend this in the years to come, but we can't know that we'll be as fortunate in the future with our revenues and expenses so right now it would not be fiscally sensible to commit to doing so. Because the best way I know to have the good times continue is to act responsibly now.

We will also seek permission from the State Legislature to continue the $400 property tax rebate. We expect they will approve our request since the original law said the rebate would be continued only if the city reduced the overall rate— exactly what I am proposing today.

The other $250 million in tax relief we propose will be included in three other measures.

One: we will seek to help small businesses grow by reducing the Unincorporated Business Tax through a combination of deductions and credits. This tax hurts our ability to attract and retain small businesses; reducing it will strengthen our long term business climate. And remember, one of every two people working in New York are employed by small businesses.

Two: to create the jobs that will continue to fuel our economy and to benefit businesses large and small. We will also propose three targeted reductions in the General Corporate Tax, including a credit to owners of small, or "S," Corporations, as Speaker Quinn has championed.

And three: to make sure that shoppers and visitors continue to flock to great stores in all five boroughs, we will totally eliminate the city sales tax for all clothing and footwear.

And as to the rest of our surplus, we will be prudent and dedicate it to reducing future deficits.

Working With NY State on Medicaid and Pensions

On the expense side of the budget, we will work hard to make sure that all of our money is well spent. And this year, we'll take aim at a problem that has cried out for attention: Medicaid fraud. Working with the State, we'll attempt to root out fraud and waste—and return the savings to city taxpayers.

We'll also put forward state legislation that will help us control costs in a second area that threatens our long-term fiscal health, the unchecked growth of pensions.

It's no secret that the State Legislature has been giving away the store getting no productivity in return and saddling our children with costly pension giveaways. It's time for Albany to stop playing Santa Claus with the city's money!

If they want to fund pension increases, they should pay for it. But this year, let's put the city's pension decisions where they belong, on the collective bargaining table. That's what accountability is all about!

Helping Poorer New Yorkers Achieve More "Self-Sufficiency"

To control our destiny, we must control our budget, so we can invest in a better city for all New Yorkers. And that includes pragmatic ways to help more people achieve the dignity of work and to help more working people achieve the goal of self-sufficiency.

Over the past five years, we've moved more than 400,000 people from welfare to work. Our welfare rolls are down 18% from 2002—and are now lower than at any time since 1964. Still. . . nearly one in five New Yorkers—many of whom set the alarm clock and punch the time clock every working day—live below the Federal poverty line.

Last fall, our Commission for Economic Opportunity presented a realistic, cost-effective roadmap to help thousands of poor New Yorkers help themselves. We're already realizing many of the Commission's recommendations.

And today, let me describe just three of the ways more New Yorkers will begin to achieve further self-sufficiency this year.

First–building on the great work our Department of Consumer Affairs does each year, we're going to help even more hard-working New Yorkers claim tax credits to which they're entitled. This week, the Department of Finance will start sending tax forms to about 120,000 households who were eligible for City, State and Federal Earned Income Tax Credits in 2003 and 2004 but who never claimed them.

The average household is due well over $1,000 — and some are owed considerably more. We're so determined to help New Yorkers get that money that we've already done the math on their tax forms!

Now they will simply have to sign the forms, mail them in and get ready to receive money they've already earned. For working families with children, that money is going to make a huge difference in helping them get ahead and it's money that will be spent in their local communities, thereby helping local businesses, as well.

By the way, this will generate more in sales tax revenue for the city than our share of the EITC expense.

The second Commission recommendation we're announcing today will help working students at CUNY's community colleges step forward to earn higher degrees–and then, higher incomes. Right now, the demands of their jobs prevent far too many of them from completing their studies and without degrees, they often remain among our working poor.

So this September the City University will establish dedicated morning, afternoon, and evening tracks, enabling some working students to do all their schoolwork during hours convenient for them. As far as we know, no community college system anywhere has ever attempted this approach. But every successful business offers services that reflect customer needs. And so should government!

Finally, the third recommendation that we'll put into action will help break the long-term cycle of poverty in our city.

When it comes to improving the odds for poor mothers and infants, it's hard to beat our Nurse Family Partnership program. Through one-on-one nurturing and guidance, NFP helps first-time mothers build stronger futures for themselves and their children. And by this September, we'll have expanded this proven program by more than 50%. Because of its track record of success, I'm a big believer in NFP.

But you don't have to take my word for it. Just ask Sheena Persaud. She was 17 when she enrolled in NFP. And she wasn't attending school and didn't plan to. But with the guidance of her nurse, Carol Coleman, she not only learned about taking care of her beautiful little girl, Serena, she also stepped forward and got her GED. By the time she finished the Partnership last November, she had her current full time job in a bakery and she hopes someday to have her own catering business. Sheena, Carol, we're all very proud of you. Now we're going to help more New Yorkers like Sheena step forward and create better futures for themselves and their children.

As the NFP shows, improving public health is key to reducing poverty. So in the year ahead, we'll also focus on reducing chronic illnesses that take their heaviest toll in low-income communities. We are, for example, rapidly expanding voluntary HIV testing.

And with more than $40 million in city and federal funds, we will expand the electronic health records that help doctors and patients in poor neighborhoods improve preventive care. We'll continue to be a national leader in promoting systems that shift focus from reacting to illness, to preventing it. We know that reducing poverty won't be easy, but over the past five years, we've shown that we can craft solutions to our toughest problems.

Protecting Children

That includes protecting children who are most at risk. Last year—in the wake of Nixzmary Brown's appalling death—we took a hard look at the Administration for Children's Services, and then took decisive steps. Now, police officers and case workers collaborate more efficiently on the most severe cases of abuse. Medical providers have better training in recognizing and reporting the warning signs of child abuse or neglect and later this year, we'll expand such training to child care providers, too.

During 2007, we'll take the next steps in protecting our most vulnerable children. In March, we'll open a Leadership Academy for Child Safety which will serve ACS social work managers. We'll also propose amending State law to give ACS the power to check criminal records when child abuse allegations arise. Because how can we thoroughly determine a child's safety, if we can't find out about prior criminal convictions in the home?

Public Safety

Public safety—in the home and on the streets—is the foundation of civil society. And there's no stronger bedrock than the FDNY and the NYPD and let's not forget our Boldest, the Department of Correction! Today, we're joined by members of all three Departments—Edgar Pitre and Kelly Lonergan of the FDNY, NYPD Detective Diane Menig and Police Officer Cyrus Johnson, and Correction Officers Emmanuel Pierre-Lewis and Lashana Taylor.

Over the past five years, the FDNY has reduced fire deaths in our city to the lowest number during any five-year period in modern history. The members of the FDNY are famous for always working to find better ways to carry out their mission. We share that commitment. And that's why this year, we're going to launch a major expansion of FDNY training. Currently, our newly appointed firefighters receive 13 weeks of training.

This year, we'll start to lengthen that to 23 weeks. That will give FDNY recruits one of the most comprehensive training programs offered by any fire department anywhere handling hazardous materials, and fire prevention with extended instruction in terrorism preparedness.

We'll step up our protections against terrorism in other ways too. In the next fiscal year, for example, we will invest city capital funds in the Lower Manhattan Security Initiative. It will protect our bridges, tunnels and other critical infrastructure, as well as all those who live, work, and do business Downtown. We will always do whatever it takes to protect our city and we expect the Federal government to do its part to keep the nation's economic engine safe, too.

Keeping our city safe, of course, begins with fighting crime—and no one does it better than the NYPD. Last year, even as violent crime began to rise in the rest of the nation, the men and women of the NYPD continued to reduce violent and property crime in our city. Today, crime is more than 20 percent lower than it was five years ago.

One reason we've been so successful is because we've always been ready to look the facts straight-on—whether we liked them or not. And last year, the fact was that even as overall crime went down, homicides in our city went up. Most of those murders were committed with illegal guns. So this year we'll continue to step up our fight against the deadly menace of illegal guns in several key ways.

We'll build on the NYPD's increased enforcement activities, which last year raised gun arrests by 13 percent. But we did more than simply make arrests. We also expanded the NYPD's work with the district attorneys, intensifying debriefings of gun offenders to learn more about where they buy their guns.

Now, beginning with a pilot program in the Bronx, we'll take the next steps forward. We'll mine that new information to map the illegal gun market and then identify—and go after—gun traffickers to stop the flow of guns onto our streets.

Illegal guns are not just a problem for New York City. Two weeks ago, across the river in New Jersey, an off-duty Paterson police officer, Tyron Franklin, was gunned down at a restaurant when he refused to turn over his wallet. The City of Paterson lost one of its finest and a 16-month-old child lost a father.

New Yorkers know the ache and anger of such losses all too well. We remember so many—including Detectives James Nemorin and Rodney Andrews and Detectives Dillon Stewart and Daniel Enchautegui. And we also know that in 2005, when we lost Detectives Stewart and Enchautegui, 55 law enforcement officers were murdered across our country, 50 of them with guns. This has got to stop.

Today, we're joined by the Mayor of Paterson, Jose "Joey" Torres. Mayor Torres, New York City offers its deepest condolences to you and your city. And we'll also join you in working to bring sanity to gun policy in our nation. Next week, more than 50 mayors from across the country—who are part of our coalition of

Mayors Against Illegal Guns—will gather in Washington, DC, to take up this challenge.

And I'm happy to say that Mayor Torres will be with us. Our goal will be getting Congress to overturn a wrong-headed law—one that blocks access at the local level to federal data that would let us hold gun dealers accountable for illegally selling to gun traffickers. Mayor Torres and I have a simple message for Congress: It's time to take ideology out of crime-fighting and time to give mayors—the people who are responsible for policing our streets—the tools we need to protect our citizens.

To make New York even safer, this year we'll also launch the most significant restructuring of our juvenile justice system in decades. We're going to do more than ever to hold accountable the children and teens who run afoul of the law and also help them get the services they need.

For the first time, we'll give judges objective, data-based analysis that will accurately assess the real threat posed by young offenders. And we'll provide judges more options for keeping those offenders in the community—but out of trouble.

We'll take aim at chronic truancy so often a precursor to serious delinquency with dedicated truancy courts in Red Hook and Harlem—holding children and their families accountable for school attendance.

We'll also launch a $9 million initiative to reduce the number of kids sent away to Upstate facilities and, instead, provide intensive family-based services and monitoring. And we'll partner with John Jay College on an initiative linking young offenders released from detention with the mental health services they need.

At the same time, we have to face facts: more than 50 percent of all gun arrests involve young offenders. We have got to stop treating illegal gun possession among minors as though it were a trivial, youthful indiscretion.

It is not. It is a serious, potentially deadly crime and those arrested for illegal gun possession are the most likely to commit violent crimes in the future. That's why this year—as we work to keep more young people away from guns—we will also ask Albany to eliminate youthful offender status for any violent felony committed with a firearm.

As we step up the fight against crime, we're also going to make sure that the NYPD treats every New Yorker equally and with dignity and that all complaints are taken seriously.

We call our police "New York's Finest." That's our term of respect for those who have sworn to protect us. And we must always insist that such respect flows in both directions! This year, we will expand the resources and staffing at the Civilian Complaint Review Board to ensure that all complaints are dealt with swiftly and seriously.

To build stronger trust and cooperation between the public and the police, we're also going to empower more New Yorkers to step forward and join the fight against crime.

This year, we'll begin a revolutionary innovation in crime-fighting: Equipping "911" call centers to receive digital images and videos New Yorkers send from cell phones and computers something no other city in the world is doing.

If you see a crime in progress or a dangerous building condition, you'll be able to transmit images to 911, or online to NYC.gov. And we'll start extending the same technology to 311 to allow New Yorkers to step forward and document non-emergency quality of life concerns holding City agencies accountable for correcting them quickly and efficiently.

Finally, we are going to work to improve training of our police department by identifying a site for a modern new police academy. Our police department deserves a 21st century, consolidated facility to continue to fulfill its important mission. Making government more accountable also means fighting patronage and strengthening ethics.

A Future of Limitless Promise

All the steps we've discussed today, will build on the progress, and the promise, that are so evident in this hall and throughout our city today.

You can see that hope and dynamism in these photos and charts behind me. . . and more importantly, in the faces of the people of our city. Every reform—every step forward—that we're proposing today springs from a belief that we New Yorkers deserve to hold our own destiny, one filled with such tremendous potential, in our own hands.

And now New Yorkers are ready to take all the next steps forward that we've described today. Because over the past five years, we've shown what independence, accountability, and making decisions based on the facts can accomplish.

Together, we've achieved more in turning our schools around, improving our quality of life, and bringing our city back than most people ever thought possible. And because we've done all that's necessary and then some, the future of our magnificent city is one of limitless promise.

It's time to fulfill that promise for all who are here and all who will come. With confidence and courage, let's take those next steps together.

And let's start today!

Thank you.

And God bless.

Discussion Questions

1. In general, do your agree with Bloomberg's optimistic forecast for the city's current situation and future. What parts do you agree with? Where do you disagree? Explain your answers with concrete examples.

2. In his speech Bloomberg mentions several heroes worthy of mention. Can you suggest other names?

3. The mayor talks a great deal about his education reforms relating to principals, educators, students, and funding. Which of these do you see as a priority? What exactly do you think he means by the term "accountability" in education?

4. The mayor speaks of several economic development projects such as Columbia University's move into West Harlem and the Atlantic Yards project in Brooklyn. Do you see here any need for concern?

5. How do you feel about the mayor's efforts to increase funding for transportation infrastructure and cultural institutions. Which do you feel is more urgent? Why?

6. Do you think the mayor is serious when he talks of making housing affordable to all? What do think he should do to ensure that this happens? Why is this issue so significant to all New Yorkers?

7. How do you feel about Bloomberg's commitment to CUNY? Do you think his plan sufficiently help working-class students?

8. The mayor talks at length about the many security measures he has in place to ensure public safety. How safe do you feel living in NYC?

9. What is the Mayor looking at specifically to curb gun violence in the city? What else can be done?

Writing Tasks

1. Write a letter to the mayor explaining the particular concerns you have relating to your own New York.

2. Do you think the Juvenile justice system in particular needs reform? What can be done to keep youths from commiting crimes and keeping them out of prison?

3. Look up the Weeksville Historical Society on the Web (and perhaps even take a visit). Write a report on Weeksville's significance to African Americans during the nineteenth century.

4. Research the issue of gun control. What steps are needed to make our cities safer?

5. Discuss further one of the urban concerns Bloomberg views as important for a better city.

East Harlem Develops, And Its Accent Changes

Timothy Williams and Tanzina Vega

Inside a wooden shack set in a garden on East 117th Street, a group of Puerto Rican men, many of them in their 70s and 80s, are playing a spirited game of dominoes on a rainy winter afternoon. A painting of a woman wearing a burgundy shawl over a flamenco-style dress hangs on a wall, and in the garden, tomatoes, peppers, corn and culantro, an herb used in Caribbean cooking, grow in the summer.

But outside their little retreat, a thick dust, the pounding of hammers and the shouts of construction workers inundate the block, signaling the transformation of East Harlem, also known as Spanish Harlem or El Barrio (the neighborhood). Many see it changing from the Puerto Rican enclave it has been for decades to a more heterogeneous neighborhood with a significant middle-class presence, luxury condominiums and a Home Depot.

It is a familiar story of gentrification in New York City, but this one comes with a twist: the many newcomers who are middle-class professionals from other parts of the city are joining a growing number of working-class Mexicans and Dominicans. The result is a high degree of angst among many Puerto Ricans who worry they will be unable to prevent their displacement from a neighborhood that is far more than a place to live and work. "We're in crisis mode right now, and as far as retaining the Puerto Rican and Latino identity in the neighborhood, we're in red alert," said Rafael Merino, who is on the local community board. "If we don't pick up speed, we'll lose a lot of it." While East Harlem—which had previously been an Italian neighborhood—was not the first place Puerto Ricans settled after arriving in large numbers in New York after World War II, it became the de facto center of cultural life after large-scale displacement from Chelsea, Hell's Kitchen, the Upper West Side, and more recently, Williamsburg and the Lower East Side.

East Harlem is the place where people come to celebrate Three Kings Day and quinceañeras, to gather the night before the Puerto Rican Day Parade, and to play dominoes on weekends. But in recent years, rising rents have caused many Puerto Ricans to leave for more affordable Hudson Valley towns, or for cities like Allentown and Bethlehem in Pennsylvania and Stamford and Bridgeport in Connecticut. "You have a choice, try to pay that rent, or move out," said Tony Ramirez, a plumber who has lived in East Harlem for 43 of his 47 years.

"Puerto Ricans in El Barrio is like being extinct. None of the people I grew up with are around. People feel like strangers in their own town."

An illustration of his lament can be seen on several blocks of 116th Street, long Puerto Rican East Harlem's main shopping strip, which are now filled with shops selling Mexican food, flags and pastries. In 1980, there were 856,440 people of Puerto Rican descent living in New York City, compared with 787,046 in 2005, according to census data. In East Harlem, the number of Puerto Ricans has also been declining, to 37,878 in 2005, from 40,542 in 1990, according to the census. They now make up about 35.3 percent of the neighborhood's population, down from 39.4 percent in 1990.

Carmen Vasquez, public relations manager for Hope Community Inc., a private, nonprofit real estate and cultural organization in the neighborhood, said that the concentration of public housing and other low-income apartment units in East Harlem would keep the Puerto Rican population stable for now. 'There will be some displacement, but we will retain our heritage and our culture," she said. "You won't stop gentrification, but you can contain it and slow it down." But the changes are unmistakable.

For decades, there had been no doubt about where the Upper East Side ended and East Harlem began: 96th Street, the last major east-west street before the start of East Harlem's clusters of high-rise public housing projects. Taxi drivers sometimes dropped off passengers at 96th Street rather than venture farther north to what they considered to be a crime-ridden area. Some courier services also refused to cross the line. Even the row of upscale shops along Second and Third Avenues stopped just short of 96th Street. That demarcation line is softer now, and nicknames for the southern tier of East Harlem abound: the Upper East Side, Upper Yorkville and SpaHa—short for Spanish Harlem.

Peter Lorusso, 25, who works for a shipping company, has lived for about a year in the Aspen, a 234-unit luxury apartment complex at 101st Street and First Avenue, where one-half of the units rent at market rates. The three-year-old building has its own garage with valet parking and a 10,000-foot courtyard with bamboo trees. It also offers a free shuttle van every 20 minutes to nearby subways during the morning and evening commutes—as do several other new upscale buildings in the neighborhood. Mr. Lorusso said he does not usually go north of 101st Street. Instead, he and his friends "do the pub crawl" on the Upper East Side along Second Avenue. The Aspen, he said, is "an extension of the Upper East Side." "People are bringing more money north, which is a good thing," he said. "You just got to be street smart."

Jon Rich, 30, a stockbroker who lives in the Aspen, had previously rented apartments in TriBeCa, Battery Park City and Midtown. He now splits the $2,800 rent for his two-bedroom apartment with a roommate. "I couldn't afford to stay where I was," he said. Fifteen blocks north of the Aspen, on the site of the former Washburn Wire Factory at 116th Street and the Franklin D. Roosevelt

Drive, workers have dismantled the plant to make way for the $300 million East River Plaza shopping center, which will feature a Home Depot, a Best Buy and a Target store. A second large development in the area was derailed by the Bloomberg administration last year after widespread opposition. The $1 billion project, known as Uptown New York, had called for retail space and 1,500 apartments in an area between 125th and 127th Streets and Second and Third Avenues. Eighty percent of the apartments would have been rented or sold at market rates.

Still, residents say many of East Harlem's new residential developments are unreasonably expensive. On 117th Street between First and Pleasant Avenues—a block that the police say has been home to a thriving drug market and where two people were killed in the past six months—more than eight buildings are being renovated or constructed. One of the buildings is the Nina, nine units of "luxury condominiums" where a one-bedroom penthouse is on the market for $850,000. "The Upper East Side is now the playground for the sophisticated bohemian," reads the Nina's Web site. "East Harlem will be known as the area that will feature SoHo-type lofts, with a NoHo sensibility, and a Village flair, without the hefty price tag."

Jose Hidalgo, 76, one of the men playing dominoes in the shack on 117th Street next door to the Nina, has lived in the neighborhood for 55 years. He grew up in Santa Isabel, Puerto Rico. "Where am I going to live with these people and their condominiums?" he asked. "If I have to leave, I'll go back to my country. I don't have to pay rent; and I have a house there." But Mr. Hidalgo said he believes that even if the new condos and co-ops find buyers, their owners won't stay. "These people come here and they don't last long," Mr. Hidalgo said. "Once they see what the neighborhood is really like, especially in the summer," he said, when the streets become noisy and the crime rate typically climbs, they will sell their apartments and leave. His friend, Jose Vazquez, 65, who has lived in East Harlem since 1959, said poor people are going to be forced out. "People who used to pay $600 a month are now paying $900 a month."

But Henry M. Calderon, a real estate broker and president of the East Harlem Chamber of Commerce, said some Puerto Ricans believe they are entitled to live in East Harlem, although they failed to buy property when it was cheaper. "Is it a right to live here or a privilege?" Mr. Calderon asked. "Is it a right to have an apartment facing Park Avenue? We cannot expect that we have a right to live where we want to live."

Nicholas L. Arture, executive director of the Association of Hispanic Arts and treasurer of the East Harlem Board of Tourism, said even without significant rates of Puerto Rican home ownership, one way to preserve the area's pedigree is to market it to visitors. One plan calls for transforming 106th Street east of Fifth Avenue into a "cultural corridor" showcasing Puerto Rican heritage through murals and cultural centers, art galleries and restaurants.

Mr. Arture said the area's Puerto Rican flavor has already attracted visitors who want to know more about the neighborhood. Recently, a group of graduate students from Kenya said they wanted to visit after having read about the neighborhood on the Internet. "They wanted to eat rice and beans," Mr. Arture said. "They wanted to experience the culture."

Discussion Questions

1. Describe what is currently happening in East Harlem. How do you feel about this process known as gentrification?

2. What does "El Barrio" mean to large numbers of New York Puerto Ricans? Why are they worried about its disappearance?

3. What is the leading cause of displacement for current residents residing in East Harlem? Is there a solution to this problem?

4. Why do so many areas take on new names like Upper Yorkville and SpaHa once they get developed? Can you think of other renamed neighborhoods?

5. Do you agree with Mr. Lorusso's comment that "people are bringing more money north, which is a good thing"?

6. Do you believe New Yorkers have a "right" to live where they want? Carefully justify your response.

Writing Tasks

1. Use this article as a reference to a discussion of the story "Chango's Fire" by Ernesto Quinonez found in the Literary New York section.

2. Write an essay that elaborates on the advantages and disadvantages of gentrification and development of a neighborhood. Be sure also to establish where you stand in this debate.

3. Look up an apartnat advertisement for Spanish Harlem and discuss how and to who it seems to be marketed.

Legalization and De-Legalization

Aarti Shahani

Aarti Shahani is a co-founder of Families for Freedom, a Brooklyn-based defense network for immigrant families facing deportation.

As thousands of students walked out of their schools to protest pending immigration bills in Congress, 17-year-old Julio Beltre stood in front of New York's Federal Plaza last month to tell the story of his father, Juan Beltre: On a morning a year ago, in April 2005, before the sun rose, six agents from the Department of Homeland Security had woken up his father and dragged him away from their Bronx home, while his wife and four children—all U.S. citizens—watched in horror.

Why was he being seized? Juan Beltre had committed a single drug possession offense dating back to 1995. But in those ten long years, Beltre had completed probation, was a long-term greencard holder—and was now suffering from a brain tumor.

"Now my mom has to raise us alone," his son recounted at the demonstration. His father was deported back to the Dominican Republic.

The testimonies of Julio Beltre and a dozen other citizen-children with similar stories came in a week of marches, walkouts, hearings, and headlines. Immigration is *the issue* everywhere, from the hearts of protesters to the halls of the Capitol to the editorial pages of *The New York Times.*

More Legalization—Or More Deportations?

The debate is as complex as it is heated. On March 27th, the Senate Judiciary Committee approved an immigration bill that would, if passed into law:

- expand the grounds of deportation
- use domestic military bases for immigration detention
- legalize the indefinite detention of noncitizens
- authorize New York City police and other local officers to enforce federal immigration laws
- erect a border fence
- enable Homeland Security agents to expel suspected foreigners indiscriminately
- create a national identification system for all workers.

Yet the following morning, the front page of New York's largest Spanish language paper, *El Diario*, exclaimed "TRIUMFAMOS." Meanwhile, restrictionist commentator Lou Dobbs campaigned against the bill on television and in Mexico.

This ironic role reversal stems from one section of the proposed bill, the guestworker legalization provisions. Under the leadership of Senator Arlen Specter of Pennsylvania, the Judiciary Committee voted 12-6 to approve a new visa program, devised by Senators Edward Kennedy and John McCain, under which undocumented workers would have to register with the government, maintain continuous employment for six years, pay back and future taxes, and pass civics and English lessons in order to apply for a green card. Some hail the Senate bill as a victory because, for the first time since the amnesty passed by President Ronald Reagan in 1986, undocumented workers would have a potential pathway to work and live lawfully in the U.S.

Fighting to Keep the Legalization Provisions

In the coming weeks, the Judiciary proposal faces the scrutiny of the full Senate. Advocates are fighting to prevent the "earned legalization" provisions from being watered down. The main variable is whether or not the visa granted to undocumented workers will lead to a green card and eventual citizenship.

We are now at a crossroads. While the nation's attention is focused on the legalization question, lawmakers have guaranteed only one thing: there will be no legalization-only bill. If the Senate ultimately approves anything, it will go to a closed-door conference committee to be resolved with the House bill passed in December 2005 under the leadership of Wisconsin Republican James Sensenbrenner. The House bill concedes no greencards. It's only common ground with the Senate provisions to expand detentions, deportations, and border police.

A shared history underlies the consensus. September 11th transformed immigration into a national security debate, with Democrats and Republicans both convinced that any immigration reform must come with tighter controls. But as the Beltre family illustrates, the New York congressional delegation has to resolve the national security agenda with a powerful reality: non-citizens are not the only affected population. Citizen spouses and children left behind are devastated because of decade-old deportation laws.

Ten Years of Deportations

It's not the act of terror we remember best. In April 1995, a white veteran of the first Gulf War blew up the Oklahoma City federal building. One year later, to memorialize that tragedy, then-President Bill Clinton signed a sweeping immigration enforcement measure: the Anti-Terrorism and Effective Death Penalty Act.

A sister bill, the Illegal Immigration Reform and Immigrant Responsibility Act, passed just months later.

Together, the 1996 laws transformed the meaning of membership in America and substantially ramped up policing based on citizenship. There was no legalization or guestworker program. Instead, there were sweeping deportation measures that empowered the executive branch to more easily expel people already within our borders.

Prior to the 1996 laws, a New Yorker placed in deportation proceedings could typically go before an immigration judge and seek a pardon if she could demonstrate that she was no threat to society and had significant ties to her U.S. community. But the new laws instituted a system of mandatory deportation and detention whereby the vast majority of New Yorkers facing deportation are held in immigrant prisons without bail and have no opportunity to plead their case before an immigration judge. These judges are appointees of the U.S. attorney general, yet they cannot pardon or postpone the deportation of a noncitizen—even if they believe the punishment would harm U.S. citizen children and communities.

With detention and deportation as the new mandatory minimums, more than 1.3 million people have been expelled from the U.S. in the last 10 years, and immigrants have become the fastest-growing segment of our prison population. (Homeland Security does not make city-specific statistics available.) Taxpayers are footing the bill for the ever-growing deportation budget. American veterans, breadwinners, and people who have lived here since infancy have been deported through this process.

Just before September 11th, lawmakers on both sides of the aisle agreed that 1996 went too far. One of its leading proponents, former Republican Congressman Bill McCollum of Florida, called the unintended impacts on families a "manifest injustice." But such wisdom crumbled with the Twin Towers. America was left with the inflexible, even cruel legal infrastructure of 1996. Since the tragedy, the Bush Administration has poured billions into even more vigilant enforcement of these laws.

Plea Bargains Lead To Deportations

In New York as in other urban centers, the criminal justice system is a cornerstone of the immigration policing strategy. The criminal courts rely on a plea system to expedite the high volume of cases. Prosecutors issue lengthy indictments. Defense attorneys advise clients to plea to lesser charges, in order to secure a deal with little or no jail time.

Every week, hundreds of immigrant New Yorkers arrested for garden-variety crimes plead guilty under this plea-bargain system. But neither the judge nor attorney warn them that after they complete their sentence, a second punishment will follow: detention and deportation. As the federal immigration authorities' reliance on local criminal institutions grows, there is no countervailing process to ensure that the rights of immigrants are observed.

Connecting Past and Present Policy

The criminalization trends of 1996 pervade the bills in Congress today. Proposals consistently extend mandatory deportation and detention to a wider net of immigrants. Even the most progressive proposals bar immigrants who admit to crimes—like using a fake ID to get a job—from obtaining green cards.

The New York congressional delegation has been nearly mute on how America's immigration are harming families—with one recent exception. On March 28, 2006, Congressman Jose Serrano of the Bronx introduced the Child Citizen Protection Act, a bill to restore partial discretion to immigration judges in cases where removal of an immigrant is clearly against the best interests of a U.S. citizen child. Serrano called the bill "common-sense legislation" that would protect children and families from unnecessary separation. But the other members of Congress from New York are largely silent, despite the New York families who flood their district offices—families already devastated by deportation.

"Our leaders need to change the laws," Julio Beltre concluded his speeech during the demonstration at Federal Plaza, "before more young people like me get hurt." On April 24th, the 10-year anniversary of the 1996 laws, he and other New Yorkers will converge in Washington D.C. with families from other cities whose lives have changed because of deportation.

Discussion Questions

1. How does the anecdote of Julio Beltre's deportation set up this essay's central theme?

2. Why exactly is immigration "*the issue* everywhere" as Shahani claims? Do you see it as an important concern?

3. What is your response to the Senate Judiciary Committee's recommendations for an immigration bill?

4. What exactly is the "guestworker legalization provision?" How does this affect support for the Senate's immigration bill?

5. What has the effect of 9/11 been on immigration reform?

6. How did the immigration laws of 1996 affect illegal immigrants in this country?

7. What is the problem with the current plea bargain system for immigrants?

Writing Tasks

1. Write an essay in which you argue either for stricter or more lenient immigration laws. Be sure to cite key legislation and bring in concrete examples that support your assertions.

2. Research the current deliberations on immigration reform in America today. Where does the debate over legalization and de-legalization seem to be heading?

3. Look up familiesforfreedom.org. Report on what articles and statistics you find there.

Arts Education

Jonathan Mandell

The principal of St. Nicholas School in the Bronx makes it clear what she thinks of arts education when one of her teachers enters her office unbidden.

"Who's watching your class?" the principal, Sister Aloysius, asks her teacher, Sister James.

"They're having Art," Sister James replies.

"Art," the senior nun snorts. "Waste of time."

"It's only an hour a week," Sister James replies.

"Much can be accomplished in 60 minutes."

This exchange is near the beginning of John Patrick Shanley's hit Broadway play, "Doubt," and serves in part to establish the principal's rigid character. But while the principal and the school may be fictional ("a parable," Shanley calls it), the attitude is for real.

"Many educational leaders in New York City. . . do not value art as a core academic subject that requires time and the attention of . . . principals, teachers and parents," concludes a report on arts education in New York City public schools released by the City Council in June of 2003.

That report and three hearings of the education committee of the City Council picture arts education as spotty and undervalued, with inequitable resources, inadequate instruction, insufficient facilities, and a shortage of qualified arts educators—but also find much to feel hopeful about: In the New York City public school system, "you can find absolute state-of-the-art enlightened arts education," Richard Kessler, executive director of the Center for Arts Education, testified at the third of the council hearings last month. "It's the best of times and the worst of times."

From Anti-Art To "The Arts Administration"

The still-widespread attitude that the arts are a "frill" helps explain why funding for them always seems endangered. A New Yorker cartoon in 2003 depicted one caveman complaining to another: "Why is the arts budget always the first thing to be cut, when you know damn well it's the only thing that separates us from the monkeys?" This was no joke during the 1970s fiscal crisis, when the arts were virtually eliminated from the city's public schools; all art, music, drama and dance teachers were laid off. Although the city's cultural institutions and individual

Reprinted by permission of Gotham Gazette.

artists tried to fill in the gaps, with the aid of newly-created private non-profit organizations like *ArtsConnection* and the *Center for Arts Education*, it took more than two decades before City Hall and the school system itself committed to restoring arts funding and the arts curriculum. The New York City Department of Education says it spent roughly $250 million for arts education in the last school year (out of a total budget of some $13 billion.)

It is a sign of progress that Sharon Dunn, who is newly in charge of arts education for the Department of Education, officially acknowledged that an anti-art attitude is part of the problem, though she couched this politely: "One of the areas identified as most in need of development," Dunn testified last month, "is the need to acquaint school administrators with the benefits and elements of arts education."

Dunn's testimony at the October 31 council hearing was intended to emphasize that the Bloomberg administration, Dunn said, "has made arts education a priority." She gave as one small example among many the creation of a "cultural pass program for school leaders," with funding from the Bank of America, that enables school principals and other educators to attend cultural events for free.

But the "embodiment of a deep commitment" by the mayor, chancellor and school system, she said, is the "Blueprint for Teaching and Learning in the Arts." This echoes statements that Mayor Michael Bloomberg made during his re-election campaign. In answer to a *questionnaire by an education advocacy group*, he wrote that he was "dedicated to developing and improving access to quality arts education for every public school student in our city." Evidence of this commitment, he said, was that his administration "created and implemented the city's first comprehensive kindergarten through twelfth grade art curriculum in visual arts, music, theater and dance."

The *New York Times* more or less reiterated this point, in a laudatory article on the front page of the Arts and Leisure section entitled "The Arts Administration" that asserted that the Bloomberg administration "has done more to promote and support the arts than any in a generation" and singled out its "development of a mandated arts curriculum for public school students . . . the first of its kind since the city gutted arts education during the 1970's fiscal crisis."

But that article itself has been *criticized for its omissions* (mostly involving criticism of Bloomberg budget cutbacks to cultural organizations) and for its timing — just two weeks before the election. And, as the most recent hearing made clear, some critics see a sharp disconnect between what officials say and what actually exists.

Why Arts Education Is Not a Frill

It should be self-evident that learning to play a musical instrument or to appreciate a painting or to know how to respond to performances at Lincoln Center would give students a sense of discernment and delight that would last their entire lives. But merely providing a lifetime of pleasure and fulfillment seems a hard sell at a time when there is so much worry that American youth (all Americans, actually) are ill-prepared for the economic challenges of the future. The result of such concerns has been a emphasis on teaching "the basics"—and on test scores.

The arts can easily seem an "obscure" consideration, said Richard Kessler, "when you look at the push being made in reading and math . . . and [at] the ways in which school leaders are evaluated"—i.e. by test scores.

But if it may be difficult to test and grade individual achievement in the arts, the arts have been shown to offer concrete and measurable scholastic benefits. Research studies indicate that involvement in the arts—whether in school or after school; as a participant or a spectator—enhances young people's ability to learn in other subjects. Sustained participation in music, for example, was shown to be connected to success in mathematics; and participating in theater was correlated with success in reading. One study found that young people exposed to the arts are far more likely to be recognized for academic achievement, to participate in a math or science fair, and to win an award for writing an essay or a poem.

The arts have proven a reliable way of reaching students who, for one reason or another, were alienated from their studies. The arts involve parents and other members of the community in a way that other "schoolwork" usually cannot.

The arts also can develop empathy and instill confidence in young people, and (in the words of the City Council report) "provides them with a language to understand and contribute to the world around them." This was demonstrated in an especially compelling way in *Born Into Brothels,* an Academy Award-winning documentary about the children of prostitutes, whose lives were transformed when they were taught how to take photographs.

To Xanthe Jory, executive director of the Bronx Charter School for the Arts, "the arts can be a catalyst for change, not only in individual students, but also in the life of the school."

The City's Blueprint for Teaching and Learning in the Arts

The core of the city's efforts in arts education is called Project ARTS (standing for Arts Restoration Throughout the Schools), and the core of Project ARTS are the recently-completed blueprints for the arts—there is one blueprint each for theater, for visual arts, for music and for dance.

In each of the four artistic fields, and in every grade, the blueprints offer five "strands" of learning that begin with the making of art, but go beyond it. A well-rounded arts education would mean growing mastery in all five approaches. To use the terminology that the blueprints use, the five elements include (with examples randomly selected from the blueprints to illustrate):

1. "Making Art"
In theater, for example, students are expected to achieve certain "benchmarks" in each grade, in acting, directing, designing, technical work and playwriting. Second-grade actors, for example, should be able to "make appropriate use of costumes and props in activities, sharings and performances" while fifth-grade actors should "demonstrate the ability to memorize spoken word and staging within a performed work" and eighth-grade actors would be able to "apply a knowledge of the characteristics of various genres in performance, including tragedy, comedy, farce, improvisation and musical theater."

2. "Literacy in the Arts"
In the visual arts, a 12th grader would be asked to "identify issues raised by a controversial work of art," and expected to know enough about art history and the vocabulary used in interpreting a painting to write both a review of a museum exhibition, and "wall text, labels, catalogues and promotional materials for a student-curated exhibition."

3. "Making Connections"
A fifth-grade music student learning how to play "This Land Is Your Land" could be assigned to research the period in which Woody Guthrie composed the song, what issues engaged him, and how his song compares to Irving Berlin's "God Bless America." The student, while improvising harmonies for "Ode To Joy," could be assigned to explore other examples of harmony—in poetry, in painting, in architecture. The connections being made are to other fields and to society in general.

4. "Working with Community and Cultural Resources"
A dancer in the eighth grade would be asked to attend professional dance performances and report on them for her schoolmates, or use the New York Public Library for the Performing Arts to research American social dances.

5. "Exploring Careers and Lifelong Learning"
The point here, said Sharon Dunn, is to drive home to the student that "as you learn to look at art and find that you have a passion for it, there's actually a place at the end of this path [where] you can earn a living."

But Dunn stresses that an arts education is for every student, not just those who might one day become professionals, and the blueprints should also function as resources for teachers in every discipline.

Falling Short

At the recent City Council hearing, Eva Moskowitz, the chair of the council's education committee, seemed unimpressed with the blueprints. "I'm all for being ambitious," she said at one point, "but given . . . the fact that there's chaos in many of our schools, it just seems like I'll have great grandchildren before we'll have this implemented . . . I mean we barely have schools that have bands."

Moskowitz and other members of the council were especially taken aback when Dunn said she did not know what percentage of the public schools currently offer their students an excellent arts education—nor, when pushed, would she offer an estimate or even hazard a guess.

"I find it profoundly troubling," Moskowitz said, "that either they don't want to say that only five percent of their schools are meeting the standard . . . or they honestly don't know."

While Bloomberg talks of having "created and implemented" a "comprehensive" curriculum, in other words, there's proof only of the blueprint having been created, not implemented, and, to Moskowitz and others, the blueprint is not even really a curriculum (much less a comprehensive one) but a sometimes vaguely-worded and often obvious set of goals and guidelines.

At the hearing, and in its report, the education committee enumerated other concrete challenges, among them a lack of such facilities as art or dance studios, an inadequate supply of basic material and equipment such as musical instruments, and a shortage of arts teachers. Some 150 public schools — more than one in ten — still have no full-time arts teachers of any kind. (Currently, there are *reportedly* 2,343 licensed art teachers across the city, including only 136 teaching theater and 124 teaching dance.) While the school system is hoping to hire more, they are having trouble finding them, in part because schools of education (taking their cue from New York City's long-time lack of interest) eliminated their programs to train arts teachers. To make things worse, Richard Kessler observed, "we are hearing regularly from schools where arts specialists are being let go."

If there is one Web site that offers the most compelling information about the state of arts education in New York City public schools, it is probably not the Department of Education's pages on the blueprint for teaching and learning in the arts, but DonorsChoose, a site that tries to match classroom needs with individual philanthropists. Here an elementary school teacher in the Bronx asks for help in taking her students on a trip to visit the Guggenheim Museum, and one in Brooklyn asks for help in funding a similar trip to the Brooklyn Museum. A middle school teacher in Queens asks for a few hundred dollars to build a theater library: "Our kids are talented, creative, and energetic. Most of them have never seen a play, much less been a part of one." A high school teacher in Brooklyn asks for money for three-dollar magic markers. "Our markers have run dry. The students are eager to finish their intricate design work but there is no money for new markers . . . This is just one more frustration and disappointment in . . . lives that are full of substandard supplies and facilities."

Discussion Questions

1. Why do you think so many educational leaders in NYC? think that the arts (visual art, music, drama, and dance) are "a waste of time?" How do you feel about this response?

2. Explain the New Yorker cartoon caption: "Why is the arts budget always the first thing to be cut, when you know damn well it's the only thing that separates us from the monkeys."

3. How does Mandell defend arts education? How well has the arts served you in other areas of your education and life?

4. What does "Literacy in the Arts" actually mean? How important is this?

5. Do you think it's a good idea for school to require students to attend and then write about their experiences at cultural institutions?

6. According to Mandell, how does studying art serve life-long needs?

7. Why is Eva Moskowitz, the chair of the City Council's Education Committee, skeptical of the plan to improve arts education in NYC schools? Do you share her skepticism?

Writing Task

1. Write a defense of a well-funded arts education in public schools.

2. Design and complete your own urban arts assignment based on the suggestions given by Project ARTS.

9/11 and The Rise of the Blogosphere

Aaron Barlow

Aaron Barlow is a Professor of English at New York City College of Technology of the City University of New York. He has been involved with blogs since the early 1990s and continues to participate in Web discussions as part of ePluribus Media, an Internet-based "citizen journalist" group that has grown out of blogs. This article first appears as a chapter in his book *The Rise of the Blogosphere.*

It was soon after I returned from two long stints of living in Africa that I began to get seriously interested in what was happening on the Internet. The year was 1991. Through a modem, I found The WELL, CompuServe, and (a little later) America Online and involved myself in the bulletin-board discussions and then in AOL's chat rooms. Though I was fascinated by what I imagined all of this could become, these weren't particularly satisfying to me, for I wanted more substance than online discussion was providing at the time. Though I could keep a log of them, the conversations were ephemeral and, in many respects, characterless and directionless. The posts tended to be brief and with minimal follow-up, perhaps a result of the minute-by-minute charges that participation incurred.

One of the things I thirsted for was international news. Europe had changed dramatically while I was in Africa, listening in through the BBC as country after country in the East threw off its rulers and turned toward the West. Now, back home, I was finding little enough news from Europe and even less from Africa. Frustrated, I signed up for a variety of USENET newsgroups. The Internet, I hoped, could fill me in on what was going on in the rest of the world.

It did not—not sufficiently, at least. In 1993, I was as shocked as anyone else in New York City when a truck bomb went off in the World Trade Center. Who were these people? Why had I never heard of them? Then, in 1998, explosions rocked U.S. embassies in Dar es Salaam, Tanzania, and in Nairobi, Kenya—something was up, but what? Having been in and out of the Nairobi embassy a number of times, I really did have an interest—but there was little to find out and little follow-up in the media beyond desultory reporting on the misguided retaliatory bombing of a chemical plant in Sudan.

By then, I had completely stopped watching network evening news programs. It was no deliberate decision; they just did not interest me any longer.

Reprinted by permission of Aaron Barlow.

Why? Because, as Fenton describes the situation, on "some nights prior to 9/11, the network news shows featured no foreign news at all":

> This was a major shift from the heyday of network news in the 1970s, when the networks dominated the airwaves—and almost half the content of most network evening news broadcasts was devoted to foreign news. The same phenomenon occurred in the newspaper business: foreign news fell from 10 percent of the average daily's news content in 1971 to roughly 2 percent [by 9/11]. The major news magazines cut back their foreign news from 22 percent in 1985 to 13 percent in 1995. And yet the popularity of news broadcasts fell consistently throughout those years. The more they dumbed down in the race for ratings, the more viewers they lost.[5]

They certainly had lost me, though I was so uninterested that I did not even bother to think about why. Like so many Americans, I just stopped watching.

Though I knew much more about the wider world than most Americans (I had even traveled to Eastern Europe and Russia in 1992, to see for myself what was going on), I had no real idea what was happening—and the news media weren't helping me learn. I read *The New York Times* daily, but even that often proved fruitless. Subscriptions to *Harper's, The Atlantic Monthly,* and *The New York Review of Books* helped, but I felt increasingly out of touch with what was going on in the greater world—more so than I had even as a Peace Corps Volunteer in northern Togo.

For me, personally, the professional news media had failed, though I really had no idea how or why. Certainly, I was not yet at the point of recognizing what was going on—unlike Fenton, who, with many of the old-time correspondents, clearly saw that the press had stopped doing its job: "At the very least, it is our job to keep our public informed of events that will affect them. We should serve as a kind of alert mechanism, an early warning system. Yet we abdicated that position in the months and years leading up to 9/11—and, in real and important ways, we have still not yet returned to the post."[6] He is right—and there were thousands upon thousands like me who thirsted for the news we weren't getting, but who weren't expert enough students of the news media to see what was happening or to do anything about it, just as there were many in the news media who also felt helpless. Like me, many who wanted news were already turning to the Internet as an alternative—though it had not yet reached its stride and was not yet able to offer the panoply of sources for news, from the professional to the personal, from every corner of the globe. It had not yet given *us* a way to replace the failed news media.

It was in 2001 that I first established a blog. It wasn't much: a crude and early blogger.com site—and I posted rarely. I did not fully recognize just what the blogs could do and did not have the time to spend to learn how to manipulate them expertly. Though they were easy to establish and to use, successful blogging was a demanding task even then. One of the things it took, was regularity and effort in development of an interested audience. I had the time for neither.

Even so, I knew that the blogs were going to be important, somehow—it was just that my own life (I was running one store, closing another, and beginning to teach for the first time in almost a decade) did not really have room for them. Their flexibility and the already apparent diversity they could encompass made it clear to me that these could develop into an entirely new type of communication. Their public nature, the ability to accept comments, and the fact that multiple bloggers could work from one site added up to something that could only expand the way we presented ourselves as individuals and kept track of our interactions with others. . . .

It wasn't until the morning of September 11, 2001, that I finally realized just how important the blogs were going to become, though, ironically, that day also stopped my blogging for three years. I had experienced the cacophony of much less significant "breaking" news events on the web, going back to the death of Princess Diana, four years and a little more than a week earlier, and had not been impressed. At the time of the princess's death, I'd been in an AOL chat room discussing some other topic completely—yet every minute or so, someone would enter the room, type a line about the car crash, and then leave—presumably to do the same elsewhere. All other discussion got completely sidetracked. A level of hysteria that I would not have thought possible on the Web was generated.

I wasn't about to get involved in that sort of thing, not on 9/11, not in face of that event. But I did want to communicate what I was experiencing, walking through Brooklyn close enough to ground zero to watch sheets of half-burned paper flutter to the ground around me, to feel and taste the ash in the air, and—soon—to watch the ashen and ash-covered who had walked across the Brooklyn Bridge and were now trudging down Court Street past my store, heading for their homes in Carroll Gardens, Red Hook, and even further away, many walking to Bay Ridge, Gravesend, and Coney Island.

Unable to listen to the radio with its stunned, nattering announcers—and not having television available at the store—I resorted to my computer for news. There, for the first time, I recognized the incredible power of the Web as a source of information—and misinformation—in breaking-news situations. I also thought immediately of my blog, for I needed to say something, but like those around me, I didn't really want to start talking. Like everyone else, I was in shock; all we could do was look at each other, eyes replacing speech. So, instead, I composed something, there at my store, as people walked by in the lingering dust. I sent it to everyone on my email address list and posted it on my blog.

For the first time, I felt one of the real powers of the blogs, the power to bring people together in a time of tragedy. Over the following days, I posted a couple of further thoughts on 9/11, but even though I now saw how important the blogs were likely to become, my heart wasn't in it, and I felt pulled to deal primarily with the people directly around me. My last post until 2005 came less than two weeks after 9/11.

Coming out of my own shock, I found that the news media were once again focusing on the wider world. Perhaps I thought that the blogs wouldn't be needed, that the news media would once again be doing their job. Though I never got back into the evening news habit, I did find that I could turn on the radio or the television or pick up a magazine and find something about events outside the borders of the United States. However, that wasn't destined to last. American journalism, after seeming to wake from its long nap, soon turned over and went back to sleep, dashing all hopes that a newly invigorated news media would help the American population and government deal with the aftermath of 9/11. By the end of 2001, the news media had fallen back into its old patterns of concentration on the easy stories of missing women and other meaningless fluff.

As those same months passed, I began to get more involved in my new second career as a teacher—extending my classroom work to scholarship. The writing I was doing was directed toward books and journals (some of them online) and not toward what I (in my ignorance) saw as the much more personal world of the blogs. Because coverage continued on U.S. actions abroad in Afghanistan and then Iraq, I was satisfied that there was, at least, a little more coverage than there had been, even though it was again shrinking. So I didn't actively look for alternatives.

Strangely—for I am rather much of a political junkie—I had not participated in the political blogs that had begun to come online in the months before 9/11 and did not do so as they exploded in popularity over the next couple of years. It amused me when the commercial news media made a big deal of bloggers getting press passes to the 2004 presidential conventions—I wondered what the big deal was and why anyone should think bloggers shouldn't be there—but I had no urge to even look at my own blog again, let alone post to it.

I didn't know what I was missing. Having used the blogs as an emotional aide during a crisis, I somehow didn't want to turn to them for anything else, though I certainly knew how powerful that could be. Perhaps I didn't want to lose the emotions of that time in what was sure to be a much more raucous blog experience.

Not surprisingly, what I found when I did start to read the political blogs in 2004 startled me. Here, finally, was opinion that did not masquerade as objective observation. Here, there was no attempt to provide balance between competing views. Though slightly shocking, is was certainly refreshing—even from points of view I disagreed with completely.

More important, no agenda was hidden on the blogs. Everything was right out in the open. Though the arguments were nasty and fierce, at least they weren't cloaked under a mantle of collegiality and false respect. It was then, reading through the arguments on the blogs, that I began to understand the ways in which the professional and commercial news media had failed me. Like much of the public, I had already become jaded to claims of "balance" and "objectivity." No one believed that anymore. On the right, it was all the "liberal media." To the left, it was "the corporate media." Neither side felt any trust at all for the news media, and both were as right as they were wrong in their beliefs. Both saw the news media, also, as essentially commercial, as turning news into entertainment for profit—a much more accurate judgment than simply seeing the news media in thrall to some liberal or corporate establishment that was forcing certain views on a reluctant public. Like millions of others, on discovering the blogs, I felt I had been released from a straightjacket, that I could now move for myself rather than waiting for the media to place me on one side or another. It was exhilarating.

In the preceding two years, the commercial news media had reached a new low, unable to question the administration of a president who, in the aftermath of 9/11, had popularity ratings in the stratosphere, a news media suddenly unwilling to be anything more than a means of transmittal of government-produced statements. There seemed to be only one source of information, really, though it wore a number of faces. I wasn't alone in my increasing frustration. Dissatisfaction with the news media had risen to the point of overt anger with what were seen as the poseurs of feigned neutrality and seriousness who were claiming to bring important information into American homes.

Many of us reacted to this by seeking the other extreme: if we couldn't have neutrality, if we could trust none of those who had once claimed our trust, then as a new venue was established, one that bypassed questions of trust, we would most certainly embrace it and the overt bias it expressed. Furthermore, we were starting to understand that it wasn't a problem with the information we were getting, but rather, what was bothering us was that it was *selected* information. Quite clearly, we weren't getting the whole picture—but we couldn't get anyone in the news media to admit that, let alone address the issue. We were "thirsty for *real* information—news unfiltered by editors who 'know what's best for us,' facts boldly stated and supported, and unvarnished opinion openly expressed for all to see and judge. And blogs gave it . . . in spades."[7]

It was in 2004, the year that I started reading the political blogs, that they really started to have an impact on the political and media worlds. The numbers were startling and tell the story. Certainly, I was not alone in turning to the blogs. As Kline records, "during the crucial August period leading up to the 2004 presidential election, the ten most popular political blogs collectively had 28 million visits from readers, which rivaled traffic to the three 24/7 online cable news networks. One of those, the liberal blog Daily Kos, drew 7 million reader visits alone that month, which beat Fox News's 5.7 million online visits."[9]

What was attractive about the blogs was the freedom they represented. There were so many of them, from an infinite variety of viewpoints, that one could always find another if the first did seem agreeable. Though many didn't see it that way (seeing what was happening as a retreat from debate), what was going on was a necessary step toward the reestablishment of a public sphere—and toward a discovery that seems to have been as shocking to American politicians (many of whom believed that Iraqis, for example, wanted to be the same as Americans) as to journalists. The discovery, in Fenton's words, was that the "freer flow of information, apparently, does not lead all societies toward the same values. Given the freedom to do so, we don't even *perceive* the same things. The truth gets fractured, everybody takes sides, no one knows what's going on, *so people watch the news that confirms their views.*"[10] But once they have absorbed that information, people also do start to look around for other viewpoints, if for no other reason than to prove them wrong. People, after all, *like* debate and *want* to be involved personally in the public sphere. Because each blog is limited, and most recycle much of the same set of ideas over and over again, no one blog, ultimately, proves sufficient for most bloggers—not even their own.

Just as no blog in itself will be sufficient for revitalization of the public sphere, not even the blogs as a whole will be able to bring back debate among an engaged public. Even with them, someone doing what journalism is supposed to do will be necessary—for, without that, many people may get stuck watching only "news that confirms their views." For the past two centuries, (as James Fallows points out), journalism has been "the main tool we have for keeping the world's events in perspective. It is the main source of agreed-upon facts we can use in public decisions."[11] And that tool has been important in focusing the debate. Fallows goes on to say that the "excesses of journalism have been tolerated because no other institution can provide the benefits journalism can."[12] Although that may have been the case once, it may not be today and certainly will not be much longer. People have already started to blog about events they witness, and this will continue and expand. One day, no major event will occur anywhere in the world without people recording it on cell phones and broadcasting it on a blog. In face of this, unless journalists do begin to reform themselves, thereby providing something that these amateurs can't do in the aggregate, the profession of journalism will atrophy.

My own engagement with the blogs as an active writer for a sustained period of time began in early 2005, when I was finally convinced that they could be a venue for sustained discussion of a positive nature—even if each individual blog was a belligerent advocate of just one viewpoint. I had begun to see longer posts based on research by the blogger and thoughtful essays that did much more than cry and scream about this issue or that, and I now wanted to join in the growing discussion.

Along with many thousands of others, that's just what I did.

Discussion Questions

1. What advantage does the field of reporting have today that has never been possible before? What does it mean to be both a citizen and a reporter?

2. How does Barlow describe American media coverage of the rest of the world in the 1990s? How does Barlow explain this?

3. Do Americans regard the news they get today from the media useful or even accurate? What are your views on the media in this regard? Are there other sources you go to find out what is really happening?

4. What is the difference between being given the news and taking it?

5. How does one become a successful blogger?

6. How did Barlow view the world wide web in 1991? How did he view it after 9/11? How does he explain his change of heart?

7. What should the role of the media be? Where does it succeed? Where does it fail?

8. According to Barlow, how will the growing number of bloggers revitalize the public sphere?

Writing Tasks

1. Go to the blogger's section at NewYorkTimes.com, Salon.com, or Gothamgezette.com. Write an essay that responds to the views expressed on a current debate.

2. Find three blogs on the Internet and evaluate them as credible or non-credible sources of information.

Section II:
Literary New York

"Nighthawks" Edward Hopper (1942)
Image courtesy of The Art Institute of Chicago.

The city seen from the Queensborough Bridge is always the city seen for the first time, in its wild promise of all the mystery and the beauty in the world.

F. Scott Fitzgerald (from *The Great Gatsby*)

Writing is the hardest work in the world not involving heavy lifting.

Pete Hamill

Literary New York

There is no city like New York to inspire great writing. A quick perusal of some of our finest classics from the poetry of Walt Whitman, to the down and out reportage of Stephen Crane in *Maggie: A Girl of the Streets,* to the memorable vivisections of the upper crust in Henry James' *Washington Square,* Edith Wharton's *House of Mirth,* and F. Scott Fitzgerald's *The Great Gatsby,* to exciting exposés of the marginalized in Ann Petry's *The Street,* Ralph Ellison's *Invisible Man* and Jack Kerouac's *The Town and the City,* to modern classics like Tom Wolfe's *Bonfire of the Vanities,* Chang-Rae Lee's *Native Speaker,* and Jonathan Lethem's *Fortress of Solitude,* New York is the unrivalled setting for fiction that both entertains and instructs on a deeply personal and universal level. Indeed, the setting for enduring writers like Whitman *has* to be New York. Nowhere else, after all, can one find such energy, diversity, spectacle, tension and movement as in this most "unruly, musical, self-sufficient" city— "My City!"

The selections collected here are but a microcosm of a much larger field, but they are representative of the types of themes and approaches New York fiction often contains. In them we find moments of pure feeling; histories of desperation or hope; musings on loneliness, connection, isolation and joy. The first three selections, for example, contrast the varied emotions that the city invokes, from Whitman's euphoria to the metaphysical lament "Ah Humanity!" that completes "Bartleby, the Scrivener." The city also encourages new forms of fiction to arise as we see in the modernist pieces of Pound and e.e. cummings. Like the jazzlike montage of the New York skyline, the same jagged edge and urban tempo are captured in their poems.

As Edwidge Danticat shows, the granite city can be a place that teaches us how to better understand those closest to us. Ultimately, it is a place of constant transformation, a process that, as "Chango's Fire" so vividly demonstrates, can startle the urban soul. For better and for worse, the place where we dwell forever surprises us, broadening our perceptions and changing who we are.

Walt Whitman

Walt Whitman (1819–1892), America's most famous poet, reveled in the "faces and streets" of Manhattan and Brooklyn, where he was born. He viewed the crowd as the embodiment of democracy and a spiritual force and wrote about his urban experiences incessantly. He was particularly fascinated with the spectacle of early mass transit such as the Brooklyn Ferry and the omni-buses on Broadway, which symbolized to him the relentless tide of human energy.

MANNAHATTA

I was asking for something specific and perfect for my city,   1
    Whereupon lo! upsprang the aboriginal name.

Now I see what there is in a name, a word, liquid, sane,
    unruly, musical, self-sufficient,
I see that the word of my city is that word from of old,   5
Because I see that word nested in nests of water-bays, superb,
Rich, hemm'd thick all around with sailships and steamships,
    an island sixteen miles long, solid-founded,
Numberless crowded streets, high growths of iron, slender,
    strong, light, splendidly uprising toward clear skies,   10
Tides swift and ample, well-loved by me, toward sundown,
The flowing sea-currents, the little islands, larger adjoining
    islands, the heights, the villas,
The countless masts, the white shore-steamers, the lighters,
    the ferry-boats, the black sea-steamers well-model'd,   15
The down-town streets, the jobbers' houses of business,
    the houses of business of the ship-merchants and
    money-brokers, the river-streets,
Immigrants arriving, fifteen or twenty thousand in a week,
The carts hauling goods, the manly race of drivers of   20
    horses, the brown-faced sailors,
The summer air, the bright sun shining, and the sailing
    clouds aloft,
The winter snows, the sleigh-bells, the broken ice in the
    river, passing along up or down with the flood-tide or
    ebb-tide,   25
The mechanics of the city, the masters, well-form'd,
    beautiful-faced, looking you straight in the eyes,
Trottoirs throng'd, vehicles, Broadway, the women, the
    shops and shows,
A million people—manners free and superb—open voices—   30
    hospitality—the most courageous and friendly young men,

City of hurried and sparkling waters! city of spires and masts!
City nested in bays! my city!

CROSSING BROOKLYN FERRY

*f*lood-tide below me! I see you face to face!   1
Clouds of the west—sun there half an hour high—I see you
   also face to face.

Crowds of men and women attired in the usual costumes,
   how curious you are to me!   5
On the ferry-boats the hundreds and hundreds that cross,
   returning home, are more curious to me than you
   suppose,

And you that shall cross from shore to shore years hence
   are more to me, and more in my meditations, than you
   might suppose.   10

2
The impalpable sustenance of me from all things at all
   hours of the day,
The simple, compact, well-join'd scheme, myself
   disintegrated, every one disintegrated yet part of the
   scheme,
The similitudes of the past and those of the future,   15
The glories strung like beads on my smallest sights and
   hearings, on the walk in the street and the passage over
   the river,
The current rushing so swiftly and swimming with me far
   away,   20
The others that are to follow me, the ties between me and
   them,
The certainty of others, the life, love, sight, hearing of others.
Others will enter the gates of the ferry and cross from shore
   to shore,   25
Others will watch the run of the flood-tide,
Others will see the shipping of Manhattan north and west,
   and the heights of Brooklyn to the south and east,
Others will see the islands large and small;
Fifty years hence, others will see them as they cross, the   30
   sun half an hour high,
A hundred years hence, or ever so many hundred years
   hence, others will see them,
Will enjoy the sunset, the pouring-in of the flood-tide, the
   falling-back to the sea of the ebb-tide.   35

3

It avails not, time nor place—distance avails not,
I am with you, you men and women of a generation, or
  ever so many generations hence,
Just as you feel when you look on the river and sky, so I
  felt,
Just as any of you is one of a living crowd, I was one of a   40
  crowd,
Just as you are refresh'd by the gladness of the river and
  the bright flow, I was refresh'd,
Just as you stand and lean on the rail, yet hurry with the
  swift current, I stood yet was hurried,   45
Just as you look on the numberless masts of ships and
  thick-stemm'd pipes of steamboats, I look'd.

I too many and many a time cross'd the river of old,
Watched the Twelfth-month sea-gulls, saw them high in the
  air floating with motionless wings, oscillating their bodies   50
Saw how the glistening yellow lit up parts of their bodies
  and left the rest in strong shadow,
Saw the slow-wheeling circles and the gradual edging
  toward the south,
Saw the reflection of the summer sky in the water,   55
Had my eyes dazzled by the shimmering track of beams,
Look'd at the fine centrifugal spokes of light round the
  shape of my head in the sunlit water,
Look'd on the haze on the hills southward and south-
  westward,   60
Look'd on the vapor as it flew in fleeces tinged with violet,
Look'd toward the lower bay to notice the vessels arriving,
Saw their approach, saw aboard those that were near me,
Saw the white sails of schooners and sloops, saw the ships
  at anchor,   65
The sailors at work in the rigging or out astride the spars,
The round masts, the swinging motion of the hulls, the
  slender serpentine pennants,
The large and small steamers in motion, the pilots in their
  pilothouses,   70
The white wake left by the passage, the quick tremulous
  whirl of the wheels,
The flags of all nations, the falling of them at sunset,
The scallop-edged waves in the twilight, the ladled cups,
  the frolicsome crests and glistening,   75
The stretch afar growing dimmer and dimmer, the gray
  walls of the granite storehouses by the docks,

On the river the shadowy group, the big steam-tug closely
    flank'd on each side by the barges, the hay-boat, the
    belated lighter,   80
On the neighboring shore the fires from the foundry
    chimneys burning high and glaringly into the night,
Casting their flicker of black contrasted with wild red and
    yellow light over the tops of houses, and down into the
    clefts of streets.   85

4

These and all else were to me the same as they are to you,
I loved well those cities, loved well the stately and rapid river,
The men and women I saw were all near to me,
Others the same—others who look back on me because I
    look'd forward to them,   90
(The time will come, though I stop here to-day and to-night.)

5

What is it then between us?
What is the count of the scores or hundreds of years
    between us?

Whatever it is, it avails not—distance avails not, and place   95
    avails not,
I too lived, Brooklyn of ample hills was mine,
I too walk'd the street of Manhattan island, and bathed in
    the waters around it,
I too felt the curious abrupt questionings stir within me,   100
In the day among crowds of people sometimes they came
    upon me,
In my walks home late at night or as I lay in my bed they
came upon me,
I too had been struck from the float forever held in solution,   105
I too had receiv'd identity by my body,
That I was I knew was of my body, and what I should be I
    knew I should be of my body.

6

It is not upon you alone the dark patches fall,
The dark threw its patches down upon me also,   110
The best I had done seem'd to me blank and suspicious,
My great thoughts as I supposed them, were they not in
    reality meagre?
Nor is it you alone who know what it is to be evil,   115
I am he who knew what it was to be evil,

I too knitted the old knot of contrariety,
Blabb'd, blush'd, resented, lied, stole, grudg'd,
Had guile, anger, lust, hot wishes I dared not speak,
Was wayward, vain, greedy, shallow, sly, cowardly, malignant,
The wolf, the snake, the hog, not wanting in me,   120
The cheating look, the frivolous word, the adulterous wish,
    not wanting,
Refusals, hates, postponements, meanness, laziness, none
    of these wanting,
Was one with the rest, the days and haps of the rest,   125
Was call'd by my nighest name by clear loud voices of
    young men as they saw me approaching or passing,
Felt their arms on my neck as I stood, or the negligent
    leaning of their flesh against me as I sat,
Saw many I loved in the street or ferry-boat or public   130
    assembly, yet never told them a word,
Lived the same life with the rest, the same old laughing,
    gnawing, sleeping.
Play'd the part that still looks back on the actor or actress,
The same old role, the role that is what we make it, as great   135
    as we like,
Or as small as we like, or both great and small.

7

Closer yet I approach you,
What thought you have of me now, I had as much of you—I
    laid in my stores in advance,   140
I consider'd long and seriously of you before you were born.

Who was to know what should come home to me?
Who knows but I am enjoying this?
Who knows, for all the distance, but I am as good as
    looking at you now, for all you cannot see me?   145

8

Ah, what can ever be more stately and admirable to me
    than masthemm'd Manhattan?
River and sunset and scallop-edg'd waves of flood-tide?
The sea-gulls oscillating their bodies, the hay-boat in the
    twilight, and the belated lighter?   150

What gods can exceed these that clasp me by the hand, and
    with voices I love call me promptly and loudly by my
    nighest name as I approach?
What is more subtle than this which ties me to the woman
    or man that looks in my face?   155
Which fuses me into you now, and pours my meaning
    into you?

We understand then do we not?
What I promis'd without mentioning it, have you not
    accepted?   160
What the study could not teach—what the preaching
    could not accomplish is accomplish'd, is it not?

9

Flow on, river! flow with the flood-tide, and ebb with the
    ebb-tide!
Frolic on, crested and scallop-edg'd waves!   165
Gorgeous clouds of the sunset! drench with your splendor
    me, or the men and women generation after me!
Cross from shore to shore, countless crowds of passengers!
Stand up, tall masts of Mannahatta! stand up, beautiful
    hills of Brooklyn!   170
Throb, baffled and curious brain! throw out questions and
    answers!
Suspend here and everywhere, eternal float of solution!
Gaze, loving and thirsting eyes, in the house or street or
    public assembly!   175
Sound out, voices of young men! loudly and musically call
    me by my nighest name!
Live, old life! play the part that looks back on the actor or
    actress!
Play the old role, the role that is great or small according a   180
    one makes it!
Consider, you who peruse me, whether I may not in
    unknown ways be looking upon you;
Be firm, rail over the river, to support those who lean idly,
    yet haste with the hasting current;   185
Fly on, sea-birds! fly sideways, or wheel in large circles
    high in the air;
Receive the summer sky, you water, and faithfully hold it
    till all downcast eyes have time to take it from you!
Diverge, fine spokes of light, from the shape of my head, or   190
    any one's head, in the sunlit water!
Come on, ships from the lower bay! pass up or down,
    white-sail'd schooners, sloops, lighters!
Flaunt away, flags of all nations! be duly lower'd at sunset!
Burn high your fires, foundry chimneys! cast black shadows   195
    at nightfall! cast red and yellow light over the tops of the
    houses!
Appearances, now or henceforth, indicate what you are,
You necessary film, continue to envelop the soul,
About my body for me, and your body for you, be hung our   200
    divinest aromas,

Thrive, cities—bring your freight, bring your shows, ample
and sufficient rivers,
Expand, being than which none else is perhaps more
spiritual,
Keep your places, objects than which none else is more   205
lasting.
You have waited, you always wait, you dumb, beautiful
ministers,
We receive you with free sense at last, and are insatiate
henceforward,   210
Not you any more shall be able to foil us, or withhold
yourselves from us,
We use you, and do not cast you aside—we plant you
permanently within us,
We fathom you not—we love you—there is perfection in   215
you also,
You furnish your parts toward eternity,
Great or small, you furnish your parts toward the soul.

From THE COLLECTED WRITINGS
OF WALT WHITMAN: PROSE WORKS *1892,*
Volume 2, New York University Press.

Bartleby, the Scrivener: A Story of Wall Street

Herman Melville

Herman Melville (1819–1891) was born in New York City and spent close to twenty-five years working as a customs inspector at the port. In addition to writing one of the greatest novels in world literature, *Moby-Dick* (which begins in Manhattan), he is also author of what is arguably the greatest New York story of them all, "Bartleby, the Scrivener." This enigmatic story explores the world of Wall Street as it was emerging in the 1850s and points to the effects of modern life on the human soul. It is a story that remains as relevant today as it was then.

Chapter 1

I am a rather elderly man. The nature of my avocations for the last thirty years has brought me into more than ordinary contact with what would seem an interesting and somewhat singular set of men, of whom, as yet, nothing that I know of has ever been written—I mean the law-copyists, or scriveners. I have known very many of them, professionally and privately, and, if I pleased, could relate divers histories at which good-natured gentlemen might smile and sentimental souls might weep. But I waive the biographies of all other scriveners for a few passages in the life of Bartleby, who was a scrivener, the strangest I ever saw or heard of. While of other law-copyists I might write the complete life, of Bartleby nothing of that sort can be done. I believe that no materials exist for a full and satisfactory biography of this man. It is an irreparable loss to literature. Bartleby was one of those beings of whom nothing is ascertainable. . . .

Ere introducing the scrivener as he first appeared to me, it is fit I make some mention of myself, my employees, my business, my chambers and general surroundings, because some such description is indispensable to an adequate understanding of the chief character about to be presented.

Imprimis: I am a man who, from his youth upwards, has been filled with a profound conviction that the easiest way of life is the best. Hence, though I belong to a profession proverbially energetic and nervous even to turbulence at times, yet nothing of that sort have I ever suffered to invade my peace. I am one of those unambitious lawyers who never addresses a jury or in any way draws down public applause, but, in the cool

1

Bartleby, the Scrivener by Herman Melville, 1853.

tranquillity of a snug retreat, do a snug business among rich men's bonds, and mortgages, and title deeds. All who know me consider me an eminently *safe* man. . . .

My chambers were upstairs at No.____ Wall Street. At one end they looked upon the white wall of the interior of a spacious skylight shaft, penetrating the building from top to bottom. This view might have been considered rather tame than otherwise, deficient in what landscape painters call "life." But, if so, the view from the other end of my chambers offered at least a contrast, if nothing more. In that direction, my windows commanded an unobstructed view of a lofty brick wall, black by age and everlasting shade . . . pushed up to within ten feet of my windowpanes.

At the period just preceding the advent of Bartleby, I had two persons as copyists in my employment, and a promising lad as an office boy. First,   5
Turkey; second, Nippers; third Ginger Nut. These may seem names the like of which are not usually found in the Directory. In truth, they were nicknames, mutually conferred upon each other by my three clerks, and were deemed expressive of their respective persons or characters. Turkey was a short, pursy Englishman, of about my own age—that is, somewhere not far from sixty. In the morning, one might say, his face was of a fine florid hue, but after twelve o'clock—his dinner hour—it blazed like a grate full of Christmas coals; and continued blazing till six o'clock, P.M. There are many singular coincidences I have known in the course of my life, not the least among which was the fact, that, exactly when Turkey displayed his fullest beams from his red and radiant countenance, just then, too, at that critical moment, began the daily period when I considered his business capacities as seriously disturbed for the remainder of the twenty-four hours. Not that he was absolutely idle or averse to business then; far from it. The difficulty was, he was apt to be altogether too energetic. There was a strange, inflamed, flurried, flighty recklessness of activity about him. He would be incautious in dipping his pen into his inkstand. All his blots upon my documents were dropped there after twelve o'clock. Indeed, not only would he be reckless and sadly given to making blots in the afternoon, but some days he went further and was rather noisy. . . . He made an unpleasant racket with his chair; in mending his pens, impatiently split them all to pieces and threw them on the floor in a sudden passion; stood up and leaned over his table, boxing his papers about in a most indecorous manner, very sad to behold in an elderly man like him. Nevertheless, as he was in many ways a most valuable person to me, and all the time before twelve o'clock was the quickest, steadiest creature, too, accomplishing a great deal of work in a style not easily to be matched—for these reasons I was willing to overlook his eccentricities, though indeed, occasionally, I remonstrated with him. . . .

Nippers, the second on my list, was a whiskered, sallow, and upon the whole rather piratical-looking young man of about five and twenty. I always deemed him the victim of two evil powers—ambition and indigestion. The ambition was evinced by a certain impatience of the duties of a mere copyist, an unwarrantable usurpation of strictly professional affairs, such as the original drawing up of legal documents. The indigestion seemed betokened in an occasional nervous testiness and grinning irritability, causing the teeth to audibly grind together over mistakes committed in copying; unnecessary maledictions, hissed rather than spoken, in the heat of business; and especially by a continual discontent with the height of the table where he worked. . . .

Ginger Nut, the third on my list, was a lad some twelve years old. His father was a carman, ambitious of seeing his son on the bench instead of a cart before he died. So he sent him to my office, as student at law, errand boy, cleaner and sweeper, at the rate of one dollar a week. . . . Copying law papers being proverbially a dry, husky sort of business, my two scriveners . . . sent Ginger Nut very frequently for that peculiar cake—small, flat, round, and very spicy—after which he had been named by them.

There was now great work for scriveners. Not only must I push the clerks already with me, but I must have additional help. In answer to my advertisement, a motionless young man one morning stood upon my office threshold, the door being open, for it was summer. I can see that figure now—pallidly neat pitiably respectable, incurably forlorn! It was Bartleby.

After a few words touching his qualifications, I engaged him, glad to have among my corps of copyists a man of so singularly sedate an aspect, which I thought might operate beneficially upon the flighty temper of Turkey and the fiery one of Nippers.

I should have stated before that ground-glass folding doors divided my premises into two parts, one of which was occupied by my scriveners, the other by myself. According to my humor, I threw open these doors or closed them. I resolved to assign Bartleby a corner by the folding doors, but on my side of them so as to have this quiet man within easy call, in case any trifling thing was to be done. I placed his desk close up to a small side window in that part of the room, a window which originally had afforded a lateral view of certain grimy back yards and bricks, but which, owing to subsequent erections, commanded at present no view at all, though it gave some light. Within three feet of the panes was a wall, and the light came down from far above, between two lofty buildings, as from a very small opening in a dome. Still further to a satisfactory arrangement, I procured a high green folding screen, which might entirely isolate

10

Bartleby from my sight, though not remove him from my voice. And thus, in a manner, privacy and society were conjoined.

At first, Bartleby did an extraordinary quantity of writing. As if long famishing for something to copy, he seemed to gorge himself on my documents. There was no pause for digestion. He ran a day and night line, copying by sunlight and by candlelight. I should have been quite delighted with his application, had he been cheerfully industrious. But he wrote on silently, palely, mechanically.

It is, of course, an indispensable part of a scrivener's business to verify the accuracy of his copy, word by word. Where there are two or more scriveners in an office, they assist each other in this examination, one reading from the copy, the other holding the original. It is a very dull, wearisome, and lethargic affair. I can readily imagine that, to some sanguine temperaments, it would be altogether intolerable. . . .

Now and then, in the haste of business, it had been my habit to assist in comparing some brief document myself, calling Turkey or Nippers for this purpose. One object I had in placing Bartleby so handy to me behind the screen was to avail myself of his services on such trivial occasions. It was on the third day, I think, of his being with me, and before any necessity had arisen for having his own writing examined, that, being much hurried to complete a small affair I had in hand, I abruptly called to Bartleby. In my haste and natural expectancy of instant compliance, I sat with my head bent over the original on my desk, and my right hand sideways, and somewhat nervously extended with the copy, so that, immediately upon emerging from his retreat, Bartleby might snatch it and proceed to business without the least delay.

In this very attitude did I sit when I called to him, rapidly stating what it was I wanted him to do—namely, to examine a small paper with me. Imagine my surprise, nay, my consternation, when, without moving from his privacy, Bartleby, in a singularly mild, firm voice, replied, "I would prefer not to."

I sat awhile in perfect silence, rallying my stunned faculties. Immediately it occurred to me that my ears had deceived me, or Bartleby had entirely misunderstood my meaning. I repeated my request in the clearest tone I could assume; but in quite as clear a one came the previous reply, "I would prefer not to."

"Prefer not to," echoed I, rising in high excitement, and crossing the room with a stride. "What do you mean? Are you moon-struck? I want you to help me compare this sheet here—take it," and I thrust it towards him.

"I would prefer not to," said he.

I looked at him steadfastly. His face was leanly composed; his gray eyes dimly calm. Not a wrinkle of agitation rippled him. Had there been

15

the least uneasiness, anger, impatience or impertinence in his manner; in other words, had there been anything ordinarily human about him, doubtless I should have violently dismissed him from the premises. I stood gazing at him awhile, as he went on with his own writing, and then reseated myself at my desk. This is very strange, thought I. What had one best do? But my business hurried me. I concluded to forget the matter for the present, reserving it for my future leisure. So calling Nippers from the other room, the paper was speedily examined.

A few days after this, Bartleby concluded four lengthy documents, being quadruplicates of a week's testimony taken before me in my High Court of Chancery. It became necessary to examine them. It was an important suit, and great accuracy was imperative. Having all things arranged, I called Turkey Nippers and Ginger Nut, from the next room, meaning to place the four copies in the hands of my four clerks, while I should read from the original. Accordingly, Turkey, Nippers, and Ginger Nut had taken their seats in a row, each with his document in his hand, when I called to Bartleby to join this interesting group.

"Bartleby! quick, I am waiting."   20

I heard a slow scrape of his chair legs on the uncarpeted floor, and soon he appeared standing at the entrance of his hermitage.

"What is wanted?" said he, mildly.

"The copies, the copies," said I, hurriedly. "We are going to examine them. There"—and I held towards him the fourth quadruplicate.

"I would prefer not to," he said, and gently disappeared behind the screen.

For a few moments I was turned into a pillar of salt, standing at the head   25
of my seated column of clerks. Recovering myself, I advanced towards the screen and demanded the reason for such extraordinary conduct.

"*Why* do you refuse?"

"I would prefer not to."

With any other man I should have flown outright into a dreadful passion, scorned all further words, and thrust him ignominiously from my presence. But there was something about Bartleby that not only strangely disarmed me, but, in a wonderful manner, touched and disconcerted me. I began to reason with him.

"These are your own copies we are about to examine. It is labor saving to you, because one examination will answer for your four papers. It is common usage. Every copyist is bound to help examine his copy. Is it not so? Will you not speak? Answer!"

"I prefer not to," he replied in a flutelike tone. It seemed to me that, while   30
I had been addressing him, he carefully revolved every statement that I made; fully comprehended the meaning; could not gainsay the irresistible

conclusion; but, at the same time, some paramount consideration prevailed with him to reply as he did.

"You are decided, then, not to comply with my request—a request made according to common usage and common sense?"

He briefly gave me to understand that on that point my judgment was sound. Yes: his decision was irreversible.

It is seldom the case that, when a man is browbeaten in some unprecedented and violently unreasonable way, he begins to stagger in his own plainest faith. He begins, as it were, vaguely to surmise that, wonderful as it may be, all the justice and all the reason is on the other side. Accordingly, if any disinterested persons are present, he turns to them for some reinforcement for his own faltering mind.

"Turkey," said I, "what do you think of this? Am I not right?"

"With submission, sir," said Turkey, in his blandest tone, "I think that   35
you are."

"Nippers," said I, "what do *you* think of it?"

"I think I should kick him out of the office."

"Ginger Nut," said I, willing to enlist the smallest suffrage in my behalf, "what do *you* think of it?"

"I think, sir, he's a little *luny*," replied Ginger Nut, with a grin.

"You hear what they say," said I, turning towards the screen, "come   40
forth and do your duty."

But he vouchsafed no reply. I pondered a moment in sore perplexity. But once more business hurried me. I determined again to postpone the consideration of this dilemma to my future leisure. . . . Meanwhile Bartleby sat in his hermitage, oblivious to everything but his own peculiar business there.

Chapter Two

Nothing so aggravates an earnest person as a passive resistance. . . . Even so, for the most part, I regarded Bartleby and his ways. Poor fellow! thought I, he means no mischief; it is plain he intends no insolence; his aspect sufficiently evinces that his eccentricities are involuntary. He is useful to me. I can get along with him. . . . But one afternoon the evil impulse in me mastered me, and the following little scene ensued:

"Bartleby," said I, "when those papers are all copied, I will compare them with you."

"I would prefer not to."

"How? Surely you do not mean to persist in that mulish vagary?"   45

No answer.

"Bartleby," said I, "Ginger Nut is away; just step around to the Post Office, won't you? (it was but a three minutes' walk), and see if there is anything for me."

"I would prefer not to."

"You *will* not?"

"I *prefer* not."   50

I staggered to my desk and sat there in a deep study. My blind inveteracy returned. Was there any other thing in which I could procure myself to be ignominiously repulsed by this lean, penniless wight?—my hired clerk? What added thing is there, perfectly reasonable, that he will be sure to refuse to do? "Bartleby!"

No answer.

"Bartleby," in a louder tone.

No answer.

"Bartleby," I roared.   55

Like a very ghost, agreeably to the laws of magical invocation, at the third summons he appeared at the entrance of his hermitage.

"Go to the next room, and tell Nippers to come to me."

"I prefer not to," he respectfully and slowly said, and mildly disappeared.

"Very good, Bartleby," said I, in a quiet sort of serenely severe self-possessed tone, intimating the unalterable purpose of some terrible retribution very close at hand. At the moment I half intended something of the kind. But upon the whole, as it was drawing towards my dinner hour, I thought it best to put on my hat and walk home for the day, suffering much from perplexity and distress of mind. . .

Now, one Sunday morning I happened to go to Trinity Church, to hear a   60
celebrated preacher, and finding myself rather early on the ground I thought I would walk round to my chambers for a while. Luckily I had my key with me, but upon applying it to the lock, I found it resisted by something inserted from the inside. Quite surprised, I called out, when to my consternation a key was turned from within, and, thrusting his lean visage at me, and holding the door ajar, the apparition of Bartleby appeared, in his shirt sleeves . . . saying quietly that he was sorry but he was deeply engaged just then, and—preferred not admitting me at present. In a brief word or two, he moreover added, that perhaps I had better walk about the block two or three times, and by that time he would probably have concluded his affairs. . . .

Full of a restless curiosity, at last I returned to the door. Without hindrance I inserted my key, opened it, and entered. Bartleby was not to be seen. I looked round anxiously, peeped behind his screen; but it was very plain that he was gone. Upon more closely examining the place, I surmised that for an indefinite period Bartleby must have ate, dressed, and slept in my office, and that too without plate, mirror, or bed. The cushioned seat of a ricketty old sofa in one corner bore the faint impress of a lean, reclining form. Rolled away under his desk, I found a blanket; under the empty grate, a blacking box and brush; on a chair, a tin basin, with soap and a ragged towel; in a newspaper a few crumbs of ginger-nuts and a morsel of cheese. Yet, thought I, it is evident enough that Bartleby has been making his home here, keeping bachelor's hall all by himself. Immediately then the thought came sweeping across me, What miserable friendliness and loneliness are here revealed! His poverty is great; but his solitude, how horrible!

That morning . . . I walked homeward, thinking what I would do with Bartleby. Finally, I resolved upon this—I would put certain calm questions to him the next morning touching his history, etc., and if he declined to answer them openly and unreservedly (and I supposed he would prefer not) then to give him a twenty-dollar bill over and above whatever I might owe him, and tell him his services were no longer required; but that if in any other way I could assist him, I would be happy to do so, especially if he desired to return to his native place, wherever that might be, I would willingly help to defray the expenses. Moreover, if, after reaching home, he found himself at any time in want of aid, a letter from him would be sure of a reply. The next morning came. "Bartleby," said I, gently calling to him behind his screen. No reply.

"Bartleby," said I, in a still gentler tone, "come here—I am not going to ask you to do anything you would prefer not to do—I simply wish to speak to you."

Upon this he noiselessly slid into view.

"Will you tell me, Bartleby, where you were born?"   65

"I would prefer not to."

"Will you tell me *anything* about yourself?"

"I would prefer not to."

"But what reasonable objection can you have to speak to me? I feel friendly towards you."

He did not look at me while I spoke, but kept his glance fixed upon my   70
bust of Cicero, which, as I then sat, was directly behind me, some six inches above my head.

"What is your answer, Bartleby," said I.

"At present I prefer to give no answer," he said, and retired into his hermitage.

It was rather weak in me I confess, but his manner, on this occasion, nettled me. Not only did there seem to lurk in it a certain calm disdain, but his perverseness seemed ungrateful, considering the undeniable good usage and indulgence he had received from me.

Again I sat ruminating what I should do. Mortified as I was at his behavior, and resolved as I had been to dismiss him when I entered my office, nevertheless I strangely felt something superstitious knocking at my
heart, and forbidding me to carry out my purpose, and denouncing me for
a villain if I dared to breathe one bitter word against this forlornest of
mankind. At last, familiarly drawing my chair behind his screen, I sat
down and said: "Bartleby, never mind, then, about revealing your history;
but let me entreat you, as a friend, to comply as far as may be with the us-
ages of this office. Say now, you will help to examine papers tomorrow
or next day: in short, say now, that in a day or two you will begin to be a
little reasonable:—say so, Bartleby."

"At present I would prefer not to be a little reasonable," was his mildly   75
cadaverous reply . . . .

The next day I noticed that Bartleby did nothing but stand at his window in his dead-wall reverie. Upon asking him why he did not write, he
said that he had decided upon doing no more writing.

"Why, how now? what next?" exclaimed I, "do no more writing?"

"No more."

"And what is the reason?"

"Do you not see the reason for yourself?" he indifferently replied.   80

I looked steadfastly at him, and perceived that his eyes looked dull and
glazed. Instantly it occurred to me that his unexampled diligence in copying by his dim window for the first few weeks of his stay with me might
have temporarily impaired his vision.

I was touched. I said something in condolence with him, I hinted that
of course he did wisely in abstaining from writing for a while; and urged
him to embrace that opportunity of taking wholesome exercise in the open
air. This, however, he did not do. A few days after this, my other clerks being absent, and being in a great hurry to dispatch certain letters by the mail,
I thought that, having nothing else earthly to do, Bartleby would surely be
less inflexible than usual, and carry these letters to the Post Office. But he
blankly declined. So, much to my inconvenience, I went myself.

Still added days went by. Whether Bartleby's eyes improved or not, I
could not say. To all appearance, I thought they did. But when I asked him
if they did, he vouchsafed no answer. At all events, he would do no copying. At last, in reply to my urgings, he informed me that he had permanently given up copying.

"What!" exclaimed I; "suppose your eyes should get entirely well—
better than ever before—would you not copy then?"

"I have given up copying," he answered, and slid aside.   85

He remained as ever, a fixture in my chamber. Nay—if that were
possible—he became still more of a fixture than before. What was to be done?

Chapter 3

Since he will not quit me, I must quit him. I will change my offices; I will move elsewhere, and give him fair notice that if I find him on my new premises I will then proceed against him as a common trespasser.

Acting accordingly, next day I thus addressed him: "I find these chambers too far from the City Hall; the air is unwholesome. In a word, I propose to remove my offices next week, and shall no longer require your services. I tell you this now, in order that you may seek another place."

He made no reply, and nothing more was said.

On the appointed day I engaged carts and men, proceeded to my chambers, and, having but little furniture, everything was removed in a few hours. Throughout, the scrivener remained standing behind the screen, which I directed to be removed the last thing. It was withdrawn; and, being folded up like a huge folio, left him the motionless occupant of a naked room. I stood in the entry watching him a moment, while something from within me upbraided me.

I re-entered, with my hand in my pocket and my heart in my mouth.

"Good-bye, Bartleby; I am going—good-bye; and God some way bless you; and take that," slipping something in his hand. But it dropped upon the floor, and then—strange to say—I tore myself from him whom I had so longed to be rid of. . . .

Several days passed, and I heard nothing more; and, though I often felt a charitable prompting to call at the place and see poor Bartleby, yet a certain squeamishness, of I know not what, withheld me.

All is over with him, by this time, thought I at last, when, through another week, no further intelligence reached me. But, coming to my room the day after, I found several persons waiting at my door in a high state of nervous excitement.

"That's the man—here he comes," cried the foremost one, whom I recognized as the lawyer who had previously called upon me alone.

"You must take him away, sir, at once," cried a portly person among them, advancing upon me, and whom I knew to be the landlord of No. _____ Wall Street. "These gentlemen, my tenants, cannot stand it any longer. Mr. B _____," pointing to the lawyer; "has turned him out of his room, and he now persists in haunting the building generally, sitting upon the banisters of the stairs by day, and sleeping in the entry by night. Everybody is concerned; clients are leaving the offices; some fears are entertained of a mob; something you must do, and that without delay."

Aghast at this torrent, I fell back before it, and would fain have locked myself in my new quarters. In vain I persisted that Bartleby was nothing to me—no more than to anyone else. In vain—I was the last person

90

95

known to have anything to do with him, and they held me to the terrible account. Fearful, then of being exposed in the papers (as one person present obscurely threatened), I considered the matter, and at length said that if the lawyer would give me a confidential interview with the scrivener, in his (the lawyer's) own room, I would, that afternoon, strive my best to rid them of the nuisance they complained of.

Going upstairs to my old haunt, there was Bartleby silently sitting upon the banister at the landing.

"What are you doing here, Bartleby?" said I.

"Sitting upon the banister," he mildly replied.   100

I motioned him into the lawyer's room, who then left us.

"Bartleby," said I, "are you aware that you are the cause of great tribulation to me, by persisting in occupying the entry after being dismissed from the office?"

No answer.

"Now one of two things must take place. Either you must do something, or something must be done to you. Now what sort of business would you like to engage in? Would you like to re-engage in copying for someone?"

"No; I would prefer not to make any change."   105

"Would you like a clerkship in a dry-goods store?"

"There is too much confinement about that. No, I would not like a clerkship; but I am not particular."

"Too much confinement," I cried; "why you keep yourself confined all the time!"

"I would prefer not to take a clerkship," he rejoined, as if to settle that little item at once.

"How would a bartender's business suit you? There is no trying of the   110
eyesight in that."

"I would not like it at all; though, as I said before, I am not particular."

His unwonted wordiness inspirited me. I returned to the charge.

"Well, then, would you like to travel through the country collecting bills for the merchants? That would improve your health."

"No, I would prefer to be doing something else."

"How, then, would going as a companion to Europe to entertain some   115
young gentleman with your conversation—how would that suit you?"

"Not at all. It does not strike me that there is anything definite about that. I like to be stationary. But I am not particular."

"Stationary you shall be, then," I cried, now losing all patience, and, for the first time in all my exasperating connection with him, fairly flying into a passion. "If you do not go away from these premises before night, I shall feel bound—indeed, I *am* bound—to—to—to quit the premises myself!" I rather absurdly concluded, knowing not with what possible threat to try to frighten his immobility into compliance.

"Bartleby," said I, in the kindest tone I could assume under such exciting circumstances, "will you go home with me now—not to my office, but my dwelling—and remain there till we can conclude upon some convenient arrangement for you at our leisure? Come, let us start now, right away."

"No; at present I would prefer not to make any change at all"

I answered nothing, but, effectually dodging everyone by the suddenness and rapidity of my flight, rushed from the building, ran up Wall Street towards Broadway, and, jumping into the first omnibus, was soon removed from pursuit . . . So fearful was I of being again hunted out by the incensed landlord and his exasperated tenants that, surrendering my business to Nippers for a few days, I drove about the upper part of the town and through the suburbs in my rockaway [carriage]; crossed over to Jersey City and Hoboken, and paid fugitive visits to Manhattanville and Astoria. In fact, I almost lived in my rockaway for the time.   120

When again I entered my office, lo, a note from the landlord lay upon the desk. I opened it with trembling hands. It informed me that the writer had sent to the police, and had Bartleby removed to the Tombs[1] as a vagrant. Moreover, since I knew more about him than anyone else, he wished me to appear at that place and make a suitable statement of the facts . . . .

The same day I received the note, I went to the Tombs, or to speak more properly, the Halls of Justice. Seeking the right officer, I stated the purpose of my call, and was informed that the individual I described was indeed within. I then assured him that Bartleby was a perfectly honest man, and greatly to be compassionated, however unaccountably eccentric. I narrated all I knew, and closed by suggesting the idea of letting him remain in as indulgent confinement as possible till something less harsh might be done—though, indeed, I hardly knew what. At all events, if nothing else could be decided upon, the almshouse must receive him. I then begged to have an interview.

Being under no disgraceful charge, and quite serene and harmless in all his ways, they had permitted him freely to wander about the prison, and, especially, in the inclosed grass-platted yards thereof. And so I found him there, standing all alone in the quietest of the yards, his face towards a high wall, while all around, from the narrow slits of the jail windows I thought I saw peering out upon him the eyes of murderers and thieves.

"Bartleby!"

"I know you," he said, without looking round—"and I want nothing to say to you."   125

---

[1] A well known New York City prison in the 19th century.

"It was not I that brought you here, Bartleby," said I, keenly pained at his implied suspicion. "And, to you, this should not be so vile a place. Nothing reproachful attaches to you by being here. And see, it is not so sad a place as one might think. Look, there is the sky, and here is the grass."

"I know where I am," he replied, but would say nothing more, and so I left him.

As I entered the corridor again, a broad meatlike man in an apron accosted me, and, jerking his thumb over his shoulder said—"Is that your friend?"

"Yes."

"Does he want to starve? If he does, let him live on the prison fare, that's all."   130

"Who are you?" asked I, not knowing what to make of such an unofficially speaking person in such a place.

"I am the grubman. Such gentlemen as have friends here hire me to provide them with something good to eat."

"Is this so?" said I, turning to the turnkey.

He said it was.

"Well, then," said I, slipping some silver into the grubman's hands (for so they called him), "I want you to give particular attention to my friend there; let him have the best dinner you can get. And you must be as polite to him as possible."   135

"Introduce me, will you?" said the grubman, looking at me with an expression which seemed to say he was all impatience for an opportunity to give a specimen of his breeding.

Thinking it would prove of benefit to the scrivener, I acquiesced, and, asking the grubman his name, went up with him to Bartleby.

"Bartleby, this is a friend; you will find him very useful to you."

"Your sarvant, sir, your sarvant," said the grubman, making a low salutation behind his apron. "Hope you find it pleasant here, sir; nice grounds—cool apartments—hope you'll stay with us some time—try to make it agreeable. What will you have for dinner today?"

"I prefer not to dine today," said Bartleby, turning away. "It would disagree with me; I am unused to dinners." So saying, he slowly moved to the other side of the inclosure and took up a position fronting the dead-wall.   140

"How's this?" said the grubman, addressing me with a stare of astonishment. "He's odd, ain't he?"

"I think he is a little deranged," said I, sadly.

Some few days after this, I again obtained admission to the Tombs, and went through the corridors in quest of Bartleby; but without finding him.

"I saw him coming from his cell not long ago," said a turnkey, "maybe he's gone to loiter in the yards."

So I went in that direction. 145

"Are you looking for the silent man?" said another turnkey, passing me. "Yonder he lies—sleeping in the yard there. Tis not twenty minutes since I saw him lie down."

The yard was entirely quiet. It was not accessible to the common prisoners. The surrounding walls, of amazing thickness, kept off all sounds behind them. The Egyptian character of the masonry weighed upon me with its gloom.

Strangely huddled at the base of the wall, his knees drawn up and lying on his side, his head touching the cold stones, I saw the wasted Bartleby. But nothing stirred. I paused, then went close up to him, stooped over, and saw that his dim eyes were open; otherwise he seemed profoundly sleeping. Something prompted me to touch him. I felt his hand, when a tingling shiver ran up my arm and down my spine to my feet.

The round face of the grubman peered upon me now. "His dinner is ready. Won't he dine today, either? Or does he live without dining?"

"Lives without dining," said I, and closed the eyes. 150

"Eh!—He's asleep, ain't he?"

"With kings and counselors,"[2] murmured I.

***

There would seem little need for proceeding further in this history. Imagination will readily supply the meager recital of poor Bartleby's internment. But ere parting with the reader, let me say, that if this little narrative has sufficiently interested him, to awaken curiosity as to who Bartleby was, and what manner of life he led prior to the present narrator's making his acquaintance, I can only reply, that in such curiosity I fully share, but am wholly unable to gratify it. Yet here I hardly know whether I should divulge one little item of rumor, which came to my ear a few months after the scrivener's decease. Upon what basis it rested, I could never ascertain; and hence, how true it is I cannot now tell. But inasmuch as this vague report has not been without a certain strange suggestive interest to me, however sad, it may prove the same with some others; and so I will briefly mention it. The report was this: that Bartleby had been a subordinate clerk in the Dead Letter Office at Washington,[3] from which he had been suddenly removed by a change in the administration. When I think over this rumor, I cannot adequately express the emotions

---

[2] From Job's Lament in the Bible: Bartleby is now dead, delivered from his troubled existence.

[3] The Dead Letter office is where letters go when recipients cannot be found.

which seize me. Dead letters! does it not sound like dead men? Conceive a man by nature and misfortune prone to a pallid hopelessness, can any business seem more fitted to heighten it than that of continually handling these dead letters and assorting them for the flames? For by the cart-load they are annually burned. Sometimes from out of the folded paper the pale clerk takes a ring:—the finger it was meant for, perhaps, moulders in the grave; a bank-note sent in swiftest charity:—he whom it would relieve, nor eats nor hungers any more; pardon for those who died despairing; hope for those who died unhoping; good tidings for those who died stifled by unrelieved calamities. On errands of life, these letters speed to death.

Ah, Bartleby! Ah, humanity!

The Making of a New Yorker

O. Henry

O. Henry (1862—1910) was a prolific American short-story writer, a master of surprise endings, who wrote about the life of ordinary people in New York City. A twist of plot, which turns on an ironic or coincidental circumstance, is typical of O. Henry's stories.

Besides many things, Raggles was a poet. He was called a tramp; but that was only an elliptical way of saying that he was a philosopher, an artist, a traveller, a naturalist, and a discoverer. But most of all he was a poet. In all his life he never wrote a line of verse; he lived his poetry. His Odyssey would have been a Limerick, had it been written. But, to linger with the primary proposition, Raggles was a poet.

Raggles's specialty, had he been driven to ink and paper, would have been sonnets to the cities. He studied cities as women study their reflections in mirrors; as children study the glue and sawdust of a dislocated doll; as the men who write about wild animals study the cages in the zoo. A city to Raggles was not merely a pile of bricks and mortar, peopled by a certain number of inhabitants; it was a thing with soul, characteristic and distinct; an individual conglomeration of life, with its own peculiar essence, flavor, and feeling. Two thousand miles to the north and south, east and west, Raggles wandered in poetic fervor, taking the cities to his breast. He footed it on dusty roads, or sped magnificently in freight cars, counting time as of no account. And when he had found the heart of a city and listened to its secret confession, he strayed on, restless, to another. Fickle Raggles!—but perhaps he had not met the civic corporation that could engage and hold his critical fancy. . . .

One day Raggles came and laid siege to the heart of the great city of Manhattan. She was the greatest of all; and he wanted to learn her note in the scale; to taste and appraise and classify and solve and label her and arrange her with the other cities that had given him up the secret of their individuality. And here we cease to be Raggles's translator and become his chronicler.

Raggles landed from a ferry-boat one morning and walked into the core of the town with the blasé air of a cosmopolite. He was dressed with care to play the role of an "unidentified man." No country, race, class, clique, union, party clan, or bowling association could have claimed him. His clothing, which had

From *The Four Million* by O' Henry.

been donated to him piece-meal by citizens of different height, but same number of inches around the heart, was not yet as uncomfortable to his figure as those specimens of raiment, self-measured, that are railroaded to you by transcontinental tailors with a suit case, suspenders, silk handkerchief and pearl studs as a bonus. Without money—as a poet should be—but with the ardor of an astronomer discovering a new star in the chorus of the milky way, or a man who has seen ink suddenly flow from his fountain pen, Raggles wandered into the great city.

Late in the afternoon he drew out of the roar and commotion with a look of dumb terror on his countenance. He was defeated, puzzled, discomfited, frightened. The greetings of the other cities he had known—their homespun kindliness, their human gamut of rough charity, friendly curses, garrulot curiosity, and easily estimated credulity or indifference. This city Manhattan gave him no clue; it was walled against him. Like a river of adamant, it flowed past him in the streets. Never an eye was turned upon him; no voice spoke to him. His heart yearned for the clap of Pittsburg's sooty hand on his shoulder; for Chicago's menacing but social yawp in his ear; for the pale and eleemosynary stare through the Bostonian eyeglass—even for the precipitate but unmalicious boot-toe of Louisville or St. Louis.

On Broadway Raggles, successful suitor of many cities, stood, bashful, like any country swain. For the first time he experienced the poignant humiliation of being ignored. And when he tried to reduce this brilliant, swiftly changing, ice-cold city to a formula he failed utterly. Poet though he was, it offered him no color similes, no points of comparison, no flaw in its polished facets, no handle by which he could hold it up and view its shape and structure, as he familiarly and often contemptuously had done with other towns. The houses were interminable ramparts loop-holed for defence; the people were bright but bloodless spectres passing in sinister and selfish array.

The thing that weighed heaviest on Raggles's soul and clogged his poet's fancy was the spirit of absolute egotism that seemed to saturate the people as toys are saturated with paint. Each one that he considered appeared a monster of abominable and insolent conceit. Humanity was gone from them; they were toddling idols of stone and varnish, worshipping themselves and greedy for though oblivious of worship from their fellow graven images. Frozen, cruel, implacable, impervious, cut to an identical pattern, they hurried on their ways like statues brought by some miracle to motion, while soul and feeling lay unaroused in the reluctant marble.

Gradually Raggles became conscious of certain types. One was an elderly gentleman with a snow-white, short beard, pink, unwrinkled face, and stony, sharp blue eyes, attired in the fashion of a gilded youth, who seemed to personify the city's wealth, ripeness and frigid unconcern. Another type was a woman, tall, beautiful, clear as a steel engraving, goddess-like, calm, clothed like the princesses of old, with eyes as coldly blue as the reflection of sunlight on a glacier. And another was a by-product of this town of marionettes—a broad, swaggering, grim, threateningly sedate fellow, with a jowl as large as a harvested wheat field, the complexion of a baptized infant, and the knuckles of a prize-fighter. This type leaned against cigar signs and viewed the world with frappéd contumely.

A poet is a sensitive creature, and Raggles soon shriveled in the bleak embrace of the undecipherable. The chill, sphinx-like, ironical, illegible, unnatural, ruthless expression of the city left him downcast and bewildered. Had it no heart? Better the woodpile, the scolding of vinegar-faced housewives at back doors, the kindly spleen of bartenders behind provincial free-lunch counters, the amiable truculence of rural constables, the kicks, arrests, and happy-go-lucky chances of the other vulgar, loud, crude cities than this freezing heartlessness.

Raggles summoned his courage and sought hand-outs from the populace. Unheeding, regardless, they passed on without the wink of an eyelash to testify that they were conscious of his existence. And then he said to himself that this fair but pitiless city of Manhattan was without a soul; that its inhabitants were mannikins moved by wires and springs, and that he was alone in a great wilderness.

Raggles started to cross the street. There was a blast, a roar, a hissing and a crash as something struck him and hurled him over and over six yards from where he had been. As he was coming down, like the stick of a rocket, the earth and all the cities thereof turned to a fractured dream.

Raggles opened his eyes. First an odor made itself known to him—an odor of the earliest spring flowers of Paradise. And then a hand soft as a falling petal touched his brow. Bending over him was the woman clothed like the princess of old, with blue eyes, now soft and humid with human sympathy. Under his head on the pavement were silks and furs. With Raggles's hat in his hand and with his face pinker than ever from a vehement outburst of oratory against reckless driving, stood the elderly gentleman who personified the city's wealth and ripeness. From a near-by café hurried the by-product with the vast jowl and baby complexion, bearing a glass full of crimson fluid that suggested delightful possibilities.

"Drink dis, sport," said the by-product, holding the glass to Raggles's lips.

Hundreds of people huddled around in a moment, their faces wearing the deepest concern. Two flattering and gorgeous policemen got into the circle and pressed back the overplus of Samaritans. An old lady in a black shawl spoke loudly of camphor; a newsboy slipped one of his papers beneath Raggles's elbow, where it lay on the muddy pavement. A brisk young man with a notebook was asking for names.

A bell clanged importantly, and the ambulance cleaned a lane through the crowd. A cool surgeon slipped into the midst of affairs.

"How do you feel, old man?" asked the surgeon, stooping easily to his task. The princess of silks and stains wiped a red drop or two from Raggles's brow with a fragrant cobweb.

"Me?" said Raggles, with a seraphic smile, "I feel fine."

He had found the heart of his new city.

In three days they let him leave his cot for the convalescent ward in the hospital. He had been in there an hour when the attendants heard sounds of conflict. Upon investigation they found that Raggles had assaulted and damaged a brother convalescent—a glowering transient whom a freight train collision had sent in to be patched up.

"What's all this about?" inquired the head nurse.

"He was runnin' down me town," said Raggles.

"What town?" asked the nurse.

"Noo York," said Raggles.

Brooklyn Bridge

Vladimir Vladimirovich Mayakovsky

Vladimir Mayakovsky (1894–1930), one of Russia's most gifted writers and a prominent member of the avant-garde, is one of the most universally recognized characters in Russian history. During his short life, he wrote a wealth of ground-breaking poems, prose, plays and art that continue to influence and inspire writers and artists to this day.

Hey, Coolidge boy,
make a shout of joy!
When a thing is good
                then it's good.
Blush from compliments
                    like our flag's calico,
even though you're
                the most super-united states
                                of
America.
Like the crazy nut
            who goes
                    to his church
or retreats
        to a monastery
                simple and rigid—
so I
    in the gray haze
                of evening
humbly
        approach
            the Brooklyn Bridge.
Like a conqueror
            on cannons with muzzles
                        as high as a giraffe
jabbing into a broken
                city beseiged,
so, drunk with glory,
            alive to the hilt,
I clamber
        proudly
            upon Brooklyn Bridge.

From *Modern Russian Poetry* by Vladimar Mayakovsky, edited by Vladimir Markov and Merrill Sparks. Reprinted by permission of HarperCollins Publishers Ltd.

Like a stupid painter
                whose enamored eyes pierce
a museum Madonna
                like a wedge.
So from this sky,
             sowed into the stars,
I look at New York
              through Brooklyn Bridge.
New York,
      heavy and stifling
                till night,
has forgotten
        what makes it dizzy
                and a hindrance,
and only
      the souls of houses
rise in the transparent
             sheen of windows.
Here the itching hum
        of the 'el'[1]
           is hardly heard,
and only by this
      hum,
        soft but stubborn,
can you feel the trains
        crawl
           with a rattle
as when dishes
      are jammed into a cupboard.
And when from
      below the started river
a merchant
      transports sugar
           from the factory bins—
then
    the masts passing under the bridge
are no bigger
      in size
        than pins.
I'm proud
     of this
       mile of steel.
In it my visions
      are alive and real—

---

[1] The elevated rail cars, now torn down.

a fight
      for structure
            instead of arty 'style',
the harsh calculation
        of bolts
          and steel.
If the end
      of the world
         comes—
and chaos
      wipes out
         this earth
and if only this
      bridge
         remains
rearing over the dust of death,
then
    as little bones,
        thinner than needles,
clad with flesh,
      standing in museums,
           are dinosaurs,—
so from this
      bridge
        future geologists
will be able
     to reconstruct
        our present course.
They will say:
       —this
        paw of steel
joined seas,
       prairies and deserts,
from here,
     Europe
        rushed to the West,
scattering
     to the wind
        Indian feathers.
This rib here
     reminds us
        of a machine—
imagine,
     enough hands, enough grip
while standing,
       with one steel leg
         in Manhattan

to drag
          toward yourself
                    Brooklyn by the lip!
By the wires
          of electric yarn
I know this
          is
          the Post-Steam Era.
Here people
          already
                    yelled on the radio,
here people
          already
                    flew by air.
For some
          here was life
                    carefree,
                              unalloyed.
For others
          a prolonged
                    howl of hunger.
From here
          the unemployed
jumped headfirst
                    into
                    the Hudson.
And finally
          with clinging stars
                    along the strings of cables
my dream comes back
                    without any trouble
and I see—
          here
                    stood Mayakovsky,
here he stood
          putting
                    syllable to syllable.
I look,
     as an eskimo looks at a train.
I dig into you,
                    like a tick into an ear.
Brooklyn Bridge.
Yes,
     you've got something here.

Translated, from the Russian, by
Vladimir Markov and Merrill Sparks

Recuerdo

Edna ST. Vincent Millay

Edna St Vincent Millay (1892-1950) was born in Rockland, Maine. When Edna was twenty her poem, *Renascence,* was published in *The Lyric Year.* As a result of this poem, Edna won a scholarship to Vassar. In 1917, the year of her graduation, Millay published her first book, *Renascence and Other Poems.* After leaving Vassar she moved to New York's Greenwich Village where she befriended writers such as Floyd Dell, John Reed and Max Eastman. The three men were all involved in the left-wing journal, *The Masses,* and she joined in their campaign against Americans involvement in the First World War.

We were very tired, we were very merry—
We had gone back and forth all night on the ferry.
It was bare and bright, and smelled like a stable—
But we looked into a fire, we leaned across a table,
We lay on a hill-top underneath the moon;
And the whistles kept blowing, and the dawn came
    soon.

We were very tired, we were very merry—
We had gone back and forth all night on the ferry;
And you ate an apple, and I ate a pear,
From a dozen of each we had bought somewhere;
And the sky went wan, and the wind came cold,
And the sun rose dripping, a bucketful of gold.

We were very tired, we were very merry,
We had gone back and forth all night on the ferry.
We hailed, "Good morrow, mother!" to a shawl-covered
    head,
And bought a morning paper, which neither of us read;
And she wept, "God bless you!" for the apples and pears,
And we gave her all our money but our subway fares.

From *Collected Poems* by Edna St. Vincent Millay, 1922

In a Station of The Metro

Ezra Pound

Ezra Pound (1885–1972) is considered one of the founding fathers of modern poetry, which sought to reduce writing to its essential features. His poem "In the Station of the Metro" is an excellent example of "imagist" writing, which strives to convey meaning concisely and vividly. Pound attended Hamilton College in New York and lived much of his life abroad. He is best known for *The Cantos*, a collection of poems he worked on throughout much of his life.

IN A STATION OF THE METRO[1]

The apparition of these faces in the crowd;
Petals on a wet, black bough.

1913, 1916

From PERSONAE by Ezra Pound, 1909.

"The Subway" George Tooker (1950) Collection of the Whitney Museum of Art

---

[1]The Paris Subway.

i was sitting in mcsorley's

e.e. cummings

Edward Estlin Cummings was born in Cambridge, MA in 1894 and lived until 1962. He earned a B.A. from Harvard and volunteered to go to France during World War I with the Ambulance Corps. After the war, he stayed in Paris, writing and painting and later returned to New York City. Cummings is one of the most innovative contemporary poets, famous for dropping or distorting punctuation and syntax. Over his life, he published over 900 poems and other works including the experimental novel *The Enormous Room.*

i was sitting in mcsorley's.   outside it was New York and beautifully snowing.

Inside snug and evil.   the slobbering walls filthily push witless
creases of screaming warmth chuck pillows are noise funnily swallows
swallowing revolvingly pompous a the swallowed mottle with smooth or
a but of rapidly goes gobs the and of flecks of and a chatter sobbings
intersect with which distinct disks of graceful oath, upsoarings the
break on   ceiling-flatness

the Bar tinking lucsious jigs dint of ripe silver with warmlyish
wetflat splurging smells waltz the glush of squirting taps plus slush
of foam knocked off and a faint piddle-of-drops she says I ploc spittle
what the lands thaz me kid in no sir hopping sawdust you kiddo he's a
palping wreaths of badly Yep cigars who jim him why gluey grins topple
together eyes pout gestures stickily point made glints squinting who's
a wink bum-nothing and money fuzzily mouths take big wobbly foot-steps
every goggle cent of it get out ears dribbles soft right old feller
belch the chap hic summore eh chuckles skulch. . . .

and i was sitting in the din thinking drinking the ale, which never
lets you grow old blinking at the low ceiling my being pleasantly was
punctuated by the always retchings of a worthless lamp.

when With a minute terrif   iceffort one dirty squeal of soiling light
yanKing from bushy obscurity a bald greenish foetal head established
It suddenly upon the huge neck around whose unwashed sonorous muscle
the fith of a collar hung gently.

(spattered) by this instant of semiluminous nausea A Vast wordless nondescript genie of trunk trickled firmly in to one exactly-multilated ghost of a chair,

a;domeshaped interval of complete plasticity, shoulders, sprouted the extraordinary arms through an angel of ridiculous velocity commenting upon an unclean table, and, whose distended immense Both paws slowly loved a dinted mug

gone Darkness   it was so near to me, i ask of shadow won't you have a drink?

(the eternal perpetual question)

Inside snugandevil.   i was sitting in mcsorley's   It, did not answer.

outside. (it was New York and beautifully, snowing. . . .

"McSorley's Bar" by John Sloan
© Founders Society Purchase, General membership Fund. Photograph © 2007 The Detroit Institute of Arts.

Langston Hughes

LENOX AVENUE: MIDNIGHT

The rhythm of life   1
Is a jazz rhythm,
Honey,
The gods are laughing at us.

The broken heart of love,   5
The weary, weary heart of pain,—
        Overtones,
        Undertones,
To the rumble of street cars,   10
To the swish of rain.

Lenox Avenue,
Honey,
Midnight,
And the gods are laughing at us.

THEME FOR ENGLISH B

The instructor said,   1

    Go home and write
    a page tonight.

    And let that page come out of you—   5
    Then, it will be true.

I wonder if it's that simple?

I am twenty-two, colored, born in Winston-Salem.   10
I went to school there, then Durham, then here
to this college on the hill above Harlem.
I am the only colored student in my class.
The steps from the hill lead down to Harlem,
through a park, then I cross St. Nicholas,
Eighth Avenue, Seventh, and I come to the Y,
the Harlem Branch Y, where I take the elevator
up to my room, sit down, and write this page: 15

It's not easy to know what is true for you or me
at twenty-two, my age. But I guess I'm what
I feel and see and hear. Harlem, I hear you:

hear you, hear me—we two—you, me talk on this page.
(I hear New York, too.) Me—who?   20
Well, I like to eat, sleep, drink, and be in love.
I like to work, read, learn, and understand life.
I like a pipe for a Christmas present,
or records—Bessie, bop, or Bach.

I guess being colored doesn't make me not like   25
the same things other folks like who are other races.
So will my page be colored that I write?
Being me, it will not be white.
But it will be
a part of you, instructor.   30
You are white—
yet a part of me, as I am a part of you.
That's American.
Sometimes perhaps you don't want to be a part of me.
Nor do I often want to be a part of you.   35
But we are, that's true!
As I learn from you,
I guess you learn from me—
although you're older—and white—
and somewhat more free.   40

This is my page for English B.

BALLAD OF THE LANDLORD

Landlord, landlord,
My roof has sprung a leak.
Don't you 'member I told you about it
Way last week?

Landlord, landlord,
These steps is broken down.

When you come up yourself
It's a wonder you don't fall down.

Ten bucks you say I owe you?
Ten bucks you say is due?
Well, that's ten bucks more'n I'll pay you
Till you fix this house up new.

What? You gonna get eviction orders?
You gonna cut off my heat?
You gonna take my furniture and
Throw it in the street?

Um-huh! You talking high and mighty.
Talk on—till you get through.
You ain't gonna be able to say a word
If I land my fist on you.

Police! Police!
Come and get this man!
He's trying to ruin the government
And overturn the land!

Copper's whistle!
Patrol bell!
Arrest.

Precinct Station.
Iron cell.
Headlines in press:

MAN THREATENS LANDLORD

. . .

TENANT HELD NO BAIL

. . .

JUDGE GIVES NEGRO 40 DAYS IN COUNTY JAIL

"Lenox Avenue: Midnight", "Theme For English B", "Ballad of the Landlord", from *The Collected Poems of Langston Hughes* by Langston Hughes, edited by Arnold Rampersad with David Roessel, Associate Editor, copyright © 1994 by The Estate of Langston Hughes. Used by permission of Alfred A. Knopf, a division of Randon House, Inc.

Going Uptown to Visit Miriam

Victor Hernandez Cruz

on the train
old ladies playing football
going for empty seats

very funny persons

the train riders
                are silly people
                i am a train rider

but no one knows where i am
going to take this train

to take this train
to take this train

the ladies   read popular
paperbacks   because they
are popular   they get off
at 42 to change for the
westside line   or off
59 for the department store
the train pulls in & out
the white walls   dark-
ness   white walls   darkness

ladies looking up i
wonder where they going
the dentist   pick up
husband pick up wife
pick up kids
pick up ?grass?
to library   to museum
to laundromat   to school

but no one knows where i am
going to take this train

to take this train

to visit miriam
to visit miriam

& to kiss her
on the cheek
& hope i don't
see sonia on the
street

but no one knows where i'm taking
this train
       taking this train
       to visit miriam.

The City in Which I Love You

Li-Young Lee

Li-Young Lee was born in 1957 in Jakarta, Indonesia, of Chinese parents. His father, who was a personal physician to Mao Zedong while in China, relocated his family to Indonesia, where he helped found Gamaliel University. In 1959 the Lee family fled the country to escape anti-Chinese sentiment and after a five-year trek through Hong Kong, Macau, and Japan, they settled in the United States in 1964. He is the author of *Book of My Nights, The City in Which I Love You* (1991), *Rose* (1986), as well as a memoir entitled *The Winged Seed: A Remembrance* (1995).

Morning comes to this city vacant of you.
Pages and windows flare, and you are not there.
Someone sweeps his portion of sidewalk,
wakens the drunk, slumped like laundry,
and you are gone.

You are not in the wind
which someone notes in the margins of a book.
You are gone out of the small fires in abandoned lots
where human figures huddle,
each aspiring to its own ghost.

Between brick walls, in a space no wider than my face,
a leafless sapling stands in mud.
In its branches, a nest of raw mouths
gaping and cheeping, scrawny fires that must eat.
My hunger for you is no less than theirs.

New York Day Women

Edwidge Danticat

Edwidge Danticat was born in Haiti and moved to the United States when she was twelve. She is the author of several books, including *Breath, Eyes, Memory, Krik? Krak!;* and *The Farming of Bones*, an American Book Award winner. She is also the editor of *The Butterfly's Way: Voices from the Haitian Diaspora in the United States.*

Today, walking down the street, I see my mother. She is strolling with a happy gait, her body thrust toward the DON'T WALK sign and the yellow taxicabs that make forty-five-degree turns on the corner of Madison and Fifty-seventh Street.

I have never seen her in this kind of neighborhood, peering into Chanel and Tiffany's and gawking at the jewels glowing in the Bulgari windows. My mother never shops outside of Brooklyn. She has never seen the advertising office where I work. She is afraid to take the subway, where you may meet those young black militant street preachers who curse black women for straightening their hair.

Yet, here she is, my mother, who I left at home that morning in her bathrobe, with pieces of newspapers twisted like rollers in her hair. My mother, who accuses me of random offenses as I dash out of the house.

***

Would you get up and give an old lady like me your subway seat? In this state of mind, I bet you don't even give up your seat to a pregnant lady.

***

My mother, who is often right about that. Sometimes I get up and give my seat. Other times, I don't. It all depends on how pregnant the woman is and whether or not she is with her boyfriend or husband and whether or not *he* is sitting down.

As my mother stands in front of Carnegie Hall, one taxi driver yells to another, "What do you think this is, a dance floor?"

My mother waits patiently for this dispute to be settled before crossing the street.

***

In Haiti when you get hit by a car, the owner of the car gets out and kicks you for getting blood on his bumper.

***

My mother who laughs when she says this and shows a large gap in her mouth where she lost three more molars to the dentist last week. My mother, who at fifty-nine, says dentures are okay.

***

You can take them out when they bother you. I'll like them. I'll like them fine.

***

Will it feel empty when Papa kisses you?

***

Oh no, he doesn't kiss me that way anymore.

***

My mother, who watches the lottery drawing every night on channel 11 without ever having played the numbers.

***

A third of that money is all I would need. We would pay the mortgage, and your father could stop driving that taxicab all over Brooklyn.

***

I follow my mother, mesmerized by the many possibilities of her journey. Even in a flowered dress, she is lost in a sea of pinstripes and gray suits, high heels and elegant short skirts, Reebok sneakers, dashing from building to building.

My mother, who won't go out to dinner with anyone.

***

If they want to eat with me, let them come to my house, even if I boil water and give it to them.

***

My mother, who talks to herself when she peels the skin off poultry.

***

Fat, you know, and cholesterol. Fat and cholesterol killed your aunt Hermine.

***

My mother, who makes jam with dried grapefruit peel and then puts in cinnamon bark that I always think is cockroaches in the jam. My mother, whom I have always bought household appliances for, on her birthday. A nice rice cooker, a blender.

I trail the red orchids in her dress and the heavy faux leather bag on her shoulders. Realizing the ferocious pace of my pursuit, I stop against a wall to rest. My mother keeps on walking as though she owns the sidewalk under her feet.

As she heads toward the Plaza Hotel, a bicycle messenger swings so close to her that I want to dash forward and rescue her, but she stands dead in her tracks and lets him ride around her and then goes on.

My mother stops at a corner hot-dog stand and asks for something. The vendor hands her a can of soda that she slips into her bag. She stops by another vendor selling sundresses for seven dollars each. I can tell that she is looking at an African print dress, contemplating my size. I think to myself, Please Ma, don't buy it. It would be just another thing that I would bury in the garage or give to Goodwill.

***

Why should we give to Goodwill when there are so many people back home who need clothes? We save our clothes for the relatives in Haiti.

***

Twenty years we have been saving all kinds of things for the relatives in Haiti. I need the place in the garage for an exercise bike.

***

You are pretty enough to be a stewardess. Only dogs like bones.

***

This mother of mine, she stops at another hot-dog vendor's and buys a frank-furter that she eats on the street. I never knew that she ate frankfurters. With her blood pressure, she shouldn't eat anything with sodium. She has to be careful with her heart, this day woman.

***

I cannot just swallow salt. Salt is heavier than a hundred bags of shame.

***

She is slowing her pace, and now I am too close. If she turns around, she might see me. I let her walk into the park before I start to follow again.

My mother walks toward the sandbox in the middle of the park. There a woman is waiting with a child. The woman is wearing a leotard with biker's shorts and has small weights in her hands. The woman kisses the child good-bye and surrenders him to my mother; then she bolts off, running on the cemented stretches in the park.

The child given to my mother has frizzy blond hair. His hand slips into hers easily, like he's known her for a long time. When he raises his face to look at my mother, it is as though he is looking at the sky.

My mother gives this child the soda that she bought from the vendor on the street corner. The child's face lights up as she puts in a straw in the can for him. This seems to be a conspiracy just between the two of them.

My mother and the child sit and watch the other children play in the sandbox. The child pulls out a comic book from a knapsack with Big Bird on the back. My mother peers into his comic book. My mother, who taught herself to read as a lit-tle girl in Haiti from the books that her brothers brought home from school.

My mother, who has now lost six of her seven sisters in Ville Rose and has never had the strength to return for their funerals.

***

Many graves to kiss when I go back. Many graves to kiss.

***

She throws away the empty soda can when the child is done with it. I wait and watch from a corner until the woman in the leotard and biker's shorts re-turns, sweaty and breathless, an hour later. My mother gives the woman back her child and strolls farther into the park.

I turn around and start to walk out of the park before my mother can see me. My lunch hour is long since gone. I have to hurry back to work. I walk through a cluster of joggers, then race to a *Sweden Tours* bus. I stand behind the bus and take a peek at my mother in the park. She is standing in a circle, chatting with a group of women who are taking other people's children on an afternoon outing. They look like a Third World Parent-Teacher Association meeting.

I quickly jump into a cab heading back to the office. Would Ma have said hello had she been the one to see me first?

As the cab races away from the park, it occurs to me that perhaps one day I would chase an old woman down a street by mistake and that old woman would be somebody else's mother, who I would have mistaken for mine.

***

Day women come out when nobody expects them.

***

Tonight on the subway, I will get up and give my seat to a pregnant woman or a lady about Ma's age.

My mother, who stuffs thimbles in her mouth and then blows up her cheeks like Dizzy Gillespie while sewing yet another Raggedy Ann doll that she names Suzette after me.

***

I will have all these little Suzettes in case you never have any babies, which looks more and more like it is going to happen.

***

My mother who had me when she was thirty-three— *I'dge du Christ*—at the age that Christ died on the cross.

***

That's a blessing, believe you me, even if American doctors say by that time you can make retarded babies.

***

My mother, who sews lace collars on my company softball T-shirts when she does my laundry.

***

Why, you can't you look like a lady playing softball?

***

My mother, who never went to any of my Parent-Teacher Association meetings when I was in school.

***

You're so good anyway. What are they going to tell me? I don't want to make you ashamed of this day woman. Shame is heavier than a hundred bags of salt.

***

Chango's Fire

Ernesto Quiñonez

Ernesto Quiñonez, who is part Ecuadoran and part Puerto Rican, was raised in El Barrio. He attended City College, where he met crime novelist Walter Mosley. His first novel *Bodega Dreams* was critically acclaimed as was his follow-up novel *Chango's Fire*, both of which are set in Spanish Harlem. He currently teaches creative writing at Cornell University.

Complaint #1

The house I'm about to set on fire stands alone on a hill. In this Westchester darkness, it resembles a lonely house Hopper might paint. A driveway wide enough for a truck. A lawn with trees and wide-open space you can picture Kennedy kids playing touch football—their smiles perfect, the knees of their khakis stained with grass. No ocean though, but a wooden porch does wrap itself around the house as if hugging it. Large windows and spacious bedrooms, an American house new immigrants dream of. The type of house America promises can be yours if you work hard, save your pennies and salute the flag.

I open the screen door, punch in the alarm code and I'm in. It's my house, really. The owner doesn't want it. It's my house for these precious few minutes. I can indulge myself in snooping through someone else's life. Walk through wooden floors that I hope to inhabit someday.

When I was first hired, I used to enter these houses with my tin gallons filled with kerosene and quickly set to work at wetting the beds, couches and curtains. Light it all up with a flick of a match and quickly take off. Now I look around, wondering why, besides the money, does this person want his house taken out? I pace around. I pick up pictures, stare at the loved ones. I see childhood secrets that were never known to me, secrets of horses and country homes, of summer vacations. I open drawers. Sift through clothes. Read the spines of books and try to find clues about this person's life. Once I burned a house where an entire set of cheerleader outfits sat in an attic closet, nicely folded. Was his wife the coach? Did he kill these girls? Who knows?

I walk around. This house is beautiful but the furniture is outdated, the lamps, doors and closets have old, yellow glows. In the living room, there's a television with knobs, a stereo with a turntable. Nailed to the wall is a black rotary telephone that hangs like an extinct breed. In the kitchen, there is not so much as a toaster. The wooden chairs in the dining room are chipped, and the walls are crowded with portraits of Catholic saints, of fruits and landscapes. But it is the faded sunflower curtains and dead plants by the windows that pretty much indicates an old woman lived here. Now that she's been put away, or is dead, this house seems to be used only as storage space, like a huge empty room where broken toys or unused objects from a previous life or a failed marriage sit lifeless. There's sadness in this house. It feels like its children deserted it many years ago and not so much as even cared to look back. Not a single tear. All around, everything carries such sorrow. A darkness attaches itself to the walls, as if no light had ever shone, even when tiny feet ran around these floors. There's a sense of neglected space in these halls. I'm stepping on unwanted family history. Nothing in this house has been deemed worthy to be saved or treasured. Everything has been condemned to be erased by fire.

But I can't really say for sure what happened here years ago that has made this house so bleak. But bleak it is. And now that the last of the old folks are gone, their grown children will light a match to unwanted memories. The house gets lit, the neighborhood stays the same color, and the property gets rebuilt with funneled insurance money.

Just as well. It's not my house, nor my memories. Even less, it's not my place to ask.

I don't ask.

I never ask.

The people I work for don't know me. I only deal with Eddie, and Eddie deals with them, and I don't know who they deal with or how the insurance is fixed, all I know is that the bread gets passed around in that order. Me getting the last of the crumbs.

I've been working for Eddie for some time now. The crumbs I get are large enough that I mortgaged an apartment floor in this old, battered, three-story walk-up. On the first floor, my friend Maritza has set up her crazy church, and the second floor is owned by a white woman I barely know. Though she seems nice, she rarely makes eye contact and is always on the go. She leaves the building early in the morning and I can usually hear her come back late at night when I'm reading in bed. She doesn't spend much time in her house or on fixing up her floor like I do.

I've been upgrading my floor slowly, because it's so goddamn expensive. But I'm happy there. At times and for no reason, I go outside and cross the street and stare at my building. I smile. See the third floor? I own it, I tell myself. I see the windows are a little crooked, not exactly fitting in their frames. Got to fix that. I smile. I own it, I tell myself. I see the paint chipping on all sides. Got to fix that. I like the gray shadow my building casts when the sun hits it from the west side of 103rd Street and Lexington Avenue, and how it's sandwiched between Papelito's botanica and a barber shop. I tell myself, I've come a long way from the club-house I built as a little kid. I had gathered refrigerator boxes, painted them, cut open windows and doors, and placed my clubhouse on a vacant lot full of rats, charred bricks and thrown-out diapers. I called it the Brown House, home to the president of Spanish Harlem.

What I was too young to know back then was that it was during the decade of my childhood that my future boss, Eddie, and guys like him were hired. Eddie burned down half of El Barrio and most of the South Bronx. He got a cut of the insurance money from the property owners, including the city, which was also in on it by cutting down half of the fire services in neighborhoods like mine. It was a free-for-all. Everyone was on the take. Everyone saw it coming. As the influx of Puerto Ricans in the fifties and sixties became more intense, many Italians sold their businesses and split town. Many Jews followed suit, as did the Irish real estate owners who witnessed the neighborhood shift to a darker color and, most of them, turned to people like Eddie.

Spanish Harlem was worthless property in the seventies and early eighties. Many property owners burned their own buildings down and handed the new immigrants a neighborhood filled with hollow walls and vacant lots. Urban Swiss cheese. The city would then place many of us in the projects, creating Latino reservations. These city blocks, full of project buildings on each corner, were built not so much to house us as to corral us. To keep us in one place. We were being slowly but surely relocated, as many who owned real estate burned the neighborhood, collected the insurance, sat on the dilapidated property and waited for better days.

Today, the wait is over, Spanish Harlem's burned out buildings are gold mines. Many of the same landlords who burned their tenements are now rebuilding. Empowerment zoning has changed the face of the neighborhood. Chain stores rise like monsters from a lake. Gap. Starbucks. Blockbuster Video. Old Navy. Like the new Berlin, El Barrio is being rebuilt from its ashes. The rents are absurdly high, and it breaks my heart, because Spanish Harlem had always been a springboard. A place where immigrants came to better themselves and, when they had reached the next plateau, they'd leave traces of their culture, a bit of themselves behind, and move on. A melting pot of past success stories—Dutch, Jews, Irish, Italians. When it came our turn to inherit these blocks, East Harlem was still a magical neighborhood made up of families dreaming of their sons hiring the men their fathers worked for. Dreaming of their daughters sleeping in the houses their mothers cleaned. And then, the bottom fell out. Yet Eddie sticks around, he grows old, seeing the neighborhood change, and he laughs, "Wha' for? Who can afford these rents? Better when the city let it burn."

Eddie has a son. I actually knew his son first, Trompo Loco, Crazy Top. He's this wonderful guy I grew up with. He was never the brightest of people, probably borderline slow. But there's a beauty to him. An imperfect beauty, like one you can detect when looking for shells at Orchard Beach. A happiness you feel when finding a shell that's chipped yet it has markings like you've never seen before. Trompo Loco is like that. He is *really skinny*, making him look taller than he really is. Trompo Loco is so skinny that he would have been nicknamed Flaco, except that when he gets mad he starts twirling himself round and round until he falls to the ground. Sometimes he passes out from the dizziness. He's done this since we were kids, and because back then we all played with wooden tops, he got the name Trompo Loco. I always felt bad for him, because all the kids from the block would make fun of him. "Yo, retardo," they'd say, "why you gotta look so stupid?" Though at times—and this I hate to admit—to prove myself to the other kids, I made fun of him as well. But later on I was always defending Trompo Loco and trying to keep others from picking on him. I didn't know what was happening in his house but I knew it was something really awful, because he'd rather be outside, where all the kids made fun of him, than go upstairs. We became friends and he'd spend a lot of time in my house. So much time that my parents would bring him to church with us. It was at church that I found out the truth about Trompo Loco's crazy mother. I then understood why he'd rather be ridiculed by the kids outside than be upstairs with a woman who yelled threats to him and to herself. It was also at church that I heard the rumors that this big Italian guy was Trompo Loco's father. How that man had driven Trompo Loco's mother crazy. Then one day Trompo Loco took me to 118th Street and Pleasant Avenue, the last remnants of the Italian part of East Harlem. From a distance, Trompo Loco pointed at this coffee shop on the corner. I saw this tall man who first helped this old Latin woman and her shopping cart cross the street before he himself went inside the coffee shop. It was the first time I saw *Eddie*. Years later I wasn't just looking out for his illegitimate son. I was working for him.

When I started working for Eddie and was ready to set my first house on fire, he came along. He told me I was a JAFO, Just Another Fucking Observer, to stay out of his way and watch. "These new houses? Ga'bage. You can burn them with firecrackers." And he spilled kerosene all over the bedrooms, like he was about to mop the floors and was getting them ready. "But you know mattresses are fire eaters. The very thing we sleep on is a box of matches." I saw Eddie take no delight in setting fires; I did see youth and longing in his eyes when he talked about his early days. "In the old days now those houses were made to withstand air raids."

That first time, when I was being schooled, I spotted a Rolex watch on top of a dresser. My heart jumped and I was about to grab it and put it in my pocket. Eddie caught my eye. "Never take anything," he said, "never even take the ice cream from the fridge. The adjuster is going to look for every valuable thing in this house, and it better be burned. You know, it's gotta look good. I have people working for me, but it gotta look good. It's my name at the end of the day." And Eddie spilled more kerosene all over the floors. I asked Eddie if the firemen would know that this was deliberate. Eddie didn't answer me. I never asked him again. I learned that first day, you never ask. So I just listened.

"Each fire, Julio, has its own life, its own personality," he said to me that first time, as we watched the house burning at a distance, us safely inside his parked car. "Depending on building design, material and how clean your kerosene is, the fire will burn at its own pace, the smoke will take its own color and smell." I noticed that night that Eddie was not obsessed by fire. He saw no beauty in the flames. "Most fires are nasty, Julio. As soon as they reach a certain growth, they are like children that you can't control, or never wanted. They pretty much become an avalanche of flames and you can't take them back or stop them, Julio. So, know what you are doing before it's too late."

Like Eddie, I'm not obsessed by fire. But I have no problems with what I do. Is my conscience clean?

My conscience is clean with God and men. I burn buildings, just like Eddie, and I burn them for the same reason, the money. But the person whose house I'm burning knows I'm coming. He even gave Eddie the keys and alarm code. And I don't know how Eddie does it, how he fixes it with the insurance company, all I know is everyone gets paid and my job is to light that house up.

Tonight, right before I set this house in Westchester ablaze, I call Eddie. I want to make sure this is the right address; even though I'm already inside, I check to make sure. I don't want to burn the wrong place.

"All right," Eddie says over the phone, "read me the address back."

I read it back to him.

"Yeah, that's the one. Read me the alarm code."

I read that back, too.

"You're set. Go wet the bed."

I tell Eddie this is my last job, that I'm quitting after this one. That I'll work at the demolition site but that's it. I don't hear anything, so I repeat that this is my last job.

"How's your friend?" Eddie always refers to his son as my friend.

I tell Eddie, Trompo Loco is fine.

"Good, good. Keep an eye out for him, okay? But keep him away from my coffee shop."

I always do, right? Then I say it again, that this is my last job.

"Are you taking him to church?"

I remind Eddie that I don't go to church anymore.

"Is he at least reading his Bible?"

"Yes," I say, and "did you hear me, Eddie, this is my last job."

"Are you getting married or something?"

"No," I say, "what's that got to do with it?"

Eddie hangs up.

I sigh and get to work.

I walk up the stairs and drench a bedroom, splashing some kerosene on the curtains. I do the other bedroom, where I hear a strange noise. Like someone or something crying. I get nervous. This house is supposed to be empty. I look for the source. I calm down some when I find under one bed a scared cat. He's afraid and wailing. I stomp my feet on the floor and, like a frightened mouse, the cat runs to the other side of the room. I chase after him and he runs down the stairs. I get a good glimpse and I see it's a beautiful Russian blue, I think it's a boy. His eyes are gray and he is too thin. The poor cat must not have eaten for days, living on mice, roaches, or whatever he could find in this house, and drinking water from the toilet bowl.

Not my problem.

It's just a cat.

I walk back down the stairs, pouring kerosene on the carpet. I take out my lighter. As soon as the lighter flame kisses the wet steps, the sound is one of thunder, and the fire quickly shoots up, running up the steps like a man possessed. The same possessed man who in the gospels asked Christ, It is not yet time to take us Son of Man? Because every time I start a fire, I think of my religious upbringing. I remember all the yelling, healing and anointing, and those sermons where the word of God was never "love" or "light" but "fire." Tongues of fire. And His angry presence was evident around a neighborhood that kept burning night after night. So often that the fires were disregarded and the people branded as sinners. In the news, we were being punished for being junkies, thieves, whores and murderers. The evidence of God's wrath was the blocks upon blocks of burned buildings we supposedly brought on ourselves. In my church it was a sign, these fires that consumed Spanish Harlem, the South Bronx, Harlem, Bed-Sty, you name the ghetto, it was being lit up. It was a sign, a pox on our houses, these fires were evidence of prophecy, of fulfillment, of . . . "The Truth."

But the truth was, it was just a guy like me, who had set those fires. A schmuck like me who had been paid by a local city politician or a slumlord. Each and every one of them a poverty czar.

Outside.

I see the house is wet in flames, not an inch of it is dry from fire. I start my car and I drive out, toward the highway. I hear that wailing sound again, the same one I heard in the bedroom. I look back and see the crying cat curled up in a ball in the back seat. I had left one car window open, and when the cat ran out of the house, he must have hopped in my car. At first I brake, and I'm ready to open the back door and shoo it away, but I'm too tired to pull over. I have to be at the site in the morning, then school, and I'm sure Mami would love it if I brought home a crying cat.

So I drive away.

When I reach the highway, the New York City skyline parades all its beauty across the Hudson River. The cat jumps to the front seat like he wants to take in those glorious lights. He sits there staring, and I wonder how the city looks to a cat. Because New York City does different things to different people, even creatures. I started building my own private New York the second I came of age. When New York City was filthy and broken and, in my mind, holy. The city left its mark on me, like a fish hook that caught me, was yanked and scarred my flesh. That first image of a dirty, broken city burned in my nine-year-old eyes and memory. And no matter how much the skyline changed over the years, what towers fell, what new buildings those, the changes have never supplanted the vision of when I first climbed up on that Spanish Harlem roof and gazed upon its bright lights. How up above on that roof, Spanish Harlem sang to a nine-year-old kid like our church choir, and the skyline shone so saintly there was no doubt I was, at that very moment, closer to God.

Now, years later, somewhere in that glorious mess of a city, I own an apartment. A real space, with walls, doors and locks. It is mine. I will not die paying rent.

And that's how it's going to stay.

"Right, cat?"

Complaint #2

I park the car and pick the cat up slowly and hesitantly, thinking he's going to scratch me. I start to like him, because he doesn't. The cat lets me pick him up as if he knew this was now going to be his home.

It's late, I'm tired, and I begin to walk toward my building. I spot the white girl who just moved in. She's ahead of me, dressed in black, and her waist is small and thin, like she could be snapped in half. She looks back and sees me carrying a cat. I know I must smell of plaster from work and of kerosene and smoke from the fire. She reaches the door before me and takes her keys out and opens it. I am about to thank her and go inside, when she turns around to face me. She has a polite expression laced with a bit of suspicion. The kind of look I've seen white people give to office janitors and delivery boys.

"Excuse me," she says, blocking the door. "Do you live here?"

"Yeah, I'm on the third floor," I say courteously. She becomes even more hesitant to move away.

"Really?" she smiles nervously. "Then you wouldn't mind ringing? I just need to be sure." She looks at the cat, thinking I'm homeless or something. "I don't want to let anyone I don't know in the building."

I want to turn street on her and just rip her to pieces. Listen white bitch, I don't have to prove I live here. I lived in this neighborhood years back, when this very block was burned and broken. So move out of the way and go back to that town in Middle America where you came from.

I would love to say that.

Instead I take a deep breath.

"It's past midnight," I sigh. "I don't want to wake my parents up."

Why am I being polite when, unlike her, I have history here?

"I've just never seen you before. These aren't rentals," she says, as if I don't know this. Then she starts digging her hand into her purse and keeps it there. Mace, I'm thinking, cell phone or something?

Truth is, I want to push her aside and walk inside my property. But I just stand there. I see how vulnerable and small her body is. How her blue-green eyes highlight the splash of freckles around her nose, mirrored by a bigger splash just above the V-neck of her shirt and around her breasts. I stare at her. I think about when I was growing up, when there were not too *many white people in Spanish Harlem*. You *only saw white people when you went to work* and clocked in, and usually they were your bosses. At school they were your teachers. On TV these white people were *always doctors, lawyers and detectives*. They lived in another part of the city, or were wealthy and lived in Dallas or ran a dynasty, and you knew you were not wanted there. You'd be arrested on the very spot where you had set foot on their lawns. Now that I dealt with white people on a regular basis, and I never let them push me around, I stood my ground, but somehow, in Spanish Harlem, I felt they were in my backyard. On my lawn. I should be the one asking questions. But the other voice tells me that if I show them politeness and education, it throws them off. They expect the rude Latino from the street, and the truth is that I am that, too. And, at times, I have a problem deciding which face to put on.

"Please, can you ring?" she says again as a smile trails her last word.

El Barrio was no longer my barrio, and the past seemed irretrievable. White people living on many blocks. Some had money, some didn't, but we were supposed to leave them all alone. We were supposed to accept them moving into our neighborhoods, as opposed to when blacks and Latinos started entering their suburbs. How they'd stare at us with evil eyes. Tell their kids to stay away from our kids. Made sure their daughters stayed away from our sons. They never warmly welcomed us into the great American Dream.

"Could you please just ring?"

Give us your tired.

Your poor.

But not on my block.

Not in my suburb.

Not in my building.

"If you don't ring, I can't let you up."

And here, in Spanish Harlem, we were supposed to take the high road. Like Christ, turn the other cheek. Welcome white people and smile as greedy real estate brokers changed the name from Spanish Harlem to Spa Ha, because El Barrio was not a cool, catchy name. They needed a new name, something that would attract yuppies and make them feel hip while they wear all that black.

All that black, just like the girl blocking me from home is wearing.

"Sure," I say to her, "I don't mind ringing," which I do, because I have to ring a lot and wake up my family.

"*Quien?*"

"*Pa', soy yo.*"

"*Coño*, don't you have keys?" my father grumbles over the intercom and she giggles with reassurance, now that she is sure I live there.

"Nice cat," she takes her hand out of her bag and holds the door for me to walk inside.

"Thanks," I say. I can smell the booze on her breath, and her cheeks are bubble-gum pink. She must have been out drinking late with her friends. Because with the influx of yuppies, bars are springing all over the neighborhood. It's actually brave of her to confront me. I wonder if she would have done it if she wasn't tipsy.

We walk inside the lobby, and I hear my father ring me up.

"You live with your parents?" We start walking up the creaky stairs.

I mutter, "Yeah well, even if I had the money, I'm never putting them in a home."

"Excuse me?" she says.

"Nothing," I say, wondering if I said that too loud. "Yeah, we help each other out."

She becomes really friendly and tells me that her name is Helen and that Manhattan is so expensive and how she always wanted to buy an apartment.

"My god, I don't know how much you paid, but even in *this* neighborhood, it's so goddamned expensive."

This neighborhood? This has been my home for three decades.

"Yeah, it's not a good neighborhood," I say.

"Do you know where there's a good, cheap place to eat around here?"

"La Fonda, it's good food and cheap. It's on 105th between Lexington and Third."

I say this nicely, but I know that if it was the other way around, if I moved into an all-white neighborhood, my neighbors wouldn't want me around. Even if I hit the lotto jackpot of a hundred million dollars, I'd still not be in their class. The board members of the luxurious Dakota building on 72nd and Central Park West wouldn't let me buy even if I could. I'd be rejected on the spot. It's not all about money. And I really wanted to do the same to Helen. Let this white girl know how it feels to be invisible and hated. Even feared.

"Go check it out, great Puerto Rican dishes," I say.

"Great," she says, smiling again, "want to get coffee at Starbucks sometime?"

"Sure," I say, thinking that I wouldn't be caught dead in that place.

"Bye." She then strokes the cat, "Bye cat," and opens the door to her floor. "I'm Helen, by the way," she says again.

"Julio," I say.

"Great," she says, closing the door.

I'm happy she's gone.

I walk upstairs and hold the cat with one hand while I fumble for the door key with the other. When I finally find it, my father opens the door.

"*Mira un gato?*" my father says, half asleep, "wha' you doing with a cat?"

"Sorry Pa'," I say as I kiss him hello. My father, who is getting old before his time because of all that work and fast living in his youth, groans at the cat.

"Not a mean cat," he says and takes the cat from my arms.

"I brought it for Ma'." And just then I hear Mom get up and walk toward the living room.

"*Mira*, it's late. Where's the *vi-va-poru? Quien ha visto el vi-va-poru?*" Mom is looking for the Vicks VapoRub. I laugh. Whatever linguists say about Spanglish being invented in the street is wrong. It was invented in the home. By our parents, who weren't born in America or didn't come as children. "Where's the *vi-va-poru?*" Our parents never had a chance to grasp the English language. They just worked and worked and worked. With no schooling, they made English their own. *Pichon* for pigeon, *rufo* for roof, and so on. It's a language of family, of home, not street.

Mom sees the cat and forgets about the medicine. "*Que lindo, de quien es ese gato?*"

"Ours," I say. Mom takes it from Pop's arms.

Hot potato with a cat.

"It's hungry and skinny," she says, then lifts its tail. "*Un macho.* Kaiser," she holds the cat up, "*te vamos a llamar Kaiser.*"

"No that's a terrible name," I protest, "that's not a cat name."

"Let's call him Hector Lavoe," my father says and we pay him no mind.

"Kaiser is a German king, Ma'."

"No it's not." She goes to the kitchen to pour the cat some milk. I follow her. The dishes are dirty. Mom looks at Pops and points at the dishes.

"You better start *dishwashando*," she says to Pops and then tells me, "Is not a German king," picks up a clean plate, "*ese nombre esta en la biblia*." She takes the milk from the fridge, pours a plateful of milk, and places it on the floor.

"Kaiser?" I say. "I never read that name in the Bible."

The cat starts licking the milk clean, like it hasn't eaten in ten years.

"Well it's there, in the Book of Job," Mom says.

"How you spell that? *Cómo se escribe, Ma'.*"

My father starts doing the dishes. This late, and he's doing the dishes. Why? Because like me, Pops can never say no to Mom.

"*No se*, but it's in the Bible." She strokes the cat as he drinks. "I've seen it. *Mira*, Trompo Loco was around looking for you."

"What he want?"

"*Nada*, I guess he just wanted to play. *Bendito*, Trompo Loco, he should just move in with us," Mom says to me, not looking up, admiring Kaiser licking his whiskers.

"Barretto, let's call the cat Barretto," my father says as he washes, "after Ray Barretto."

"You forget about those old musicians and just keep *dish-washando*," Mom tells him as she strokes the cat's fur.

Having both my parents up, I decide I might as well tell them that things are going to be tight.

"I quit my second job," I say, and Mom takes her eyes off the cat and embraces me. Her hair smells of almonds.

"*Gracias al Señor*," she says. "Now you'll be a full-time student?"

"No, I'll still have to work, at the construction site," I say. I know they had their suspicions about my second job, but they never asked me what it was. I see Pops start to nod and smile as he keeps washing. "I want to pay more attention to graduating next year. It's taken me seven years," I say.

"*Mijo*," Mom says, "now see, see," she says, pointing a finger at me, "now all you have to do is find a good girl, get married, have kids, come back to the Truth, *mira que el fin está cerca*."

"Ma', please," I say, and she gets a little embarrassed; because we had this discussion already, years ago when I broke away from the church.

"Look at what happened in September, those are signs, Julio. *Cristo viene y pronto*."

"Whatever, Ma'." I'm not going to get into it with her.

"Then at least get married, let Christ come back and at least find you married. *Mira, que bay una blanquita, muy linda que se mudó aquí*." Mom whispers about our new neighbor. "She seems nice."

"Ma', please. You sound like Papelito."

"Oh no, not that man," Mom shoots the wall a dirty look, "that *pato es hijo del Diablo*."

"I like him, Ma,' and Pentecostals have their little weird shit, too—"

"Don't curse, Julio. Every time you curse the Devil takes a little piece of you."

"If that were true, Ma'," I say, "there would be no Puerto Ricans. Come on, Ma'."

She calms down. "'*Ta bien*, he's your friend. But why don't you make that *blanquita* your friend, too?"

I stay quiet.

"The thing is, those blanquitas don't clean their houses," Mom says. "We may never be rich but we will always be clean. Our cup may be small but it will never leak. These women dress nice but their apartments are a mess. But I hope you find someone soon. You're almost thirty."

"Jesus never got married," I say. "I'm just following in his footsteps."

"You're so funny today," she smirks, and I await another of her favorite expressions. "Did you swallow clown for lunch?"

"Yes," I say, "how did you know?"

"All I'm saying Julio, is I can pray *al Señor*." Mom shrugs, looking at me, "I can pray that you'll get married, see the signs and come back to truth."

"Keep praying, Ma'," I say, "*al Señor y al doctor chino*."

"*Mira cuidado*," she says, knowing I'm making fun of her praying. "*Cuidado*. You can't talk to me like that, I carried you for nine months. So you can't talk to me like that. Nine months I carried you."

"Oh yeah, Ma'," I say and lift her up, "well I'm going to carry you for nine minutes."

"She's heavy," Pops says, "like nine seconds is all you gonna make."

I put her down after she complains.

"*Mira que sinvergüenzas los do'*," she says, laughing.

My father cleans his last dish, wipes his hands dry on his shorts, and joins Mom, who is petting the cat again.

"*Mira* Julio," my father says, looking up at me, "I'm happy you're leaving that other job, too." His stare holds my eyes. I know what he means. "You did a good thing."

"*Gracias, Pa'*."

"But your mother's right, you should get married."

"You can't force marriage Pops."

"No you're right, you can't force it," he says.

Mom puts the cat on the floor and places her hands on her hips.

"Yes you can," she says to him.

"No you can't," Pops shakes his head.

"But if Julio was a girl, you'd then be forcing him to get married, *verdad?*"

"That's different. A woman is different."

"No it's not," she says.

"*Oh sí*," he says.

"*Oh no, señor*," she says.

"*Oh sí*," he says, and I leave them arguing as Kaiser finishes his milk and starts sniffing around his new home.

I go get ready to shower. Maybe later get in a bit of studying for class tomorrow night. I leave my parents in the kitchen talking. My parents always talk in the kitchen. It's like their conference room. When I was a kid, the kitchen was always warm, even when there wasn't enough heat. I'd usually see my parents sitting at the table, with the oven door open, emitting its warmth at full blast as they argued, laughed, or just stared at the walls. The kitchen had food and water, and so it was the ideal room to discuss matters of survival, rent, family, God.

My parents had met during the glory years of salsa, when the neighborhood was full of people and not projects. My mom was the religious one, really. She loved singing hymns with that voice of hers that went high enough to break glass and low enough to make you shiver. My father, Angel Santana, could play the timbales like Puente. Okay I'm lying, no one could play like Puente, but my father came close. I have the tapes to prove it. My father played with the greats, though—Barretto, Blades, De Leon, Colon, Palmeri, Cuba, Feliciano, Pacheco, and "*el cantante de los cantantes,*" Lavoe. He was partying with Lavoe, when my father said, "*el Señor se me presentó.*" When the Lord appeared to him. Lavoe and Pops had shot up everything "*hasta gasolina,* and when we ran out of that, we cooked the Pepto-Bismol in the medicine cabinet and shot that up, too." Hector Lavoe was always late to his concerts, and many times it was because he was living it up with my father. All this hard living led Pops to fall into a deep depression. He stopped playing music and one day, while sitting alone in his apartment, ready to jump off the fire escape, my father asked God to give him a sign that He loved him. At that instant, he heard a knock on the door, and it was my mother, preaching with her fellow sisters, the Good News of Jehovah. Not only did he convert, he married Mom, who helped him kick the habit, and years later Pops even played his music at church.

They are a pair, those two. I love them dearly, and as insane as Mom can be and as wimpy as Pops gets, I never doubt their love for me and they never doubt mine for them.

Getting ready to shower, I hear my parents talk about helping me pay the mortgage. I hear my father regret how he threw his life away doing too many drugs. And that his disability check is nothing. Mom thanks the Lord for what we have and how her job at the hospital can help me pay the bills. They talk about fixing some of the bedrooms that are not fit for anyone to live in them. Especially the walls. What a mess. That will be expensive. Mom would rather have new wooden floors put in. That is expensive, too.

But they are happy. Especially now that I am doing the right thing. My parents aren't stupid. They know that I have done things God wouldn't approve of. But they never questioned me. And if I had told them, given them the choice, your son can be an arsonist and buy a place in five years or just work a nine-to-five job, go to church, and die paying rent?

I know what they would have said.

So I made my own choice.

Not just because I love this town but because I also know this town. And New York City, like the country it's in, is a place that promises you everything but gives you nothing. And those things that can't be worked for must be taken, conned, or traded for with bits of your soul and sometimes even the morals of your parents. In America, it's where you end up that matters, not how you get there. As long as you get there, no one asks questions. You don't ask. You never ask. And if someone does ask how you got there? It's usually a harmless person who never got anything, never got out, died paying rent as he waited for God to deliver him.

A P P E N D I X

Researching New York

We recommend beginning with *The Encyclopedia of New York City,* edited by Kenneth T. Jackson. Every imaginable topic relating to New York is briefly discussed in this reference book. Also included are citations for related books and articles. For topics relating to New York history, see Jane Mushabac's *A Short and Remarkable History of New York City* and the websites for the Gotham Center for New York City History (gothamcenter.org) and the New York Public Library (nypl.org). Another useful place to begin your research is Gothamgazette.com. This on-line journal offers links to a range of web sites and articles on a vast array of urban topics including crime, education, arts, immigration, health services, housing, transportation, and more. We also recommend cityjournal.org, nytimes.com (the *New York Times* web-site), amnewyork.com, and mrbellersneighborhood (for publishing your own work). The library databases EBSCO-Academic Premier and Lexis/Nexis are also useful places to search for journal and newspaper articles.

New York Museums:
Brooklyn Museum of Art
Ellis Island Immigration Museum
Guggenheim Museum
International Center for Photography
Lower East Side Tenement Museum
Metropolitan Museum of Art
Museum of Modern Art
Museum of the City of New York
Museum of the Moving Image (Queens)
Museo del Barrio
New York Transit Museum (Brooklyn)
Visual Arts Museum
Whitney Museum of American Art

New York City History Web Sites:
Gotham Center for New York City History
New York Historical Society
Bronx Historical Society
Brooklyn Historical Society

Queens Historical Society
Staten Island Historical Society
Weeksville Society

Urban Art Web Site:
stylewars.com

Films About New York:

Literature and History:
Ric Burns *New York: A Documentary*
Gangs of New York (2002)
Malcolm X (1992)
Age of Innocence (1993)
The Great Gatsby (1974)
Ragtime (1981)
Breakfast at Tiffany's (1961)

City Life:
Blue on the Face (1995)
Subway Stories (1997)
A Bronx Tale (1993)
Sidewalk Stories (1991)
Straight Out of Brooklyn (1991)
Wall Street (1987)
Stranger Than Paradise (1984)
Manhattan (1979)
Taxi Driver (1976)
The Producers (1968)
Rear Window (1954)
On the Town (1949)

Immigrant/Ethnic Life:
Man Push Cart (2006)
Washington Heights (2002)
In America (2004)
Raising Victor Vargas (2003)
The Brothers McMullen (1995)
The Mambo Kings (1992)
Eat a Bowl of Tea (1989)
Mascow on the Hudson (1984)
The Chosen (1982)
Hester Street (1975)

Crime and Violence:
New Jack City (1991)
Bonfire of the Vanities (1990)
Do the Right Thing (1989)
Fort Apache, The Bronx (1981)
The Warriors (1979)
The Godfather II (1974)
Mean Streets (1973)
The Cross and the SwitchBlade (1970)
Angels with Dirty Faces (1938)

Urban Education:
Freedom Writers (2007)
Blackboard Jungle (1955)

Urban Art:
The Hip Hop Project (2006)
Style Wars (2004)
Basquiat (1996)

The City and the Imagination:
Madagascar (2005)
Spider-Man 2 (2004)
Blade Runner (1994)
Superman (1978)
King Kong (1933)
Metropolis (1927)

INDEX